Technical Writing

Principles, Strategies, and Readings

FOURTH EDITION

Diana C. Reep
The University of Akron

Allyn and Bacon

Boston London Toronto Sydney Tokyo Singapore

Vice President, Humanities: Joseph Opiela
Editorial Assistant: Mary Varney
Marketing Manager: Kate Sheehan
Editorial Production Service: Chestnut Hill Enterprises, Inc.
Manufacturing Buyer: Suzanne Lareau
Cover Administrator: Linda Knowles

Internet: www.abacon.com

Between the time Website information is gathered and published, some sites may have closed. Also, the transcription of URLs can result in typographical errors. The publisher would appreciate notification where these occur so that they may be corrected in subsequent editions.

Library of Congress Cataloging-in-Publication Data

Reep, Diana C.
    Technical writing : principles, strategies, and readings / Diana
    C. Reep — 4th ed.
        p.   cm.
    Includes bibliographical references and index.
    ISBN 0–205–29861–3
    1. English language—Technical English.   2. English language–
    –Rhetoric.   3. Technical writing.   4. College readers.   I. Title.
    PE1475.R44   1999
    808′.0666—dc21   99–25449
                                                                    CIP

Credits are on pages 569–572, which constitute an extension of the copyright page.

Printed in the United States of America

10 9 8 7 6 5 4 3 2 1   RRD-VA   04 03 02 01 00 99

For Faye, Sid, Sonia, Kim, Trisha and Tom

Contents

4   Organization   67

5   Document Design   94

11   Short and Long Reports   269

12   Types of Reports   305

Appendix A: Guidelines for Grammar, Punctuation, and Mechanics   421

Appendix B: Frequently Confused Words   439

PART **2:** Technical Writing Advice from the Workplace   443

Thematic Contents
for Part 2 Readings

Ethics

Etiquette

Graphics: Oral Presentations

Graphics: Written Communication

International Communication

Internet

Job Search

Oral Presentations: Graphic Aids

Oral Presentations: Organization

Proofreading

Style

Teleconferencing

Preface

I appreciate the enthusiastic response from instructors and students using *Technical Writing: Principles, Strategies, and Readings.* This fourth edition preserves its unique combination of instructional chapters covering the standard technical communication topics; models illustrating a variety of documents and purposes; exercises providing challenging in-class and out-of-class writing assignments; discussion topics; and articles from professional journals, offering advice on communication topics. This new edition also retains the flexible organization that instructors said they prefer, and it can be easily used in conjunction with an instructor's personal teaching materials. *Technical Writing: Principles, Strategies, and Readings* is designed for students who study technical writing as part of their career preparation in science, business, engineering, social services, and technical fields. Because of its practical features and guidelines, many students decide to keep the book as a later reference for their on-the-job writing.

INSTRUCTIONAL CHAPTERS

The 14 chapters of instruction cover the writing process, ethics and collaboration, audience analysis, organization, graphics, revision, definition, description, instructions and process explanations, formal report elements, short and long reports, types of reports, correspondence, and oral presentations. This new edition contains key changes:

- The topics of **ethics** and **collaboration** are now in a separate Chapter 2, making it easier for instructors to focus on the writing process in Chapter 1 and incorporate ethics and collaboration at another point.

- **Strategy boxes** appear in every chapter, providing tips for students on such topics as e-mail etiquette, voice mail, Internet sources for job hunting, job interviews, and graphics for oral presentations.

- Chapter 10, "Formal Report Elements," has been updated to include the latest versions of **citations** for Internet research sources, such as Web pages and on-line newspapers.

- Chapter 11, "Short and Long Reports," has been revised to cover **electronic information sources,** as well as search engines for the Internet.
- Chapter 13, "Correspondence," includes expanded coverage of **e-mail** with style and format guidelines. Also expanded is the discussion of **scannable résumés.**

Chapters include (1) checklists and guidelines for students planning, drafting, and revising documents; (2) strategy boxes with useful tips on various topics; (3) sample outlines for specific document types; (4) models of technical documents; (5) exercises for in-class and out-of-class assignments; (6) chapter summaries that highlight major points for students; and (7) lists of relevant readings in Part 2 to supplement the chapters and provide further discussion topics.

MODELS

This new edition includes **91 models** representing a variety of technical documents, graphics, and suggested outlines for document types. The models illustrate technical writing aimed at various audiences for various purposes.

Several models show successive drafts of a document, so students can analyze the changes made during the drafting process. The end-of-chapter models are accompanied by commentary that explains the purpose of the document and the rhetorical strategies used by the writer. The end-of-chapter models also are accompanied by discussion questions and, usually, writing tasks specific to the model or to the type of document under discussion. Since no writing is ever "perfect," students should be encouraged to analyze the text and visuals in the models and discuss possible changes.

WRITING ASSIGNMENTS

New writing assignments appear in every chapter. The assignments vary in difficulty and may require students to (1) revise a sample of poor writing; (2) develop a full, original document; (3) read one or more articles in Part 2 and incorporate the information into a class discussion or writing task; (4) prepare an oral presentation; or (5) collaborate with other students in drafting a document or making an oral presentation.

New to this edition are exercises requiring students to use the Internet or write an e-mail message.

APPENDIXES

This edition includes a useful new feature. **Appendix B: Frequently Confused Words** explains the meaning of words that often confound writers, such as affect/effect, amount/number, imply/infer, and sight/site/cite. Appendix A offers a convenient reference for the fundamentals of grammar, punctuation, and mechanics of style.

READINGS

Part 2 contains 26 short articles by specialists in professional communication. **Ten new articles** present information on the following topics:

- **Ethics:** "Ethics in Technical Communication" discusses designing graphics. "Technical Documentation and Legal Liability" describes a court case involving a writer's legal responsibility to present information clearly.

- **Electronic Communication:** Four new articles expand the coverage of topics concerning electronic communication. "Be Succinct! (Writing for the Web)" gives style tips for electronic documents. "It's All in the Links" discusses how to choose and write hypertext links. "Send the Right Messages about E-mail" offers guidelines for the style and content of e-mail messages. "Meeting Technology: From Low-Tech to High-Tech" explains how to choose appropriate equipment for presenting information at meetings.

- **International Communication:** Two new articles, "Doing Business in Mexico" and "Tips, Tricks and Pitfalls to Avoid When Doing Business in the Tough but Lucrative Korean Market," offer advice on handling these diverse business cultures.

- **Job Search:** Two new articles expand the advice for students beginning a job search. "Prepare, Listen, Follow up" explains how to obtain and conduct an information interview to learn about a field. "What Skills Will You Need to Succeed?" identifies the skills employers seek most.

The "Thematic Contents for Part 2 Readings" provides an easy way to find an article on a specific topic. Also, each chapter includes a list of the articles in Part 2 that complement the chapter topic.

INSTRUCTOR'S RESOURCES

The instructor's manual available with this textbook offers suggestions to those instructors who wish to try new approaches with familiar topics and to new instructors who are teaching technical communication for the first time. The manual includes suggestions for course policies, sample syllabi, a directory of document types that appear in the book, chapter-by-chapter teaching suggestions, reading quizzes for each chapter, a list of additional readings, and a list of academic journals that include research in professional communication topics.

Also, visit the Allyn and Bacon Web site <www.abacon.com> for new information on writing research and classroom ideas.

TO STUDENTS

Use this book as a resource. Your instructor will assign specific chapters, readings, and exercises, but you can also explore new topics in the chapters and in the readings.

- The models show typical on-the-job documents. Remember that no document is ever "perfect." Writers do many drafts before the final version. As you analyze a model for writing, design, and strategy, you may have a new idea for the document. Discussing possible changes helps you develop your own perceptions of the kinds of choices writers have to make in preparing technical documents.

- Use the chapter checklists as guides when planning your writing. Checklists are a useful tool for getting started and for reviewing the final draft.

- Use the readings in Part 2 as an extra resource beyond your technical communication class. If you are giving an oral presentation in another class, read the relevant articles in Part 2 to help you prepare.

- The appendixes are for your convenience in checking your written work before turning it in.

Consider this book as a tool you can use for communication tasks in school and on the job.

ACKNOWLEDGMENTS

I am grateful to the many people who have contributed to this book through four editions. My thanks to those who provided technical writing models and information about on-the-job writing practices: Maggie R. Kohls, Tishman Construction Company of Illinois, Chicago, Illinois; Trisha L. Kohls, Anderson Graduate School of Business at UCLA, Los Angeles, California; Sidney Dambrot, Ford Motor Company, Brook Park, Ohio; Charles Groves, Americhem, Inc., Akron, Ohio; Jacquelyn Biel, Kompas/Biel Associates, Milwaukee, Wisconsin; Debra Canale, Roadway Express, Inc., Akron, Ohio; Michele A. Oziomek, Lewis Research Center, Cleveland, Ohio; Mary H. Bailey, Construction Specifications Institute, Alexandria, Virginia; Ellen Heib, Reinhart, Boerner, Van Dueren, Norris & Rieselbach, Attorneys at Law, Milwaukee, Wisconsin; Steven C. Stultz, Babcock & Wilcox Co., Barberton, Ohio; Michelle Merritt, Ciba Corning Diagnostics, Oberlin, Ohio; Brian S. Fedor, LTV Steel, Cleveland, Ohio; and Michael J. Novachek, Akron, Ohio. Colleagues who offered advice and support include Gerald J. Alred, University of Wisconsin–Milwaukee, and Thomas Dukes and Janet Marting, The University of Akron. Special thanks to Faye H. Dambrot for all her help and encouragement.

At Allyn and Bacon, Joseph Opiela has guided this project from the initial idea through this fourth edition. Thanks also to the reviewers of this edition: Laura Brady, West Virginia University; Lauri Fitzgerald, Madison Area Technical College; Judith Gardner, University of Texas at San Antonio; Lynn Levy, Wisconsin State University, Pullman; and Steven Stedman, Tennessee Technical University. Finally, my intense gratitude to Sonia Dial, who cheerfully typed, retyped, sorted, and copied multiple drafts of every page.

DIANA C. REEP, dreep@uakron.edu

PART 1

Technical Writing: Ways of Writing

CHAPTER 1

Technical Writing on the Job

WRITING IN ORGANIZATIONS

No matter what your job is, writing will be important to your work because you will have to communicate your technical knowledge to others, both inside and outside the organization. Consider these situations. An engineer writes an article for a professional engineering journal, describing a project to restructure a city's sewer pipelines. A police officer writes a report for every arrest and incident that occurs on a shift. An artist writes a grant application asking for funds to create a large, postmodern, steel sculpture. A dietitian writes a brochure about choosing foods low in cholesterol for distribution to participants in a weight-control seminar. Anyone who writes about job-related information prepares technical documents that supply information to readers who need it for a specific purpose.

Surveys of people on the job indicate that writing consumes a significant portion of their working time. One study reported that engineers spend 25% of their job-related time writing technical documents and 23% reading technical and business materials.[1] Another study reported that 62.8% of the upper-level managers, 39.3% of the mid-level managers, and 43.5% of the low-level managers surveyed said that written communication was "extremely important" as a management tool.[2] And a survey of people in four different career areas reported that 39.4% in management positions, 22.2% in technical fields, 20.8% in clerical positions, and 31% in social-service occupations said they spend 21% to 40% of their job-related time writing.[3] Finally, a survey of 60 front-line manufacturing supervisors–none with college degrees—indicated that 70% spent up to 14 hours a week writing.[4]

Writing skill is important in getting a job. A survey of personnel directors indicated that written and oral communication skills were two of the top four skills college graduates need to get employment. For successful job performance, the personnel directors ranked written and oral communication in the top three factors, and for entry-level management, written communication skill was ranked number one.[5] Another survey of personnel directors at companies that hire large numbers of new college graduates revealed that 43% were dissatisfied with the writing ability of recent college graduates.[6] It is understandable, therefore, that job advertisements often list communication skills as requirements. A review of one issue of *National Business Employment Weekly* found communication skills required in 85 of 120 job listings. Employers asked for such skills as "ability to write proposals," "able to conduct reviews of company operations and procedures and report findings," and "able to write quality procedures."[7] All these studies indicate that writing is an important element in most careers.

Reader/Purpose/Situation

Three elements to consider in writing any technical documents are reader, purpose, and writing situation. The reader of a technical document seeks information for a specific purpose, and the writer's goal is to design a document that will serve the reader's needs and help the reader understand and use the information efficiently. The writing situation consists of both reader and purpose, as well as such factors as the sponsoring organization's size, budget, ethics, deadlines, policies, competition, and priorities. Consider this example of a writing situation.

Lori Vereen, an occupational therapist, must write a short article about the new Toddler Therapy Program, which she directs, at Children's Hospital. Her article will be in the hospital's monthly newsletter, which is sent to people who have donated funds in the past ten years. Newsletter readers are interested in learning about hospital programs and new medical technology, and many of the readers will donate funds for specific programs. Reading the articles in the newsletter helps them decide how to allocate their donations.

Lori understands her readers' purpose in using the newsletter. She also knows that the hospital's management wants to encourage readers to donate to specific programs (writer's purpose). Although she could include in her article much specialized information about new therapy techniques for children with cerebral palsy, she decides that her readers will be more interested in learning how the children progress through the program and develop the ability to catch a ball or draw a circle. Scientific details about techniques to enhance motor skills will not interest these readers as much, or inspire as many donations, as will stories about children needing help. Lori's writing situation is restricted further by hospital policy (she cannot use patients' names), space (she is limited to 700 words), and time (she has one day to write her article).

Like Lori, you should consider reader, purpose, and situation for every on-the-job writing task you have. These three elements will influence all your decisions about the document's content, organization, and format.

Diversity in Technical Writing

Science and engineering were once considered the only subjects of technical writing, but this limitation no longer applies. All professional fields require technical documents that help readers perform tasks and understand specific tasks. These sentences are from technical documents that provide readers with guidelines for properly completing a specific procedure:

- "Retired employees who permanently change their state of residence must file Form 176-B with the Human Resources Office within 90 days of moving to transfer medical coverage to the regional plant serving their area." (This sentence is from a manufacturing company's employee handbook. Readers are employees who need directions for keeping their company benefit records up to date.)

- "Be sure your coffeemaker is turned OFF and unplugged from the electrical outlet." (This sentence is from a set of instructions packed with a new product. Readers are consumers who want to know how to use and care for their new coffeemaker properly.)

- "The diver must perform a reverse three-and-a-half somersault tuck with a 3.4 degree of difficulty from a 33-ft platform." (This sentence is from the official regulations for a college diving competition. The readers are coaches who need to train their divers to perform the specific dives required for the meet.)

- "For recover installations, pressure-relieving metal vents should be installed at the rate of 1 for every 900 square feet of roof area." (This sentence is from a catalog for roofing products and systems. The readers are architects and engineers who may use these products in a construction project. If they do, they will include the manufacturer's specifications for the products in their own construction design documents.)

Although these sentences involve very different topics, they all represent technical writing because they provide specific information to clearly identified readers who will use the information for a specific purpose.

WRITING AS A PROCESS

The process of writing a technical document includes three general stages—planning, multiple drafting, and revising—but remember, this process is not strictly linear. If you are like most writers, you will revise your decisions about the document many times as you write. You may get an entirely new idea about format or organization while you are drafting, or you may change your mind about appropriate content while you are revising. You probably will also develop a personal writing process that suits your working conditions and preferences. Some writers compose a full draft before tailoring the document to their readers' specific needs; others analyze their readers carefully before gathering any information for the document. No one writing system is appropriate for all writers, and even experienced writers continue to develop new habits and ways of thinking about writing.

One Writer's Process

Margo Keaton is a mechanical engineer who works for a large construction firm in Chicago. Presently, her major project is constructing a retirement community in a Chicago suburb. As the project manager, she meets frequently with the general contractor, subcontractors, and construction foremen. At one meeting with the general contractor and six subcontractors, confusion arises concerning each subcontractor's responsibility for specific construction jobs, including wiring on control motors and fire-safing the wall and floor openings. Because no one appears willing to take the responsibility for the jobs or to accept statements at the meeting as binding, Margo realizes that, as project manager, she will have to determine each subcontractor's precise responsibility.

When she returns to the office she shares with five other engineers, she considers the problem. Responsibility became confused because some subcontractors were having trouble keeping their costs within their initial bids for the construction project. Eliminating some work would ease their financial burden. Then too, no one, including the general contractor, is certain about who has definite responsibilities for the wiring system and for fire-safing the openings. Margo's task is to sort out the information and write a report that will delegate responsibility to the appropriate subcontractors. As Margo thinks about the problem, she realizes that her audience for this report consists of several readers who will each use the report differently. The general contractor needs the information to understand the chain of responsibility, and the subcontractors need the report as an assignment of duties. All the readers will have to accept Margo's report as the final word on the subject.

While analyzing the situation, Margo makes some notes on the problem, the objectives of her report, and the information that should be included. She decides that she needs the original specifications for the project, previous reports, and the original bids. When she calls the design engineer, he offers to send her the original specifications via e-mail. After looking at her notes again, Margo decides that she also needs to find correspondence with the subcontractors to check for records of any changes in the original agreements. She next lists the people she regards as her readers at this point.

The next morning, Margo checks her e-mail and finds the specifications sent by the design engineer. She then calls up her computer files for the project and locates the correspondence with the subcontractors. She finds several progress reports and the minutes of past meetings, but they do not mention the specific responsibilities under dispute. After she checks all her material, she decides to enlarge her list of readers to include the design engineer, whose specifications she intends to quote, and the owner's representative, who attended all the construction meetings and heard the arguments over responsibilities. Although the design engineer and the owner's representative are not directly involved in the argument over construction responsibilities, Margo knows they want to keep up to date on all project matters.

Margo needs to compile and organize relevant information, so she opens two new files—FIRESAFE and WIRING. As she reads through the specifications and her own correspondence files, she selects relevant paragraphs and data and saves them to her clipboard. She then sorts and enters these items in either the FIRESAFE file or the WIRING file.

Margo makes her first decision about organization because she knows that some of her readers will resent any conclusions in her report that assign them more responsibility. The opening summary she usually uses in short reports will not suit this situation. Some of her readers might become angry and stop reading before they reach the explanation based on the specifications. Instead, Margo decides to structure the report so that the documentation and explanation come first, followed by the assignment of responsibilities. She plans to quote extensively from the specifications.

In her opening she will review the misunderstanding and remind her readers why this report is needed. Because the general contractor ultimately has the task of enforcing assignment of responsibilities, she decides to address the report to him and send copies of it to all other parties.

The information in the FIRESAFE and WIRING files is not in any particular order, so Margo prints a hard copy of each file and makes notes about organization in the margins. She groups her information according to specific task, such as wiring the control motors, and puts a code in the margin. All the information about wiring the control motors is coded "B". She also notes in the margins the name of the subcontractor responsible for each task.

Because the original design specification indicated which subcontractor was to do what and yet everyone seems confused, she decides that she should not only quote from the documents, but also paraphrase the quotations to ensure that her readers understand. By the end of the report, she will have assigned responsibility for each task in the project.

When she is fairly confident about her organizational decisions, she reorders the material in the FIRESAFE and WIRING files, adds her marginal notes, such as "put definition here," and prints another hard copy of both files. After making a few more notes in the margins, Margo opens a new file on her computer and begins a full draft of her report, using the information she has gathered, but rewriting completely for her readers and purpose. As she writes her draft, she also chooses words carefully because her readers will resent any tone that implies they have been trying to avoid their responsibilities or that they are not intelligent enough to figure out the chain of responsibility for themselves. She writes somewhat quickly because she has already made her major organizational decisions. The report turns out to be longer than she expected because of the need to quote and paraphrase so extensively, but she is convinced that such explanations are crucial to her purpose and her readers' understanding. Looking at her first draft again, she changes her mind about the order of the sections and decides to discuss the least controversial task first to keep her readers as calm as possible for as long as possible.

Her second draft reflects the organization she thinks her readers will find most helpful. Margo's revision at this stage focuses on three major considerations: (1) Is all the quoted material adequately explained? (2) Are there enough quotations to cover every issue and clearly establish who is to do what? (3) Is her language neutral, so no one will think she is biased or dictatorial? She decides that she does have enough quoted material to document each task and that her explanations are clear. Finally, she runs her spell-check and grammar-check programs. The spell-check stops at every proper name, and she reviews her records to ensure she has the correct spelling. The grammar-check stops at the use of passive voice, but Margo wants passive voice in some places to avoid an accusatory tone when she talks about tasks that have not been completed.

Because the situation is controversial, she takes the report to her supervisor and asks him whether he thinks it will settle the issue of job responsibilities. When Margo writes a bid for a construction project, her supervisor always reads the document carefully to be sure that special conditions and costs applying to the project are covered thoroughly. For this report, he assumes that Margo has included all the pertinent data. He suggests adding a chart showing division of responsibilities.

Margo agrees and creates a chart to attach to her report. Knowing her spell-check and grammar-check cannot find all errors, she then edits for *surface accuracy*—clear sentence structure and correct grammar and punctuation. She reads the report aloud, so she can hear any problems in sentence structure or word choice. Her edit reveals a dangling modifier and three places where she inadvertently wrote "assign" instead of "assigned." She makes all the corrections, prints a final draft, and gives her report to Kimberly, the secretary, who will make copies and distribute them.

STRATEGIES—Internet Sources for Job Hunting

America's Job Bank (www.ajb.dni.us): Offers easy access to government data on occupational trends and lists jobs nationwide.

Career Path (www.careerpath.com): Lists classified ads from newspapers across the country.

Head Hunters (www.headhunter.net): Lists over 100,000 jobs that can be searched by educational field along with job type and location.

Yahoo Classifieds (www.classifieds.yahoo. com): Lists jobs by location and type.

Stages of Writing

Margo Keaton's personal writing process enables her to control her writing tasks even while working at a busy construction company where interruptions occur every few minutes. She relies on notes and lists to keep track of both information and her decisions about a document because she often has to leave the office in the middle of a writing task. Her notes and lists enable her to pick up where she left off when she returns.

Aside from using personal devices for handling the writing process, most writers go through the same three general stages as they develop a document. Remember that all writers do not go through these stages in exactly the same order, and writers often repeat stages as they make new decisions about the content and format of a document.

Planning

In the planning stage, a writer analyzes the reader, purpose, and writing situation; gathers information; and tentatively organizes the document. All these activities may recur many times during the writing.

Analyzing Readers.   No two readers are exactly alike. They differ in knowledge, needs, abilities, attitudes, relation to the situation, and their purpose in using the document. All readers are alike, however, in that they need documents that provide information they can understand and use. As a writer, your task is to create a document that will fit the precise needs of your readers. Margo Keaton's readers were all technical people, so she was free to use technical terms without defining them. Because she knew some readers would be upset by her report, she made her first organizational decision—she would not use an opening summary. Detailed strategies for thinking about readers are discussed in Chapter 3. In general, however, consider these questions whenever you analyze your readers and their needs:

- Who are my specific readers?
- Why do they need this document?
- How will they use it?
- Do they have a hostile, friendly, or neutral attitude toward the subject?
- What is the level of their technical knowledge about the subject?
- How much do they already know about the subject?
- Do they have preferences for some elements, such as tables, headings, or summaries?

Analyzing Purpose.   A document should accomplish something. Remember that a document actually has two purposes: (1) what the writer wants the reader to know or do and (2) what the reader wants to know or do. The writer of instructions, for example, wants to explain a procedure so that readers can perform it. Readers of instructions want to follow the steps to achieve a specific result. The two purposes obviously are closely related, but they are not identical. Margo Keaton wrote her report to assign responsibilities (writer's purpose), as well as to enable her readers to understand the situation and plan their actions accordingly (reader's purpose). A writer should consider both in planning a document. Furthermore, different readers may have different purposes in using the same document, as Margo Keaton's readers did. In analyzing your document's purpose, you may find it helpful to think first of these general purposes:

> *To instruct*—The writer tells the reader how to do a task and why it should be done. Documents that primarily instruct include training and operator manuals, policy and procedure statements, and consumer instructions. Such documents deal with
> - The purpose of the procedure
> - Steps in performing the procedure
> - Special conditions that affect the procedure

To record—The writer sets down the details of an action, decision, plan, or agreement. The primary purpose of minutes, file reports, and laboratory reports is to record events both for those currently interested and for others who may be interested in the future. Such documents deal with

- Tests or research performed and results
- Decisions made and responsibilities assigned
- Actions and their consequences

To inform (for decision making)—The writer supplies information and analyzes data to enable the reader to make a decision. For decision making, a reader may use progress reports, performance evaluations, or investigative reports. Such documents deal with

- Specific facts that materially affect the situation
- The influence the facts have on the organization and its goals
- Significant parts of the overall situation

To inform (without decision making)—The writer provides information to readers who need to understand data but do not intend to take any action or make a decision. Technical writing that informs without expectation of action by the reader includes information bulletins, literature reviews, product descriptions, and process explanations. Such documents deal with

- The specific who, what, where, when, why, and how of the subject
- A sequence of events showing cause and effect
- The relationship of the information to the company's interests

To recommend—The writer presents information and suggests a specific action. Documents with recommendation as their purpose include simple proposals, feasibility studies, and recommendation reports. Such documents deal with

- Reasons for the recommendation
- Expected benefits
- Why the recommendation is preferable to an alternative

To persuade—The writer urges the reader to take a specific action or to reach a specific conclusion about an issue. To persuade, the writer must convince the reader that the situation requires action and that the information in the report is relevant and adequate for effective decision making. A report recommending purchase of a specific piece of equipment, for instance, may present a simple cost comparison between two models. However, a report that argues the need to close a plant in one state and open a new one in another state must persuade readers about the practicality of such a move. The writer will have to (1) explain why the facts are relevant to the problem, (2) describe how they were obtained, and (3) answer potential objections to the plan. Documents with a strong persuasive purpose include construction bids, grant applications, technical advertisements, technical news releases, and reports dealing with sensitive topics, such as production changes to reduce acid rain. Such documents emphasize

- The importance or urgency of the situation
- The consequences to the reader or others if a specific action is not taken or a specific position is not supported
- The benefits to the reader and others if a specific action is taken or a specific position is supported

To interest—The writer describes information to satisfy a reader's intellectual curiosity. Although all technical writing should satisfy readers' curiosity, writing that has interest as its main purpose includes science articles in popular magazines, brochures, and pamphlets. Such documents deal with

- How the subject affects daily life
- Amusing, startling, or significant events connected to the subject
- Complex information in simplified form for general readers

The general purpose of Margo Keaton's report was to inform her readers about construction responsibilities. Her specific purpose was to delegate responsibilities so that the subcontractors could work efficiently. The readers' specific purpose was to understand their duties. Remember that technical documents have both a general purpose and a specific purpose relative to the writing situation. Remember also that documents generally have multiple purposes because of the specific needs of the readers. For instance, a report that recommends purchasing a particular computer model also must provide enough information about capability and costs so that the reader can make a decision. Such a report also may include information about the equipment's design to interest the reader and may act as a record of costs and capability as of a specific date.

Strategies for analyzing readers' purpose are included in Chapter 3. Consider these questions in determining purpose:

- What action (or decision) do I want my reader to take (or make)?
- How does the reader intend to use this document?
- What effect will this document have on the reader's work?
- Is the reader's primary use of this document to be decision making, performing a task, or understanding information?
- If there are multiple readers, do they all have the same goals? Will they all use the document in the same way?
- Do my purpose and my reader's purpose conflict in any way?

Analyzing the Writing Situation.   No writer on the job works completely alone or with complete freedom. The organization's environment may help or hinder your writing and certainly will influence both your document and your writing process. The organizational environment in which you write includes (1) the roles and authority both you and your readers have in the organization and in the writing situation, (2) the communication atmosphere, that is, whether information is readily available to employees or only to a few top-level managers, (3) preferences for specific documents, formats, or types of information, (4) the organization's relationship with the community, customers, competitors, unions, and government agencies, (5) government regulations controlling both actions and communication about those actions, and (6) trade or professional associations with standards or ethical codes the organization follows. You can fully understand an organization's environment only by working in it because each is a unique combination of individuals, systems, relationships, goals, and values.

When Margo Keaton analyzed her writing situation, she realized that (1) her readers were hostile to the information she was providing, (2) work on the retirement community could not continue until the subcontractors understood and accepted her information about construction responsibilities, and (3) the delay caused by the dispute among subcontractors jeopardized her own position because she was responsible for finishing the project on time and within budget. Margo's writing situation, therefore, included pressures from readers' attitudes and time constraints. In analyzing your writing situation, consider these questions:

- Is this subject controversial within the organization?

- What authority do my readers have relative to this subject?

- What events created the need for this document?

- What continuing events depend on this document?

- Given the deadline for this document, how much information can be included?

- What influence will this document have on company operations or goals?

- Is this subject under the control of a government agency or specific regulations?

- What external groups are involved in this subject, and why?

- Does custom indicate a specific document for this subject or a particular organization and format for this kind of document?

Gathering Information.   Generally, you will have some information when you begin a writing project. Some writers prefer to analyze reader, purpose, and situation and then gather information; others prefer to gather as much information as possible early in the writing process and then decide which items are needed for the readers and purpose. Information in documents should be (1) accurate, (2) relevant to the readers and purpose, and (3) up to date or timely. Margo Keaton's information gathering was focused on existing internal documents because she had to verify past decisions. Many sources of information are available beyond your own knowledge and company documents. Chapter 11 discusses how to find information from outside sources.

Organizing the Information.   As you gather information, you will probably think about how best to organize your document so that your readers can use the information efficiently. As Margo Keaton gathered information for her report, she separated it into major topics in two computer files. She then grouped the information according to specific tasks and made notes about additions. She printed a hard copy of her reordered notes for easy reference before starting her first full draft. General strategies for organizing documents are discussed in Chapter 4. In organizing information, a writer begins with two major considerations: (1) how to group the information into specific topics and (2) how to arrange the information within each topic.

Grouping Information into Topics.   Arranging information into groups requires looking at the subject as a whole and recognizing its parts. Sometimes you know the main topics from the outset because the subject of the document is usually organized in a specific way. In a report of a research experiment, for example, the information would probably group easily into topics, such as research purpose, procedure, specific results, and conclusions. Always consider what groupings will help the reader use the information most effectively. In a report comparing two pieces of equipment, you might group information by such topics as cost, capability, and repair costs to help your reader decide which model to purchase. If you were writing the report for technicians who will maintain the equipment, you might group information by such topics as safety factors, downtime, typical repairs, and maintenance schedules. Consider these questions when grouping information:

- Does the subject matter have obvious segments? For example, a process explanation usually describes a series of distinct stages.

- Do some pieces of information share one major focus? For example, data about equipment purchase price, installation fees, and repair costs might be grouped under the major topic "cost," with subtopics covering initial cost, installation costs, and maintenance costs.

- Does the reader prefer that the same topics appear in a specific type of document? For example, some readers may want "benefits" as a separate section in any report involving recommendations.

Arranging Information within a Topic.   After grouping the information into major topics and subtopics, organize it effectively within each group. Consider these questions:

- Which order will enable the reader to understand the material easily? For example, product descriptions often describe a product from top to bottom or from bottom to top so that readers can visualize the connecting parts.

- Which order will enable the reader to use this document? For example, instructions should present the steps in the order in which the reader will perform them. Many managers involved in decision making want information in descending order of importance so that they can concentrate on major issues first.

- Which order will help the reader accept this document? For example, when Margo Keaton organized her sections, she held back information her readers were not eager to have until the end of the report.

By making a master list of your topics in order or by reorganizing your notes in computer files as Margo Keaton did, you will be able to visualize your document's structure. The master list of facts in order is an *outline*. Although few writers on the job take the time to make a formal outline with Roman numerals or decimal numbering, they usually make some kind of informal outline because the information involved in most documents is too lengthy or complicated to be organized coherently without using a guide. Some writers use lists of the major topics; others prefer more detailed outlines and list every major and minor item. Outlines do not represent final organization decisions. You may reorganize as you write a draft or as you revise, but an outline will help you control a writing task in the midst of on-the-job interruptions. After a break in the writing process, you can continue writing more easily if you have an outline.

Multiple Drafting

Once you have tentatively planned your document, a rough draft is the next step. At this stage, focus on thoroughly developing the information you have gathered, and do not worry about grammar, punctuation, spelling, and fine points of style. Thinking about such matters during drafting will interfere with your decisions about content and organization. Follow your initial plan of organization, and write quickly. When you have a completed draft, then think about revision strategies. A long, complicated document may require many drafts, and most documents except the simplest usually require several drafts. Margo Keaton wrote her first rough draft from beginning to end using the notes she had organized; other writers may compose sections of the document out of order and then put them in order for a full draft. Keep your reader and purpose firmly in mind while you write, because ideas for new information to include or new ways to organize often occur during drafting.

Revising and Editing

Revision takes place throughout the writing process, but particularly after you have begun drafting. Read your draft and rethink these elements:

- *Content*—Do you need more facts? Are your facts relevant for the readers and purpose?

- *Organization*—Have you grouped the information into topics appropriate for your readers? Have you put the details in an order that your readers will find easy to understand and use? Can your readers find the data easily?

- *Headings*—Have you written descriptive headings that will guide your readers to specific information?

- *Openings and closings*—Does your opening establish the document's purpose and introduce the readers to the main topic? Does your closing provide a summary, offer recommendations, or suggest actions appropriate to your readers and purpose?

- *Graphic aids*—Do you have enough graphic aids to help your readers understand the data? Are the graphic aids appropriate for the technical knowledge of your readers?

- *Language*—Have you used language appropriate for your readers? Do you have too much technical jargon? Have you defined terms your readers may not know?

- *Reader usability*—Can your readers understand and use the information effectively? Does the document format help your readers find specific information?

After you are satisfied that you have revised sufficiently for your readers and purpose, edit the document for correct grammar, punctuation, spelling, and company editorial style. For Margo Keaton, revision centered on checking the report's content to be sure that every detail relative to assigning construction responsibilities was included. She also asked her supervisor to read the report to check that the information was clear and that the tone was appropriate for the sensitive issue. Her final editing focused on grammar and punctuation. Remember that no one writes a perfect first draft. Revising and editing are essential for producing effective technical documents.

CHAPTER SUMMARY

This chapter discusses the importance of writing on the job and the writing process. Remember:

- Writing is important in most jobs and often takes a significant portion of job-related time.

- Technical writing covers many subjects in diverse fields, and every writing task involves analyzing reader, purpose, and writing situation.

- Each writer develops a personal writing process that includes the general stages of planning, multiple drafting, and revising and editing.

- The planning stage of the writing process includes analyzing the reader, purpose, and writing situation; gathering information; and organizing the document.

- The multiple drafting stage of the writing process involves developing a full document and redrafting as writers rethink their original planning.

- The revising and editing stage of the writing process includes revising the document's content and organization and editing for grammar, punctuation, spelling, and company style.

SUPPLEMENTAL READINGS IN PART 2

Graham, J. R. "What Skills Will You Need to Succeed?" *Manager's Magazine,* p. 487.

ENDNOTES

1. Charlene M. Spretnak, "A Survey of the Frequency and Importance of Technical Communication in an Engineering Career," *The Technical Writing Teacher* 9.3 (Spring 1982): 133–136.

2. Marie E. Flatley, "A Comparative Analysis of the Written Communication of Managers at Various Organizational Levels in the Private Business Sector," *Journal of Business Communication* 19.3 (Summer 1982): 35–49.

3. Mary K. Kirtz and Diana C. Reep, "A Survey of the Frequency, Types and Importance of Writing Tasks in Four Career Areas," *The Bulletin of the Association for Business Communication* 53.4 (December 1990): 3–4.

4. Mark Mabrito, "Writing on the Front Line: A Study of Workplace Writing," *Business Communication Quarterly* 60.3 (September 1997): 58–70.

5. Dan B. Curtis, Jerry L. Winsor, and Ronald D. Stephens, "National Preferences in Business and Communication Education," *Communication Education* 38.1 (January 1989): 6–14.

6. Leslie J. Davison, James M. Brown, and Mark L. Davison, "Employer Satisfaction Ratings of Recent Business Graduates," *Human Resource Development Quarterly* 4.4 (Winter 1993): 391–399.

7. Vanessa Dean Arnold, "The Communication Competencies Listed in Job Descriptions," *The Bulletin of the Association for Business Communication* 55.2 (June 1992): 15–17.

This model shows a writer's first two outlines for an administrative bulletin at a manufacturing company. Because the company has defense contracts, many written and visual materials include classified information that must be coded according to Department of Defense regulations. The company administrative bulletin will describe the correct procedures for marking classified materials. Readers are the six clerks who work in the Security Department and are responsible for marking the materials correctly. The clerks are accustomed to following company guidelines in administrative bulletins.

The writer begins planning the document by reading through the Department of Defense regulations and noting those that apply to his company. He jots down a list of the items as he reads, creating his first rough outline of the content that must appear in the document.

Next, he interviews several Security Department clerks about the kinds of classified materials they handle and their preferences for written guidelines. In his office, the writer drafts a second and longer outline on his computer.

In his second list, he adds specific detail to each item. Based on his interviews with the clerks, he now lists the most common classified materials first and the least common last. He also records two special items that he must explain in the bulletin: (1) materials that cannot be marked in the usual manner and (2) documents that include paragraphs classified at different levels.

Discussion

1. Assume you are the writer in this situation. Discuss what kinds of information you would want to have about your readers and about how they intend to use the bulletin.

2. In his second list, the writer includes more detail under each item. Identify the types of information he added to his list. Discuss why he probably chose to draft a second list at this stage, rather than write his first full draft of the bulletin.

3. After talking to the clerks, the writer rearranged items in his second list according to how frequently they appear. Discuss what other principle he appears to be using in grouping his items.

MARKING CLASSIFIED INFORMATION
- BOOKS, PAMPHLETS, BOUND DOCS
- CORRESPONDENCE + NONBOUND DOCS
- ARTWORK
- PHOTOS, FILM, MICROFILM
- LETTERS OF TRANSMITTAL
- SOUND TAPES
- MESSAGES
- UNMARKABLE MATERIAL
- CHARTS, TRACINGS, DRAWINGS

AUTHORITY FOR CLASSIFYING
- CONTRACTING AGENCY

CLASSIFIED - ALL INFO CONNECTED TO PROJECT

OTHER INFO - COMPANY MAY CLASSIFY -
REGIONAL OFFICE REVIEWS

MARKING PARAGRAPHS FOR DIFFERENT CLAS-
SIFICATIONS
- PREFERRED
- OR STATEMENT ON FRONT
- OR ATTACH CLASSIFICATION GUIDE FOR
CONTENT

NOTE: MATERIAL IN PRODUCTION
- EMPLOYEES NOTIFIED OF CLASSIFI-
CATION

First Outline

Military Security Bulletin

Authority to classify—contracting agency
Classified info—according to Form 264
Info not in contract—company can classify
If needed—regional office should review

Marking classified info—no typing—use date—classification—name and address of facility

1. bound docs—books, pamphlets: top and bottom, covers, title, first and last pages
2. correspondence and nonbound: top and bottom; if parts differ, highest classification prevails
3. letters of transmittal: first page
4. charts, tracings, and drawings: under legend, title block or scale, top and bottom
5. artwork: top and bottom of board and page
6. photos, films, microfilms: outside of container beginnings and ends of rolls, title block
7. sound tapes: on containers and beginning and end of recording
8. messages: top and bottom, first and last words of transmitted oral message
9. unmarkable material: tagged, production employees notified
10. paragraphs: if varying classifications in force, each marked for degree
    —or statement on front or in text
    —or attach guide for each part

**Mark each paragraph if possible.

Second Outline

This model shows the first two drafts of the administrative bulletin. The writer's first draft is based on his expanded outline, and he follows company style guidelines by numbering items and giving the bulletin a title and number. He also capitalizes "company" wherever it appears. He develops each point from his second outline into full, detailed sentences, including instructions for each item and special considerations for specific items.

Before writing his second draft, the writer asks the senior clerk to read his first version and suggest changes. The writer then revises based on her comments.

In the second draft, the writer uses a headline that clarifies the purpose of the bulletin and includes headings in the document to separate groups of information. In addition to numbering the classified materials, the writer uses bold face for key words that identify each item.

Item 10 in the first draft becomes a separate section in the second draft because the senior clerk noticed that the information about marking paragraphs applies to all written material.

Discussion

1. Discuss the changes in format and headings the writer made from his first to his second draft. Why will these changes be helpful to the readers?

2. In his discussion with the clerks, the writer learned that they prefer to divide their work so that each handles only specific types of classified materials. Discuss further changes in format and organization that might help the clerks use the bulletin efficiently. For instance, what changes would help a clerk who worked only with items 1, 2, and 3?

3. Compare the first draft and second draft as if you were a clerk who must mark a 20-page booklet in which the sections have different classifications. Discuss how the organization changes will help you find the information you need.

Military Security Guide—Bulletin 62A

The contracting federal agency shall have the authority for classifying any information generated by the Company. All information developed or generated by the Company while performing a classified contract will be classified in accordance with the specifications on the "Contract Security Classification Specification," Form 264. Information generated by the Company shall not be classified unless it is related to work on classified contracts; however, the facility management can classify any information if it is believed necessary to safeguard that information in the national interest. Moreover, the information classified by Company management should be immediately reviewed by the regional security office.

MARKING CLASSIFIED INFORMATION AND MATERIAL

All classified information and material must be marked (not typed) with the proper classification, date of origin, and the name and address of the facility responsible for its preparation.

1. Bound Documents, Books, and Pamphlets shall be marked with the assigned classification at the top and bottom on the front and back covers, the title page, and first and last pages.

2. Correspondence and Documents Not Bound shall be marked on the top and bottom of each page. When the separate components of a document, such as sections, etc., have different classifications, the overall classification is the highest one for any section. Mark sections individually also.

3. Letters of Transmittal shall be marked on the first page according to the highest classification of any component. A notation may be made that, upon removal of classified material, the letter of transmittal may be downgraded or declassified.

4. Charts, Drawings, and Tracings shall be marked under the legend, title block, or scale and at the top and bottom of each page.

5. Artwork shall be marked on the top and bottom margins of the mounting board and on all overlays and cover sheets.

6. Photographs, Films, and Microfilms shall be marked on the outside of the container. In addition, motion picture films shall be marked at the beginning and end of each roll and in the title block.

First Draft

7. Sound tapes shall be marked on their containers and an announcement made at the beginning and end of the recording.

8. Messages, sent electronically, such as e-mail, shall have the classification marking at the top and bottom of each page. In addition, the first and last word of the message shall be the classification.

9. Classified Material that cannot be marked shall be tagged with the classification and other markings. Material still in production that cannot be tagged requires that all employees be notified of the proper classification.

10. Paragraphs in documents, bound or nonbound, which are of different classifications, shall be marked to show the degree of classification, if any, of the information contained therein. Or a statement on the front of the document or in the text shall identify the parts of the document that are classified and to what degree. Or an appropriate classification guide shall be attached to cover the classified contents of the document. Marking paragraphs individually is the preferred method. Neither of the other two alternatives may be used until it is determined that paragraph marking is not possible.

Military Security Guide—Bulletin 62A

MARKING CLASSIFIED INFORMATION AND MATERIAL

Authority

The contracting federal agency shall have the authority for classifying any information generated by the Company. All information developed or generated by the Company while performing a classified contract will be classified in accordance with the specifications on the "Contract Security Classification Specification," Form 264. Information generated by the Company shall not be classified unless it is related to work on classified contracts; however, management can classify any information that may affect the national interest. The information classified by Company management should be immediately reviewed by the regional security office.

Required Marking

All classified information and material must be marked (not typed) with (1) the proper classification, (2) date of origin, and (3) the name and address of the facility responsible for its preparation.

Types of Information and Material

1. **Bound Documents, Books, and Pamphlets** shall be marked with the assigned classification at the top and bottom on the front and back covers, the title page, and first and last pages.

2. **Correspondence and Documents Not Bound** shall be marked on the top and bottom of each page. If the components of a document, such as sections or chapters, have different classifications, the overall classification is the highest one for any section. Individual sections shall be marked also.

3. **Letters of Transmittal** shall be marked on the first page according to the highest classification of any component. A notation may be made that, upon removal of classified material, the letter of transmittal may be downgraded or declassified.

4. **Charts, Drawings, and Tracings** shall be marked under the legend, title block, or scale and at the top and bottom of each page.

Second Draft

5. **Artwork** shall be marked on the top and bottom margins of the mounting board and on all overlays and cover sheets.

6. **Photographs, Films, Microfilms, and Disks** shall be marked on the outside of the container. Disks shall be marked on labels. In addition, motion picture films shall be marked at the beginning and end of each roll and in the title block.

7. **Sound Tapes** shall be marked on their containers and an announcement made at the beginning and end of the recording.

8. **Electronic Messages** shall have the classification marking at the top and bottom of each hard-copy page. In addition, the first and last word of the message shall be the classification.

9. **Classified Material that cannot be marked** shall be tagged with the classification and other markings. All employees shall be notified of the proper classification for material still in production that cannot be tagged.

Individual Paragraphs

Paragraphs of documents, bound or nonbound, which are of different classifications, shall be marked to show the degree of classification. Material shall be marked in one of three ways:

- Individual paragraphs shall be marked separately.

- A statement on the front of the document or in the text shall identify the parts of the document that are classified and to what degree.

- An appropriate classification guide shall be attached to provide the classifications of each part of the document.

Marking paragraphs individually is the preferred method. Neither of the other two alternatives may be used until facility management determines that paragraph marking is not possible.

Chapter 1 Exercises

1. In groups, make notes on your individual writing processes. Decide which steps fit the outline of the writing process in this chapter. Identify any individual elements, such as needing a peanut butter sandwich to get started. Discuss how these individual preferences may contribute to the person's writing process.

2. In groups, assume you are an intern in the office of the president of your school. You have been told to write a welcoming letter to new students. Discuss the reader, purpose, and writing situation you would have to consider for this assignment. The president will sign the letter.

3. Find a science or technical article in your field and identify the reader and purpose. In groups, discuss the elements in the articles that helped you identify reader and purpose.

4. Interview someone you know who has a job that requires some writing. Ask the person about his or her personal writing process. What kinds of documents and for whom does the person write? How do company requirements affect the writing process? Is team writing or management review usually involved? What activity in the writing process does the person find most difficult? How much rewriting does the person do for a typical writing task? What part of the person's writing process would he or she like to change or strengthen? Write a memo to your instructor describing how this person handles a typical writing task. Use the memo format shown in Chapter 13.

CHAPTER 2

Collaboration and Ethics

WRITING WITH OTHERS

Writing on the job usually means collaborating with others. A survey of members of six professional associations, such as the American Institute of Chemists and the American Consulting Engineers Council, found that 87% of those responding said they sometimes wrote in collaboration with others, and 98% said that effective writing was "very important" or "important" to successfully doing their work.[1]

You may informally ask others for advice when you write, or you may write a document with a partner or a team of writers. When writers work together to produce a document, problems often arise beyond the usual questions about content, organization, style, and clarity. Overly harsh criticism of another's work can result in a damaged ego; moreover, frustration can develop among writers when their writing styles and paces clash. In addition to other writers, you may also collaborate with a manager who must approve the final document, or you may work with a technical editor who must prepare the document for publication.

Writing with a Partner

Writing a document with a partner often occurs when two people report research or laboratory tests they have conducted jointly. In other situations, two people may be assigned to a feasibility study or field investigation, and both must write the final report. Sometimes one partner will write the document and the other will read, approve, and sign it. More often, however, the partners will collaborate on the written document, contributing separate sections or writing the sections together. Here is a checklist for writing with a partner:

- Plan the document together so that you both clearly understand the document's reader and purpose.

- Divide the task of gathering information so that neither partner feels overworked.

- Decide who will draft which sections of the document. One partner may be strong in certain topics and may prefer to write those sections.

- Consult informally to clarify points or to change organization and content during the drafting stage.

- Draft the full document together so that you both have the opportunity to suggest major organizational and content changes.

- Edit individually for correctness of grammar, punctuation, usage, and spelling, and then combine results for the final draft. Or if one partner is particularly strong in these matters, that person may handle the final editing alone.

Writing on a Team

In addition to writing alone or with a partner, writers frequently work on technical documents with a group. An advantage to writing with a team is that several people, who may be specialists in different areas, are working on the same problem, and the final document will reflect their combined knowledge and creativity—several heads are better than one. A disadvantage of writing with a group is that conflicts arise among ideas, styles, and working methods—too many cooks in the kitchen. An effective writing team must become a cohesive problem-solving group in which conflict is used productively.

Team Planning

The initial meetings of the writing team are important for creating commitment to the project as well as mutual support. All team writers should feel equally involved in planning the document. Here is a checklist for team planning:

- Select someone to act as a coordinator of the team, call meetings, and organize the agenda. The coordinator also can act as a discussion leader, seeking consensus and making sure that all questions are covered.

- At meetings, select someone to take notes on decisions and assignments. These notes should be distributed to team members as soon as possible.

- Clarify the writing problem so that each team member shares the same understanding of reader and purpose.

- Generate ideas about strategy, format, and content without evaluating them until all possible ideas seem to be on the table. This brainstorming should be freewheeling and noncritical so that members feel confident about offering ideas.

- Consult the graphic artist; planning should include decisions about graphics to enhance the text.

- Discuss and evaluate the ideas about content and graphics; then narrow the suggestions to those that seem most suitable.

- Arrive at a group agreement on overall strategy, format, and content for the document.

- Organize a tentative outline for the major sections of the document so that individual writers understand the shape and boundaries of the sections they will write.

- Divide the tasks of collecting information and drafting sections among individual writers.

- Schedule meetings for checking progress, discussing content, and evaluating rough drafts.

- Schedule deadlines for completing rough drafts.

STRATEGIES—Electronic Collaboration

Electronic communication can enhance collaboration. Establish guidelines during the planning stage.

- Decide which documents you will exchange.
- Decide the file format you will use for e-mail or File Protocol Transfer.
- Send documents by fax for final document review.
- Determine a mutually convenient time to use the telephone or exchange e-mail to discuss progress.

Team Drafting

Meetings to work on the full document generally focus on the drafts from individual writers. Team members can critique the drafts and offer revision suggestions. At these meetings, the group also may decide to revise the outline, add or omit content, and further refine the format. Here is a checklist for team drafting:

- Be open to suggestions for changes in any area. No previous decision is carved in stone; the drafting meetings should be sessions that accommodate revision.

- Encourage each team member to offer revision suggestions at these meetings. Major changes in organization and content are easier to incorporate in the drafting stage than in the final editing stage.

- Ask questions to clarify any points that seem murky.

- Assign the coordinator to assemble the full draft and, if needed, send it for review to people not on the team, such as technicians, marketing planners, lawyers, and upper-level management.

- Schedule meetings for revising and editing the full draft.

Team Revising and Editing

The meetings for revising and editing should focus on whether the document achieves its purpose. This stage includes final changes in organization or content as well as editing for accuracy. Here is a checklist for revising and editing:

- Evaluate comments from outside reviewers and incorporate their suggestions or demands.

- Assign any needed revisions to individual writers.

- Assign one person to evaluate how well the format, organization, and content fit the document's reader and purpose.

- Check that the technical level of content and language is appropriate for the audience.

- Decide how to handle checking grammar, punctuation, and spelling in the final draft. One writer who is strong in these areas might volunteer to take on this editing.

Handling Conflict among Writers

Even when writers work well together, some conflict during a project is inevitable; however, conflict can stimulate effort and creativity. Remember these strategies for turning conflict into productive problem solving:

- Discuss all disagreements in person rather than through memos or third parties.

- Assume that others are acting in good faith and are as interested as you in the success of the project.

- Avoid feeling that all conflict is a personal challenge to your skills and judgment.

- Listen carefully to what others say; do not interrupt them before they make their points.

- Paraphrase the comments of other people to make sure you understand their meaning.

- Solicit ideas for resolving conflicts from all team members.

- Acknowledge points on which you can agree.

- Discuss issues as if a solution or compromise is possible instead of trying to prove other people wrong.

By keeping the communication channels open, you can eliminate conflict and develop a document that satisfies the goals of the writing team.

Writing for Management Review

The procedure called *management review*—in which a writer composes a document that must be approved and perhaps signed by a manager—holds special problems. First, management review almost inevitably involves criticism from a writer's superior. Second, the difference in company rank between manager and writer makes it difficult for the two to think of themselves as partners. Finally, the writer often feels responsible for the real work of producing the document, while the manager is free to cast slings and arrows at it without having struggled through the writing process. Management review works best when writers feel that they share in making the decisions instead of merely taking orders as they draft and redraft a document. Here are guidelines for both writers and managers who want a productive management review:

- Hold meetings in a quiet workplace where the manager will not be interrupted with administrative problems.

- Discuss the writing project from the beginning so that you both agree on purpose, reader, and expected content.

- Review the outline together before the first draft. Changes made at this point are less frustrating than changes made after sections are in draft.

- As the project progresses, meet periodically to review draft sections and discuss needed changes.

- Be certain that meetings do not end before you both agree on the goals of the next revision and the strategies for changes.

The manager involved in a management review of a document is ultimately responsible for guiding the project. In some cases, the manager is the person who decides what to write and to whom. In other situations, the manager's primary aim is to direct the writer in developing the final document's content, organization, and format. Here are guidelines for a manager who wants a successful management review:

- Criticize the problem, not the person.

- Avoid criticism without specifics. To say, "This report isn't any good," without pinpointing specific problems will not help the writer revise.

- Criticize the project in private meetings with the writer; do not discuss the review process publicly.

- Analyze the situation with the writer rather than dictate solutions or do all the critiquing yourself.

- Project an objective, calm frame of mind for review meetings.

- Concentrate on problem solving rather than on the writer's "failure."

- Have clear-cut reasons for requesting changes, and explain them to the writer. Avoid changes made for the sake of change.

- If the standard company format does not fit the specific document very well, encourage the writer to explore new formats.

- Seek outside reviewers for technical content or document design before a final draft.

- Listen to the writer's ideas and be flexible in discussing writing problems.

- Begin the review meetings by going over the successful parts of the document.

Most managers dislike having to give criticism, but subordinates dislike even more having to accept it. Dwelling on the criticism itself will interfere with the writing process. Here are guidelines for a writer involved in a management review:

- Concentrate on the issues that need to be solved, not on your personal attachment to the document.

- Accept the manager's criticism as guidance toward creating an improved document rather than as an attack on you.

- Remember that every document can be improved; keep your ego out of the review process.

- Ask questions to clarify your understanding of the criticism. Until you know exactly what is needed, you cannot adequately revise.

Writing with a Technical Editor

A writer of technical documents may also work with a technical editor during the review. Documents with a large and diverse audience, such as policy and procedures manuals or consumer booklets, usually require a technical editor. The editor may work with the writer in the development stage to (1) help plan the content and organization, (2) clarify the purpose and audience, and (3) anticipate difficulties in format and production or spot potential legal problems. In some cases, the editor may not see the document until it has gone through several drafts and technical reviews. If the schedule permits, the editor should begin work before the final technical review to avoid last-minute conflicts between necessary changes and pending deadlines.

The writer should present a draft that is accurate and free of errors in grammar, punctuation, and spelling. The editor will review several areas. First, the editor will review the document's structure, ensure that graphic aids are placed appropriately, and check for consistent terminology throughout the sections. Second, the editor will mark the draft for clarity; revise sentences that seem overly long, garbled, ambiguous, or awkward; and review word choice. Third, the editor will check punctuation, grammar, mechanics, and spelling. Last, the editor will mark for standard company style. Both the editor and writer need to think of themselves as a team rather than as adversaries. Here are some guidelines for writers and editors working together:

- Prepare for editorial conferences. The writer should receive the editor's marked copy before a scheduled conference, so the writer can review changes and comments and prepare for the meeting.

- Discuss how editorial changes clarify the document's meaning or serve the reader's purpose rather than focusing on personal preferences in style or format.

- Do not try to cover all editorial matters for a long document in one editorial conference. Schedule separate meetings for format, content, grammar and mechanics, organization, and consistency.

- Check to ensure that editorial changes do not alter the document's meaning or appropriate tone.

- Be open-minded and flexible. Listen to each other's ideas and ask each other questions about purpose, audience, strategy, and content.

After each editorial conference, the writer incorporates the agreed-upon changes. The editor will review the production checklist to be sure the final draft is complete, correct, and properly formatted. The editor is responsible for overseeing the production process. Remember, the editor and writer have a common goal—to produce a document that serves its readers efficiently.

WRITING ETHICALLY

Ethics is a broad term that refers to a set of moral principles. These principles vary according to someone's culture, religion, and personal values. Many companies now have a written corporate code of ethics that includes statements outlining the company's goals and its responsibilities to customers, employees, dealers, stockholders, and others.

In producing technical documents, writers who want to behave ethically should consider how their communication choices affect readers, the company, and other writers on the project. Review the following when writing a document:

- Have you included enough information to avoid harming the reader or damaging equipment?

- Have you warned readers of all possible hazards in specific terms?

- Have you presented comparable facts (e.g., sales figures) similarly to avoid manipulating the reader's understanding?

- Are your facts accurate and do your graphics present data without distortion or bias?

- Have you differentiated clearly between fact and opinion?

- Have you checked for potentially misleading word choice, such as "minor leak," referring to a flow that could cause serious damage if left unchecked?

- Are your research sources reliable and appropriate for an unbiased presentation of data?

- Is your information presented in a context that helps readers understand the implications of the facts?

- Have you tested the document for usability, or, if no interaction with the reader is possible, have you anticipated the reader's needs?

- Have you included any potentially libelous statements or misrepresentations that could cause the company to lose its reputation or that could result in lawsuits?

- Have you used confidential or classified company information inappropriately in the document?

- Have you been receptive to other writers' suggestions for the document and worked with them in a cooperative spirit?

A recent survey asked technical communicators the question, "What would you advise a new technical communicator to do if he or she were asked to do something that he or she thought was unethical?" The top three answers were (1) talk to the supervisor, (2) talk to the person who requested the action, and (3) talk to colleagues.[2]

As a writer, consider the ethical aspects of each document from the perspectives of those who provide information and those who use it, and seek advice if you have questions.

CHAPTER SUMMARY

This chapter discusses guidelines for effective collaborative writing on the job and the ethical questions every writer should consider. Remember:

- Writing on the job often requires collaborating with others by writing with a partner, writing on a team, writing for management review, or writing with a technical editor.

- Conflict among writers working together can be productive if writers exchange ideas freely.

- A writer must consider the ethical implications in the content and design of every technical document.

SUPPLEMENTAL READINGS IN PART 2

Allen, L., and Voss, D. "Ethics in Technical Communication," p. 446.

Caher, J. M. "Technical Documentation and Legal Liability," *Journal of Technical Writing and Communication*, p. 469.

Porter, J. E. "Ideology and Collaboration in the Classroom and in the Corporation," *The Bulletin of the Association for Business Communication,* p. 522.

Wicclair, M. R., and Farkas, D. K. "Ethical Reasoning in Technical Communication: A Practical Framework," *Technical Communication,* p. 556.

ENDNOTES

1. Andrea Lunsford and Lisa Ede, "Why Write . . . Together: A Research Update," *Rhetoric Review* 5.1 (Fall 1986): 71–81.

2. Sam Dragga, "A Question of Ethics: Lessons from Technical Communicators on the Job, *Technical Communication Quarterly* 6.2 (Spring 1997): 161–178.

Model 2-1 Commentary

This model shows two drafts of a safety bulletin for workers who are renovating buildings that contain lead-based paint. In his first assignment at the company, the writer was told to prepare readable bulletins for the work site. In a planning meeting, the project manager and the writer agreed that they needed separate bulletins for the workers, the engineers, and the contractors, who all had different on-the-job requirements. After writing his first draft of the bulletin for workers, the writer submitted it to the project manager for review. The project manager sent the draft back with the following comments.

> This draft looks like a good start. I have some questions:
>
> 1. You have the items separated into before, during, and after work, but they don't stand out very well. Maybe underlining or all capitals? Headings?
> 2. Rearrange the first section. If a worker fails the physical, there is no need for the safety course. The last section looks out of order too.
> 3. The suit information is hard to read—reformat?
>
> Let's get together when you have a second draft.

The writer considered the project manager's comments and then wrote the second draft.

Discussion

1. Discuss the changes the writer made in his second draft in response to the project manager's comments. How do the changes make the bulletin more useful to workers on the job site?

2. Discuss the project manager's comments. How helpful are they in directing the writer? Does the project manager sound objective? flexible? supportive?

3. Assume you are the project manager. What comments would you make about the second draft? Write a third draft based on those comments.

BULLETIN 128—SAFETY GUIDELINES FOR WORKERS RENOVATING BUILDINGS CONTAINING LEAD-BASED PAINT

In accordance with OSHA Regulations CFR 1910.1200 and 1910.1025, all workers must complete medical testing and safety training before work begins. Testing and training must be finished no later than one week before renovation begins. The following is included:

- A six-hour Lead Paint Abatement Health and Safety Training course conducted by site engineers

- a thorough physical examination

- A baseline whole blood test

- a Respiratory Protection Program and test administered **one day prior to the beginning work**

During daily work, OSHA regulations require workers to wear the following equipment (approved by OSHA):

- full-body disposable TYVEK suits with hoods, gloves, booties, and goggles with protective side shields (suits must be worn prior to entering the work area and remain on until the area passes final clearance inspection). Disposable suits may be worn **once** and then discarded in designated bins. Nylon clothing may be worn under TYVEK suits but must be laundered separately.

- Half-faced respirators approved by OSHA and NIOSH must be worn before entering the work area and remain on until the washing area.

Workers may not eat, drink, smoke, or apply cosmetics in the work areas. These activities must be at least 100 feet from any work area.

After work, the following clean-up procedures must be followed:

- Properly dispose of all protective suits, safety equipment, and respirators.

- Shower immediately.

- Wash and dry hands and face thoroughly before entering shower.

First Draft

BULLETIN 128—SAFETY GUIDELINES FOR WORKERS RENOVATING BUILDINGS CONTAINING LEAD-BASED PAINT

Before Work Begins

OSHA Regulations CFR 1910.1200 and 1910.1025 require the following medical testing and safety training to be completed **no later than one week before renovation begins:**

1. A base-line whole blood test

2. A thorough physical examination

3. A six-hour course, Lead Paint Abatement Health and Safety Training, conducted by site engineers

4. A Respiratory Protection Program and test administered **one day prior to beginning work**

During Daily Work

Workers must wear the following equipment approved by OSHA and NIOSH **before entering the work area and until reaching the washing area:**

- Full-body disposable TYVEK suits with hoods, gloves, booties, and goggles with protective side shields
  Note: (1) Disposable suits may be worn **once** and discarded in designated bins; (2) Nylon clothing may be worn under the TYVEK suit, but it must be laundered separately.

- Half-faced respirators

Workers may **not** eat, drink, smoke, or apply cosmetics within 100 feet of any work areas.

After Work

Workers must follow these clean-up procedures:

1. Properly dispose of all protective suits, safety equipment, and respirators.

2. Wash and dry hands and face thoroughly before entering the shower.

3. Shower immediately.

Second Draft

Chapter 2 Exercises

1. Identify the ethical dilemmas in the following situations. Discuss how you would have handled each situation.

   a. The proposal for construction of a biomedical waste incinerator stated, "At a public meeting on December 3, 1998, no opposition to the plan was expressed." A snowstorm had dropped 10 inches on the community during the day of the meeting, and the four people who attended were members of the town council that was supporting the project.

   b. The cover of a collection of four novellas by different writers featured the name of the most popular writer in print twice as large as that used for the other names and in a brighter color. The popular writer's novella was the shortest in the collection, only half as long as any of the other three.

   c. A report on a new pesticide cited data from a previous study that showed favorable results. The report did not discuss the data from the same study that indicated workers might be at risk for breathing problems when using the pesticide. The writer had been told to emphasize the effects of the pesticide on grasshoppers.

2. Read "Ethics in Technical Communication" by Allen and Voss in Part 2. Find an advertisement for a technical product. Analyze the advertisement and decide whether the writer has made ethical choices in language, content, and graphics.

3. Read "Ethical Reasoning in Technical Communication: A Practical Framework" by Wicclair and Farkas in Part 2. In groups, discuss Case 3 described in the article. Assume your group represents the technical writer's friend at another government agency and draft a memo advising the writer how to handle the ethical dilemma. Compare your group's draft with the drafts of other groups. Next, discuss your group's collaborative process. Did someone take the role of coordinator? How were decisions made? How was the drafting process handled? Compare your group's collaborative process with that of the other groups.

CHAPTER 3

Audience

ANALYZING READERS

Each reader represents a unique combination of characteristics and purpose that will affect your decisions about document content and format. To prepare an effective technical document, therefore, analyze your readers during the planning stage of the writing process. Consider your readers in terms of these questions:

- How much technical knowledge about the subject do they already have?
- What positions do they have in the organization?
- What are their attitudes about the subject or the writing situation?
- How will they read the document?
- What purpose do they have in using the document?

If you have multiple readers for a document, you also need to consider the differences among your readers.

Subject Knowledge

Consider how much information your readers already have about the main subject and subtopics in the document. In general, you can think of readers as having one of these levels of knowledge about any subject:

- *Expert level*—Readers with expert knowledge of a subject understand the theory and practical applications as well as most of the specialized terms related to the subject. Expert knowledge implies years of experience and/or advanced training in the subject. A scientist involved in research to find a cure for emphysema will read another scientist's report on that subject as an expert, understanding the testing procedures and the discussion of results. A marketing manager may be an expert reader for a report explaining possible strategies for selling a home appliance in selected regions of the country.

  Expert readers generally need fewer explanations of principles and fewer definitions than other readers, but the amount of appropriate detail in a document for an expert reader depends on purpose. The expert reader who wants to duplicate a new genetic test, for instance, will want precise information about every step in the test. The expert reader who is interested primarily in the results obtained will need only a summary of the test procedure.

- *Semiexpert level*—Readers with semiexpert knowledge of a subject may vary a great deal in how much they know and why they want information. A manager may understand some engineering principles in a report but probably is more interested in information about how the project affects company planning and budgets, subjects in which the manager is an expert. An equipment operator may know a little about the scientific basis of a piece of machinery but is more interested in information about handling the equipment properly. Other readers with semiexpert knowledge may be in similar fields with overlapping knowledge. A financial analyst may specialize in utility stocks but also have semiexpert knowledge of other financial areas. Semiexpert readers, then, may be expert in some topics covered in a document and semiexpert in other topics. To effectively use all the information, the semiexpert reader needs more definitions and explanations of general principles than the expert reader does.

- *Nonexpert level*—Nonexpert readers have no specialized training or experience in a subject. These people read because (1) they want to use new technology or perform new tasks or (2) they are interested in learning about a new subject. Nonexperts using technology for the first time or beginning a new activity are such readers as the person using a stationary exercise bike, learning how to play golf, or installing a heat lamp in the bathroom. These readers need information that will help them use equipment or perform an action. They are less interested in the theory of the subject than in its practical application. Nonexperts who read to learn more about a subject, however, are often interested in some theory. For instance, someone who reads an article in a general science magazine about the disappearance of the dinosaurs from Earth will probably want information about scientific theories on the cause of the dinosaurs' disappearance. If the reader becomes highly interested in the topic and reads widely, he or she then becomes a semiexpert in the subject, familiar with technical terms, theories, and the physical qualities of dinosaurs. For nonexpert readers, include glossaries of technical terms, checklists of important points, simple graphics, and summaries.

All readers, whatever their knowledge level, have a specific reason for using a technical document, and they need information tailored to their level of knowledge. Remember that one person may have different knowledge levels and objectives for different documents. A physician may read (1) a report on heart surgery as an expert, seeking more information about research, (2) a report recommending new equipment for a clinic as a semiexpert who must decide whether to purchase the equipment, (3) an article about space travel as a nonexpert who enjoys learning about space, and (4) an owner's manual for a new camera as a consumer who needs instructions for operating the camera.

Position in the Organization

Your reader's hierarchical position in the company and relationship with you are also important characteristics to consider. Readers are either external (outside the company) or internal (inside the company). Those outside the company include customers, vendors, stockholders, employees of government agencies or industry associations, competitors, and the general public. The interests of all these groups center on how a document relates to their own activities. Within all companies, the hierarchy of authority creates three groups of readers:

- *Superiors*—Readers who rank higher in authority than the writer are superiors. They may be executives who make decisions based on information in a document. Superiors may be experts in some aspects of a subject, such as how cost projections will affect company operations, and they may be semiexperts in the production systems. If you are writing a report to superiors about a new company computer system, your readers would be interested in overall costs, the effect of the system on company operations, expected benefits company wide, and projections of future computer uses and needs.

- *Subordinates*—Readers who rank lower in authority than the writer are subordinates. They may be interested primarily in how a document affects their own jobs, but they also may be involved in some decision making, especially for their own units. If your report on the new computer system is for subordinates, you will probably emphasize information about specific models and programs, locations for the new computers, how these computers support specific tasks and systems, and how the readers will use the computers in their jobs.

- *Peers*—Those readers on the same authority level as the writer are peers, although they may not be in the same technical field as the writer. Their interests could involve decision making, coordinating related projects, following procedures, or keeping current with company activities. Your report on the new computer system, if written for peers, might focus on how the system will link departments and functions, change current procedures, and support company or department goals.

Personal Attitudes

Readers' personal responses to a document or a writing situation often influence the document's design. As you analyze your writing situation, assess these considerations for your readers:

- *Emotions*—Readers can have positive, negative, or neutral feelings about the subject, the purpose of the document, or the writer. Even when readers try to read objectively, these emotions can interfere. If your readers have a negative attitude about a subject, organizing the information to move from generally accepted data to less accepted data or starting with shared goals may help them accept the information.

- *Motivation*—Readers may be eager for information and eager to act. On the other hand, they may be reluctant to act. Make it easy for your readers to use the information by including items that will help them. Use lists, tables, headings, indexes, and other design features to make the text more useful. Most important, tell readers why they should act in this situation.

- *Preferences*—Readers sometimes have strong personal preferences about the documents they must use. Readers may demand features such as lists or charts, or they may refuse to read a document that exceeds a specified length or does not follow a set format. If you discover such preferences in your readers, adjust your documents to suit them.

Reading Style

Technical documents usually are not read, nor are they meant to be read, from beginning to end like a mystery novel. Readers read documents in various ways, determined partly by their need for specific information and partly by personal habit. These reading styles reflect specific readers' needs:

- *Readers use only the summary or abstract.* Some readers want only general information about the subject, and the abstract or opening summary will serve this purpose. An executive who is not directly involved in a production change may read only the abstract of a report. This executive needs up-to-date information about the change, but only in general form. A psychologist who is looking for research studies about abused children may read the abstract of an article in order to decide whether the article contains the kind of information needed. Relying on the abstract for an overview or using the abstract to decide whether to read the full document saves time for busy readers.

- *Readers check for specific sections of information.* A reader may be interested only in some topics covered in a lengthy document. A machine operator may read a technical manual to find the correct operating procedures for a piece of equipment, but a design engineer may look for a description of the machine, and a service technician will turn to the section on maintenance. Long reports and manuals often have multiple readers who are interested only in the information relevant to their jobs or departments. Use descriptive headlines to direct these readers to the information they need.

- *Readers scan the document, pausing at key words and phrases.* Sometimes readers quickly read a document for a survey of the subject, but they concentrate only on information directly pertaining to topics that affect them. The manager of an insurance company annuity department may scan a forecasting report to learn about company planning and expected insurance trends over the next ten years. The same manager, however, will read carefully all information that in any way affects the annuity department. Such information may be scattered throughout the report, so the manager will look for key words. To help such a reader, use consistent terms throughout.

- *Readers study the document from beginning to end.*   Readers who need all the information in order to make a decision are likely to read carefully from beginning to end. A reader who is trying to decide what automobile to buy may read the manufacturers' brochures from beginning to end, looking for information to aid in the decision. Someone who needs to change an automobile tire will read the instructions carefully from beginning to end in order to perform the steps correctly. For these readers, highlight particularly important information in lists or boxes, direct their attention to information through headings, and summarize main points to refresh their memories.

- *Readers evaluate the document critically.*   Someone who opposes a project or the writer's participation in it may read a document looking for information that can be used as negative evidence. The multiple readers of a report recommending a company merger, for instance, may include those opposed to such a plan. Such readers will focus on specific facts they believe are inadequate to support the recommendation. If you know that some of your readers are opposed to the general purpose of your report, anticipate criticisms of the plan or of your data and include information that will respond to these criticisms.

Multiple Readers

Technical documents usually have multiple readers. Sometimes the person who receives a report will pass it on informally to others. Manuals may be used by dozens of employees in all departments of an organization. Readers inside and outside a company study annual reports. Consumer instruction manuals are read by millions. This diversity among readers presents extra problems in document design. In addition to analyzing readers based on technical knowledge, positions in the organization, attitudes, and reading styles, consider whether readers are primary or secondary.

Primary Readers

Primary readers will take action or make decisions based on the document. An executive who decides whether to accept a recommendation to change suppliers and purchase equipment is a primary reader. A consumer who buys a blender and follows the enclosed instructions for making drinks is a primary reader. The technical knowledge, relationship to the organization and to the writer, and personal preferences of these two primary readers are very different, but each is the person who will use the document most directly.

Secondary Readers

Secondary readers do not make decisions or take direct action because of the document, but they are affected or influenced by it. A technician may be asked to read a report about changing suppliers and to offer an opinion. If the change takes place, the technician will have to set up maintenance procedures for the new equipment. A report suggesting new promotion policies will have one or more primary readers who are authorized to make decisions. All the employees who have access to the report, however, will be secondary readers with a keen interest in the effect of any changes on their own chances for promotion. Remember that secondary readers are not necessarily secondary in their interest in a subject, but only in their power or authority to act on the information.

If your document has multiple primary readers, plan for those who need the most help in understanding the subject and the technical language. For instance, when preparing a bulletin for dozens of regional sales representatives, some of whom have been with the company many years and some of whom are newly hired, include the amount of detail and the language most appropriate for the least experienced in the group. New sales representatives need full explanations, but experienced people can skim through the bulletin and read the sections they have a specific interest in if you include descriptive headings.

In some situations, the differences among primary readers or between primary and secondary readers may be so great that you decide to write separate documents. For example, one report of a medical research program cannot serve both the general public and experts. The two groups of readers have entirely different interests and abilities for dealing with the specialized medical information. Even within a company, if the amount of technical information needed by one group will shut out other readers, separate documents may be the easiest way to serve the whole audience.

International Readers

Growing international trade, company branch offices in foreign markets, and booming immigration into the United States have created new challenges for writers. Many documents you write may be used by people for whom English is a second language or who must rely on translations. If you have international readers, you must research their specific communication customs and expectations in order to write an effective document. Even if your international readers use English to conduct business, you need to find out about cultural customs, so you can avoid offending or confusing people who rely on the documents you write. Here are only a few areas for you to consider when developing documents for use by international readers:

- *Graphics.*   In the United States, we expect readers to scan pictures or drawings from left to right, but some cultures scan graphics in a circular direction or up and down. "Universal" symbols are not necessarily universal. One computer company discovered that the trash-can icon was not useful in foreign markets because people put their trash in different types of containers.[1]

- *Colors.*   Cultures attach different meanings to colors. In the United States, a blue ribbon is first prize, but in England first prize is a red ribbon. Red, however, represents witchcraft and death in some African countries. In Japan, white flowers symbolize death, but in Mexico purple flowers symbolize death.[2]

- *Shapes.*   The meaning of shapes and gestures differs among countries. The OK sign we make in the United States by putting thumb and forefinger together is a symbol for money in Japan and is considered vulgar in Brazil.[3]

- *Numbers.*   Some countries do not use an alphabet with the telephone system. Therefore, telephone numbers or fax numbers should be given only in figures, even if the company uses a word in its telephone number for advertising in the United States.[4]

- *Names and rank.*   Countries differ widely on the correct use of names and titles. First names are seldom used in Germany during business transactions, but in Thailand, first names are used except on the most formal occasions. In Belgium, French-speaking people are addressed differently than Dutch-speaking people are.[5]

- *Format.*   Acceptable document format varies by country. Dates are often given in a different style from that in the United States. The day May 15, 1998, for instance, is written as 15.mai 1998 in Germany. The time 10:32 P.M. is 22.32 in France.[6] Correspondence salutations and closings differ from country to country. You also must adopt the formality or informality expected by your international readers.

There are thousands of variations in communication style among the world's cultures. Taking the time to research the customs of your international readers shows respect, but it is also the only way to ensure that your document fulfills its purpose.

STRATEGIES—E-mail Etiquette

Do not use icons, for example, ":)" or abbreviations, for example, "IMHO" in business messages because they may confuse the receiver.

Do not erase the incoming message and send back a simple yes or no answer. The receiver may not remember exactly what the original topic or question was. Paraphrase the original statement or retain the original material in your reply.

Do not respond to a flame. Any response may start an extended exchange of nasty messages.

Do not forward someone's message to a third party without permission.

FINDING OUT ABOUT READERS

Sometimes you will write for readers whom you know well. But how do you find out about readers whom you do not know well or whom you will never meet? Gathering information about your readers and how they plan to use a document can be time consuming, but it is essential at the planning stage of the writing process. Use both informal inquiries and formal interviews to identify readers' characteristics and purposes.

Informal Checking

When you are writing for people inside your organization, you often can find out about them and their purposes by checking informally in these ways:

- Talk in person or by telephone with the readers themselves or with those who know them, such as the project director, the person who assigned you the writing task, and people who have written similar documents. If you are writing to a high-level executive, you may not feel comfortable calling the executive, but you can talk with others who are familiar with the project, the purpose of the document, and the reader's characteristics.

- Check the readers' reactions to your drafts. You can find out how your readers will use the information in your document by sharing drafts during the writing process. If you are writing a procedures manual, sharing drafts with the employees who will have to follow the procedures will help you clarify how they intend to use the document and what their preferences are.

- Analyze your organization's chain of responsibility relative to the document you are writing. For example, the marketing director may supervise 7 regional managers, who, in turn, supervise 21 district managers, who, in turn, supervise the sales representatives. Perhaps all are interested in some aspects of your document. By analyzing such organizational networks, you can often identify secondary readers and adjust your document accordingly.

- Brainstorm to identify readers' characteristics for groups. If you are writing a document for a group of readers, such as all registered nurses at St. Luke's Hospital, list the characteristics that you know the readers have in common. You may know, for example, that the average nurse at St. Luke's has been with the hospital for 4.5 years, has a B.S.N. degree, grew up in the area, and attends an average of two professional training seminars a year. Knowing these facts about your readers will help you tailor your document to their needs.

Interviewing

Writers on the job use interviews as part of the writing process in two ways: (1) to gather information about the subject from experts and technicians and (2) to find out readers' purposes and intended uses of a document. Whether you are interviewing experts for information about the subject or potential readers to decide how to design the document, a few guiding principles will help you control the interview and use the time effectively.

Preparing for the Interview

Interviewers who are thoroughly prepared get the most useful information while using the least amount of time.

- *Make an appointment for the interview.*   Making an appointment shows consideration for the other person's schedule and indicates that the interview is a business task, not a casual chat. Be on time, and keep the interview within the estimated length.

- *Do your background research before the interview.*   Interview time should be as productive as possible. Do not try to discuss the document before having at least a general sense of the kinds of information and overall structure required. You are then in a position to ask more specific questions about content or ask for and use opinions about document design.

- *Prepare your questions ahead of time.*   Write out specific questions you intend to ask. Ask the expert for details that you need to include in the document. Project yourself into your readers' minds and imagine how the document might serve their purposes; then frame your questions to pinpoint exactly how your readers will respond to specific sections, headings, graphic aids, and other document features.

- *Draft questions that require more than yes or no answers.* Interview time will be more productive if each question requires a detailed answer. Notice the following ineffective questions and their more effective revisions:

    Ineffective: Do you expect to use the manual daily for repair procedures?

    Effective: For which repair and maintenance procedures do you need to consult the manual?

This revision will get more specific answers than the first version.

    Ineffective: What do you think operators need in a manual like this one?

    Effective: Which of the following features are essential in an operator's manual for this equipment? (List all that you can think of and then ask if there are others.)

The first version may get a specific answer, but it will not necessarily be comprehensive. Check all possibilities during an interview to avoid repeating questions later.

Conducting the Interview

Think of the interview as a meeting that you are leading. You should guide the flow of questioning, keep the discussion on the subjects, and cover all necessary topics.

- *Explain the purpose of the interview.* Tell the person why you want to ask questions and how you think the interview will affect the final document.

- *Break the ice if necessary.* If you have never met the person before, spend a few minutes discussing the subject in general terms so that the two of you can feel comfortable with each other.

- *Listen attentively.* Avoid concentrating on your questions so much that you miss what the other person is saying. Sometimes in the rush to cover all the topics, an interviewer is more preoccupied with checking off the questions than with listening carefully to the answers.

- *Take notes.* Take written notes so that you can remember what the reader told you about special preferences or needs. If you want to tape the interview, ask permission before arriving. Remember, however, that some people are intimidated by recording devices.

- *Group your questions by topic.*   Do not ask questions in random order. Thoroughly cover each topic, such as financial information, before moving on to other subjects.

- *Ask follow-up questions.*   Do not stick to your list of questions so rigidly that you miss asking obvious follow-up questions. Be flexible, and follow a new angle if it arises.

- *Ask for clarification.*   If you do not understand an answer, ask the person for more detail immediately. It is easier to clarify meaning on the spot than days later.

- *Maintain a sense of teamwork.*   Although you need to control the interview, think of the meeting as a partnership to solve specific questions of content and format.

- *Keep your opinions out of the interview.*   What you think about the project or the purpose of the document is not as relevant during an interview as what the other person thinks about these topics. Concentrate on gathering information rather than on debating issues.

- *Ask permission to follow up.*   End the interview by requesting a chance to call with follow-up questions if needed.

- *Thank the interviewee.*   Express your appreciation for the person's help and cooperation.

Immediately after the interview, write up your notes in a rough draft so that you can remember the details.

TESTING READER-ORIENTED DOCUMENTS

Along with analyzing and interviewing readers, writers sometimes evaluate audience needs through user tests of a document while it is still in draft. Manuals and instructions are particularly good candidates for user tests because their primary purpose is to guide readers in performing certain functions and because they are meant for groups of readers. When potential readers test a document's usefulness before the final draft stage, a writer can make needed changes in design and content based on actual experience with the document. There are three types of user tests.

Readers Answering Questions

Asking readers to answer questions after reading a document helps a writer decide whether the content will be easily understood by the audience. A utility company may want to distribute a brochure that explains to consumers how electricity use is computed and how they can reduce their energy consumption. Through a user test, the writer can determine if the brochure answers consumers' questions. Several versions of the same brochure also can be tested to determine which version readers find most useful. The test involves these steps:

1. A group of typical consumers reads the draft or drafts of the brochure.

2. The consumers then answer a series of questions on the content and perhaps try to compute an energy-consumption problem based on the information in the brochure.

3. The consumers also complete a demographic questionnaire, which asks for age, sex, job title, education level, length of time it took to complete the questions, and their opinions as to the readability of the brochure.

4. The writer then analyzes the results to see how correctly and how fast the consumers answered the questions and what the demographic information reveals about ease of use for different consumer groups.

5. Finally, the writer revises any portions of the brochure that proved difficult for readers and then retests the document.

Readers Performing a Task

In another situation, a writer may be most concerned about whether readers will be able to follow instructions and perform a task correctly. A manual may be tested in draft by operators and technicians who will use the final version. This user test follows the same general pattern as the preceding one, but the emphasis is on performing a task.

1. Selected operators follow the written instructions to perform the steps of a procedure.

2. The length of time to complete the task is recorded, as well as how smoothly the operators proceeded through the steps of the procedure.

3. The operators next complete a demographic questionnaire, comment on how effective they found the instructions, and point out areas that were unclear.

4. Analysis of the results focuses on correctness in completing the task, the length of time required, and the portions of the document that received most criticism from the readers.

5. The writer revises the sections that were not clear to the readers and retests the document.

Readers Thinking Aloud

Another type of user test requires readers to think aloud as they read through a document. This method (called *protocol analysis*) allows the writer or design-review team to record readers' responses everywhere in the document, analyze readers' comments, and revise content, structure, and style accordingly. Readers may be puzzled by the terminology, the sequence of items, too much or too little detail, the graphics, or sentence clarity. The writer can then revise these areas before the final draft.

CHAPTER SUMMARY

This chapter discusses analyzing readers and testing reader use of documents. Remember:

- Writers analyze readers according to the level of their readers' technical knowledge, positions in the organization, attitudes, reading styles, and positions as primary or secondary readers.

- Readers generally have one of three levels of technical knowledge—expert, semiexpert, and nonexpert.

- A reader's position in the organization may be as the writer's superior, subordinate, or peer.

- A reader's response to a document may be influenced by emotions, motivation, and preferences.

- Readers may differ in their reading styles. Some read only the abstract or introduction; others look for specific sections or topics; others read from beginning to end; and some may read in order to criticize the information or project.

- When a document has multiple readers, the writer must develop content, organization, and style to serve both primary and secondary readers.

- When writing for international readers, a writer must research cultural differences in communication style.

- Writers find out about their readers through informal checking and formal interviewing.

- Writers test document effectiveness by asking readers to (1) read the document and answer questions about content, (2) read the document and then perform the task explained in the document, and (3) talk about their reactions to the document.

SUPPLEMENTAL READINGS IN PART 2

Alessi, R. J. "Doing Business in Mexico," *Association Management,* p. 444.

Ridgway, L. "The Writer as Market Researcher," *Technical Communication,* p. 529.

Tarutz, J. H. "Editing for an International Audience," *Technical Editing,* p. 545.

"Tips, Tricks and Pitfalls to Avoid When Doing Business in the Tough but Lucrative Korean Market," *Business America,* p. 549.

ENDNOTES

1. Emily A. Thrush, "Bridging the Gaps: Technical Communication in an International and Multicultural Society," *Technical Communication Quarterly* 2.3 (Summer 1993): 271–283.

2. "Recognizing and Heeding Cultural Differences Can Be Key to International Business Success," *Business America* 115.10 (October 1994): 8–11.

3. "Recognizing and Heeding."

4. Ernest Plock, "Understanding Cultural Traditions Is Critical When Doing Business with the Newly Independent States," *Business America* 115.10 (October 1994): 14.

5. "Recognizing and Heeding."

6. William Horton, "The Almost Universal Language: Graphics for International Documents," *Technical Communication* 40.4 (1993): 682–692.

MODEL 3-1   Commentary

This brochure is designed to help arthritis patients understand their disease. Other readers might be family members or friends of the patients. The brochure begins by defining the disease and the types of arthritis that typically occur. The drawing shows readers the differences between a normal hip and an arthritic one. The brochure concludes with an explanation of the kinds of treatment available and offers the assurance that the disease is treatable if not curable.

Discussion

1. Discuss the section headings. Why are they appropriate for the readers of the brochure?

2. Discuss the purpose of the photo in the brochure. Is it worth the space it uses or should more information about the disease be included?

3. This brochure is written for multiple readers—all nonexperts in the subject. In groups, decide what information you would include in a 500-word summary to be read by the spouses of arthritis patients. What information would you omit? Draft the 500-word summary, and compare your draft with those written by other groups.

4. Individually, or in groups if your instructor prefers, develop a reader test as discussed in this chapter under "Testing Reader-oriented Documents." Bring to class a short brochure intended for general readers and distributed by a utility company, a charitable organization, or a consumer-products company. Develop five questions designed to test a reader's understanding of the information in the brochure. Follow the testing procedure described under "Readers Answering Questions." Analyze the results and identify any sections of the brochure that could be improved. Rewrite one section of the brochure based on your reader test. Submit both the original brochure and your revision of one section to your instructor.

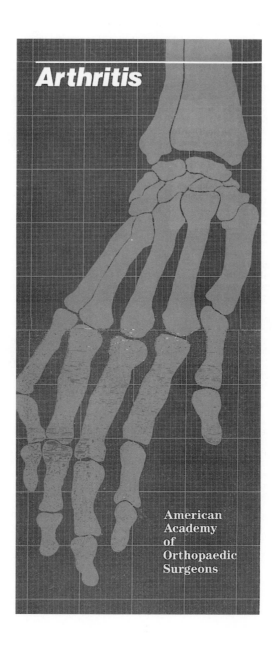

Model 3-1

What is arthritis?

The word "arthritis" means joint inflammation (*arthr* = joint; *itis* = inflammation). As many as 36 million people in the United States have some form of arthritis. It is a major cause of lost work time and causes serious disability in many persons. Although arthritis is mainly a disease of adults, children may also have it.

What is a joint?

A joint is a special structure in the body where the ends of two or more bones meet. For example, a bone of the lower leg called the tibia and the thigh bone, which is called the femur, meet to form the knee joint. The hip is a simple ball and socket joint. The upper end of the femur is the ball. It fits into the socket, a part of the pelvis called the acetabulum.

The bone ends of a joint are covered with a smooth, glistening material called hyaline cartilage. This material cushions the underlying bone from excessive force or pressure and allows the joint to move easily without pain. The joint is enclosed in a capsule with a smooth lining called the synovium. The synovium produces a lubricant, synovial fluid, which helps to reduce friction and wear in a joint. Connecting the bones are ligaments, which keep the joint stable. Crossing the joint are muscles and tendons, which also help to keep the joint stable and enable it to move.

What is inflammation?

Inflammation is one of the body's normal reactions to injury or disease. When a part of the body is injured, infected, or diseased, the body's natural defenses work to repair the problem. In an injured or diseased joint, this results in swelling, pain, and stiffness. Inflammation is usually temporary, but in arthritic joints, it may cause long-lasting or permanent disability.

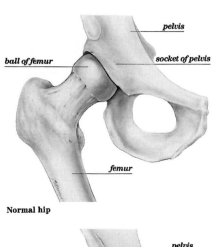

pelvis
ball of femur
socket of pelvis
femur

Normal hip

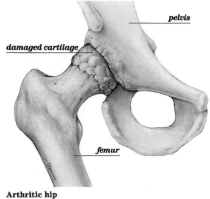

pelvis
damaged cartilage
femur

Arthritic hip

Types of arthritis

What is osteoarthritis?

There are more than 100 different types of arthritis. One major type is osteoarthritis, which is sometimes called degenerative joint disease. It occurs to some extent in most people as they age. Osteoarthritis can begin earlier as a result of a joint injury or overuse. Often, weightbearing joints such as the knee, hip, and spine, are involved. The wrists, elbows, and shoulders are usually not affected by osteoarthritis. These joints may be affected if they are used extensively in either work or recreational activities, or if they have been damaged from fractures or other injuries.

In osteoarthritis, the cartilage surface covering the bone ends becomes rough and eventually wears away. In some cases, an abnormal bone growth called a "spur" can develop. Pain and swelling result from joint inflammation. Continued use of the joint produces more pain. It may be relieved somewhat by rest.

What is rheumatoid arthritis?

Rheumatoid arthritis is a chronic, or long-lasting disease that can affect many parts of the body, including the joints. In rheumatoid arthritis, the joint fluid contains chemical substances that attack the joint surface and damage it. Inflammation occurs in response to the disease. The joints most commonly involved are those in the hands, wrists, feet, and ankles, but large joints such as hips, knees, and elbows may also be involved. Swelling, pain, and stiffness are usually present even when the joint is not used. These are the main signs of rheumatoid arthritis and its related diseases. Rheumatoid arthritis can affect persons of all ages, even children, although more than 70% of persons with this disease are over thirty. Many joints of the body may be involved at the same time.

How is arthritis diagnosed?

Diagnosing arthritis includes noting the patient's symptoms, performing a physical examination, and taking x-rays, which are important in showing the extent of damage to the joint. Blood tests and other laboratory tests, such as examination of the joint fluid, may help to determine the type of arthritis the patient has. Once the diagnosis has been made, treatment can begin.

In most cases, people with arthritis can continue to perform the activities of daily living.

How is arthritis treated?

The goals of treatment are to provide pain relief and also to maintain or restore function to the arthritic joint. There are several kinds of treatment:

Medication—Many medications, including aspirin and other anti-inflammatory drugs, may be used to control pain and inflammation in arthritis. The physician chooses a particular medication by taking into account the type of arthritis, its severity, and the patient's general physical health. At times, injections of a substance called cortisone directly into the joint may help to relieve pain and swelling. It is important to know, however, that repeated frequent injections into the same joint can have undesirable side effects.

Joint protection—Canes, crutches, walkers, or splints may help relieve the stress and strain on arthritic joints. Protection of the joint also includes learning methods of performing daily activities that are the least stressful to painful joints. In addition, certain exercises and other forms of physical therapy, such as heat treatments, are used to treat arthritis. They can help to relieve stiffness and to strengthen the weakened muscles around the joint. The type of physical therapy depends on the type and severity of the arthritis and the particular joints involved.

Surgery—In general, an orthopaedist will perform surgery for arthritis when other methods of non-surgical treatment have failed to give the patient sufficient relief. The physician and patient will choose the type of surgery by taking into account the type of arthritis, its severity, and the patient's physical condition. Surgical procedures include
■ removal of the diseased or damaged joint lining;
■ realignment of the joints;
■ total joint replacement; and
■ fusion, which permanently places the bone ends of a joint together to prevent joint motion.

Is there a cure for arthritis?

At present, most types of arthritis cannot be cured. Researchers continue to make progress in finding the underlying causes for the major types of arthritis. Often, when a cause is found for a disease, preventive measures can be undertaken. In the meantime, orthopaedists, working with other physicians and scientists, have developed effective treatments for arthritis.

In most cases, persons with arthritis can continue to perform the activities of daily living. Weight reduction for obese persons with osteoarthritis, physical therapy, and anti-inflammatory drugs are measures that can be taken to reduce pain and stiffness.

In persons with severe cases of arthritis, orthopaedic surgery can provide dramatic pain relief and restore lost joint function. A total joint replacement, for example, can enable a person with severe arthritis in the hip or the knee to walk without pain or stiffness.

Some types of arthritis, especially the rheumatoid form, are best treated by a team of health care professionals with special abilities. These professionals include rheumatologists (nonsurgeons who are arthritis specialists), physical and occupational therapists, social workers, as well as orthopaedic surgeons.

This page is the first in a set of instructions from a company service manual. The instructions cover one stage of the complicated procedure of installing a hard disk drive. The opening paragraph identifies the intended reader and states the purpose of the instructions. The writer also refers the reader to other manuals that will be needed to complete the installation. A list of parts appears before the instruction steps.

Discussion

1. The parts for this procedure are packaged in a kit. Discuss why the writer decided to list the parts separately.

2. Discuss the format. What is the purpose of the detailed heading at the top right? Compare the format to that in Model 3-1. How does format aid the reader of each model?

3. Discuss whether the reader of Model 3-2 is probably a nonexpert, semiexpert, or expert in the subject.

4. Find a user manual for a word-processing program. Rewrite one page of the introductory material for an eighth-grade student who is going to start using the program.

CIBA·CORNING

ACS:*180°PLUS*
ACS:*180°*
Express® Plus
Hard Disk Drive Kit
Part No. 1458x390

Installation Instructions

These instructions are intended for Field Service Engineers trained by Ciba Corning to service ACS:180® and Express® Plus systems. Use these instructions to install the hard disk drive on the ACS:180 or the Express Plus systems.

NOTE: This procedure requires you to format the new hard disk drive, load the software, restore the calibrations, and restore the customer parameters. Refer to the current version of the *ACS:180 Software Installation Instructions* or the *Express Plus Software Installation Instructions*.

Hard Disk Drive Kit:

Item	Part Number	Quantity
Quantum LPS 170S or 270S Hard Disk Drive	27307	1
LED Cable	1458x328	1

For the ACS:180 Systems

1. Turn the system off and disconnect the power cord.
2. Remove the CRT module:
   a. Disconnect the cable from position J36 on the Backplane board.
   b. Remove the top two screws and the bottom right screw from the front of the bracket that holds the CRT module.
   c. Slide the CRT module forward.

 CAUTION: The hard disk data cable is not keyed; therefore, if this cable is incorrectly connected to the hard disk drive, the system will not operate properly and could cause damage to the hard disk drive.

3. Remove the following cables from the hard disk drive:
   - Hard disk data cable
   - Power cable
   - LED cable assembly
4. Remove the floppy disk drive from the system.
5. Remove the hard disk drive from the bracket, as shown in Figure 1. Set the screws and washers aside.

Model 3-2

This model shows the opening page of a report by research chemists for the U.S. Bureau of Mines. The report is an investigative study of the thermodynamics of certain chemical compounds. Readers are other research scientists interested in this experiment and the results that might influence their own research. The abstract is written for expert readers and does not provide a summary for nonexpert readers. You probably cannot understand the language or the content of this document.

The report language is highly specialized. None of the technical terms or chemical symbols is defined because the writer expects only experts to read the report.

Discussion

1. Compare the language, kinds of information, and formats of Models 3-1, 3-2, and 3-3, and discuss how each document is appropriate for its readers.

2. Find a set of instructions used in your workplace. Bring a copy to class. In groups, exchange instructions and read them from the perspective of a new employee. Discuss what items might confuse a reader and what information may need to be added to the instructions to help the reader.

Enthalpy of Formation of 2CdO • CdSO$_4$

by H. C. Ko[1] and R. R. Brown[1]

Abstract

The Bureau of Mines maintains an active program in thermochemistry to provide thermodynamic data for the advancement of mineral science and technology. As part of this effort, the standard enthalpy of formation at 298.15 K, ΔHf°, for 2CdO • CdSO$_4$ was determined by HCl acid solution calorimetry to be −345.69 ±0.61 kcal/mol.

Introduction

Cadmium oxysulfate (2CdO • CdSO$_4$) is known as an intermediate compound in the decomposition process of cadmium sulfate (CdSO$_4$). There is only one reported value (4)[2] for the enthalpy of formation at 2CdO • CdSO$_4$, and that value was determined by a static manometric method. The objective of this investigation was to establish the standard enthalpy of formation for this compound by HCl solution calorimetry, which is inherently a more accurate method. This investigation was conducted as part of the Bureau of Mines effort to provide thermodynamic data for the advancement of mineral technology.

Materials

Cadmium oxide: Baker[3] analyzed reagent-grade CdO was dried at 500°C for 2 hr. X-ray diffraction analysis indicated that the pattern matched the one given by PDF card 5–640 (2). Spectrographic analysis indicated 0.05 pct Pb to be present as the only significant impurity.

Cadmium oxysulfate: 2CdO • CdSO$_4$ was prepared by reacting stoichiometric quantities of anhydrous CdSO$_4$ and CdO in a sealed, evacuated Vycor tube according to the following procedure. The materials were blended and transferred to a Vycor reaction tube. The reaction tube was evacuated and heated to 330°C for 17 hr to remove traces of water that may have been introduced during blending and transferring. The tube was then sealed and heated to 600°C for 19 hr. The temperature was. . . .

---

[1]Research chemist, Albany Research Center, Bureau of Mines, Albany, Oreg.
[2]Underlined numbers in parentheses refer to items in the list of references at the end of this report.
[3]Reference to specific trade names does not imply endorsement by the Bureau of Mines.

Model 3-3

Chapter 3   Exercises

1. At a large law firm, one of the items in a packet labeled "Information for New Employees" was the following memo. Identify the difficulties a new employee would have in understanding this memo. In groups, draft a new memo to cover the topic. Add or change any information you wish.

> To: All Employees
> From: Social Committee
> Because of the increased work loads, staff shortages, and absences from the coffees, the following procedure will be followed beginning Monday. When a staff member leaves, gets married, or has a baby, doughnuts will be placed in the upstairs and downstairs lounges. A notice will be placed on the bulletin board and a member of the social committee will present the gift. Should you have any questions, contact one of the Social Committee members.

2. Do a Web search for the general topic of automobile repair. Identify four information sites and decide whether the sites are directed at expert, semiexpert, or nonexpert readers. What specific elements at the sites indicate the level of reader? Bring your list to class and share your findings with your classmates. Or, if your instructor prefers, select a topic in your field and search the Web for relevant sites.

3. In groups, discuss the following situations and decide what kinds of information the reader will want and need.

a. A committee from the state historical society will visit the Montello House in Santa Fe to decide whether to include the house as an official stop in its "Tour of Historical New Mexico" program. You must write an information bulletin to help the committee members evaluate the house, which was built in 1803 by a wealthy Mexican cattleman, remodeled in 1889 as the official mayor's house, fell into disrepair as it was used by a series of owners, and then was restored by a community group in 1992. Several famous people have lived in the 28-room house.

b. Your company, Health Wise Food Stores, is switching its health plan to a new Health Maintenance Organization (HMO). A 96-page booklet describing the details of the program will be given to all 68 employees. You are told to write a memo that explains the four or five topics of most concern to employees so that they will not have to read the booklet immediately.

c. As a member of your college orientation committee, you need to write an information bulletin about one of your favorite campus activities. Your readers are international students who have never participated in the activity. In groups, select an activity and decide what kinds of information you would include.

4. Select either (1) a document used by most students on campus (e.g., parking regulations, instructions for library use) or (2) a consumer document (e.g., leaflet from a utility company, instructions packed with a product) and interview an international student about what changes in language or graphics would be necessary in that student's country. Discuss the results.

CHAPTER 4

Organization

SORTING INFORMATION

The organization of a document has a strong influence on how well the reader understands and is able to use the information. If a document is well organized with headings, lists, and key words that trigger a reader's memory of prior knowledge of the subject, a reader can learn and use new information effectively. Reading studies show that if adults are given poorly organized information, they tend to reorganize it themselves and to omit information that does not clearly fit into their prior knowledge.[1] As a writer you must organize documents to help readers learn and remember new information.

In some writing situations, documents have predetermined organizational patterns. Social workers at a child welfare agency may be directed to present information in all case reports under the major topics of living conditions, parental attitudes, previous agency contact, and suspected child abuse. Because these major topics appear in all the agency case reports, readers who use them regularly, such as attorneys and judges, know where to look for the specific details they need. Such consistency is useful to readers if the documents have a standard format—only the details change from situation to situation.

If you are writing a document that does not have standard categories for information, however, your first step will be to organize the information into major topics and identify appropriate subtopics.

Select Major Topics

Begin organizing your document by sorting the information into major topics. Select the topics based on your analysis of your readers' interest in and need for information. If you are writing a report about columns or pillars, you should group your information into major topics that represent what your readers want to know about the subject. If your readers are interested in Greek and Roman column design, you can group your information according to classic column type—Doric, Ionic, and Corinthian. Readers interested in learning about column construction may prefer an organization based on construction materials, such as brick, marble, wood, stone, and metal. Readers interested in the architectural history of columns may prefer an organization based on time period, such as Ancient, Medieval, and Renaissance. Readers interested in the cultural differences in column design may prefer the information grouped according to geographic region, such as Asian, Mediterranean, and North American.

As you sort your information into major topics, remember that the topics should be similar in type and relatively equal in importance. You should not have one major topic based on column design and one based on time period. Such a mix of topics would confuse your readers. You should also be certain that the major topics you select are distinct. You would not want to use time periods that overlap, such as the Renaissance and the fifteenth century, or column designs that overlap, such as Doric and Tuscan. Consider carefully which major topics represent appropriate groups of information for your readers.

Identify Subtopics

After you determine your major topics, consider how to sort the information into appropriate subtopics. Do not simply lump facts together. Instead, think about what specific information you have that will support each major topic. If your major topics are based on classic column types, your readers may be interested in such subtopics as Greek design, Roman design, changes in design over time, and how the Greeks and Romans used the columns. These subtopics, or specific pieces of information, should appear under each of the major topics because your readers want to know how these details relate to each column type. When you have identified your major topics and have selected appropriate subtopics, you are ready to begin outlining.

CONSTRUCTING OUTLINES

Think of an outline as a map that identifies the major topics and shows their location in a document. Outlines provide three advantages to a writer:

1. A writer can "see" the structure of a document before beginning a rough draft in the same way that a traveler can follow the route of a journey on a road map before getting into a car.

2. Having a tentative organizational plan helps a writer concentrate on presenting and explaining the information in the rough draft, rather than on writing and organizing at the same time.

3. A writer can keep track of organizational decisions no matter how many interruptions occur in the writing process.

An outline usually begins as a short, informal list of topics and grows into a detailed list that includes all major topics and subtopics and groups them into chunks of information most appropriate for the reader. Consider this situation: Al Martinez's first project as a summer intern in the Personnel Department of Tri-Tech Chemical Company is to write a bulletin explaining the company rules on travel and business expenses. Al's readers will be both the managers who travel and the secretaries who handle the paperwork. At present, the pertinent information is scattered through more than a dozen memos written over the last three years. After reading all these memos and noting appropriate items, Al begins to organize his information. He begins with an informal outline.

Informal Outlines

An *informal outline* is a list of main topics in the order the writer expects to present them in the rough draft. Computers have made outlining faster and easier than it used to be. With word processing, a writer can quickly (1) add or delete items and rearrange them without recopying sections that do not change and (2) keep the outline up to date by changing it to match revisions in rough drafts. In developing an informal outline, remember these guidelines:

1. List all the relevant topics in any order at first. Al listed the main topics for his bulletin in the order in which he found them discussed in previous memos in company files.

2. Identify the major groups of related information from your list. Looking at his list of items, Al saw immediately that most of his information centered around types of expenses and reimbursement and approval procedures. Al, therefore, clustered his information into groups representing these topics.

3. Arrange the information groups in an order that will best serve the readers' need to know. Al decided to present reimbursement procedures first because readers would need to know about those before traveling. He then organized groups representing types of expenses from most common to least common so that the majority of readers could find the information they needed as quickly as possible.

Model 4-1 shows Al's informal outline for his bulletin. Writers usually use informal outlines to group and order information in the planning stage. Often, an informal outline is all that a writer needs. For some documents, such as a manual, however, a writer must prepare a formal outline that will be part of the document. Also, some writers prefer to work with formal outlines in the planning stage.

Formal Outlines

A *formal outline* uses a special numbering system and includes subtopics under each major section. A formal outline is a more detailed map of the organization plan for a document. Writers usually use one of two numbering

1. Travel Authorization and Reimbursement Rules
2. Meals
3. Hotels
4. Transportation
5. Daily Incidental Expenses
6. Spouse's Travel
7. Entertainment
8. Gifts
9. Loss or Damage
10. Nonreimbursed Items

MODEL 4-1   Al's Informal Outline

systems for outlines: (1) Roman and Arabic numerals or (2) decimals (also called the *military numbering system*). Choose whichever numbering system you prefer unless your outline will be part of the final document. In that case, use the numbering system most familiar to your readers or the one your company prefers. Model 4-2 shows a set of topics organized by both numbering systems.

Al Martinez decided to develop his informal outline into a formal one because he wanted a detailed plan before he began his rough draft.

Topic Outlines

A *topic outline* lists all the major topics and all the subtopics in a document by key words. Like the major topics, all subtopics should be in an order that the readers will find useful. Al developed his formal topic outline by adding the items he knew he had to explain under each major topic and using the Roman–Arabic numbering system. Model 4-3 shows Al's formal topic outline.

In drafting his formal topic outline, Al knew that he wanted to begin his bulletin by explaining the process of applying for and receiving reimbursement for travel expenses because his readers needed to understand that system before they began collecting travel-expense information and preparing expense reports. He organized expense topics in the order in which they appeared on the forms his readers would have to submit and then listed specific items under each main topic. While redrafting his outline, Al revised some of his earlier organizational decisions. First, he decided that the topic "Spouse's Travel" was not really a separate item and ought to be covered under each travel expense item, such as "Hotels." He also decided that the topic "Gifts" was really a form

Roman-Arabic Numbering System
I. Costs
   A. Equipment
      1. Purchase
      2. Maintenance
         a. Weekly
         b. Breakdown
   B. Employees
      1. Salaries
      2. Benefits
II. Locations
   A. European
      1. France

Decimal Numbering System
1.0 Costs
   1.1 Equipment
      1.1.1. Purchase
      1.1.2. Maintenance
         1.1.2.1. Weekly
         1.1.2.2. Breakdown
   1.2 Employees
      1.2.1. Salaries
      1.2.2. Benefits
2.0 Locations
   2.1 European
      2.1.1. France

MODEL 4-2   Formal Outline Numbering Systems

of entertainment for clients, so he listed gifts under "Entertainment" in his formal topic outline.

Sentence Outlines

A *sentence outline* develops a topic outline by stating each point in a full sentence. When a project is long and complicated or the writer is not confident about the subject, a sentence outline helps clarify content and organization before drafting begins. Some writers prefer sentence outlines because they can use the sentences in their first drafts, thereby speeding up the initial drafting. Al Martinez also decided to expand his topic outline into a sentence outline as a way of moving closer to his first draft. Model 4-4 shows a portion of Al's sentence outline.

I. Travel Authorization and Reimbursement
  A. Approval
  B. Forms
     1. Form 881
     2. Form 669
     3. Form 40-A
     4. Form 1389
  C. Submission
II. Meals
  A. Breakfast
  B. Lunch
  C. Dinner
III. Hotels
  A. Chain Guaranteed Rates
  B. Suites
IV. Transportation
  A. Automobile
     1. Personal Cars
        a. Mileage
        b. Maintenance
     2. Rental Cars
        a. Approved Companies
        b. Actual Costs Only
  B. Airplane
     1. Tri-Tech Aircraft
     2. Other Companies' Aircraft
     3. Commercial Aircraft
  C. Railroad
  D. Taxi, Limousine, Bus
V. Daily Incidental Expenses
  A. Parking and Tolls
  B. Tips
  C. Laundry and Telephone
VI. Entertainment
  A. Parties
     1. Home
     2. Commercial
  B. Meals
  C. Gifts
     1. Tickets
     2. Objects
VII. Loss or Damage
VIII. Nonreimbursed Items
  A. Personal Items
  B. Legal, Insurance Expenses

MODEL 4-3   Al's Formal Topic Outline

I. Travel Authorization and Reimbursement. Tri-Tech will pay travel expenses directly or reimburse an employee for costs of traveling on company business.
   A. All official travel for Tri-Tech must be approved in advance by supervisors.
   B. Several company forms must be completed and approved.
      1. Form 881, "Travel Authorization," is used for trip approval if travel reservations are needed.
      2. Form 669, "Petty Cash Requisition," is used if no travel reservations are needed.
      3. Form 40-A, "Domestic Travel Expenses," is used to report reimbursable expenses in the United States.
      4. Form 1389, "Foreign Expense Payment," is used to report reimbursable expenses outside the United States.
   C. Travel authorization forms should be submitted to the employee's supervisor, but posttravel forms should be sent directly to the Travel Coordinator in the Personnel Department.
II. Meals. Tri-Tech will reimburse employees for three meals a day while traveling.
   A. Breakfast expenses are reimbursed if the employee is away overnight or leaves home before 6:00 a.m.

MODEL 4-4   A Portion of Al's Formal Sentence Outline

DEVELOPING EFFECTIVE PARAGRAPHS

Each paragraph in a document is a unit of sentences that focuses on one idea and acts as a visual element to break up the text into manageable chunks of information. Effective paragraphs guide readers by

- Introducing individually distinct but related topics
- Emphasizing key points
- Showing relationships between major points
- Providing visual breaks in pages to ease reading

For effective paragraphs, writers should consider unity, coherence, development, and an organizational pattern for presenting information.

Unity

Unity in a paragraph means concentration on a single topic. One sentence in the paragraph is the *summary sentence* (also called the *topic sentence*), and it establishes the main point. The other sentences explain or expand the main point. If a writer introduces several major points into one paragraph without developing them fully, the mix of ideas violates the unity of the paragraph and leaves readers confused. Here is a paragraph that lacks unity:

> Many factors influence the selection of roofing material. Only project managers and engineers have the authority to change the recommendations, and the changes should be in writing. The proper installation of roofing material is important, and contractors should be trained carefully. Roof incline, roof deck construction, and climatic conditions must be considered in selecting roofing material.

The first sentence appears to be a topic sentence, indicating that the paragraph will focus on factors in selecting roofing. Readers, therefore, would expect to find individual factors enumerated and explained. However, the second and third sentences are unrelated to the opening and instead introduce two new topics: authority to select roofing and the training of contractors. The fourth sentence returns to the topic of selecting roofing material. Thus the paragraph actually introduces three topics, none of which is explained. The paragraph fails to fulfill the expectations of the reader. Here is a revision to achieve unity:

> Three factors influence the selection of roofing material. One factor is roof incline. A minimum of ¼ in. per foot incline is recommended by all suppliers. A second factor is roof deck construction. Before installing roofing material, a contractor must cover a metal deck with rigid installation, prime a concrete deck to level depressions, or cover a wooden deck with a base sheet. Finally, climatic conditions also affect roofing selection. Roofing in very wet climates must be combined with an all-weather aluminum roof coating.

In this version, the paragraph is unified under the topic of which factors influence the selection of roofing materials. The opening sentence establishes this main topic; then the sentences that follow identify the three factors and describe how contractors should handle them. Remember, readers are better able to process information if they are presented one major point at a time.

Coherence

A paragraph is *coherent* when the sentences proceed in a sequence that supports one point at a time. Transitional, or connecting, words and phrases help coherence by showing the relationships between ideas and by creating a smooth flow of sentences. Here are the most common ways writers achieve transition:

- Repeat key words from sentence to sentence.
- Use a pronoun for a preceding key term.
- Use a synonym for a preceding key term.

- Use demonstrative adjectives (*this* report, *that* plan, *these* systems, *those* experiments).

- Use connecting words (*however, therefore, also, nevertheless, before, after, consequently, moreover, likewise, meanwhile*) or connecting phrases (*for example, as a result, in other words, in addition, in the same manner*).

- Use simple enumeration (*first, second, finally, next*).

Here is a paragraph that lacks clear transitions, and the sentences are not in the best sequence to explain the two taxes under discussion:

> Married couples should think about two taxes. When a person dies, an estate tax is levied against the value of the assets that pass on to the heirs by will or automatic transfer. Income tax on capital gains is affected by whatever form of ownership of property is chosen. Under current law, property that one spouse inherits from the other is exempt from estate tax. Married couples who remain together until death do not need to consider estate taxes in ownership of their homes. The basic rule for capital gains tax is that when property is inherited by one person from another, the financial basis of the property begins anew. For future capital gains computations, it is treated as though it were purchased at the market value at the time of inheritance. When the property is sold, tax is due on the appreciation in value since the time it was inherited. No tax is due on the increase in value from actual purchase to time of inheritance. If the property is owned jointly, one-half gets the financial new start.[2]

This paragraph attempts to describe the impact of two federal taxes on married couples who own their homes jointly. The writer begins with the topic of estate tax, but he or she quickly jumps to the capital gains tax, then returns to the estate tax, and finally concludes with the capital gains tax. Since readers expect information to be grouped according to topic, they must sort out the sentences for themselves in order to use the information efficiently. The lack of transition also forces readers to move from point to point without any clear indication of the relationships between ideas. Here is a revision of the paragraph with the transitions highlighted:

> For financial planning, married couples must think about two taxes. **First,** is the estate tax. When an individual dies, **this tax** is levied against the value of the assets that pass on to the heirs by will or automatic transfer. Under current law, any amount of property that one spouse inherits from the other is exempt from **estate tax. Therefore,** married couples who remain together until death do not need to consider **estate taxes** in planning ownership of their home. The **second** relevant tax is capital gains. Unlike **estate tax, capital gains tax** is affected by what form of ownership of property a couple chooses. The basic rule for **capital gains tax** is that when property is inherited by one person from another, it begins anew for tax purposes. **That is,** for future **capital gains** computation, the **property** is treated as though it were purchased at the market value at the time of inheritance. When the **property** is sold, tax is due

on the appreciation in value since the time it was inherited. No tax, **however,** is due on the increase in value from actual purchase to time of inheritance. If the **property** is owned jointly, one-half begins anew for tax purposes.

In this revision, the sentences are rearranged so that the writer gives information first about the estate tax and then about the capital gains tax. Transitions come from repetition of key words, pronouns, demonstrative adjectives, and connecting words or phrases.

Coherence in paragraphs is essential if readers are to use a document effectively. When a reader stumbles through a paragraph trying to sort out the information or to decide the relationships between items, the reader's understanding and patience diminish rapidly.

Development

Develop your paragraphs by including enough details so that your reader understands the main point. Generally, one- and two-sentence paragraphs are not fully developed unless they are used for purposes of transition or emphasis or are quotations. Except in these circumstances, a paragraph should contain a summary or topic sentence and details that support the topic.

Here is a poorly developed paragraph from a brochure that explains diabetes to patients who must learn new eating habits.

> People with insulin-dependent diabetes need to plan meals for consistency. Insulin reactions can occur if meals are not balanced.

This sample paragraph is inadequately developed for a new patient who knows very little about the disease. The opening sentence suggests that the paragraph will describe meal planning for diabetics. Instead, the second sentence tells what will happen without meal planning. Either sentence could be the true topic sentence, and neither point is developed. The reader is left, therefore, with an incomplete understanding of the subject and no way to begin meal planning. Here is a revision:

> People with insulin-dependent diabetes need to plan meals for consistency. To control blood sugar levels, schedule meals for the same time every day. In addition, eat about the same amounts of carbohydrates, protein, and fat every day in the same combinations and at the same times. Your doctor will tell you the exact amounts appropriate for you. This consistency in eating is important because your insulin dose is based on a set food intake. If your meal plan is not balanced, an insulin reaction may occur.

In this revision, the writer develops the summary sentence by giving examples of what consistency means. The paragraph is developed further by an explanation of the consequences if patients do not plan balanced meals. The point about an insulin reaction is now connected to the main topic of the paragraph—meal planning.

In developing paragraphs, think first about the main idea and then determine what information the reader needs to understand that idea. Here are some ways to develop your paragraphs:

- Provide examples of the topic.

- Include facts, statistics, evidence, details, or precedents that confirm the topic.

- Quote, paraphrase, or summarize the evidence of other people on the topic.

- Describe an event that has some influence on the topic.

- Define terms connected with the topic.

- Explain how equipment operates.

- Describe the physical appearance of an object, area, or person.

In developing your paragraphs, remember that long, unbroken sections of detailed information may overwhelm readers, especially those without expert knowledge of the subject, and may interfere with the ability of readers to use the information.

STRATEGIES—Emphasis

Emphasize a key term by placing it at the beginning or the end of a sentence.

No: In the past decade, an analytical technique called **x-ray fluorescence** has become important in the cement industry.

Yes: **X-ray fluorescence,** an analytical technique, has become important in the cement industry in the past decade.

Yes: In the past decade, the cement industry has accepted an analytical technique called **x-ray fluorescence.**

Patterns for Presenting Information

The following patterns for presenting information can be effective ways to organize paragraphs or entire sections of a document. Several organizational patterns may appear in a single document. A writer preparing a manual may use one pattern to give instructions, another to explain a new concept, and a third to help readers visualize the differences between two procedures. Select the pattern that will best help your readers understand and use the information.

Ascending or Descending Order of Importance Pattern

To discuss information in order of importance to the reader, use the ascending (lowest-to-highest) or descending (highest-to-lowest) pattern. If you are describing the degrees of hazard of several procedures or the seriousness of several production problems, you may want to use the descending pattern to alert your readers to the matter most in need of attention. In technical writing, the descending order usually is preferred by busy executives because they want to know the most important facts about a subject first and may even stop reading once they understand the main points. However, the ascending order can be effective if you are building a persuasive case on why, for example, a distribution system should be changed.

This excerpt from an advertisement for a mutual fund illustrates the descending order of importance in a list of benefits for potential investors in the fund:

> Experienced and successful investors select the Davies-Meredith Equity Fund because
>
> 1. The Fund has outperformed 98% of all mutual funds in its category for the past 18 months.
> 2. The Fund charges no investment fees or commissions.
> 3. A 24-hour toll-free number is available for transfers, withdrawals, or account information.
> 4. Each investor receives the free monthly newsletter, "Investing for Your Future."

Although a reader may be persuaded to invest in the fund by any of these reasons, most potential investors would agree that the first item is most important and the last item least important. The writer uses the descending order of importance to attract the reader's attention.

The writer, however, uses the ascending order of importance to illustrate the gains in an investment over time:

> Long-term investment brings the greatest gains. An initial investment of $1000 would have nearly doubled in six years:
>
> | | |
> |---|---|
> | 1 year | $1045 |
> | 2 years | $1211 |
> | 4 years | $1571 |
> | 6 years | $1987 |

The ascending order pattern here emphasizes to the investor the benefits of keeping money in the fund for several years.

Cause-and-Effect Pattern

The cause-and-effect pattern is useful when a writer wants to show readers the relationship between specific events. If you are writing a report about equipment problems, the cause-and-effect pattern can help readers see how one breakdown led to another and interrupted production. Be sure to present a clear relationship between cause and effect and give readers evidence of that relationship. If you are merely speculating about causes, make this clear:

> The probable cause of the gas leak was a blown gasket in the transformer.

Writers sometimes choose to describe events from effects back to cause. Lengthy research reports often establish the results first and then explain the causes of those results.

This excerpt from a pamphlet for dental patients uses cause and effect to explain how periodontal disease develops:

> Improper brushing or lack of flossing and regular professional tooth clean-ing allows the normal bacteria present in the mouth to form a bacterial plaque. This plaque creates spaces or pockets between the gums and roots of the teeth. Chronic inflammation of the gums then develops. Left untreated, the inflam-mation erodes the bone in which the teeth are anchored, causing the teeth to loosen or migrate. Advanced periodontal disease requires surgery to reconstruct the supporting structures of the teeth.

Chronological Pattern

The chronological pattern is used to present material in stages or steps from first to last when readers need to understand a sequence of events or follow spe-cific steps to perform a task. This excerpt from consumer instructions for a popcorn maker illustrates the chronological pattern:

> 1. Before using, wash cover, butter-measuring cup, and popping cham-ber in hot water. Rinse and dry. *Do not immerse housing in water.*
> 2. Place popcorn container under chute.
> 3. Preheat the unit for 3 minutes.
> 4. Using the butter-measuring cup, pour ½ cup kernels into popping chamber.

Instructions should always be written in the chronological pattern. This pat-tern is also appropriate when the writer needs to describe a test or a process so that the reader can visualize it, as in this description of the test method from a media research report:

> The television viewers ($N = 923$) first completed a demographic question-naire. They then watched a 2- to 3-minute clip of the television program they were rating. After seeing the clip, viewers used the Personal Attributes Ques-tionnaire to rate the male and female characters for stereotypical traits. Finally, viewers rated themselves on the Personal Attributes Questionnaire for com-parison purposes.

Classification Pattern

The classification pattern involves grouping items in terms of certain characteristics and showing your readers the similarities within each group. The basis for classification should be the one most useful for your purpose and your readers. You might classify foods as protein, carbohydrate, or fat for a report to dietitians. In a report on foods for a culinary society, however, you might classify them as beverages, appetizers, and desserts. Classification is useful when you have many items to discuss, but if your categories are too broad, your readers will have trouble understanding the distinctiveness of each class. Classifying all edibles under "food" for either of the two reports just mentioned would not be useful because you would have no basis for distinguishing the individual items. This paragraph from a student report uses classification to explain types of sugars:

> When analyzing a patient's nutritional needs, dietitians generally sort sugars into five types. Sucrose comes from sugar cane and sugar beets and is found in table sugar. Dextrose is derived from corn and is used in many commercially produced foods. Lactose is found in milk and milk products, and some people find it difficult to digest. Fructose is in fruits and is somewhat sweeter than the other sugars. Lastly, glucose is found in a variety of fruits, honeys, and vegetables.

Partition Pattern

The partition pattern, in contrast to the classification pattern, involves separating a topic or system into its individual features. This division allows readers to master information about one aspect of the topic before going on to the next. Instructions are always divided into steps so that readers can perform one step at a time. The readers' purpose in needing the information should guide selection of the basis for partition. For example, a skier on the World Cup circuit would be interested in a discussion of skis based on their use in certain types of races, such as downhill or slalom. A manufacturer interested in producing skis might want the same discussion based on materials used in production. A sales representative might want the discussion based on costs of the different types of skis. This excerpt from a weather information brochure for consumers uses partition to explain Earth's atmosphere:

> Earth's atmosphere is divided into five layers. The first layer, the troposphere, is next to Earth's surface and extends about 7 miles up. It contains most of the clouds and weather activity. The next layer is the stratosphere extending to about 30 miles up and containing relatively little water or dust. The third layer is the mesosphere extending 30 to 50 miles up. The mesosphere is very cold, dropping to about minus 100 Fahrenheit. The fourth layer, the thermosphere, is also called the ionosphere and extends to about 250 miles up. The thermosphere has rapidly increasing temperatures because of solar radiation. The final layer is the exosphere in which the traces of atmosphere fade into space.

Comparison and Contrast Pattern

The comparison and contrast pattern focuses on the similarities (comparison) or differences (contrast) between subjects. Writers often find this pattern useful because they can explain a complex topic by comparing or contrasting it with another familiar topic. For this pattern, the writer has to set up the basis for comparison according to what readers want to know. In evaluating the suitability of two locations for a new restaurant, a writer could compare the two sites according to accessibility, neighborhood competition, and costs. There are two ways to organize the comparison and contrast pattern for this situation. In one method (topical), the writer could compare and contrast location A with location B under specific topics, such as

Accessibility
1. Location A
2. Location B

Neighborhood competition
1. Location A
2. Location B

Costs
1. Location A
2. Location B

In the other method (complete subject), the writer could present an overall comparison by discussing all the features of location A and then all the features of location B, keeping the discussion in parallel order, such as

Location A
1. Accessibility
2. Neighborhood competition
3. Costs

Location B
1. Accessibility
2. Neighborhood competition
3. Costs

In choosing one method over another, consider the readers' needs. For the report on two potential restaurant locations, readers might prefer a topical comparison to judge the suitability of each location in terms of the three vital factors. The topical method does not force readers to move back and forth between major sections looking for one particular item, as the complete subject method does. In comparing two computers, however, a writer may decide that readers need an overall description of the two in order to determine which seems to satisfy more office requirements. In this case, the writer would present all the features of computer A and then all those of computer B.

This excerpt showing comparison is taken from a report written by a swimming coach to a university director of athletics who needs to know about coaching techniques used on campus:

> This year the swim team has been using a nontraditional training regimen. As you may know, the traditional training method relies on swimmers developing a good aerobic base by swimming between 10,000 and 20,000 yards a day at a steady pace for two months before the meet season. The new training method we are using involves lower yardage but higher swimming pace. This new method calls for 4000 yards of swimming daily, but all swimming is to be at race pace. The two methods both develop an aerobic base, but the second emphasizes race conditions.

Definition Pattern

The purpose of definition is to explain the meaning of a term that refers to a concept, process, or object. Chapter 7 discusses writing definitions for objects or processes. Definition also can be part of any other organizational pattern when a writer decides that a particular term will not be clear to readers. An *informal definition* is a simple statement using familiar terms:

> A drizzle is a light rainfall.

A *formal definition* places the term into a group and then explains the term's special features that distinguish it from the group:

term   group   special features

A pronator is a muscle in the forearm that turns the palm downward.

Writers use *expanded definitions* to identify terms and explain individual features when they believe readers need more than a sentence definition. Definitions can be expanded by adding examples, using an analogy, or employing one of the organization patterns, such as comparison and contrast or partition.

This excerpt from a student's biology report uses the cause-and-effect pattern to expand the definition of arteriosclerosis:

> Arteriosclerosis is a disease of the arteries, commonly known as hardening of the arteries. As we age, plaques of fatty deposits, called atheromas, form in the blood and cling to the walls of the arteries. These deposits build up and narrow the artery passage, interfering with the flow of blood. Fragments of the plaque, called emboli, may break away and block the arteries, causing a sudden blockage and a stroke. Even if no plaque fragments break away,

eventually the artery will lose elasticity, blood pressure will rise, and blood flow will be sufficiently reduced to cause a stroke or a heart attack.

Spatial Pattern

In the spatial pattern, information is grouped according to the physical arrangement of the subject. A writer may describe a machine part by part from top to bottom so that readers can visualize how the parts fit together. The spatial pattern creates a path for readers to follow. Features can be described from top to bottom, side to side, inside to outside, north to south, or in any order that fits the way readers need to "see" the topic.

This excerpt is from an architect's report to a civic restoration committee about an old theater scheduled to be restored:

> The inside of the main doorway is surrounded by a Castilian castle facade and includes a red-tiled parapet at the top of the castle roof. A series of parallel brass railings just beyond the doorway creates corridors for arriving movie patrons. Along the side walls are ornamented white marble columns behind which the walls are covered with 12-ft-high mirrors. The white marble floor sweeps across the lobby to the wall opposite the entrance, where a broad split staircase curves up from both sides of the lobby to the triple doors at the mezzanine level. The top of the staircase at the mezzanine level is decorated with a life-size black marble lion on each side.

CHAPTER SUMMARY

This chapter discusses organizing information by sorting it into major topics and subtopics, constructing outlines, and developing effective paragraphs. Remember:

- Information should be grouped into major topics and subtopics based on the way the readers want to learn about the subject.

- An informal outline is a list of major topics.

- A formal outline uses a special numbering system, usually Roman and Arabic numerals or decimals, and lists all major topics and subtopics.

- A topic outline lists all the major topics and subtopics by key words.

- A sentence outline states each main topic and subtopic in a full sentence.

- Effective paragraphs need to be unified, coherent, and fully developed.

- Organizational patterns for effective paragraphs include ascending or descending order of importance, cause and effect, chronological, classification, partition, comparison and contrast, definition, and spatial.

SUPPLEMENTAL READINGS IN PART 2

Benson, P. J. "Writing Visually: Design Considerations in Technical Publications," *Technical Communication,* p. 454.

Hartman, D. B., and Nantz, K. S. "Send the Right Messages about E-Mail," *Training & Development,* p. 489.

Nielsen, J. "Be Succinct! (Writing for the Web)," *Alertbox,* p. 513.

Plunka, G. A. "The Editor's Nightmare: Formatting Lists within the Text," *Technical Communication,* p. 515.

"Six Graphics Guidelines," *Simply Stated,* p. 535.

ENDNOTES

1. Duin, Ann Hill. "Factors That Influence How Readers Learn from Text: Guidelines for Structuring Technical Documents," *Technical Communication* 36.1 (February 1989): 97–101.
2. Adapted from Allen Bernstein, *1998 Tax Guide for College Teachers* (Washington, DC: Academic Information Service, 1997).

This model is a company bulletin for supervisors. The purpose is to advise supervisors how to reduce heat stroke and other problems in employees who are working in extremely hot conditions. The writer begins with a brief introduction that establishes the importance of the topic. Also, the writer groups the suggestions for reducing heat stress under descriptive headings.

Discussion

1. Discuss why the writer directed the reader's attention to another bulletin in the introduction to this one.

2. Discuss the headings in this bulletin. How helpful are they to the reader? Do you have any suggestions for changes?

3. Discuss the order of the sections. How helpful is it to the reader?

4. Analyze why the writer decided to use a list in one section.

5. In groups, draft a bulletin for new students at your school on one of the following topics:
- Study tips and good study locations
- Student center activities and conveniences
- Sports opportunities on campus

BULLETIN 321a
April 27, 1998

PREVENTING HEAT STRESS

Working in hot conditions often can create health hazards as the body reacts to high temperatures. This bulletin suggests methods supervisors can use to reduce heat-related problems in the workplace. See also Bulletin 321b for definitions of heat disorders.

Cooling Methods

A variety of devices other than air conditioning will help reduce heat.

- Place fans in key locations so that the air reaches workers.
- Use shielding to block radiant heat sources.
- Use power tools to reduce manual labor.
- Eliminate steam leaks.

Work and Rest Periods

If possible, schedule heavy work in the cooler early hours of the day. Alternating the standard work and rest periods with longer rest periods in a cool area can help workers avoid heat disorders. If a worker reports extreme discomfort, allow a longer rest period and call first-aid personnel.

Employee Awareness

Employees must be conscious of the need to replace fluids. Keep water supplies (one quart per worker per hour) available at the work site. Post the names and numbers of first aid personnel in an accessible location. Urge workers to report distress.

Resistance Buildup

New workers and workers returning from two weeks or more off the job should build up heat resistance over a five-day period. Arrange work schedules to allow 50 percent of the normal workload and time exposure the first day. Increase exposure each day until worker is up to 100 percent exposure by the end of the fifth day.

MODEL 4-6   Commentary

This letter report was written by an engineer to a client who had requested an analysis of suitable roadway improvement processes and a recommendation for future work. The engineer reviews the current conditions of the city's roads, then describes the two available types of recycled asphalt processes, and concludes with the firm's recommendation. The writer also offers to discuss the subject further and to provide copies of the reports he mentions in his letter.

Discussion

1. Discuss the headings the writer uses in his letter report. How helpful are they to the reader? Are there any revisions you would make in the headings?

2. In his "Recommendation" section, the writer mentions environmental concerns. How much impact does this mention of the environment have in this section? What revisions in content or organization would you make to increase the emphasis on the environmental reasons for using recycled asphalt?

3. Identify the organizational strategies the writer uses throughout his report.

MANNING-HORNSBY ENGINEERING CONSULTANTS
3200 Farmington Drive
Kansas City, Missouri 64132
(816) 555–7070

November 23, 1999

Mr. Marvin O. Thompson
City Manager
Municipal Building, Suite 360
Ridgewood, MO 64062

Dear Mr. Thompson:

This report covers the Manning-Hornsby review of the current roadway conditions in Ridgewood, Missouri, analysis of the available recycled asphalt processes, and our recommendation for the appropriate process for future Ridgewood roadway improvement projects.

Current Ridgewood Maintenance Program

The City of Ridgewood has 216 miles of roadways. Half of these have curbs and gutters, while the other half have bermed shoulders with drainage ditches. About 95 percent of the roadways are of asphalt composition. The remaining 5 percent are of reinforced concrete construction or are unimproved.

Condition: Over the last five years, 40 miles of existing roadways have been improved. Improvements generally consist of crack sealing and removal and replacement of minor sections of pavement followed by a resurfacing overlay. Roadways with curbs and gutters are typically overlayed with 3–4 inch layers of hot-mix asphalt. Roadways with berms and drainage ditches are typically overlayed with 3–4 inch layers of cold-mix asphalt, also known as "chip and seal." No form of recycled asphalt has ever been used on these roadways.

Both these processes are appropriate for Ridgewood roadways. Hot-mix asphalt is a bituminous pavement, mixed hot at an asphalt plant, delivered hot to the site, and rolled to a smooth compacted state. The cold-mix asphalt is mixed and placed at lower temperatures with higher asphalt contents. Cold-mix asphalt is usually covered with bitumen and stone chips. Generally, the hot mix provides a smoother surface than the cold mix but is more susceptible to future cracking. The cold mix is more resilient than the hot mix and will reform itself in the summer heat and high temperatures.

Mr. Marvin O. Thompson   -2-   November 23, 1999

Problem: One of the problems associated with the current maintenance process is that roadways are being overlayed without the removal of existing asphalt. Therefore, the roadway grades are increasing. In some cases, the curbs are starting to disappear. Drainage problems are occurring due to the flattening road surface, permanent cross slopes, and grade changes. These conditions cause low spots that do not drain to existing catchbasins.

So that the curb and drainage problems noted above are eliminated, future projects should include the removal of existing layers of asphalt before resurfacing begins. Plans should call for milling off a depth of existing asphalt that is equal to or greater than the proposed overlay thickness. The milling process will make it possible to achieve curb heights, pavement cross slopes, and pavement grades that are similar to the originally constructed roadway. The City must then decide what it wants to do with the milled asphalt.

Recycled Asphalt

Recycling products has become a popular operation in today's environmentally conscious world. One waste material already being used extensively is asphalt. Most experts agree that using recycled asphalt in roadways does not detract from performance. Using recycled asphalt becomes advantageous specifically in cases where existing asphalt removal is necessary on projects because past overlays are affecting curb heights and creating drainage problems. In these cases, using recycled asphalt creates two main benefits. First, by reusing existing asphalt, the municipality takes another step toward solving its environmental problems by reducing solid waste in landfills. Second, using recycled asphalt reduces project costs as noted below. There are two types of recycled asphalt appropriate for roadways such as those in Ridgewood.

Hot In-Place Recycled Asphalt: Hot in-place asphalt recycling has been used throughout the United States with satisfactory results. Hot in-place recycling consists of milling off existing asphalt to a specified depth, mixing the recycled asphalt with virgin asphalt at high temperatures, laying the hot asphalt, and rolling it to a highly compacted density. Mixing is performed either at the asphalt plant or in a mixing vehicle that follows directly behind the milling equipment and directly in front of the paver. Reports from other municipalities and states indicate using hot in-place recycled asphalt can save 10 to 30 percent in road costs.

Mr. Marvin O. Thompson   -3-   November 23, 1999

Cold In-Place Recycled Asphalt: Cold in-place asphalt recycling usually consists of milling off existing asphalt to a specified depth, mixing that asphalt with virgin materials and/or rejuvenating liquids, then laying it back in place. The mixing is done either at the plant or in a paving machine directly behind the milling machine. The advantage of this procedure is the ability to use existing material to correct road profile problems. During in-place recycling, a new roadway crown can be established. The cold mix is commonly used for base or intermediate layers on low volume roads. The main benefit here is the cold mix's ability to prevent old cracks from reflecting through the overlay. The majority of users of recycled cold mix top it with virgin asphalt or chip and seal. The latest reports indicate that using cold in-place recycled asphalt can save local governments from 6 to 67 percent in road costs.

Recommendation

The existing roadways in Ridgewood have undergone years of overlays in road maintenance. The future improvement projects will have to reestablish road grades for proper drainage and for standard curb heights. Increasing evidence shows that cost savings can be achieved by using both hot and cold in-place recycled asphalt. In addition, these processes provide an environmentally sound alternative to wasting asphalt in land fills. Manning-Hornsby recommends that the City of Ridgewood adopt this recycled asphalt process in future roadway improvement projects.

I would be happy to discuss this recommendation with you in more detail, and I can provide copies of the reports from other areas about the use of recycled asphalt. I will call your office next week to set up a time convenient to you. In the meantime, please do not hesitate to contact me with any questions.

Sincerely,

Joseph F. Lennetti

Joseph F. Lennetti
Senior Engineer
MANNING-HORNSBY ENGINEERING CONSULTANTS

Chapter 4   Exercises

1. The following bulletin from an electric power company is for homeowners and provides information for dealing with power outages. Redraft the information into a more useful organization, with headings to direct the reader to topics.

Summer storms can create damage and down trees that knock out power lines. You need to know how to handle these situations. Prepare a home emergency kit that will meet your family's needs for at least three days. Include any special items for disabled or elderly family members and infants. The electric company cannot promise to restore power at a certain time. Crews must work on removing hazards to public safety, such as burning poles and transformers or downed power lines, before they can work on restoring home power. Repairs that can help large numbers of customers receive priority. Stay in your car if a power line falls on it. Report downed power lines or broken lines immediately. Notify the police or fire department if you cannot reach the electric company. In your home supply kits, be sure to have bottled water (at least one gallon per person per day). Also, you will need food that will not spoil. Customers on life-sustaining medical equipment should have a backup plan, such as batteries or a generator, and should make arrangements with the company to be placed on a special priority list in case of power outages. Police, hospitals, nursing homes, fire stations, and radio and TV stations receive priority in repairs. Home kits should also include a first-aid kit and blankets for each person. Have extra batteries for your radio and flashlights. To preserve food as long as possible, do not open refrigerators or freezers during outages. Unplug electronic equipment, such as computers, VCRs, and TVs, in case a power surge occurs during an outage or a repair. Check your neighbors to see if your home is the only one affected. If it is, check your circuit breakers or fuse box. Many people like to keep a simple change of clothing for each family member in the home kits in case the outage continues for more than 24 hours. Stay away from downed power lines, and do not touch anyone or anything in contact with a power line. Make sure children stay away from any dangerous situations.

2. The following memo was sent to all employees at an electronics company. Revise it to improve organization and guide readers to the main points.

Any associate who believes he or she has been subjected to sexual harassment should report such behavior immediately. Sexual harassment is prohibited by law. Sexual harassment occurs when

UNDERSTANDING DESIGN FEATURES

Document design refers to the physical appearance of a document. Because the written text and its presentation work together to provide readers with the information they need, think about the design of your documents during the planning stage—even before you select appropriate information and organize it.

Readers do not read only the printed words on a page; they also "read" the visual presentation of the text, just as a television viewer pays attention not only to the main actor and the words he or she speaks, but also to the background action, noises, music, and other actors' movements. In an effective document, as in an effective television scene, the words and visuals support each other.

Desktop publishing has expanded the writer's role in producing technical documents. A writer with sophisticated computer equipment and design software packages can create finished documents with most of the design features discussed in this chapter. Desktop publishing makes it easy to produce newsletters, catalogs, press releases, brochures, training materials, reports, and proposals—all with graphic aids, columns, headlines, mastheads, bullets, and any design feature needed by readers.

Rapidly developing computer technology increases the capabilities of desktop publishing with each new scanner, printer, and software package. It is not an exaggeration to say that desktop publishing has launched a printing revolution as more companies produce more of their own documents. No matter whether a document is produced on centuries-old movable type or on the latest computer technology, however, the writer's goal is the same—to provide readers with the information they need in a form they can use.

Purpose of Design Features

Some documents, such as business letters, have well-known, conventional formats, but letters and other documents also benefit from additional design features—graphic aids and the format elements of written cues, white space, and typographic devices. These design features increase the usefulness of documents in several ways.

1. They guide readers through the text by directing attention to individual topics and increasing the ability of readers to remember the important, highlighted sections.

2. They increase reader interest in the document. Unbroken blocks of type have a numbing effect on most readers, but eye-catching graphic aids and attention-getting format devices keep readers focused on the information they need.

3. They create a document that reflects the image you wish readers to have. A conservative law firm may want to project a solid, traditional,

no-nonsense image with its documents, whereas a video equipment company may prefer to project a trendy, dramatic image. Both images can be enhanced by specific design features.

Design Principles

The principles of design are qualities important to any visual presentation regardless of topic or audience. Experienced designers use the principles of design to create the "look" they want for a document. The general principles most designers consider in all documents are balance, proportion, sequence, and consistency.

Balance

Page balance refers to having comparable visual "weight" on both sides of a page or on opposing pages in a longer document. A page in a manual filled with text and photographs followed by a page with only a single paragraph in the center would probably jar the reader. If this unsettling effect is not your intent, avoid such imbalance in page design.

Think of page balance as similar to the scales held by the figure of Justice, which you have seen so often. Formal balance on a page would be the same as two evenly filled scales hanging at the same level. Informal balance, which is used more often by experienced page designers, would be represented by a heavily weighted scale on one side balanced by two smaller scales equal to the total weight of the larger scale on the other side.

One large section of a page, then, can be balanced by two smaller sections. Every time an element is added to or removed from a page, however, the balance shifts. A photograph that is dominant on one page may not be dominant on another page. Remember these points about visual "weight":

- Big weighs more than small.

- Dark weighs more than light.

- Color weighs more than black and white.

- Unusual shapes weigh more than simple circles or squares.

Proportion

Proportion in page design refers to the size and placement of text, graphic aids, and format elements on the page. Experienced designers rarely use an equal amount of space for text and graphics page after page. Not only would this be monotonous for readers, but it would interfere with the readers' ability to use the document. Reserving the same amount of space for one heading called "Labor" and another called "Budgetary Considerations" would result in the long heading looking cramped and the short heading looking lost in the space available. In a similar fashion, you would not want every drawing in a parts manual to be the same size regardless of the object it depicts. Each design feature should be the size that is helpful to the readers and appropriate for the subject.

Sequence

Sequence refers to the arrangement of design features so that readers see them in the best order for their use of the document. Readers usually begin reading a page at the top left corner and end at the bottom right corner. In between these two points, readers tend to scan from left to right and up to down. Readers also tend to notice the features with the most "weight" first. Effective design draws readers through the page from important point to important point.

Consistency

Consistency refers to presenting similar features in a similar style. Keep these elements consistent throughout a document:

- *Margins.* Keep uniform margins on all pages of a document.
- *Typeface.* Use the same size and style of type for similar headings and similar kinds of information.
- *Indentations.* Keep uniform indentations for such items as paragraphs, quotations, and lists.

Do not mistake consistent format for boring format. Consistency helps readers by emphasizing similar types of information and their similar importance. A brochure published by the Ohio Department of Health to alert college students to the dangers of AIDS is designed as a series of questions. Each question (e.g., "What is AIDS?" and "How Do You Get AIDS?") is printed in all capital letters in light blue. The answers are printed in black. This consistency in design helps the readers quickly find the answers to their questions.

CREATING GRAPHIC AIDS

Graphic aids, called *figures* and *tables,* are not merely decorative additions to documents or oral presentations. Often graphic aids are essential in helping readers understand and use the information in a document. Instructions may be easier to use when they have graphics that illustrate some steps, such as directions for gripping a tennis racquet properly or for performing artificial respiration.

Purpose of Graphic Aids

Think about which graphic aids would be appropriate for your document during the planning stage. Graphic aids are important in technical documents in these ways:

- Graphic aids provide quick access to complicated information, especially numerical data. For example, a reader can more quickly see the highs and lows of a production trend from a line graph than from a long narrative explanation.

- Graphic aids isolate the main topics in complex data and appeal particularly to general and nonexpert readers. Newspapers, for instance, usually report government statistics with graphic aids so that their readers can easily see the scope of the information.

- Graphic aids help readers see relationships among several sets of data. Two pie graphs side by side will illustrate more easily than a narrative can the differences between how the federal government spent a tax dollar in 1980 and in 2000.

- Graphic aids, such as detailed statistical tables, can offer expert readers quick access to complicated data that would take pages to explain in written text.

Readers of some documents expect graphic aids. Scientists reading a research report expect to see tables and formulas that show the experimental method and results. Do not, however, rely solely on graphic aids to explain important data. Some readers are more comfortable with written text than with graphics, and for these readers, your text should thoroughly analyze the facts, their impact on the situation or on the future, their relevance for decision making or for direct action, and their relation to other data. For consistency and reader convenience, follow these guidelines for all graphic aids.

1. Identify each graphic aid with a specific title, such as "1990–1998 Crime Rates" or "Differences in Patient Response to Analgesics."

2. Number each graphic aid. All graphics that are not tables with words or numbers in columns are called figures. Number each table or figure consecutively throughout the document, and refer to it by number in the text:

> The results shown in Table 1 are from the first survey. The second survey is illustrated in Figure 2.

3. Place each graphic aid in the text as near after the first reference to it as possible. If, however, the document has many tables and charts or only some of the readers are interested in them, you may decide to put them all in an appendix to avoid breaking up the text too frequently.

The guidelines in this chapter for creating various types of graphic aids provide general advice for such illustrations. Effective graphic aids, however, can violate standard guidelines and still be useful to the readers who need them. The daily newspaper *USA Today* contains many innovative illustrations of data for its readers who are interested in a quick understanding of the latest statistical or technical information. The key to creating effective graphic aids is to analyze purpose and reader before selecting graphic formats. While an industrial psychologist may prefer a detailed statistical table of the results of a survey of construction workers, a general reader may want—and need—a simple pie chart showing the key points.

Tables

A table shows numerical or topical data in rows and columns, thus providing readers with quick access to quantitative information and allowing readers to make comparisons among items easily. Model 5-1 shows a table that presents a comparison of data from company service centers over a 2-year period.

Here are general guidelines for setting up tables:

1. Provide a heading for each column that identifies the items in the column.

2. Use footnotes to explain specific items in columns. Footnotes for specific numbers or columns require lowercase superscript letters (e.g., [a], [b], [c]). If the footnote is for a specific number, place the letter directly after the number (e.g., 432[a]). If the footnote applies to an entire column, place the letter directly after the column heading (e.g., Payroll[b]). List all footnotes at the left margin of the table, directly below the data.

3. Space columns sufficiently so that the data do not run together.

4. Give the source of your data below the table. If you have multiple sources and have compiled the information into a table, explain this in the text, if necessary.

5. Use decimals and round off figures to the nearest whole number.

6. Indicate in the column heading if you are using a particular measure for units, such as "millions of dollars" or "per 5000 barrels."

TABLE 1   Shipments from Service Centers

	1997	1998	% Change
Liberty, MO	4,167	4,012	− 3.72
Saukville, WI	4,857	4,118	− 15.22
Franklin, TN[a]	623	5,106	+719.58
Medina, OH	3,624	3,598	− 0.72
Salem, OR	3,432	3,768	+ 9.79
Lafayette, LA	2,740	3,231	+ 17.92
Tucson, AZ	5,024	5,630	+ 12.06
Sweetbriar, KY[b]	2,616	3,967	+ 51.64
TOTALS	27,083	33,430	+ 23.44

[a]Opened in June 1997.
[b]Opened in March 1997.

MODEL 5-1   A Typical Table Comparing Data from Two Different Years

Figures

All graphic aids that are not tables are considered figures. Information in tables can often be presented effectively in figures as well, and sometimes readers can use figures more readily than tables. A geologist seeking information about groundwater levels may want a table giving specific quantities in specific geologic locations. Someone reading a report in the morning newspaper on groundwater levels across the United States, however, may be better served by a set of bars of varying lengths representing groundwater levels in regions of the country, such as the Pacific Northwest. Before selecting graphic aids for your document, consider your readers and their ability to interpret quantitative information and, particularly, their need for specific or general data. The most common types of graphic aids are bar graphs, pictographs, line graphs, pie graphs, organization charts, flowcharts, line drawings, cutaway drawings, exploded drawings, maps, and photographs.

Bar Graphs

A *bar graph* uses bars of equal width in varying lengths to represent (1) a comparison of items at one particular time, (2) a comparison of items over time, (3) changes in one item over time, or (4) a comparison of portions of a single item. The horizontal and vertical axes represent the two elements being illustrated, such as time and quantity. Model 5-2 is a typical vertical bar graph in which bars represent different types of pollution-reduction costs incurred by a company.

Bars can extend in either a vertical direction, as in Model 5-2, or in a horizontal direction, as in Model 5-3. In Model 5-3, the bars emphasize the increasing sales over the 5-year period. Notice that in both Models 5-2 and 5-3, a specific figure indicating a dollar amount is printed at the top or the end of the bar.

Bars can also appear on both sides of the axis to indicate positive and negative quantities. Model 5-4 uses bars on both sides of the horizontal axis, indicating positive and negative quantities. Notice that the zero point in the vertical axis is about one-third above the horizontal axis and that the quantities are labeled positive above the zero point and negative below it.

Bar graphs cannot represent exact quantities or provide comparisons of quantities as precisely as tables can, but bar graphs are generally useful for readers who want to understand overall trends and comparisons.

Depending on the size of the graph and the shading or color distinctions, up to four bars can represent different items at any point on an axis. Label

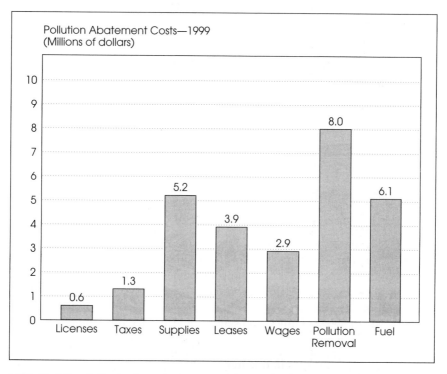

MODEL 5-2   A Typical Vertical Bar Graph Showing Costs for Different Items

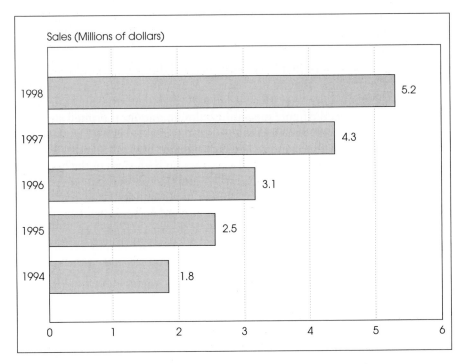

Sales (Millions of dollars)

1998 — 5.2
1997 — 4.3
1996 — 3.1
1995 — 2.5
1994 — 1.8

0   1   2   3   4   5   6

MODEL 5-3   A Typical Horizontal Bar Graph Showing Sales Growth

each bar or provide a key to distinguish among shadings or colors. Model 5-5 shows a bar graph with multiple bars representing three different kinds of fish.

Pictographs

A *pictograph* is a variation of a bar graph that uses symbols instead of bars to illustrate specific quantities of items. The symbols should realistically correspond to the items, such as, for example, a cow representing milk production. Pictographs provide novelty and eye-catching appeal, particularly in documents intended for consumers. Pictographs are limited, however, because symbols cannot adequately represent exact figures or fractions. When using a pictograph, (1) make all symbols the same size, (2) space the symbols equally on the axis, (3) show increased quantity by increasing the number of symbols rather than the size of the symbol, (4) round off the quantities represented instead of using a portion of a symbol to represent a portion of a unit, and (5) include a key indicating the quantity represented by a symbol. Model 5-6 uses houses to represent the trend in housing sales during a 6-month period.

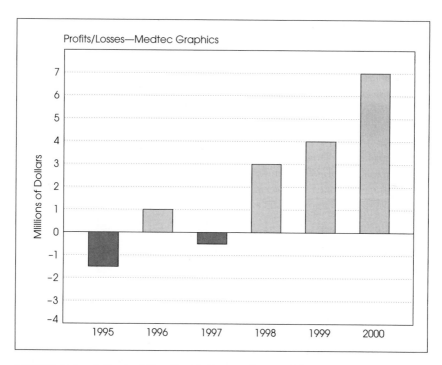

MODEL 5-4 A Typical Bar Graph Presenting Positive and Negative Data for Profits and Losses

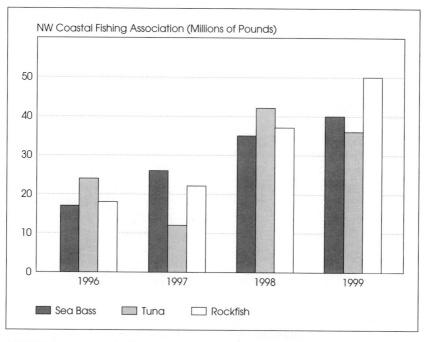

MODEL 5-5 A Typical Bar Graph with Multiple Bars Showing Differences in Three Items

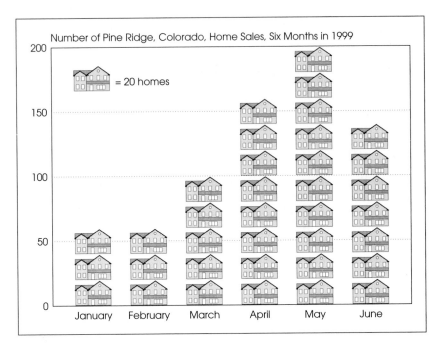

MODEL 5-6   A Typical Pictograph Showing Housing Sales

Line Graphs

A *line graph* uses a line between the horizontal and vertical axes to show changes in the relationship between the elements represented by the two axes. The line connects points on the graph that represent a quantity at a particular time or in relation to a specific topic. Line graphs usually plot changes in quantity or in position and are particularly useful for illustrating trends. Three or four lines representing different items can appear on the same graph for comparison. The lines must be distinguished by color or design, and a key must identify them. Label both vertical and horizontal axes, and be sure that the value segments on the axes are equidistant. Model 5-7 uses three lines, each representing sales for a specific corporation. The lines plot changes in sales (vertical axis) during specific years (horizontal axis). The amounts indicated are not exact, but readers can readily see differences in the corporate sales over time.

Model 5-8 uses three lines, each representing energy consumption by a different type of user. Notice that the lines are distinguished by design and are labeled in the graph rather than by a key, as in Model 5-7.

Pie Graphs

A *pie graph* is a circle representing a whole unit, with the segments of the circle, or pie, representing portions of the whole. Pie graphs are useful if the whole

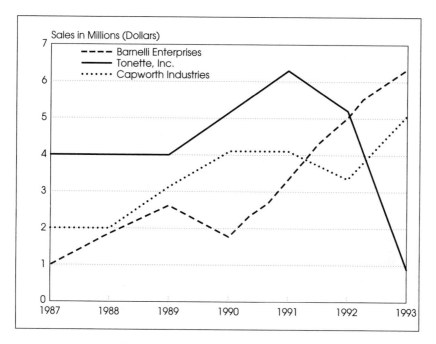

MODEL 5-7   A Typical Line Graph Comparing Sales of Three Companies

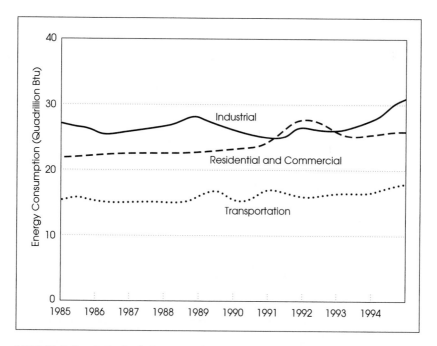

MODEL 5-8   A Typical Line Graph Comparing Energy Consumption by Three Types of Users

unit has between three and ten segments. Use colors and shadings to highlight segments of special importance, or separate one segment from the pie for emphasis. In preparing a pie graph, start the largest segment at the 12 o'clock position and follow clockwise with the remaining segments in descending order of size. If one segment is "Miscellaneous," it should be the last. Label the segments, and be sure their values add up to 100% of the total. Model 5-9 is a pie graph with six segments. The segments represent four different companies—those heating and cooling contractors with the largest share of the Chicago area business. The segment representing Wisconsin-based contractors appears ahead of the "Other" segment because it is the more specific group. One section of a pie chart may be separated from the pie to emphasize the item or quantity represented by that section, as in Model 5-10. In this case, the writer wants to emphasize the percentage spent on computers. Notice that the computer section of the pie is also distinguished by stripes to further highlight it for the reader.

Pie charts and other figures often have call-outs to identify specific parts of the illustration. Call-outs consist of lines leading from a specific part of the illustration to a number, often circled, which corresponds to an item in a separate list. The call-out line may also lead to a written term. Notice that the call-outs in Model 5-9 are small arrows that connect a specific section of the pie to the identification of the contractors and percentages represented. The call-out lines in Model 5-10 lead to the type of expenditure and the percentage. Call-out lines should always touch the edge of the section or part being identified.

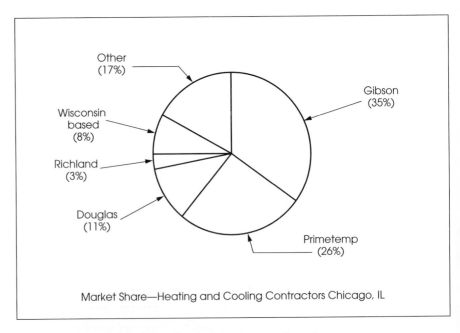

Market Share—Heating and Cooling Contractors Chicago, IL

MODEL 5-9   A Typical Pie Graph Showing Market Share

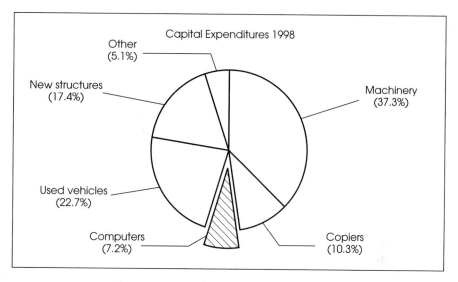

MODEL 5-10   A Pie Graph That Emphasizes One Segment

Organization Charts

An *organization chart* illustrates the individual units in a company or any group and their relationships to each other. Organization charts are most often used to illustrate the chain of authority—the position with the most authority at the top and all other positions leading to it in some way. Organization charts also indicate the lines of authority between units or positions and which positions are on the same level of authority. Rectangles or ovals usually represent the positions in an organizational chart. Label each clearly. Model 5-11 is an organization chart showing the committees at a charitable foundation.

Flowcharts

A *flowchart* illustrates the sequence of steps in a process. A flowchart can represent an entire process or only a specific portion of it. As a supplement to a written description of a process, a flowchart is useful in enabling readers to visualize the progression of steps. An open-system flowchart shows a process that begins at one point and ends at another. A closed-system flowchart shows a circular process that ends where it began. Use rectangles, circles, or symbols to represent the steps of the process, and label each clearly. Model 5-12 uses rectangles to show the steps of coal-cleaning operations. Model 5-13 uses drawings to show the stages of mass burning of refuse. The truck dumps refuse into storage pits. The refuse then moves through the hopper onto stoker grates and finally emerges as ash at the end of the process. The simple drawings guide the reader through the process.

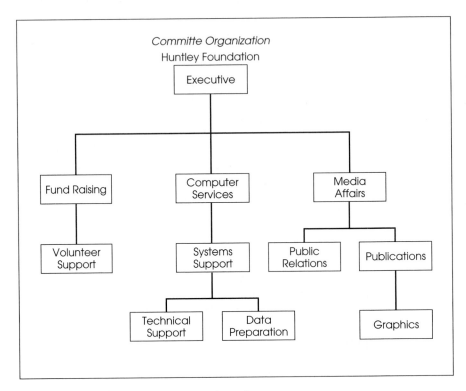

MODEL 5-11   A Typical Organization Chart

Line Drawings

A *line drawing* is a simple illustration of the structure of an object or the position of a person involved in some action. The drawing may not show all the details but, instead, highlights certain areas or positions that are important to the discussion. If details of the interior of an object are important, a cutaway drawing is more appropriate. If the relationship of all the components is important, an exploded drawing is more appropriate. Model 5-14 is a line drawing of a police officer conducting a driver sobriety test. The drawing shows the customary positions of the driver and police officer as the driver tries to walk a straight line.

Cutaway Drawings

A *cutaway drawing* shows an interior section of an object or an object relative to a location and other objects so that readers can see a cross section below the surface. Cutaway drawings show the location, relative size, and relationships of interior components. Use both horizontal and vertical cutaway views if your

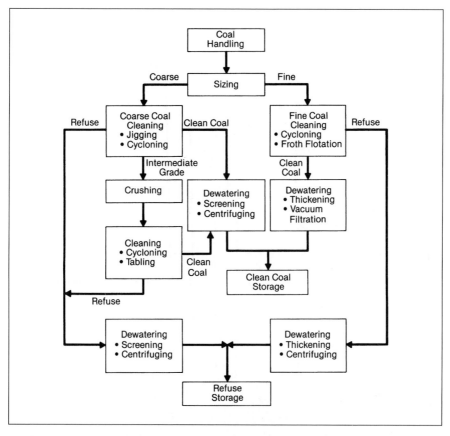

MODEL 5-12   A Typical Flowchart: Coal-Cleaning Operations

readers need a complete perspective of an interior. Model 5-15 is a cutaway drawing of a suction dredge revealing its parts and its position in the water.

Model 5-16 shows another cutaway drawing, this time showing the interior of a specialized furnace used in testing the transmission qualities of nonsilicon-based glass.

Exploded Drawings

An *exploded drawing* shows that individual components of an object as separate, but in the sequence and location they have when put together. Most often used in manuals and instruction booklets, exploded drawings help readers visualize how the exterior and interior parts fit together. Model 5-17 is an exploded drawing of a cart used to illustrate assembly instructions for a consumer.

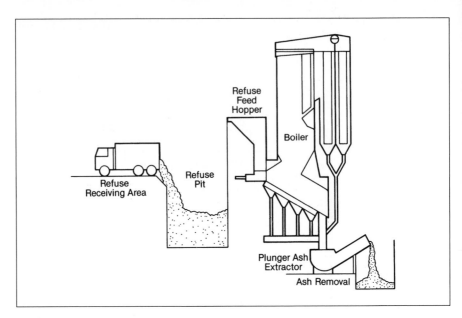

MODEL 5-13   A Typical Flowchart Using Drawings: Mass Burning

MODEL 5-14   A Line Drawing of a Police Officer Conducting a Driver Sobriety Test

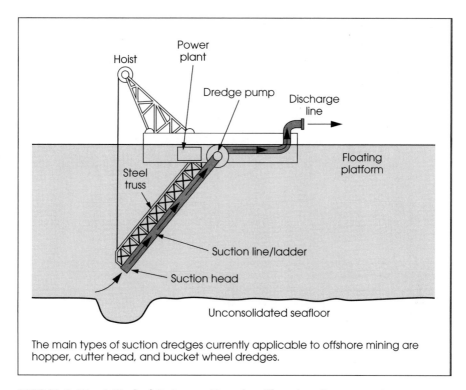

The main types of suction dredges currently applicable to offshore mining are hopper, cutter head, and bucket wheel dredges.

MODEL 5-15   A Typical Cutaway Drawing Showing Components of a Suction Dredge

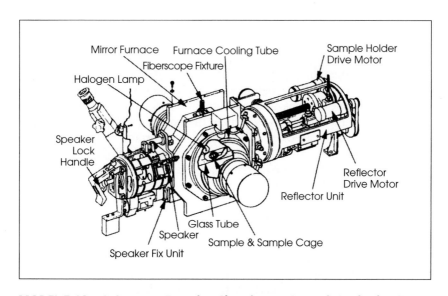

MODEL 5-16   A Cutaway Drawing Showing an Acoustic Levitation Furnace

111

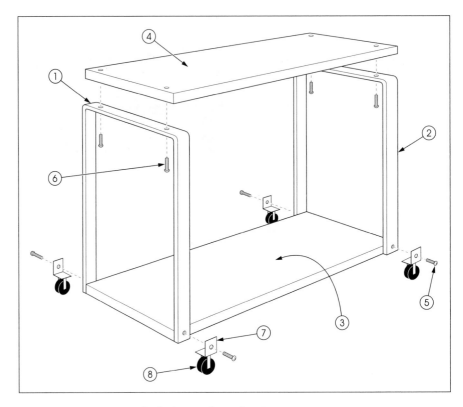

MODEL 5-17   An Exploded Drawing of a Cart

Maps

A *map* shows (1) geographic data, such as the location of rivers and highways, or (2) demographic and topical data, such as density and distribution of population or production. If demographic or topical data are featured, eliminate unnecessary geographic elements and use dots, shadings, or symbols to show distribution or density. Include (1) a key if more than one topical or demographic item is illustrated, (2) a scale of miles if distance is important, and (3) significant boundaries separating regions. Model 5-18 uses shading to distinguish differences in rental vacancies. Notice also that the map is exploded to emphasize the geographic divisions named.

Photographs

A *photograph* provides a surface view of an object or event. To be effective, photographs must be clear and focus on the pertinent item. Eliminate distracting backgrounds or other objects from the photograph. If the size of an object is important, include a person or well-known item in the photograph to illustrate the comparative size of the object. Model 5-19 is a typical product photograph.

MODEL 5-18   A Map Showing Changes in Rental Vacancy Rates by State

**MODEL 5-19   A
Product Photograph
of HealthRider**

USING FORMAT ELEMENTS

For many internal documents, such as reports, company procedures, and bulletins, the writer is responsible for determining the most effective format elements. Just as you use graphic aids to provide readers with easy access to complicated data, use format elements to help readers move through the document, finding and retaining important information. For printed documents, the writer often does not have the final word on which format elements to use. However, always consider these elements, and be prepared to consult with and offer suggestions to the technical editor and art director about document design. The following guidelines cover three types of format elements: (1) written cues, (2) white space, and (3) typographic devices.

Written Cues

Written cues help readers find specific information quickly. The most frequently used written cues are headings, headers and footers, jumplines, icons, and company logos.

Headings

Headings are organizational cues that alert readers to the sequence of information in a document. Use headings

- To help readers find specific data
- To provide an outline that helps readers see the hierarchical relationship of sections
- To call attention to specific topics
- To show where changes in topics occur
- To break up a page so that readers are not confronted with line after line of unbroken text.

Include headings for major sections and for topics within the sections. If one heading is followed by several pages of text, divide that section into subsections with more headings. If, on the other hand, every heading is followed by only two or three sentences, regroup your information into fewer topics. Headings are distinguished by level and style. Model 5-20 illustrates the placement and style of the four levels of headings most commonly used in technical documents.

Placement.   *First-level* headings represent major sections or full chapters. Center first-level headings and use all capital letters. Begin the text two lines below the heading. *Second-level* headings represent major sections. Center second-level headings and use upper- and lowercase letters. Begin the text two lines below the heading. *Third-level* headings are flush with the left margins and in

---

SAFETY IN SHIP BUILDING

This bulletin provides information about worker safety. . . .

Deck Openings and Edges

When workers are near unguarded hatches or edges, they. . . .

Edges of Decks

Guard rails must be in place at edges more than 5 ft above a solid surface. . . .

Personal Flotation Devices.   Workers near unguarded edges on a vessel afloat must wear. . . .

MODEL 5-20   Heading Placement and Style

upper- and lowercase letters. Begin the text two lines below the heading. *Fourth-level* headings are flush with the left margin, in upper- and lowercase letters, followed by a period. Begin the text on the same line.

You do not have to use all four levels of headings in any one document. A two-page report, for example, may have only third-level headings. Never use only one heading at any level. Divide your text so that you have at least two or more headings at whatever level you have selected. Always include at least one or two lines of text between headings. Most writers prefer boldface for headings because it stands out more than underlining or italics.

Style.   Use nouns, phrases, or sentences for headings. All headings of the same level, however, should be the same part of speech. If you want to use a noun for a heading, all headings of that level should be nouns. If one heading is a phrase, all headings of that level should be phrases. Here are three types of headings:

Nouns:	**Protein**
	Fat
	Carbohydrate
Phrases:	**Use of Tests**
	Development of Standards
	Rise in Cost
Sentences:	**Accidents Are Rising.**
	Support Is Not Available.
	Reductions Are Planned.

Nouns and phrases are the most commonly used headings. Be sure also that your headings clearly indicate the topic of the section they head so that readers do not waste time reading through unneeded information. Keep sentence headings short. Headings such as "Miscellaneous" or "General Principles" provide no guide to the information covered in the section. Write headings with specific terms and informative phrases so that readers can scan the document for the sections of most interest.

Headers and Footers

A *header* or *footer* is a notation on each page of a document identifying it for the reader and including one or more of the following: (1) document date, (2) title, (3) document number, (4) topic, (5) author, or (6) title of the larger publication the document is part of. Place headers at the tops of pages and footers at the bottoms flush with either the right or left margin. Here is an example:

Interactive Systems Check, No. 24-X,
May 1, 2000.

Jumplines

A *jumpline* is a notation indicating that a section is continued in another part of a document. Place a jumpline below the last line of text on the page. Here is an example:

Continued on page 39

Logos

A *company logo* is a specific design used as the symbol of a company. It may be a written cue or a visual one or a combination. Examples include the red cross of the American Red Cross, the golden arches of McDonald's, and the line drawing of a bell for the regional telephone companies. A logo identifies an organization for readers, and it also may unify the document by appearing at the beginning of major sections or on each page.

Icons

An *icon* is a drawing or visual symbol of a system or object, such as a mailbox representing e-mail or a suitcase representing the airport baggage pickup. Icons are often used on public signs, as links on Web pages, or as guides in documents, directing readers to certain sections. Computer clip art supplies many common icons, but use them for specific purposes, not just as decoration. For international readers, check whether an icon has the same meaning in their culture as in yours. Avoid using national flags or religious symbols as icons.

White Space

White space is the term for areas on a page that have no text or graphics. Far from being just a wasted spot on a page, white space helps readers process the text efficiently. In documents with complicated data and lots of detail, white space rests readers' eyes and directs them to important information. Think of white space as having a definite shape on the page, and use it to create balance and proportion in your documents. White space commonly appears in margins, heading areas, columns, and indentations.

Margins

Margins of white space provide a frame for the text and graphics (called the "live area") on a page. To avoid monotony, experienced designers usually vary the size of margins in printed documents. The bottom margin of a page is generally the widest, and the top margin is slightly smaller. If a document, such as a manual, is bound with facing pages, the inside margin is usually the narrowest, and the outside margin is slightly wider than the top margin.

Heading Areas

White space provides the background and surrounding area to set off headings. Readers need sufficient white space around headings to be able to separate them from the rest of the text.

Columns

In documents with columns of text, the white space between the columns both frames and separates the columns. Too much or too little space here will upset the balance and proportion of the page. Generally, the wider the columns, the more space that is needed between columns to help readers see them as separate sections of text.

Indentations

The white space at the beginning of an indented sentence and after the last word of a paragraph sets off a unit of text for readers, as does the white space between lines, words, and single-spaced paragraphs. Add extra space between paragraphs to increase readability. Youhaveonlytotrytoreadalinewithout whitespacebetweenwordstoseehowimportantthistinywhitespaceis.

White space is actually the most important format element, because without it most readers would quickly give up trying to get information from a document.

STRATEGIES—Color in Documents

- Draw reader attention to similar topics or sections by using the same color in the text or background
- Limit the number of colors in a document. Too much color decreases readability.
- Use black on white for maximum contrast and readability. Colored type recedes unless the type is also boldface.

Typographic Devices

Typographic devices are used to highlight specific details or specific sections of a document. Highlighting involves selecting different typefaces or using boldface type, lists, and boxes.

Typefaces

Type is either *serif* or *sans serif*. Serif type has small projections at the top or bottom of the major vertical strokes of a letter. Sans serif type does not have these little projections.

This sentence is printed in serif type.

This sentence is printed in sans serif type.

A *typeface* is a particular design for the type on a page. Typeface should be appropriate to readers and purpose. An ornate, script typeface suitable for a holiday greeting card would be out of place in a technical manual.

Poor: *Feasibility Tests in Mining Ventures*

Better: **Feasibility Tests in Mining Ventures**

Follow these general guidelines if you are involved in selecting the typeface for a printed document:

1. Stay in one typeface group, such as Times New Roman, throughout each document. Most typefaces have enough variety in size and weight to suit the requirements of one document.

2. Use the fewest possible sizes and weights of typeface in one document. A multitude of type sizes and weights, even from the same typeface, distracts readers.

3. Avoid type smaller than 10 points because readers over age 40 will have trouble reading it.

4. Use both capital and lowercase letters for text. This combination is more readable than all capitals or all lowercase letters.

5. Use italics sparingly. Appendix A in this book explains the conventional use of italics. Avoid using them for emphasis because they are harder to read than regular type.

Boldface

Boldface refers to type with extra weight or darkness. Use boldface type to add emphasis to (1) headings, (2) specific words, such as warnings, or (3) significant topics. This example shows how boldface type sets off a word from a sentence:

Depending on the type of incinerator, **gas temperatures** could vary more than 2000 degrees.

Lists

Lists highlight information and guide readers to the facts they specifically need. In general, lists are distinguished by numbers, bullets, and squares.

Numbers.   Traditionally, lists in which items are numbered imply either that the items are in descending order of importance or that the items are sequential stages in a procedure. Here is a sample from an operator's manual:

1. Clean accumulated dust and debris from the surface.

2. Run the engine and check for abnormal noises and vibrations.

3. Observe three operating cycles.

4. Check operation of the brake.

Because numbered lists set off information so distinctly from the text, they are often used even when the items have only minor differences in importance. If a list has no chronology, you may use bullets to set off the items.

Bullets.   *Bullets* are small black circles that appear before each item in a list just as a number would. On a typewriter or word processor without a bullet symbol, use the small o and fill it in with black ink. Use bullets where there is no distinction in importance among items and where no sequential steps are involved. Here is an example from a company safety bulletin:

> A periodic survey is needed to check for the following:
>
> - Gasoline and paint vapors
> - Alkaline and acid mists
> - Dust
> - Smoke

Squares.   Squares are used with checklists if readers are supposed to respond to questions or select items on the page itself. A small square precedes each item in the same position as a number or a bullet would appear. Here is an example from a magazine subscription form:

> ☐ Please bill me for the total cost.
>
> ☐ Please bill me in three separate installments.
>
> ☐ Please charge to my credit card.

Boxes

A box is a frame that separates specific information from the rest of the text. In addition to the box itself, designers often use a light color or shading to further set off a box. Here is an example of boxed information:

> Boxes are used
>
> - to add supplemental information that is related to the main subject but not part of the document's specific content.
> - to call reader attention to special items such as telephone numbers, dates, prices, and return coupons.
> - to highlight important terms or facts.

Boxes are effective typographic devices, but overuse of them will result in a cluttered, unbalanced page. Use restraint in boxing information in your text.

CHAPTER SUMMARY

- This chapter discusses document design features—graphic aids and format elements. Remember:

- Design features guide readers through the text, increase reader interest, and contribute to a document "image."

- Basic page design principles include balance, proportion, sequence, and consistency.

- Graphic aids (1) provide readers with quick access to information, (2) isolate main topics, (3) help readers see relationships among sets of data, and (4) offer expert readers quick access to complicated data.

- All graphic aids should be identified with a descriptive heading and a number and should be placed as near as possible to the reference in the text.

- The most frequently used graphic aids are tables, bar graphs, pictographs, line graphs, pie graphs, organization charts, flowcharts, line drawings, cutaway drawings, exploded drawings, maps, and photographs.

- Written format elements such as headings, headers and footers, jumplines, logos, and icons help readers find special information.

- White space, the area without text or graphics, directs readers to information sections.

- Typographic devices such as typefaces, boldface type, lists, and boxes highlight specific sections or specific details.

SUPPLEMENTAL READINGS IN PART 2

Allen, L., and Voss, D. "Ethics in Technical Communication," p. 446.

Benson, P. J. "Writing Visually: Design Considerations in Technical Publications," *Technical Communication*, p. 454.

McAdams, M. "It's All in the Links," *The Editorial Eye*, p. 502.

Plunka, G. A. "The Editor's Nightmare: Formatting Lists within the Text," *Technical Communication*, p. 515.

"Six Graphics Guidelines," *Simply Stated*, p. 535.

White, J. V. "Color: The Newest Tool for Technical Communicators," *Technical Communication*, p. 551.

Model 5-21   Commentary

These pages are from a brochure prepared by Moen Incorporated. The brochure, written for consumers, presents the special features in a filtering faucet system.

Discussion

1. Identify and discuss the design elements used in these pages. In what ways do they assist the reader in understanding the information?

2. This brochure is written for nonexpert readers. Discuss how the headings direct the reader's attention to relevant topics.

3. Discuss the use of white space and how it helps or hinders the reader of these pages.

4. Discuss the text. How does the language appeal to consumers?

5. Bring a brochure for a consumer product to class. Identify the special design elements and discuss how they help the reader understand the information in the brochure.

The Filtering System *Reduces Impurities • Improves Taste • Eliminates Odors*

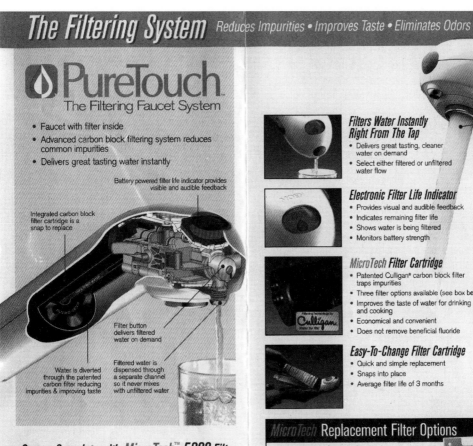

PureTouch
The Filtering Faucet System

- Faucet with filter inside
- Advanced carbon block filtering system reduces common impurities
- Delivers great tasting water instantly

Battery powered filter life indicator provides visible and audible feedback

Integrated carbon block filter cartridge is a snap to replace

Filter button delivers filtered water on demand

Water is diverted through the patented carbon filter reducing impurities & improving taste

Filtered water is dispensed through a separate channel so it never mixes with unfiltered water

Filters Water Instantly Right From The Tap
- Delivers great tasting, cleaner water on demand
- Select either filtered or unfiltered water flow

Electronic Filter Life Indicator
- Provides visual and audible feedback
- Indicates remaining filter life
- Shows water is being filtered
- Monitors battery strength

MicroTech Filter Cartridge
- Patented Culligan® carbon block filter traps impurities
- Three filter options available (see box below)
- Improves the taste of water for drinking and cooking
- Economical and convenient
- Does not remove beneficial fluoride

Easy-To-Change Filter Cartridge
- Quick and simple replacement
- Snaps into place
- Average filter life of 3 months

Comes Complete with *MicroTech* 5000 Filter

- Removes Chlorine (93.3%)
- Removes lead (99.5%)
- Removes Cryptosporidium & Giardia (99.98%)
- Does not remove beneficial fluoride
- Improves taste, reduces odor
- Each Cartridge Filters Approximately 200 Gallons (3 months average use)

MicroTech Replacement Filter Options

MicroTech 1000 Filter Cartridge
Reduces chlorine, improves taste and odor
MicroTech 3000 Filter Cartridge
Also reduces lead
MicroTech 5000 Filter Cartridge
All the benefits of MicroTech 3000 **plus** reduces cysts (cryptosporidium and giardia)

The contaminants or other substances removed or reduced by this filter are not necessarily in all users' water

Replacement filters available in single or two-packs.

Great Tasting Filtered Water With Just One Touch™

MODEL 5-21

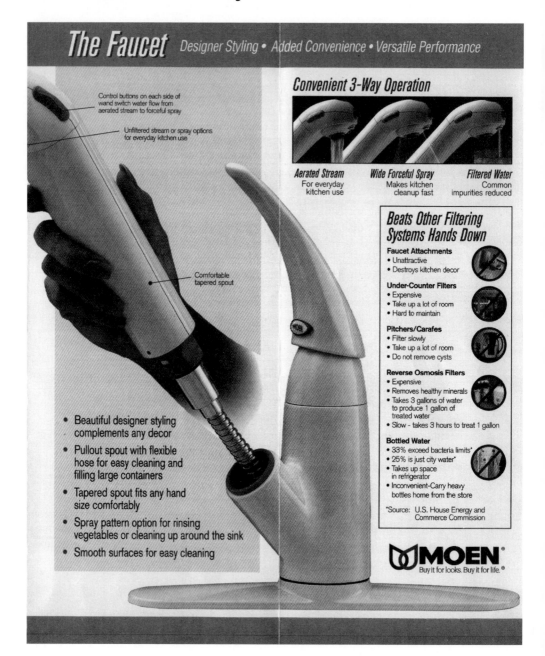

The Faucet   *Designer Styling • Added Convenience • Versatile Performance*

Control buttons on each side of wand switch water flow from aerated stream to forceful spray

Unfiltered stream or spray options for everyday kitchen use

Comfortable tapered spout

- Beautiful designer styling complements any decor
- Pullout spout with flexible hose for easy cleaning and filling large containers
- Tapered spout fits any hand size comfortably
- Spray pattern option for rinsing vegetables or cleaning up around the sink
- Smooth surfaces for easy cleaning

Convenient 3-Way Operation

Aerated Stream
For everyday kitchen use

Wide Forceful Spray
Makes kitchen cleanup fast

Filtered Water
Common impurities reduced

Beats Other Filtering Systems Hands Down

Faucet Attachments
- Unattractive
- Destroys kitchen decor

Under-Counter Filters
- Expensive
- Take up a lot of room
- Hard to maintain

Pitchers/Carafes
- Filter slowly
- Take up a lot of room
- Do not remove cysts

Reverse Osmosis Filters
- Expensive
- Removes healthy minerals
- Takes 3 gallons of water to produce 1 gallon of treated water
- Slow - takes 3 hours to treat 1 gallon

Bottled Water
- 33% exceed bacteria limits*
- 25% is just city water*
- Takes up space in refrigerator
- Inconvenient-Carry heavy bottles home from the store

*Source: U.S. House Energy and Commerce Commission

MOEN®
Buy it for looks. Buy it for life.®

MODEL 5-22   Commentary

This model is a page from a 91-page catalog published by the Hunter Fan Company. The catalog, written for consumers, explains the advantages of using fans for energy conservation and cost savings, describes the principles of fan construction, and features photographs and descriptions of dozens of fan designs. This page shows a cutaway view of the fan mechanism and lists the special features of the company fans.

Discussion

1. Discuss why the company would want to feature this illustration ahead of all photographs of decorative fans suitable for various rooms and purposes.

2. Discuss balance, proportion, sequence, and consistency in this page design.

3. Discuss the text. Why might the writer have listed features in this particular order? What is the advantage of using a list here?

4. Discuss the use of white space and how it helps or hinders the reader of this page.

5. Bring a consumer catalog to class. In groups, analyze the design of a single page from each catalog. As a group, select which one of these pages is most effective for a consumer, and explain your choice to the rest of the class.

THE HUNTER ORIGINAL®

For the Customer Demanding the Very Best . . . The Original.
Made for a Lifetime – Tested for a Lifetime – Backed for a Lifetime!

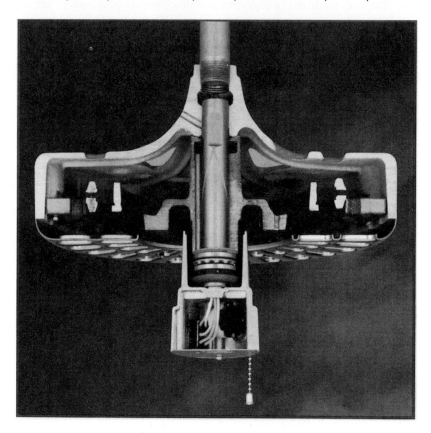

- Made in USA
- Lifetime Warranty
- 15° Blade Pitch for Maximum Air Movement
- Indestructible Cast Iron Housing
- Maintenance Free Oil Bath Design

- Unique Motor Design Accommodates 4 or 5 Blades
- 3 Speeds, Electrically Reversible
- No Rubber Flywheel to Replace
- Swivel Mount Canopy for Angled Ceiling Mount (2nd Century Models)
- Hardwood Veneer Blades

THE ORIGINAL®

MODEL 5-22

MODEL 5-23   Commentary

This model is from NASA educational materials for use in classrooms. The writer explains an atmospheric phenomenon, the Aurora Australis, and includes an illustration.

Discussion

1. Identify the graphic aid used in this model. What difficulty exists in this kind of situation that would not be present if the designer were illustrating a machine?

2. Look at Models 3-1, 7-1, 7-2, 8-4, 8-5, 9-2, and 9-8 and discuss the graphic aids and format elements used in these documents. How do the features help readers interpret the information?

3. In groups, develop an illustration for one of the following items. Add whatever setting or extra conditions you wish. Your readers are fifth-grade students. When your graphic is finished, write a paragraph to accompany it.

- Mud slide
- Cold-weather front (low) meeting a warm-weather front (high) over your state
- Tornado
- Flash flood
- Difference between National Weather Service "warning" and "watch"
- Difference between freezing rain and snow
- Water evaporation from a body of water into the air
- Difference between light rain (0.1 in. per hour) and heavy rain (more than 0.30 in. per hour)

Aurora Australis (Southern Lights) from Orbit

Outer space is like a shooting gallery crisscrossed by charged particle bullets. Most of these particles, electrons and protons, are ejected from the Sun and stream outward throughout the solar system. When these streams pass by Earth's magnetic field, they produce and control electrical processes that give rise to beautiful light shows in the night sky.

Auroras are the visible manifestation of electrical processes that occur in Earth's upper atmosphere and in outer space. The streams of charged particles from the Sun interact with Earth's magnetic field like a generator to create current systems with electric potentials of as much as 100,000 volts. Charged particles (electrons), possibly derived from Earth's ionosphere and contained by Earth's magnetic field, are energized by this process and sent spiraling along magnetic field lines toward Earth's upper atmosphere.

When these energized charged particles strike the upper atmosphere, they excite the gases present and cause them to emit light, which we call the aurora. The colors seen both from Earth's surface and by astronauts in orbit are characteristic of atoms and molecules of oxygen and nitrogen.

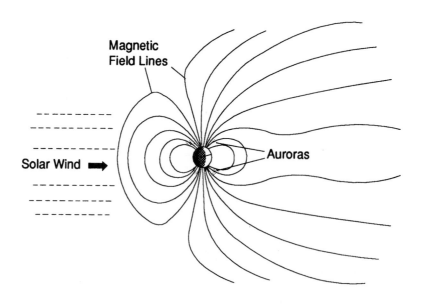

1. As a summer intern working at WKYC-TV, you have been assigned to prepare a set of weather information sheets. The sheets are intended for the general public, and elementary school teachers often use them in classes. After sorting through the current information, you decide to create graphics to illustrate the following facts:

   a. People are killed by lightning in open fields (27%), under trees (14%), during water sports (8%), golfing (5%), using heavy machinery (3%), using the telephone (2.4%), and the rest in unknown locations. More men (84%) than women (16%) are killed.

   b. The average number of deaths every year in the United States from lightning is 100, and about 245 people are injured. Lightning-generated fires destroy 30,000 buildings a year. The worst months for lightning deaths are June (21%), July (30%), and August (22%).

   c. The top five states for lightning-related deaths and the average number of deaths per year are Florida (9.78), North Carolina (4.96), Texas (4.62), New York (3.87), and Tennessee (3.65).

   d. A cloud-to-ground stroke of lightning can be 9 miles long; a cloud-to-cloud stroke can be 90 miles long; contact with a high object, such as a tree, begins a return stroke, which travels upward at about 60,000 miles per second.

After finishing the graphics, write a paragraph for general readers about the significance of these facts.

2. While working part-time at National Motors, you are given the job of preparing an information sheet about the company production and ranking. The sheet will be available on the company's Web site. You use the following information to prepare graphics that will illustrate the facts for the general public:

   a. The company sales include industrial electric motors (64%), adjustable speed drives (22%), electronic controls (12%), and other (2%).

   b. Last year, the company opened 14 sales offices worldwide: 3 in London; 1 in Rio de Janeiro; 1 in Mexico City; 2 in Melbourne; 2 in Singapore; 3 in Athens; 2 in Toronto. The U.S. offices in Atlanta, Omaha, and San Antonio were opened in 1990. The company headquarters is in Denver.

   c. U.S. sales totaled $550 million in 1999, $510 million in 1998, $490 million in 1997, and $200 million in 1996. Market share was 13% in 1999, 12.5% in 1998, 12% in 1997, and 7.9% in 1996. International sales were $89 million in 1999, $82 million in 1998, $76 million in 1997, and $13 million in 1996.

   d. In an industrial survey, the company motors were ranked the first choice of food processors (31%), design engineers (34%), packaging manufacturers (48%), industrial distributors (43%), and heating equipment manufacturers (32%).

Write a brief analysis of these figures so that your Web readers will understand how well the company is doing.

3. Read "Color: The Newest Tool for Technical Communicators" by White and "It's All in the Links" by McAdams in Part 2. Find three company home pages and evaluate the graphics, layout, color, and links. How effective are the pages in leading readers to specific information? How appealing to the eye are the pages? If possible, print out the pages, bring them to class, and discuss any changes you would make. *Or,* write an informal report to your instructor, evaluating the page designs. Informal reports are discussed in Chapter 11.

4. Find a technical document from a company and make enough copies for the other students in class. Prepare an oral critique of the document relative to the design guidelines given in this chapter. Explain how you would revise the document for a more effective format.

CHAPTER **6**

Revision

CREATING A FINAL DRAFT

As you plan and draft a document, you probably will change your mind many times about content, organization, and style. In addition to these changes, however, you should consider revision as a separate stage in producing your final document. During drafting, you should concentrate primarily on developing your document from your initial outline. During revision, concentrate on making changes in content, organization, and style that will best serve your readers and their purpose. These final changes should result in a polished document that your readers can use efficiently.

Thinking about revision immediately after finishing a draft is difficult. Your own writing looks "perfect" to you, and every sentence seems to be the only way to state the information. Experienced writers allow some time between drafting and revising whenever possible. The longer the document, the more important it is to let your writing rest before final revisions so that you can look at the text and graphic aids with a fresh attitude and read as if you were the intended reader and had never seen the material before. Most writers divide revision into two separate stages—global, or overall document revision, and fine-tuning, or style and surface-accuracy revision.

Global Revision

The process of *global revision* involves evaluating your document for effective content and organization. At this level of revision, you may add or delete information; reorganize paragraphs, sections, or the total document; and redraft sections.

Fine-tuning Revision

The process of *fine-tuning revision* involves the changes in sentence structure and language choice that writers make to ensure clarity and appropriate tone. This level also involves checking for surface accuracy, such as correct grammar, punctuation, spelling, and mechanics of technical style. Many organizations have internal style guides that include special conventions writers must check for during fine-tuning revision.

With word processing, both global and fine-tuning revisions can be fast and easy. Depending on your type of word-processing program, you can make revisions using these capabilities:

1. *Delete and insert.*   You can omit or add words, sentences, and paragraphs anywhere in the text.

2. *Search for specific words.*   You can search through the full text for specific words or phrases that you want to change. If you want to change the word *torpid* to *inactive* throughout the document, the computer will locate every place *torpid* appears so that you can delete it and insert *inactive*.

3. *Moving and rearranging text.*   You can take your text apart as if you were cutting up typed pages and arranging the pieces in a new order. You can move whole sections of text from one place to another and reorder paragraphs within sections. You also may decide that revised sentences should be reorganized within a paragraph.

4. *Reformat.*   You can easily change margins, headlines, indentations, spacing, and other format elements.

5. *Check spelling and word choice.*   Most software programs have spelling checkers that scan a text and flag misspelled words that are in the checker's dictionary. Spelling checkers, however, cannot find usage errors, such as *affect* for *effect*, or correctly spelled words that you have used incorrectly, such as *personal* for *personnel*. A thesaurus program will suggest synonyms for specific words. You can select a synonym and substitute it wherever the original word appears in the text.

6. *Check grammar and punctuation.*   Many grammar checkers are now available, and they can find such problems as fragments, comma splices, and agreement errors. The checkers can also flag wordy phrases, passive voice, and jargon. However, do not accept the grammar checkers as "always right." They cannot substitute for a solid understanding of grammar and punctuation on your part. Dangling modifiers and verb tense problems, for example, usually slip past the grammar checkers. As a careful writer, you should reread your document slowly and make appropriate decisions about corrections and style.

Revision on a computer is so convenient that some people cannot stop making changes in drafts. Do not change words or rearrange sentences simply for the sake of change. Revise until your document fulfills your readers' needs, and then stop.

MAKING GLOBAL REVISIONS

For global revisions, rethink your reader and purpose, and then review the content and organizational decisions you made in the planning and drafting stages. Consider changes that will help your readers use the information in the document efficiently.

Content

Evaluate the content of your document and consider whether you have enough information or too little. Review details, definitions, and emphasis.

Details.   Have you included enough details for your readers to understand the general principles, theories, situations, or actions? Have you included details that do not fit your readers' purpose and that they do not need? Do the details serve both primary and secondary readers? Are all the facts, such as dates, amounts, names, and places, correct? Are your graphic aids appropriate for your readers? Do you need more? Have you included examples to help your readers visualize the situation or action?

Definitions.   Have you included definitions of terms that your readers may not know? If your primary readers are experts and your secondary readers are not, have you included a glossary for secondary readers?

Emphasis.   Do the major sections stress information suitable for the readers' main purpose? Do the conclusions logically result from the information provided? Is the urgency of the situation clear to readers? Are deadlines explained? Do headings highlight major topics of interest to readers? Can readers easily find specific topics?

After evaluating how well the document serves your readers and their need for information, you may discover that you need to gather more information or that you must omit information you have included in the document. Reaching the revision stage and finding that you need to gather more information can be frustrating, but, remember, readers can only work with the information they are given. The writer's job is to provide everything readers need to use the document efficiently for a specific purpose.

Organization

Evaluate the overall organization of your document as well as the organization of individual sections and paragraphs. Review these elements:

Overall Organization.   Is the information grouped into major topics that are helpful and relevant to your readers? Are the major topics presented in a logical order that will help readers understand the subject? Are the major sections divided into subsections that will help readers understand the information and highlight important subtopics? Do some topics need to be combined or further divided to highlight information or to make the information easier to understand? Do readers of this document expect or prefer a specific organization, and is that organization in place?

Introductions and Conclusions.   Consider the introductions and conclusions both for the total document and for major sections. Does the introduction to the full document orient readers to the purpose and major topics covered? Do the section introductions establish the topics covered in each section? Does the conclusion to the full document summarize major facts, results, recommendations, future actions, or the overall situation? Do the section conclusions summarize the major points and show why these are important to readers and purpose?

Paragraphs.   Do paragraphs focus on one major point? Are paragraphs sufficiently developed to support that major point with details, examples, and explanations? Is each paragraph organized according to a pattern that will help readers understand the information, such as chronological or spatial?

Headings.   Are the individual topics marked with major headings and subheadings? Do the headings identify the key topics? Are there several pages in a row without headings, or is there a heading for every sentence, and therefore, do headings need to be added or omitted?

Format.   Are there enough highlighting devices, such as headings, lists, boxes, white space, and boldface type, to lead readers through the information and help them see relationships among topics? Can readers quickly scan a page for key information?

After evaluating the organization of the document and of individual sections, make necessary changes. You may find that you need to write more introductory or concluding material or reorder sections and paragraphs. Remember that content alone is not enough to help readers if they have to hunt through a document for relevant facts. Effective organization is a key element in helping readers use a document quickly and efficiently.

MAKING FINE-TUNING REVISIONS

When you are satisfied that your global revisions have produced a complete and well-organized draft, go on to the fine-tuning revision stage, checking for sentence structure, word choice, grammar, punctuation, spelling, and mechanics of technical style. This level of revision can be difficult because by this time you probably have the document or sections of it memorized. As a result, you may read the words that should be on the page, rather than the words that are on the page. For fine-tuning revisions you need to slow your reading pace so that you do not overlook problems in the text. You also should stop thinking about content and organization and think instead about individual sentences and words. Experienced writers sometimes use these techniques to help them find trouble spots:

- *Read aloud.*   Reading a text aloud will help you notice awkward or overly long sentences, insufficient transitions between sentences or paragraphs, and inappropriate language. Reading aloud slows the reading pace and helps you hear problems in the text that your eye could easily skip over.

- *Focus on one point at a time.*   You cannot effectively check for sentence structure, word choice, correctness, and mechanical style all at the same time, particularly in a long document. Experienced writers usually revise in steps, checking for one or two items at a time. If you check for every problem at once, you are likely to overlook items.

- *Use a ruler.*   By placing a ruler under each line as you read it and moving the ruler from line to line, you will focus on the words, rather than on the content of the document. Using a ruler also slows your reading pace, and you are more likely to notice problems in correctness and technical style.

- *Read backward.*   Some writers read a text from the bottom of the page up in order to concentrate only on the typed lines. Reading from the bottom up will help you focus on words and find typographic errors, but it will not help you find problems in sentence structure or grammar because sentence meaning will not be clear as you move backward through the text.

You may find a combination of these methods useful. You may use a ruler, for example, and focus on one point at a time as you look for sentence structure, word choice, and grammar problems. As a final check when you proofread, you may read backward to look for typographic errors.

The following items are those most writers check for during fine-tuning revision. For a discussion of grammar, punctuation, and mechanical style, see Appendix A.

Overloaded Sentences

An overloaded sentence includes so much information that readers cannot easily understand it. This sentence is from an announcement to all residents in a city district:

> You are hereby notified, in accordance with Section 107–27 of the Corinth City Code, that a public hearing will be held by a committee of the Common Council on the date and time, and at the place listed below, to determine whether or not to designate a residential permit parking district in the area bounded by E. Edgewood Avenue on the north, E. Belleview Place on the south, the Corinth River on the west, and Lake McCormick on the east, except the area south of E. Riverside Place and west of the north/south alley between N. Oakland Avenue and N. Bartlett Avenue and the properties fronting N. Downer Avenue south of E. Park Place.

No reader could understand and remember all the information packed into this sentence. Here is a revision:

> As provided in City Code Section 101–27, a committee of the Common Council of Corinth will meet at the time and place shown below. The purpose of the meeting is to designate a residential permit parking district for one area be-

tween the Corinth River on the west and Lake McCormick on the east. The area is also bounded by E. Edgewood Avenue on the north and E. Belleview Place on the south. Not included is the area south of E. Riverside Place and west of the north/south alley between N. Oakland Avenue and N. Bartlett Avenue and the properties fronting N. Downer Avenue south of E. Park Place.

To revise the original overloaded sentence, the writer separated the pieces of information and emphasized the individual points in shorter sentences. The first sentence in the revision announces the meeting. The next two sentences identify the meeting's purpose and the streets included in the parking regulations. A separate sentence then identifies streets not included. Readers will find the shorter sentences easier to understand and, therefore, the information easier to remember. Because so many streets are involved, readers will also need a graphic aid—a map with shading that shows the area in question. Avoid writing sentences that contain so many pieces of information that readers must mentally separate and sort the information as they read. Even short sentences can contain too much information for some readers. Here is a much shorter sentence than the preceding one, yet if the reader were a nonexpert interested in learning about cameras, the sentence holds more technical detail than he or she could remember easily:

> The WY–30X camera is housed in a compact but rugged diecast aluminum body, including a 14X zoom lens and 1.5-in. viewfinder, and has a signal-to-noise ratio of 56 dB, resolution of more than 620 lines on all channels, and registration of 0.6% in all zones.

In drafting sentences, consider carefully how much information your readers are likely to understand and remember at one time.

Clipped Sentences

Sometimes when writers revise overloaded sentences, the resulting sentences become so short they sound like the clipped phrases used in telegrams. Do not cut these items from your sentences just to make them shorter: (1) articles (*a, an, the*), (2) pronouns (*I, you, that, which*), (3) prepositions (*of, at, on, by*), and (4) linking verbs (*is, seems, has*). Here are some clipped sentences and their revisions:

Clipped:	Attached material for insertion in Administration Manual.
Revised:	The attached material is for insertion in the Administration Manual.
Clipped:	Questioned Mr. Hill about compensated injuries full-time employees.
Revised:	I questioned Mr. Hill about the compensated injuries of the full-time employees.
Clipped:	Investigator disturbed individual merits of case.
Revised:	The investigator seems disturbed by the individual merits of the case.

Do not eliminate important words to shorten sentences. The reader will try to supply the missing words and may not do it correctly, resulting in ambiguity and confusion.

Lengthy Sentences

Longer sentences demand that readers process more information, whereas shorter sentences give readers time to pause and absorb facts. A series of short sentences, however, can be monotonous, and too many long sentences in a row can overwhelm readers, especially those with nonexpert knowledge of the subject. Usually, short sentences emphasize a particular fact, and long sentences show relationships among several facts. With varying sentence lengths you can avoid the tiresome reading pace that results when writers repeat sentence style over and over. This paragraph from a letter to bank customers uses both long and short sentences effectively:

> Your accounts will be automatically transferred to the Smith Road office at the close of business on December 16, 1999. You do not need to open new accounts or order new checks. If for some reason another Federal location is more convenient, please stop by 2900 W. Manchester Road and pick up a special customer courtesy card to introduce you to the office of your choice. The Smith Road office is a full-service banking facility. Ample lobby teller stations, auto teller service, 24-hour automated banking, night depository, as well as a complete line of consumer and commercial loans are all available from your new Federal office. You will continue to enjoy the same fine banking service at the Smith Road office, and we look forward to serving you. If you have questions, please call me at 555-8876.

In this paragraph the writer uses short sentences to emphasize the fact that customers do not have to take action, as well as that the new bank office is a full-service branch. Longer sentences explain the services and how to use them. The offer of help is also in a short sentence for emphasis.

Passive Voice

Active voice and passive voice indicate whether the subject of a sentence performs the main action or receives it. Here are two sentences illustrating the differences:

Active: The bridge operators noticed severe rusting at the stone abutments.
Passive: Severe rusting at the stone abutments was noticed by the bridge operators.

The active-voice sentence has a subject (*bridge operators*) that performs the main action (*noticed*). The passive-voice sentence has a subject (*rusting*) that receives the main action (*was noticed*). Passive voice is also characterized by a form of the verb *to be* and a prepositional phrase beginning with *by* that identifies the performer of the main action—usually quite late in the sentence. Readers generally prefer active voice because it creates a faster pace and is more direct. Passive voice also may create several problems for readers:

1. Passive voice requires more words than active voice because it includes the extra verb (*is, are, was, were, will be*) and the prepositional phrase that introduces the performer of the action. The preceding passive-voice sentence has two more words than the active-voice sentence. This may not seem excessive, but if every sentence in a 10-page report has two extra words, the document will be unnecessarily long.

2. Writers often omit the *by* phrase in passive voice, decreasing the number of words in the sentence but also possibly concealing valuable information from readers. Notice how these sentences offer incomplete information without the *by* phrase:

   Incomplete: At least $10,000 was invested in custom software.

   Complete: At least $10,000 was invested in custom software by the vice president for sales.

   Incomplete: The effect of welded defects must be addressed.

   Complete: The effect of welded defects must be addressed by the consulting engineer.

3. Writers often create dangling modifiers when using passive voice. In the active-voice sentence below, the subject of the sentence (*financial analyst*) is also the subject of the introductory phrase.

   Active: Checking the overseas reports, the company financial analyst estimated tanker capacity at 2% over the previous year.

   Passive: Checking the overseas reports, tanker capacity was estimated at 2% over the previous year.

   In the second sentence, the opening phrase (*Checking . . .*) cannot modify *tanker capacity* and is a dangling modifier.

4. Passive voice is confusing in instructions because readers cannot tell *who* is to perform the action. Always write instructions and direct orders in active voice.

   Unclear: The cement should be applied to both surfaces.

   Revised: Apply the cement to both surfaces.

   Unclear: The telephone should be answered within three rings.

   Revised: Please answer the telephone within three rings.

In technical writing, passive voice is sometimes necessary. Use passive voice when

1. You do not know who or what performed the action:

    The fire was reported at 6:05 A.M.

2. Your readers are not interested in who or what performed the action:

    Ethan McClosky was elected district attorney.

3. You are describing a process performed by one person, and naming that person in every sentence would be monotonous. Identify the performer in the opening and then use passive voice:

    The carpenter began assembling the base by gluing each long apron to two legs. The alignment strips were then cut for the tray bottoms to finished dimensions. The tabletop was turned upside down and. . . .

4. For some reason, perhaps courtesy, you do not want to identify the person responsible for an action:

    The copy machine jammed because a large sheaf of papers was inserted upside down.

Jargon

Jargon refers to the technical language and abbreviated terms used by people in one particular field, one company, or one department or unit. People in every workplace and every occupation use some jargon. A server may refer to "watering the tables" (putting water glasses on the tables), a public relations executive may ask a secretary to get "the glossies" (glossy photographs), or a psychologist may remark to another psychologist that the average woman has a "24F on the PAQ" (a femininity score of 24 on the Personal Attributes Questionnaire). In some cases, jargon may be so narrow that employees in one department cannot understand the jargon used in another department. Use jargon in professional communications only when you are certain your readers understand it.

Here is a sentence from a memo sent by a purchase coordinator to his supervisor:

Guttenhausen (Deutsche) big R price is list less 40 to Inventory versus rest to Corporate.

When the supervisor included this information in a memo he prepared for the division head about the weekly orders, he revised it as follows:

Guttenhausen Industries (Bonn) will pay our standard price less 40% (in deutsche marks) for the Model RR–28 transformer, charged to the Inventory account. The difference between this price and our usual cost plus 15% will be charged to the Corporate account.

The supervisor cut the original jargon and clarified the message by fully identifying the company, the transformer model, and the prices and by explaining how the costs would be charged. The revision required two sentences. Jargon allows employees to exchange briefer messages, but only if the readers understand every term and the abbreviated references. When in doubt, cut out jargon and clarify your terms.

Sexist Language

Sexist language refers to words or phrases that indicate a bias against women in terms of importance or competence. Most people would never use biased language to refer to ethnic, religious, or racial groups, but sexist language often goes unnoticed because many common terms and phrases that are sexist in nature have been part of our casual language for decades. People now realize that sexist language influences our expectations about what women can accomplish and also relegates women to an inferior status. Using such language is not acceptable any longer. In revising documents, check for these slips into sexist language:

1. Demeaning or condescending terms. Avoid using casual or slang terms for women.

   Sexist: The girls in the Records Department will prepare the reports.

   Revised: The clerks in the Records Department will prepare the reports.

   Sexist: The annual division picnic will be June 12. Bring the little woman.

   Revised: The annual division picnic will be June 12. Please bring your spouse.

2. Descriptions for women based on standards different from those for men. Avoid referring to women in one way and men in another.

   Sexist: The consultants were Dr. Dennis Tonelli, Mr. Robert Lavery, and Debbie Roberts.

   Revised: The consultants were Dr. Dennis Tonelli, Mr. Robert Lavery, and Ms. Debra Roberts.

   Sexist: There were three doctors and two lady lawyers at the meeting.

   Revised: There were three doctors and two lawyers at the meeting.

   Sexist: The new mechanical engineers are Douglas Ranson, a graduate of MIT and a Rhodes scholar, and Marcia Kane, an attractive redhead with a B.S. from the University of Michigan and an M.S. from the University of Wisconsin.

   Revised: The new mechanical engineers are Douglas Ranson, a graduate of MIT and a Rhodes scholar, and Marcia Kane, with a B.S. from the University of Michigan and an M.S. from the University of Wisconsin.

3. Occupational stereotypes. Do not imply that all employees in a particular job are the same sex.

Sexist: An experienced pilot is needed. He must. . . .

Revised: An experienced pilot is needed. This person must. . . .

Sexist: The new tax laws affect all businessmen.

Revised: The new tax laws affect all businesspeople.

Although some gender-specific occupational terms remain common, such as *actor/actress* and *host/hostess*, most such terms have been changed to neutral job titles.

Sexist: The policeman should fill out a damage report.

Revised: The police officer should fill out a damage report.

Sexist: The stewardess reported the safety problem.

Revised: The flight attendant reported the safety problem.

4. Generic *he* to refer to all people. Using the pronoun *he* to refer to unnamed people or to stand for a group of people is correct grammatically in English, but it might be offensive to some people. Avoid the generic *he* whenever possible, particularly in job descriptions that could apply to either sex. Change a singular pronoun to a plural:

Sexist: Each technical writer has his own office at Tower Industries.

Revised: All technical writers have their own offices at Tower Industries.

Eliminate the pronoun completely:

Sexist: The average real estate developer plans to start his construction projects in April.

Revised: The average real estate developer plans to start construction projects in April.

Use *he* or *she* or *his* or *hers* very sparingly:

Sexist: The x-ray technician must log his hours daily.

Revised: The x-ray technician must log his or her hours daily.

Better: All x-ray technicians must log their hours daily.

Concrete versus Abstract Words

Concrete words refer to specific items, such as objects, statistics, locations, dimensions, and actions that can be observed by some means. Here is a sentence using concrete words:

The 48M printer has a maximum continuous speed of 4000 lines per minute, with burst speeds up to 5500 lines per minute.

Abstract words refer generally to ideas, conditions, and qualities. Here is a sentence from a quarterly report to stockholders that uses abstract words:

> The sales position of Collins, Inc., was favorable as a result of our attention to products and our response to customers.

This sentence contains little information for readers who want to know about the company activities. Here is a revision using more concrete language:

> The 6% rise in domestic sales in the third quarter of 1999 resulted from our addition of a safety catch on the Collins Washer in response to over 10,000 requests by our customers.

This revision in concrete language clarifies exactly what the company did and what the result was. Using concrete or abstract words, as always, depends on what you believe your readers need. However, in most professional situations, readers want and need the precise information provided by concrete words.

The paragraphs that follow are from two reports submitted by management trainees in a large bank after a visit to the retail division of the main branch. The trainees wrote reports to their supervisors, describing their responses to the procedures they observed. The paragraph from the first report uses primarily abstract, nonspecific language:

> The first department I visited was very interesting. The way in which the men buy and investigate the paper was very interesting and informative. This area, along with the other areas, helped me where I am right now—doing loans. Again, the ways in which the men deal with the dealers was quite informative. They were friendly, but stern, and did not let the dealers control the transaction.

The paragraph from the second report uses more concrete language:

> The manual system of entering sales draft data on the charge system seems inefficient. It is clear that seasonal surges in charge activity (for example, Christmas) or an employee illness would create a serious bottleneck in processing. My talk with Eva Lockridge confirmed my impression that this operation is outdated and needs to be redesigned.

The first writer did not identify any specific item of interest or explain exactly what was informative about the visit. The second writer identified both the system that seemed outdated and the person with whom she talked. The second writer is providing her reader with concrete information rather than generalities.

Gobbledygook

Gobbledygook is writing that is indirect, vague, pompous, or longer and more difficult to read than necessary. Writers of gobbledygook do not care if their readers can use their documents because they are interested only in demonstrating how many large words they can cram into convoluted sentences. Such writers are primarily concerned with impressing or intimidating readers rather than helping them use information efficiently. Gobbledygook is characterized by these elements:

1. Using jargon the readers cannot understand.

2. Making words longer than necessary by adding suffixes or prefixes to short, well-known words (e.g., *finalization, marginalization*). Another way to produce gobbledygook is to use a longer synonym for a short, well-known word. A good example is the word *utilize* and its variations to substitute for *use. Utilize* is an unnecessary word because *use* can be substituted in any sentence and mean the same thing. Notice the revisions that follow these sentences:

   Gobbledygook: The project will utilize the Acme trucks.
   Revision: The project will use the Acme trucks.

   Gobbledygook: By utilizing the gravel already on the site, we can save up to $5000.
   Revision: By using the gravel already on the site, we can save up to $5000.

   Gobbledygook: Through the utilization of this high-speed press, we can meet the deadline.
   Revision: Through the use of this high-speed press, we can meet the deadline.

   The English language has many short, precise words. Use them.

3. Writing more elaborate words than are necessary for document purpose and readers. The writer who says "deciduous perennial, genus *Ulmus*" instead of "elm tree" is probably engaged in gobbledygook unless his or her readers are biologists.

This paragraph from a memo sent by a unit supervisor to a division manager is supposed to explain why the unit needs more architects:

In the absence of available adequate applied man-hours, and/or elapsed calendar time, the quality of the architectural result (as delineated by the drawings) has been and will continue to be put ahead of the graphic quality or detailed completeness of the documents. In order to be efficient, work should be consecutive not simultaneous, and a schedule must show design and design development as scheduled separately from working drawings on each project, so that a tighter but realistic schedule can be maintained, optimizing the productive efforts of each person.

You will not be surprised to learn that the division manager routinely threw away any memos he received from this employee without reading them.

STRATEGIES—Fad Words

A **fad word** usually comes from a particular field and drifts into general use. **Bottom line** in accounting means the final figure showing profit or loss; in general use, it means a deadline or result. A fad word also may be a common word used in a new way. **Access** is a noun meaning the ability to reach someone or something; the computer industry uses **access** as a verb meaning to retrieve files from a database.

Avoid confusing readers with the latest fad words whenever a clearer, standard word is available.

No: The governor referenced the dam project in his speech.

Yes: The governor mentioned the dam project in his speech.

Wordiness

Wordiness refers to writing that includes superfluous words that add no information to a document. Wordiness stems from several causes:

1. *Doubling terms.* Using two or more similar terms to make one point creates wordiness. These doubled phrases can be reduced to one of the words:

   final ultimate result (result)
   the month of July (July)
   finished and completed (finished or completed)
   unique innovation (innovation)

2. *Long phrases for short words.* Wordiness results when writers use long phrases instead of one simple word:

   at this point in time (now)
   in the near future (soon)
   due to the fact that (because)
   in the event that (if)

3. *Unneeded repetition.* Repeating words or phrases too often increases wordiness and disturbs sentence clarity:

The Marshman employees will follow the scheduled established hours established by their supervisors, who will establish the times required to support production.

This sentence is difficult to read because *established* appears three times, once as an adjective and twice as a verb. Here is a revision:

The Marshman employees will follow the schedule established by their supervisors, who will set times required to support production.

4. *Empty sentence openings.* These sentences are correct grammatically but their structure contributes to wordiness:

It was determined that the home office sent income statements to all pension clients.

It is necessary that the loader valves (No. 3C126) be scrapped because of damage.

It might be possible to open two runways within an hour.

There will be times when the videotapes are not available.

There are three new checking account options available from Southwest National Bank.

These sentences have empty openings because the first words (*There will be / There are / It is / It was / It might be*) offer the reader no information, and the reader must reach the last half of the sentence to find the subject. Here are revisions that eliminate the empty openings:

The home office sent income statements to all pension clients.

The loader valves (No. 3C126) must be scrapped because of damage.

Two runways might open within an hour.

Sometimes the videotapes will not be available.

Southwest National Bank is offering three new checking account options.

Remember that wordiness does not refer to the length of a document, but to excessive words in the text. A 40-page manual containing none of the constructions discussed here is not wordy, but a half-page memo full of them is.

CHAPTER SUMMARY

This chapter discusses two stages of revision—global revision and fine-tuning revision. Remember:

- Revision consists of two distinct stages: (1) global revision, which focuses on content and organization, and (2) fine-tuning revision, which focuses on sentence structure, word choice, correctness, and the mechanics of technical style.

- For global revision, writers check content to see if there are enough details, definitions, and emphasis on the major points.

- For global revision, writers also check organization of the full document and of individual sections for (1) overall organization, (2) introductions and conclusions, (3) paragraphs, (4) headings, and (5) format.

- For fine-tuning revision, writers check sentence structure for overloaded sentences, clipped sentences, overly long sentences, and overuse of passive voice.

- For fine-tuning revision, writers also check word choice for unnecessary jargon, sexist language, overly abstract words, gobbledygook, and general wordiness.

SUPPLEMENTAL READINGS IN PART 2

Bagin, C. B. and Van Doren, J. "How to Avoid Costly Proofreading Errors," *Simply Stated*, p. 451.

"The Practical Writer," *The Royal Bank of Canada*, p. 524.

Tarutz, J. H. "Editing for an International Audience," *Technical Editing*, p. 545.

This model shows three drafts of a company bulletin outlining procedures for security guards who discover a fire while on patrol. The bulletin will be included in the company's "Security Procedures Manual," which contains general procedures for potential security problems, such as fire, theft, physical fights, and trespassing. The bulletins are not instructions to be used on the job. Rather, the guards are expected to read the bulletins, become familiar with the procedures, and follow them if a security situation arises.

Discussion

1. In the first draft, identify the major topics the writer covers, and discuss how well the general organization fits the purpose of the readers.

2. Compare the first and second drafts, and discuss the changes the writer made in organization, sentence structure, and detail. How will these changes help the readers understand the information?

3. Compare the third draft with the first two, and discuss how the specific changes will improve the usefulness of the bulletin.

4. In groups, draft a fourth version of this bulletin, making further organization changes to increase clarity. *Or*, if your instructor prefers, rewrite one section of the third draft, and make further fine-tuning revisions according to the guidelines in this chapter.

BULLETIN 46-RC   FIRE EMERGENCIES—PLANT SECURITY PATROLS

Following are procedures for fire emergencies discovered during routine
security patrols. All security personnel should be familiar with these
procedures.

General Inspection

Perimeter fence lines, parking lots, and yard areas should be observed
by security personnel at least twice per shift. Special attention should be
given to outside areas during the dark hours and nonoperating periods.
It is preferable that the inspection of the yard area and parking lots be
made in a security patrol car equipped with a spot light and two-way
radio communications. Special attention should be given to the condition
of fencing and gates and to yard lighting to assure that all necessary
lights are turned on during the dark hours and that the system is fully
operative. Where yard lights are noted as burned out, the guard should
report these problems immediately to the Plant Engineer for corrective
action and maintain follow-up until the yard lighting is in full service.
Occasional roof spot checks should be made by security patrols to
observe for improper use of roof areas and fire hazards, particularly
around ventilating equipment.

Discovery

When a guard discovers a fire during an in-plant security patrol, he should
immediately turn in an alarm. This should be done before any attempt is
made to fight the fire because all too frequently guards think they can put
out the fire with the equipment at hand, and large losses have resulted.

Whenever possible, the guard should turn in the alarm by using the
alarm box nearest the scene of the fire. If it is necessary to report the
fire on the plant telephone, he should identify the location accurately so
that he may give this information to the plant fire department or to the
guard on duty at the Security Office, who will summon the employee fire
brigade and possibly the city fire department.

Once he has turned in the alarm, the guard should decide whether he
can effectively use the available fire protection equipment to fight the
fire. If the fire is beyond his control, he should proceed to the main aisle
of approach where he can make contact with the fire brigade or firemen
and direct them to the scene of the fire. If automatic sprinklers have
been engaged, the men in charge of the fire fighting crew will make the
decision to turn off the system.

First Draft

BULLETIN 46-RC   FIRE EMERGENCIES—PLANT SECURITY PATROLS

All security guards should be familiar with the following procedures for fire emergencies that occur during routine security patrols.

Inspection Areas

Inspection of the yard area and parking lots should be made in a security patrol car equipped with a spot light and two-way radio communications. At least twice per shift, the guard should inspect (1) fence lines, (2) parking lots, and (3) yard areas. These outside areas require special attention during the dark hours and nonoperating periods. The guard should inspect carefully the condition of the fencing and gate closures. The yard lighting should be checked to ensure that all necessary lights are turned on during the dark hours and that the system is fully operative. If the guard notes that yard lights are burned out, he should report these problems to the Plant Engineer for corrective action and maintain follow-up until the yard lighting is in full service.

Roof Checks

Occasional roof spot checks should be made by the guard to observe improper use of roof areas and any fire hazards, particularly around ventilating equipment.

Fires

When a guard discovers a fire during an in-plant security patrol, he should immediately turn in an alarm before he makes any attempt to fight the fire. In the past, attempts to fight the fire without sounding an alarm have resulted in costly damage and larger fires than necessary.

Whenever possible, the guard should turn in the alarm at the alarm box nearest the scene of the fire. If he must use a plant telephone, he should identify the location accurately. This information helps the plant fire department or the guard on duty at the Security Office, who must summon the employee fire brigade or the city fire department.

Once he has turned in the alarm, the guard should decide whether he can fight the fire with the available equipment. If the fire is beyond his control, he should go to the main entrance of the area so that he can direct the fire fighters to the scene of the fire. If the automatic sprinklers are on, the supervisor of the fire fighting crew will decide when to turn off the system.

Second Draft

BULLETIN 46-RC   FIRES—PLANT SECURITY PATROLS

All security guards should be familiar with the following procedures for fires that occur during routine security patrols.

Inspection Areas

The guard should inspect the outside areas in a security patrol car equipped with a spot light and two-way radio. The outside areas require special attention after dark and during nonoperating hours. At least twice per shift, the following should be inspected:

Fence Lines—The guard should check fences for gaps or breaks in the chain and gate closures for tight links and hinges.

Parking Lots and Yards—The guard should monitor the lighting in all parking lots and open yards to ensure that all necessary lights are on after dark and that the system is fully operative. If any lights are burned out, the guard should report the locations to the Plant Engineer and maintain follow-up until the lighting is repaired.

Occasional spot checks during a shift should be made of the following:

Roofs—The guard should check for improper use of the roof areas and any fire hazards, particularly around ventilating equipment.

Fires

Discovery—Upon discovering a fire during an in-plant security patrol, the guard must turn in an alarm before attempting to fight the fire. In the past, attempts to fight the fire before turning in an alarm have resulted in costly damage and larger fires than necessary.

Alarms—Whenever possible, the guard should turn in the alarm at the alarm box nearest the scene of the fire. If a plant telephone is more convenient or safer, the guard should be sure to identify the fire location accurately. This information is needed by the plant fire department and the guard at the Security Office, who must summon the employee fire brigade or the city fire department.

Fire Fighting—Once the alarm is in, the guard should decide whether to fight the fire with the available equipment. If the fire is beyond control, the guard should go to the main entrance to the fire area and direct the fire brigade or city fire fighters to the scene of the fire. If the automatic sprinklers are on, the supervisor of the fire brigade or of the fire department crew will decide when to turn off the system.

Third Draft

1. The following memo was written by a new vice-president at a large manufacturing company. Supervisors who received the memo made joking references to each other about "writing problems at the top." Revise this memo for clarity and improved style. Add any information you need to clarify the message.

> As some of you may already be aware, the corporate control division will be conducting an internal controls review of all production units in February 2000. This review occurs every three years and culminates with a report to the Board of Directors covering the on-site reviews including the international locations. For those of you who have already completed the preliminary internal controls review last year, the new review should not pose undue difficulties or problems. Please remember that all internal audit reviews issued on a preliminary basis for your units since February 1998 should be reviewed by you, so you can identify any areas where controls were deemed to be inadequate. Discussion should address what has been done since the first review to strengthen the controls referenced in the reports, and, if an issue is still outstanding, what planned actions are underway to address the problem. Documentation of major/critical/ important issues will need to be described, including any and all use of policy manuals, etc. If these things are not in place, please describe your plans for future handling. Scheduled dates for visits to units will be announced later, but work should now begin for us to be able to provide a concise overview for the report to the board.

2. The Human Resources Director at a community physical rehabilitation center sent the following memo to nurses who traveled between the two main facilities and made home visits. Within a day, the director received several complaints about the memo. Identify the problems, and revise the message according to the principles in this chapter.

> We are all going to have to pay more attention to proper filling out of time sheets. Effective June 1, 2000, you are going to have to include mileage on your time sheets, but you are going to be responsible for traveling from facility to facility. My secretary, Helen, only knows what you tell her, so please keep accurate records. Our executive director, Dr. John Mitchell, has directed me to remind you that "comp time" is against our rules, and, therefore, you may only make scheduling adjustments within a week, so, for example, if someone works two hours more on Monday, she can have two hours off during that week, but not during the next week. Also, no one can have a half day off unpaid to attend to personal business if she has paid sick days or vacation days remaining. She will have to use sick or vacation time. Check with Julie or Sue in my office if you have any

questions about this policy. Dr. Mitchell is concerned about nurses taking their vacation days just to shop and forgetting that important matters may require time off.

3. The security director of a large electronics company sent the following memo to the loading dock supervisor. The director was surprised when the supervisor asked for clarification. Revise the memo for clarity and add any details you wish.

> For security, trucks being loaded with trash at the dock or yard area should be placed under daily surprise spot check surveillance to assure that these loads contain only trash and nonsalable waste materials. Utilization of guards on special assignment to observe shipment loading of scrap should be implemented and records maintained with a "spot check" log. Guards should peruse the loads for items that can be utilized outside the company. Variance of spot checks in terms of time must be in place so that a consistent pattern is not observable and anticipated by employees.

4. Find a "real-world" letter, memo, bulletin, pamphlet, or report. Analyze the writing style according to the guidelines in this chapter. Write a brief evaluation of the writing style and identify specific places in the document where revision would make the writing easier to understand. *Or,* if your instructor prefers, rewrite the original document to improve the style according to the guidelines in this chapter. Hand in both your revision and the original document.

CHAPTER 7

Definition

UNDERSTANDING DEFINITIONS

Definition is essential in good technical writing because of the specialized vocabulary in many documents. All definitions are meant to distinguish one object or procedure from any that are similar and to clarify them for readers by setting precise limits on each expression. In writing definitions, use vocabulary understandable to your readers. Defining one word with others that are equally specialized will frustrate your readers; no one wants to consult a dictionary in order to understand an explanation that was supposed to make referring to a dictionary unnecessary.

Certain circumstances always call for definitions:

1. When technical information originally written for expert readers is revised for nonexpert readers, the writer must include definitions for all terms that are not common knowledge.

2. A document with readers from many disciplines or varied backgrounds must include definitions enabling readers with the lowest level of knowledge to understand the document.

3. All new or rare terms should be defined, even for readers who are experts in the subject. Change is so rapid in science and technology that no one can easily keep up with every new development.

4. When a term has multiple meanings, a writer must be clear about which meaning is being used in the document. The word *slate,* for example, can refer to a kind of rock, a color, a handheld chalkboard, or a list of candidates for election.

As discussed in Chapter 4, writers frequently use definitions in reports addressed to multiple readers because some of the readers may not be familiar with the technical terminology used. Definitions in reports may range from a simple phrase in a sentence to a complete appendix at the end of the report. In all cases, the writer decides just how much definition the reader needs to be able to use the report effectively. Definitions also may be complete documents in themselves; for example, entries in technical handbooks or science dictionaries are expanded definitions. Furthermore, individual sections of manuals, technical sales literature, and information pamphlets are often expanded definitions for readers who lack expert knowledge of the field but need to understand the subject.

The three types of definitions are (1) informal, (2) formal sentence, and (3) expanded. All three can appear in the same document, and your use of one or another depends on your analysis of the needs of your readers and your purpose in using a specific item of information.

WRITING INFORMAL DEFINITIONS

Informal definitions explain a term with a word or a phrase that has the same general meaning. Here are some examples of informal definitions:

Contrast is the difference between dark and light in a photograph.

Terra cotta—a hard, fired clay—is used for pottery and ornamental architectural detail.

Viscous (sticky) substances are used in manufacturing rayon.

Leucine, an amino acid, is essential for human nutrition.

The first definition is a complete sentence; the other definitions are words or phrases used to define a term within a sentence. Notice that you can set off the definition with dashes, parentheses, or commas. Place the definition immediately after the first reference to the term. Informal definitions are most helpful for non-expert readers who need an introduction to an unfamiliar term. Be sure to use a well-known word or phrase to define a difficult term.

The advantage of informal definitions is that they do not significantly interrupt the flow of a sentence or the information. Readers do not have to stop thinking about the main idea in order to understand the term. The limitation of informal definitions is that they do not thoroughly explain the term and, in fact, are really identifications rather than definitions. If a reader needs more information than that provided by a simple identification, use a formal sentence definition or an expanded definition.

WRITING FORMAL SENTENCE DEFINITIONS

A *formal sentence definition* is more detailed and rigidly structured than an informal definition. The formal definition has three specific parts.

Term		*Group*	*Distinguishing features*
An *ace*	is	a tennis serve	that is successful because the opponent cannot reach the ball to return it.

The first part is the specific term you want to define, followed by the verb *is* or *are, was* or *were*. The second part is the group of objects or actions to which the term belongs. The third part consists of the distinguishing features that set this term off from others in the same group. In this example, the group part *a tennis serve* establishes both the sport and the type of action the term refers to. The distinguishing features part explains the specific quality that separates this tennis serve from others—the opponent cannot reach it.

These formal definitions illustrate how the group and the distinguishing features become more restrictive as a term becomes more specific:

Term		*Group*	*Distinguishing features*
A *firearm*	is	a weapon	from which a bullet or shell is discharged by gunpowder.
A *rifle*	is	a firearm	with spiral grooves in the inner surface of the gun barrel to give the bullet a rotary motion and increase its accuracy.
A *Winchester*	is	a rifle	first made about 1866, with a tubular magazine under the barrel that allows the user to fire a number of bullets without reloading.

In writing a formal sentence definition, be sure to place the term in as specific a group as possible. In the preceding samples, a rifle could be placed in the group *weapon,* but that group also includes clubs, swords, and nuclear missiles. Placing the rifle in the group *firearm* eliminates all weapons that are not also firearms. The distinguishing features part then concentrates on the characteristics that are special to rifles and not to other firearms. The distinguishing features part, however, cannot include every characteristic detail of a term. You will have to decide which features most effectively separate the term from others in the same group and which will best help your readers understand and use the information.

When writing formal sentence definitions, remember these tips:

1. Do not use the same key word in the distinguishing features part that you used in one or both of the other two units.

   Poor: A pump is a machine or device that pumps gas or liquid to a new level or position.

   Better: A pump is a machine or device that raises or moves gas or liquid to a new level or position.

   Poor: An odometer is a measuring instrument that measures the distance traveled by a vehicle.

   Better: An odometer is a measuring instrument that records the distance traveled by a vehicle.

   In the first example, the distinguishing features section includes the word *pump,* which is also the term being defined. In the second example, the distinguishing features part includes the verb *measures,* which is used in the group part. In both cases, the writer must revise to avoid repetition that will send readers in a circle. Sometimes you can assume that your readers know what a general term means. If you are certain your readers understand the term *horse* and your purpose is to clarify the term *racehorse,* you may write, "A racehorse is a horse that is bred or trained to run in competition with other horses."

2. Do not use distinguishing features that are too general to adequately specify the meaning of the term.

Poor:	Rugby is a sport that involves rough contact among players as they try to send a ball over the opponent's goal lines.
Better:	Rugby is a team sport that involves 13 to 15 players on each side who try to send a ball across the opponent's goal line during two 40-minute halves.

Poor:	A staple is a short piece of wire that is bent so as to hold papers together.
Better:	A staple is a short piece of wire that is bent so both ends pierce several papers and fold inward, binding the papers together.

In both examples, the distinguishing features are not restrictive enough. Many sports, such as football and soccer, involve rough contact between players who try to send a ball over the opponent's goal line. The revision focuses on the number of players and the minutes played, features which distinguish rugby from similar team sports. Notice also that the group has been narrowed to *team sport* to further restrict the definition and help the reader understand it. In the second poor example, the distinguishing features could apply to a paper clip as well as a staple. Remember to restrict the group as much as possible and provide distinguishing features that isolate the term from its group.

3. Do not use distinguishing features that are too restrictive.

Poor:	A tent is a portable shelter made of beige canvas in the shape of a pyramid, supported by poles.
Better:	A tent is a portable shelter made of animal skins or a sturdy fabric and supported by poles.

Poor:	A videotape is a recording device made of a magnetic ribbon of material ¾ in. wide and coated plastic that registers both audio and visual signals for reproduction.
Better:	A videotape is a recording device made of a magnetic ribbon of material, usually coated plastic, that registers both audio and visual signals for reproduction.

In the first example, the distinguishing features are too restrictive because not all tents are pyramid-shaped or made of beige canvas. The second example establishes only one size for a videotape, but videotapes come in several sizes, so size is not an appropriate distinguishing feature. Do not restrict your definition to only one brand or one model if your term is meant to cover all models and brands of that particular object.

4. Do not use *is when, is where,* or *is what* in place of the group part in a formal definition.

Poor: A tongue depressor is what medical personnel use to hold down a patient's tongue during a throat examination.

Better: A tongue depressor is a flat, thin, wooden stick used by medical personnel to hold down a patient's tongue during a throat examination.

Poor: Genetic engineering is when scientists change the hereditary code on an organism's DNA.

Better: Genetic engineering is the set of biochemical techniques used by scientists to move fragments from the genes of one organism to the chromosomes of another to change the hereditary code on the DNA of the second organism.

In both examples, the writer initially neglects to place the term in a group before adding the distinguishing features. The group part is the first level of restriction, and it helps readers by eliminating other groups that may share some of the distinguishing features. The first example, for instance, could apply to any object shoved down a patient's throat. The poor definition of genetic engineering refers only to the result and does not clarify the term as applying to specific techniques that will produce that result.

STRATEGIES—Complete Comparisons

When comparing two elements, identify them fully in the sentence.

No: The Washburn Clinic is better equipped.

Yes: The Washburn Clinic is better equipped than the Health Center.

No: Replacing the spark plugs is easier than the muffler.

Yes: Replacing the spark plugs is easier than replacing the muffler.

WRITING EXPANDED DEFINITIONS

Expanded definitions can range from one paragraph in a report or manual to an entry several pages long in a technical dictionary. Writers use expanded definitions in these circumstances:

1. When a reader must fully understand a term to successfully use the document. A patient who has just been diagnosed with hypoglycemia probably will want a more detailed definition in the patient information booklet than just a formal sentence definition. Similarly, a decision maker who is

reading a feasibility study about bridge reconstruction will want expanded definitions of such terms as *cathodic protection* or *distributed anode system* in order to make an informed decision about the most appropriate method for the company project.

2. When specific terms, such as *economically disadvantaged* or *physical therapy,* refer to broad concepts and readers other than experts need to understand the scope and application of the terms.

3. When the purpose of the document, such as a technical handbook or a science dictionary, is to provide expanded definitions to readers who need to understand the terms for a variety of reasons.

A careful writer usually begins an expanded definition with a formal sentence definition and then uses one or more of the following strategies to enlarge the definition with more detail and explanation.

Cause and Effect

Writers use the cause-and-effect (or effect-and-cause) strategy to illustrate relationships among several events. This strategy is effective in expanded definitions of terms that refer to a process or a system. The following paragraph is from a student report about various types of exercises used in athletic training. The definition explains the effect aerobic exercise has on the body.

Aerobic exercise is a sustained physical activity that increases the body's ability to obtain oxygen, thereby strengthening the heart and lungs. Aerobic effect begins when an exercise is vigorous enough to produce a sustained heart rate of at least 150 beats a minute. This exercise, if continued for at least 20 minutes, produces a change in a person's body. The lungs begin processing more air with less effort, while the heart grows stronger, pumping more blood with fewer strokes. Overall, the body's total blood volume increases and the blood supply to the muscles improves.

Classification

Classification is used in expanded definitions when a writer needs to break a term into types or categories and discuss the similarities and differences among the categories. The following expanded definition is from a report written by a public television station manager to a donors group, soliciting funds for equipment purchases. The writer uses classification to define videotape machines. Note that the writer does not begin with a formal sentence definition and that the distinguishing features actually appear in the second sentence.

The videotape recorder/player is an electronic device that is one of the most important components of television station operation. The videotape recorder creates distinct video and audio tracks during recording; then, during playback, the videotape player "reads" the images and sound information from the recorded tracks. Videotape machines fall into three categories—production, editing, and playback. A production recorder preserves images on tape for later editing. The editing recorder plays back an image on one machine and records it on a second machine. The playback machine must reproduce the best signal possible from a recorded tape so that the edit recorder can capture the best possible image and record it on another tape. The requirements for each of these VCRs vary because each is expected to do a different job.

Comparison or Contrast

Writers use comparison to show readers the similarities or differences between the term being defined and another commonly understood term. When using this strategy, be sure the term you are using for comparison or contrast is familiar to your readers. The following definition is from a book about Civil War military equipment written for general readers. The writer compares a specific style of tent to a hoop skirt and a teepee, objects most readers have seen in films or books. A third comparison occurs when the writer explains how the men arranged themselves to sleep, further illustrating the shape and size of the tent and creating an image that general readers will understand easily.

Much more popular and efficient was the Sibley tent, named for its inventor, Henry H. Sibley, now a brigadier general in the Confederate service. One Reb likened it to a "large hoop skirt standing by itself on the ground." Indeed, it resembled nothing so much as an Indian teepee, a tall cone of canvas supported by a center pole. Flaps on the sides could be opened for ventilation, and an iron replica of the tent cone called a Sibley stove heated the interior—sort of. Often more than twenty men inhabited a single tent, spread out like the spokes of a wheel, their heads at the outer rim and their feet at the center pole.[1]

Description

A detailed description of a term being defined will expand the definition. Reading about the physical properties of a term often helps readers to visualize the concept or object and remember it more readily. Chapter 8 provides a detailed discussion of developing physical descriptions. This excerpt is from a NASA description of the sections of the Space Shuttle:

The orbiter carries the crew and payload. It is 122 feet (37 meters) long and 57 feet (17 meters) high, has a wingspan of 78 feet (24 meters), and weighs from 168,000 to 175,000 pounds (76,000 to 79,000 kilograms) empty. It is about the size and general shape of a DC-9 commercial jet airplane. Orbiters may vary slightly from unit to unit.[2]

Development or History

Writers may expand definitions by describing how the subject has changed from its original form or purpose over time. When using development or history to expand a definition, you may include (1) discovery or invention of the concept or object, (2) changes in the components or design of the concept or object, or (3) changes in the use or function of the concept or object. The following excerpt from a science pamphlet for general readers expands the definition of the telegraph by briefly explaining some of its history:

> Although the term *telegraph* means a system or apparatus for sending messages over a long distance and, therefore, could include smoke and drum signals, the term now generally refers to the electric telegraph developed in the nineteenth century. In the late eighteenth century, Frenchman Claude Clappe designed a system of signals that relied on a vertical pole and movable crossbar with indicators. Using a telescope, operators in towers three miles apart read the signals and then passed the messages from tower to tower between principal French cities. The success of this system encouraged experimentation. In the early nineteenth century, researchers discovered that electric current through a wire could cause a needle to turn. The development of the electromagnet then allowed Samuel F. B. Morse to devise a practical system of transmitting and receiving electric signals over long distances, and he invented a message code of dots, dashes, and spaces. By mid-nineteenth century, telegraph systems spread across the United States and Europe.

Etymology

Etymology is the study of the history of individual words. The term derives from the Greek *etymon* (true meaning) and *logos* (word). Writers rarely use etymology as the only strategy in an expanded definition, but they often include it with other strategies. The following definition of *ligament* is from a brochure for orthopedic patients:

> In anatomy, a ligament is a band of white fibrous tissue that connects bones and supports organs. The word *ligament* comes from the Latin *ligare* (to tie or bind). Although a ligament is strong, it does not stretch, so if the bones are pulled apart, the ligament connecting them will tear.

Examples

Another way to expand a definition is to provide examples of the term. This strategy is particularly effective in expanding definitions for nonexpert readers who need to understand the variety included in one term. This definition of a combat medal is taken from a student examination on military history:

A combat medal is a military award given to commemorate an individual's bravery under fire. Medals are awarded by all branches of the armed forces and by civilian legislative bodies. The Congressional Medal of Honor, for instance, is awarded by the President in the name of Congress to military personnel who have distinguished themselves in combat beyond the call of duty. The Purple Heart is awarded by the branches of the armed services to all military personnel who sustain wounds during combat. The Navy Cross is awarded to naval personnel for outstanding heroism against an enemy.

Method of Operation or Process

Another effective strategy for expanding a definition is to explain how the object represented by the term works, such as how a scanner reads images, stores them on disks, and prints them. Also, a writer may expand a definition of a system or natural process by describing the steps in the process, such as how a drug is produced or how a hurricane occurs. Chapter 9 covers developing process explanations.

This excerpt from an American Heart Association pamphlet, *Heart Attack*, expands the definition of *coronary atherosclerosis* by explaining the process by which the artery becomes clogged:

> *Coronary atherosclerosis* causes heart attack. It's a slow process that can go on for years without causing any symptoms. Fatty deposits build up along the inner walls of the arteries to the heart. Much like lime deposits forming in a water pipe, atherosclerosis coats the inside of the artery channels and gradually narrows them. The fatty buildup reduces the flow of blood from the artery to an area of the heart muscle. When the blood flow stops due to a blockage—usually from a blood clot—a heart attack results.[3]

Negation

Writers occasionally expand a definition by explaining what a term *does not* include. This definition of *ocean* from a book about oceanography uses negation as part of the definition:

> The *ocean* is the big blue area on a globe that covers 72 percent of the earth and has a volume of 1.37 billion cubic kilometers. It does *not* include rivers, lakes, or shallow, mostly landlocked bays and estuaries whose volume is insignificant by comparison.[4]

Partition

Separating a term into its parts and explaining each part individually can effectively expand a definition and help the reader visualize the object. In a biology report on blood circulation in humans, a student uses partition to expand her definition of *artery:*

> An artery is a blood vessel that carries blood from the heart to other parts of the body. All arteries have three main layers: the intima, the media, and the adventitia. The intima is the innermost layer and consists primarily of connective tissue and elastic fibers. The media, or middle layer, consists of smooth muscle fibers and connective tissue. The outermost layer is the adventitia, which is mainly connective tissue. Each of these layers consists of sublayers of muscle and elastic fibers. The thickness of all the layers depends on the size of the artery.

Stipulation

In some circumstances, writers need to restrict the general meaning of a term in order to use it in a particular context. Such stipulative definitions are often necessary in research reports when the reader needs to understand the limitations of the term as used by the writer. Without the stipulative definition, the reader probably would assume a broader meaning than the writer intends. The following is a stipulative definition from a sociologist's report of interviews with women in homeless shelters in a large city:

> For this report, the term *homeless women* applies to females over the age of 20 who, at the time of the study, had been in a recognized homeless shelter for at least one week. In addition, the women were unemployed when they were interviewed and had been on welfare assistance at least once before going to the shelter.

PLACING DEFINITIONS IN DOCUMENTS

If a definition is part of a longer document, you need to place it so that readers will find it useful and nondisruptive. Include definitions (1) within the text, (2) in an appendix, (3) in footnotes, and/or (4) in a glossary.

Within the Text

Informal definitions or formal sentence definitions can be incorporated easily into the text of a document. If an expanded definition is crucial to the success of a document, it can also be included in the text. However, expanded definitions may interrupt a reader's concentration on the main topic. If the expanded definitions are not crucial to the main topic, consider placing them in an appendix or glossary.

In an Appendix

In a document intended for multiple readers, lengthy expanded definitions for nonexpert readers may be necessary. Rather than interrupt the text, place such expanded definitions in an appendix at the end of the document. Readers who do not need the definitions can ignore them, but readers who do need them can easily find them. Expanded definitions longer than one paragraph usually should be in an appendix unless they are essential in helping readers understand the information in the document.

In Footnotes

Writers often put expanded definitions in footnotes at the bottoms of pages or in endnotes listed at the conclusion of a long document. Such notes do not interrupt the text and are convenient for readers because they appear on the same page or within a few pages of the first reference to the term. If a definition is longer than one paragraph, however, it is best placed in an appendix.

In a Glossary

If your document requires both formal sentence definitions and expanded definitions, a glossary or list of definitions may be the most appropriate way to present them. Glossaries are convenient for readers because the terms are listed alphabetically and all definitions appear in the same location. Chapter 10 discusses preparation of glossaries.

CHAPTER SUMMARY

This chapter discusses how to write definitions of technical terms that readers need to understand. Remember:

- Definitions distinguish an object or concept from similar objects or concepts and clarify for readers the limits of the term.

- Definitions are necessary when (1) technical information for expert readers must be rewritten for nonexpert readers, (2) not all readers will understand the technical terms used in a document, (3) rare or new technical terms are used, and (4) a term has more than one meaning.

- Informal definitions explain a term with another word or a phrase that has the same general meaning.

- Formal sentence definitions explain a term by placing it in a group and identifying the features that distinguish it from other members of the same group.

- Expanded definitions explain the meaning of a term in a full paragraph or longer.

- Writers expand definitions by using one or more of these strategies: cause and effect, classification, comparison or contrast, description, development or history, etymology, examples, method of operation or process, negation, partition, and stipulation.

- Definitions may be placed within the text or in an appendix, footnotes, or glossary, depending on the needs of readers.

SUPPLEMENTAL READINGS IN PART 2

Benson, P. J. "Writing Visually: Design Considerations in Technical Publications," *Technical Communication*, p. 454.

"Six Graphics Guidelines," *Simply Stated*, p. 535.

White, J. V. "Color: The Newest Tool for Technical Communicators," *Technical Communication*, p. 551.

ENDNOTES

1. From W. C. Davis, *Rebels & Yankees: Fighting Men of the Civil War* (New York: Gallery Books, 1989), p. 132.

2. From *Space Shuttle*, NASA, PMS 013-B (KSC), December 1991.

3. Reproduced with permission. From *Heart Attack*, 1993. Copyright American Heart Association.

4. From W. Bascom, *The Crest of the Wave: Adventures in Oceanography* (New York: Doubleday, 1988), p. 294.

MODEL 7-1   Commentary

This definition of four epoxy consistencies is from a user manual prepared by Gougeon Brothers, Inc., for consumers doing boat maintenance or repair. The writer compares the epoxy texture to four common products that are well known to the average consumer. The writer also designs a table with line drawings to illustrate the differences among the four textures.

Discussion

1. Discuss the effectiveness of using common food products as comparison for the epoxy consistencies.

2. Discuss why the writer probably decided to include written descriptions of the consistencies. How do the illustrations and the text support each other? What is the advantage of placing the information in a table?

3. In groups, draft an expanded definition of one of the conditions that often affect students: writer's block, oral presentation panic, test anxiety, research resistance, or term paper deadline denial. Assume you are writing these definitions for a brochure to be distributed to incoming freshmen at your school. Include one or two tips for avoiding these conditions. Compare your definition with those of other groups.

CONSISTENCY	Unthickened mixture. SYRUP	Slightly thickened. CATSUP	Moderately thickened. MAYONNAISE	Maximum thickness. PEANUT BUTTER
GENERAL APPEARANCE				
CHARACTERISTICS	Drips off vertical surfaces.	Sags down vertical surfaces.	Clings to vertical surfaces—peaks fall over.	Clings to vertical surfaces—peaks stand up.
USES	Coating, "wetting-out" before bonding, applying fiberglass, graphite and other fabrics.	Laminating/bonding flat panels with large surface areas, injecting with a syringe.	General bonding, filleting, hardware bonding.	Gap filling, filleting, fairing, bonding uneven surfaces.

Figure 5 Epoxy can be thickened to the ideal consistency needed for a particular job. The procedures in this manual refer to four common consistencies: syrup, catsup, mayonnaise and peanut butter.

MODEL 7-1   Definition of Epoxy Consistencies

This definition of a stroke is from an American Heart Association pamphlet written for the general reader. The line drawings illustrate the location and cause of a stroke. Reproduced with permission. From *High Blood Pressure*, 1995. Copyright American Heart Association.

Discussion

Discuss the usefulness of the text and the illustrations for the nonexpert reader.

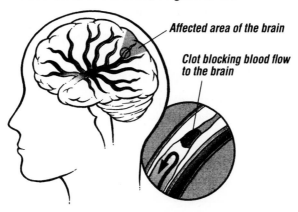

What's a **brain attack?**

A brain attack (stroke) occurs when a blood vessel in the brain bursts or gets clogged. The affected part of the brain doesn't get the blood it needs and, in minutes, begins to die.

Affected area of the brain

Clot blocking blood flow to the brain

If you have a brain attack, you could die, suffer paralysis or have trouble talking or understanding speech. Your vision could be affected. You could also lose emotional control or become depressed. Every brain attack produces its own unique effects.

If you have the warning signs of brain attack, don't wait. Call your local emergency number or have someone drive you to the nearest hospital *immediately.* Every second counts!

MODEL 7-3   Commentary

This expanded definition of solid and hazardous wastes is taken from a 667-page set of guidelines issued by the Department of Housing and Urban Development (September 1990). The guidelines cover dozens of topics, all connected to the identification and removal of lead-based paint as part of the department's public housing program. The readers include anyone involved with maintenance and renovation of public housing projects that may contain lead-based paint.

The definition begins with a reference to legislation regarding solid wastes. The writer first defines the term informally and then cites the official definition in the 1976 Resource Conservation and Recovery Act. A definition for hazardous wastes, a subcategory, follows. The writer uses a variety of expansion strategies and format devices in this appendix.

Discussion

1. Identify the strategies the writer uses to expand this definition of solid and hazardous wastes. How helpful is this definition to readers who must be able to recognize hazardous wastes?

2. Discuss how useful the format of this appendix would be to the readers.

3. Discuss changes you might make in content, organization, or format to increase the document's usefulness to readers.

4. In groups, draft an expanded definition of a computer term. Include at least one example of the term. Identify a specific audience before you begin drafting.

Appendix 6: Waste Disposal: Solid and Hazardous Wastes

6.0   THE RESOURCE CONSERVATION AND RECOVERY ACT (RCRA)

The *Resource Conservation and Recovery Act* of 1976, what we commonly refer to as RCRA, is an amendment to the first piece of Federal solid waste legislation called the Solid Waste Disposal Act of 1965. RCRA was amended in 1980 and most recently on November 8, 1984, by HSWA.

6.1   DEFINING SOLID AND HAZARDOUS WASTES

Solid wastes include such diverse wastes as household trash, sewage sludge, and discarded industrial materials. Solid wastes are not, however, necessarily solid.

They may be liquid, semisolid, or gaseous. The term "solid waste" is further defined in Section 1004(27) of RCRA as follows:

> The term "solid waste" means any garbage, refuse, sludge, from a waste treatment plant, water supply treatment plant, or air pollution control facility and other discarded material, including solid, liquid, semisolid, or contained gaseous material resulting from industrial, commercial, mining, and agricultural operations, and from community activities, but does not include solid or dissolved material in domestic sewage, or solid or dissolved materials in irrigation return flows or industrial discharges which are point sources subject to permits under Section 402 of the Federal Water Pollution Control Act, as amended (86 Stat. 880), or source, special nuclear, or byproduct material as defined by the Atomic Energy Act of 1954, as amended (68 Stat. 923).

Hazardous wastes are a sub-category of solid wastes. They can be solid, liquids, or gases. They may appear in a variety of forms:

- In barrels or drums.
- In pits, ponds, or lagoons.
- In sludges.
- As part of contaminated soil.
- In bottles or other fragile or nondurable containers.
- In aboveground or underground storage tanks.
- As part of building materials (e.g., asbestos).

In general, a waste is considered hazardous if it can endanger human health or damage the environment. Congress defined the term "hazardous waste" in Section 1004(5) of the Resource Conservation and Recovery Act (RCRA) of 1976 (42 U.S.C. S6901 *et seq.*) as follows:

> The term "hazardous waste" means a solid waste, or combination of solid wastes, which because of its quantity, concentration, or physical, chemical or infectious characteristics may:
>
> A) cause, or significantly contribute to an increase in mortality or an increase in serious irreversible, or incapacitating reversible, illness; or,
>
> B) pose a substantial present or potential hazard to human health or the environment when improperly treated, stored, transported, or disposed of, or otherwise managed.

In issuing regulations under RCRA, EPA has defined a hazardous waste to mean a solid waste that meets one of four conditions:

- It shows by observation or testing to have any of the four characteristics of hazardous waste (ignitable, reactive, corrosive, or toxic).
- It has been named and listed (see below) as a hazardous waste.
- It is a mixture containing a listed hazardous waste and a nonhazardous waste solid (unless the mixture is explicitly excluded).
- It is not excluded from regulation as a hazardous waste.

6.2 LISTING OF HAZARDOUS WASTES

The U.S. Environmental Protection Agency (EPA) has determined that certain wastes are hazardous. These wastes are incorporated into lists published by EPA. Wastes on these lists must always be handled as hazardous wastes regardless of their concentrations. The lists expand and change as new research and testing are performed; therefore, it is important to consult the lists periodically.

The lists are organized into three categories: 1) specific-source wastes (wastes from specific industries); 2) generic wastes (wastes from common manufacturing and industrial process, such as solvents); and 3) discarded commercial chemical products (such as creosote and some pesticides). The hazardous wastes associated with lead-based paint are generic wastes and discarded commercial chemical products.

Any mixture containing one or more listed hazardous wastes, or a mixture of solid waste and listed hazardous waste, is also considered a hazardous waste. This applies regardless of the percentage of the mixture that is listed as hazardous waste. There are several exemptions to this mixture rule.

If the solid waste is *not* included in the EPA list of hazardous wastes, or is *not* a mixture that contains one of these wastes, it may still be a hazardous waste if it exhibits the characteristic of ***ignitability, corrosivity, reactivity,*** or ***toxicity.*** EPA's definition of these characteristics is contained in 40 CFR, Sections 261.20 to 261.24. The standard measures specified by EPA to test for these properties are summarized in Table A-6.1.

The Resource Conservation and Recovery Act (RCRA) was passed in 1976 to address the problems posed by the improper disposal of municipal and industrial wastes. RCRA was amended in 1980 and again in 1984. The goals of RCRA are to protect human health and the environment, reduce waste and conserve energy and natural resources, and reduce or eliminate the generation of hazardous waste as expeditiously as possible. Two programs developed under RCRA affect disposal of wastes generated during lead-based paint abatement:

- *Subtitle D* governs the management of solid wastes, primarily nonhazardous wastes.

- *Subtitle C* controls hazardous waste from the time it is generated until its ultimate disposal.

1. Identify the writer's error in the following sentence definitions. Rewrite each sentence into a complete formal sentence definition.

    a. A raspberry is a fruit.

    b. Open-heart surgery is when the surgeon opens the chest to expose the heart.

    c. A sailboat is a boat used for sailing.

    d. A wristwatch is a timepiece that shows the time of day.

    e. An island is a land mass surrounded by water.

    f. A frying pan is used for frying food.

    g. A garden is a plot of land used for growing flowers.

    h. A rainbow is caused by refraction and reflection of light by water droplets.

    i. A voyage is a long journey to a distant place.

    j. A landfill is a method of solid waste disposal.

2. Write a formal sentence definition for one meaning of each of the following terms. Share your definitions with the class, and discuss how many definitions are possible for each term.

fly	bat	charge
mouse	branch	jam
nut	cell	key
port	bag	check

3. In groups, select **three terms** used in **one** of the following sports. Write a formal sentence definition for each term. Share your definitions with the class.

football	basketball
downhill skiing	soccer
golf	gymnastics
tennis	bowling
volleyball	baseball

Next, write an expanded definition of one of the terms you selected. Share your definition with the class.

4. Write an expanded definition of one of the following terms. Identify a reader and purpose for your definition. List the specific expansion strategies you used at the end of your expanded definition.

Columbus Day	Any hobby equipment
Thanksgiving Day	Any sports equipment

Memorial Day	Any musical instrument
Veteran's Day	Any video or audio equipment
Labor Day	Any public building
Valentine's Day	Any specific food

5. Research information on the Web or in the library about heat stroke, heat exhaustion, heat cramps, heat rash, and other heat disorders. Write an information bulletin that defines types of heat disorders. Your bulletin will accompany the bulletin in Model 4-5.

6. Read the articles on ethics in Part 2. Write an expanded definition of what you regard as *ethical responsibility* when a writer is preparing a technical document. Assume your reader is a beginning technical writer.

7. Identify a problem on campus, such as "inadequate parking," "unsafe hallway lighting," or "inconvenient library hours." Write an expanded definition of the problem. Assume this definition is for the president of your school who is unaware of the problem.

8. Write a memo to your supervisor at your present job to request a new piece of equipment or new supplies. You know that your supervisor is reluctant to spend money on equipment right now, but you think this equipment is necessary. Include a formal sentence definition of the item you are requesting and an expanded definition using two of the expansion strategies discussed in this chapter. *Note:* Memo format is explained in Chapter 13.

9. Write a memo to the appropriate administrator on your campus to request a piece of equipment for use in one of your classes or for a campus activity. Assume that you are the chair of a student committee that has the task of making such requests on behalf of the student body. Include a formal sentence definition of the object you are requesting and an expanded definition using two or three of the expansion strategies discussed in this chapter. *Note:* Memo format is explained in Chapter 13.

CHAPTER **8**

Description

UNDERSTANDING DESCRIPTION

Technical description provides readers with precise details about the physical features, appearance, or composition of a subject. A technical description may be a complete document in itself, such as an entry in an encyclopedia or a technical handbook. Manufacturing companies also need complete technical descriptions of each product model as an official record. Frequently, too, technical descriptions are separate sections in longer documents, such as these:

1. *Proposals and other reports.* Readers usually need descriptions of equipment and locations in a report before they can make decisions. A report discussing the environmental impact of a solid-waste landfill at a particular site, for example, would probably include a description of the location to help readers visualize the site and the potential changes.

2. *Sales literature.* Both dealers and consumers need descriptions of products—dealers so that they can advise customers and answer questions and consumers so that they can make purchase decisions. A consumer examining a new automobile in a showroom is likely to overlook certain features. A brochure containing a description of the automobile's features ensures that the consumer will have enough information for decision making.

3. *Manuals.* Descriptions of equipment help operators understand the principles behind running a piece of machinery. Technicians need a record of every part of a machine and its function in order to effectively assess problems and make repairs. Consumer instruction manuals often include descriptions to help readers locate important parts of the product.

4. *Magazine articles and brochures for general readers.* Articles and brochures about science and technology often include descriptions of mechanisms, geologic sites, or natural phenomena to help readers understand the subject. An article for general readers about a new wing design on military aircraft may include a description of the wings and their position relative to the body of the aircraft to help readers visualize the design. A brochure written for visitors at a science institute describing the development of a solar heat collector may include several descriptions of the mechanism in development so that readers can understand how the design changed over time.

Plan and draft a technical description with the same attention to readers and their need for the information that you apply to other writing tasks.

PLANNING DESCRIPTIONS

In deciding whether to include descriptions in your document, consider your readers' knowledge of the subject and why they need your information. A student in an introductory botany class has little expert knowledge about the basic parts of a flower. Such a student needs a description of these parts to understand the variations in structure of different flowers and how seeds are formed. A research report to botanists about a new hybrid flower, however, would probably not include a description of these basic parts because botanists already know them well. The botanists, on the other hand, do need a description of the hybrid flower because they are not familiar with this new variety, and they need the description to understand the research results in the report. Both types of readers, then, need descriptions, but they differ in (1) the subjects they need described, (2) the kinds of information they need, (3) the appropriate language and detail, and (4) the appropriate graphic aids.

Subjects

As you analyze your readers' level of knowledge about a subject and their need for information, consider a variety of subjects that, if described in detail, might help your readers understand and use the information in your document. Here are some general subjects to consider as you decide what to describe for readers:

1. *Mechanism*—any machine or device with moving parts, such as a steam turbine, camera, automobile, or bicycle.

2. *Location*—any site or specific geologic area, such as the Braidwood Nuclear Power Plant, the Lake Michigan shoreline at Milwaukee, or the Moon's surface.

3. *Organism*—any form or part of plant or animal life, such as an oak tree, a camel, bacteria, a kidney, or a hyacinth bulb.

4. *Substance*—any physical matter or material, such as cocaine, lard, gold, or milk.

5. *Object*—any implement without moving parts, such as a paper cup, a shoe, a photograph, or a floppy disk.

6. *Condition*—the physical state of a mechanism, location, organism, substance, or object at a specific time, such as a plane after an accident, a tumor before radiation, or a forest area after a fire.

Whenever your readers are not likely to know exactly what these subjects look like and need to know this in order to understand the information in your document, provide descriptions.

Kinds of Information

To be useful, a technical description must provide readers with a clear image of the subject. Include precise details about the following whenever such information will help your readers understand your subject better:

- Purpose or function
- Weight, shape, measurements, materials
- Major and minor parts, their locations, and how they are connected
- Texture, sound, odor, color
- Model numbers and names
- Operating cycle
- Special conditions for appropriate use, such as time, temperature, frequency

The writer of this excerpt from an architectural book about the development of greenhouses uses specific details about measurements, materials, and shapes to describe a particular building:

The wooden tie beams in the Great Conservatory at Chatsworth represent a building innovation in the application of not only cast-iron but also wrought-iron semicircular ribs, in arches and in frameworks. In this building the creation of space and the various forms of iron rib were further developed structurally. This free-standing building, 124 feet wide and 68 feet high, was created by the construction of two glass vaults, built in the ridge-and-furrow system, with a basilicalike cross-section. Rows of cast-iron columns joined by cast-iron girders carried the semicircular wooden ribs of the Paxton gutters to form a high nave with a span of 70 feet. The glass vaults of the aisles, reaching down to the low masonry base, abutted from both sides onto the main iron frame at a height of 40 feet. The aisle had the same profile, but it had quadrant-shaped ribs. The ribs of the surrounding aisles also functioned as buttresses to support the lateral thrust of the main ribs of the nave.[1]

To determine the amount and kinds of details appropriate for a technical description, assess your reader's level of knowledge about the subject and purpose in reading. The reader of this description is probably familiar with architectural terms, such as trusses and vaults. The description focuses on the components of the building's supporting structure and provides measurements—all details relevant to readers who are interested in architecture. If the readers were horticulturists, a description of the interior design and arrangement of plants and flowers would probably be of more interest.

The following description of the effects of lead poisoning in children is from a report to Congress by the Department of Housing and Urban development. The emphasis is on the typical physical condition of a child suffering from lead poisoning:

> Very severe childhood lead poisoning—involving such symptoms as kidney failure, gastrointestinal problems, comas, convulsions, seizures, and pronounced mental retardation—can occur at blood lead levels as low as 80 ug/dl. At or above 40 ug/dl, children may experience reduced hemoglobin (the oxygen-carrying substance in blood), the accumulation of a potential neurotoxicant known as ALA, and mild anemia. Near 30 ug/dl, studies have found slowed nerve conduction velocity. And between 10–15 and 25 ug/dl, researchers have documented slower reaction time, reductions in intelligence and short-term memory, other neurobehavioral deficits, and adverse effects on heme biosynthesis and vitamin D and calcium metabolism.[2]

In this description, the writer begins by naming potential diseases in general terms and then shifts to specific technical details about blood factors. Notice the informal definition included for the primary (nonexpert) readers.

This description of a location centers on the area around the site of a sunken Spanish galleon:

> The anchor has been found in 25 feet of water on the southern edge of an area known as the "Quicksands." The name didn't mean the area swallowed divers, but that the bottom was covered with a sand composed of loose shell fragments that are constantly shifted by the waves and tides. The result is a series of sinuous "dune" formations on the bottom. Tidal channels cross these dunes, running from northeast to southwest. Around the anchor, the sand is nearly 15 feet deep. Below it is a bed of limestone, the surface of which is rippled and pocked with small hollows and crevices. The sand piled on top of the limestone gradually thins out until it disappears about a quarter of a mile from the anchor. Southeast of the Quicksands, the water depth increases gradually to about 40 feet, and the sand covering the bedrock thins out to a veneer just two and a half inches thick. Small sponges and sea fans grow in this area, which we called the Coral Plateau. Continuing to the southeast, away from the anchor, the Coral Plateau slopes downward into the "Mud Deep." Here, the bedrock dips sharply, possibly following the channel of a river that may have flowed through the area when it was above sea level thousands of years ago. This channel is filled with muddy silt.[3]

In this description, the writer includes a few measurements, but he emphasizes the natural formations of sand and rock present in the area. Notice that the writer organizes spatially—the area around the anchor first and then progressively farther away, moving southeast.

Remember that descriptions may cover either (1) a particular mechanism, location, organism, substance, object, or condition, or (2) the general type. The description of the typical child with lead poisoning is a general one. Individual cases may differ, but most children with lead poisoning will fit this description in some way. The descriptions of the conservatory and the sea area, however, are specific to that building and that location. In the same manner, a product description of Model XX must be specific to that model alone and, therefore, different from a description of Model YY. Be sure to clarify for the reader whether you are describing a general type or a specific item.

Details and Language

All readers of technical descriptions need accurate detail. However, some readers need more detail and can understand more highly technical language than others. Here is a brief description from a book about the solar system written for general readers interested in science:

> The Galaxy is flattened by its rotating motion into the shape of a disk, whose thickness is roughly one-fiftieth of its diameter. Most of the stars in the Galaxy are in this small disk, although some are located outside it. A relatively small, spherical cluster of stars, called the nucleus of the Galaxy, bulges out of the disk at the center. The entire structure resembles a double sombrero with the galactic nucleus as the crown and the disk as the brim. The Sun is located in the brim of the sombrero about three-fifths of the way out from the center to the edge. When we look into the sky in the direction of the disk we see so many stars that they are not visible as separate points of light, but blend together into a luminous band stretching across the sky. This band is called the Milky Way.[4]

In this description, the writer compares the galaxy to a sombrero, something most general readers are familiar with, and then locates the various parts of the galaxy on areas of the sombrero, thus creating an image that general readers will find easy to use. The writer also uses an informal tone, drawing readers into the description by saying, "When we look into the sky. . . ." This informal tone is appropriate for general readers, but not for expert readers who need less assistance in visualizing the subject.

Here is a description of television station equipment that appeared in a magazine written for owners and technical staff of low-power television stations. The product description is used by technical staff in making decisions about future equipment purchases.

> Microdyne Corporation manufactures a complete line of fixed and motorized satellite receiving antennas, ranging in size from 1.2 meters to 7 meters and suitable for both C-band or Ku-band applications. The 3.66-meter (12-foot) antenna is specially designed for broadcast quality reception. It is a 10-piece parabolic antenna made from exceptionally strong space age fiber and polyester materials. It features a prime focus feed, superb side lobe characteristics, and high gains.

The dish can view 100° of the geostationary arc and satellites within 69° west to 139° west. This feature means easy alignment with any line-of-sight satellite in the geostationary orbit. An optional motorized actuator is available.[5]

Clearly, the expected readers for this technical description have expert knowledge because the specialized terms, such as *geostationary arc,* are not defined, and the description stresses features of this antenna and how it will function at a television station, details that expert readers need to aid their decision making. Because this description is intended to encourage readers to purchase the equipment, the features are described in persuasive language—"specially designed," "exceptionally strong," "superb side lobe," "easy alignment." A nonexpert reader interested in learning about antennas would not find this description particularly useful. Such a reader would want an overall description of antennas in general and fewer details specific to one model. The reader would want to know, for example, what is the usual appearance of a satellite-receiving antenna? Where is it mounted? What are the major parts and their functions? What is the difference between a fixed and motorized antenna? Your readers' purpose must guide your decisions about how many details and which details to include.

Follow these guidelines for using appropriate language in technical descriptions:

1. Use specific rather than general terms. Notice these examples:

General terms	*Specific terms*
short	1 in. tall
curved	S-shaped
thin	$\frac{1}{8}$ in. thick
light	cream-colored
nearby	4 in. from the base
fast	400 rpm
large	7 ft high
light	1.5 oz
heavy	16 t
noise	high-pitched shriek

2. Indicate a range in size if the description is of a general type that varies, or give an example.

   Poor: Bowling balls for adults usually weigh 12 lb.
   Better: Bowling balls for adults vary in weight from 10 to 16 lb.

3. Use precise language, but not language too technical for your readers. Do not write "a combination of ferric hydroxide and ferric oxide" if "rust" will do.

4. If you must use highly technical terms or jargon and some of your readers are nonexperts, define those terms:

The patient's lipoma (fatty tumor) had not grown since the previous examination.

5. Compare the subject to simple, well-known items and situations to help general readers visualize it:

The difference in size between the Sun and the Earth is similar to the difference between a baseball and a grape seed.

Be specific and accurate, but do not overwhelm your readers with details they cannot use. Consider carefully the language your readers need and the number of details they can use appropriately.

Graphic Aids

Graphic aids are an essential element in descriptions because readers must develop a mental picture of the subject, and words alone may not be adequate to paint that picture successfully. Chapter 5 discusses graphic aids in detail along with format devices to highlight certain facts. These graphic aids are usually effective ways to illustrate details in descriptions:

1. *Photographs.* Photographs supply a realistic view of the subject and its size, color, and structure, but they may not properly display all features or show locations clearly. Photographs are most useful for general readers who want to know the overall appearance of a subject. A guide to house plants for general readers should include photographs, for instance, so readers can differentiate among plants. A research article for botanists, however, would probably include line drawings showing stems, leaves, whorls, and other distinctive features of the plants being discussed.

2. *Line drawings.* Line drawings provide an exterior view showing key features of mechanisms, organisms, objects, or locations and special conditions, as well as how these features are connected. Line drawings are useful when readers need to be familiar with each part or area.

3. *Cutaway and exploded drawings.* Cutaway drawings illustrate interior views, including layers of materials that cannot be seen from photographs or line drawings of the exterior. Exploded drawings emphasize the separate parts of a subject, especially those that might be concealed if the object is in one piece. Often readers need both line drawings of the exterior and interior and exploded drawings to fully understand a subject.

4. *Maps, floor plans, and architects' renderings.* Maps show geographic locations, and floor plans and architects' renderings show placement of

objects within a specified area. Features that may be obscured in a photograph from any angle can be marked clearly on these illustrations, giving readers a better sense of the composition of the area than any photograph could.

Use as many graphic aids as you believe your readers need to get a clear picture of your subject. Also, be sure to direct your readers' attention to the graphic aids by references in the text, and always use the same terms in the text and in your graphic aids for specific parts or areas.

STRATEGIES—Standard American English

Avoid **regionalisms** (expressions used only in certain parts of the country).

No: The courthouse had a **bubbler** on every floor.

Yes: The courthouse had a **drinking fountain** on every floor.

Do not use **dialect** constructions that are specific to certain regions or groups and that violate standard grammatical form.

No: The boiler **needs repaired.**

Yes: The boiler **needs to be repaired.**

No: The engine **be running** too fast.

Yes: The engine **is running** too fast.

Do not use **colloquialisms** (informal terms or slang).

No: The failure of Model 6D was **a tough break.**

Yes: The failure of Model 6D was **disappointing.**

WRITING DESCRIPTIONS

After identifying your expected readers and the kinds of information they need, consider how to organize your descriptions.

Organization

In some cases, company policy or institution requirements dictate the organization of a description. An example of a predetermined description format appears in Model 8-6, a portion of a police report. Although police report formats may vary from city to city, most departments require a narrative section describing the incident that led to police intervention. The writer must follow the department's established format because readers—police, attorneys, judges, and social-service workers—handle hundreds of similar reports and rely on seeing all reports in the same format with similar information in the same place.

If you are not locked into a specific description format for the document you are writing, select an organizational pattern that will best serve your readers, usually one of these:

Spatial.   The spatial pattern is most often used for descriptions of mechanisms, objects, and locations because it is a logical way to explain how a subject looks. Remember that you must select a specific direction and follow it throughout the description, such as from base to shade for a lamp, from outside to inside for a television set, and from one end to the other for a football field. Writers often also explain the function of a subject and its main parts. This additional information is particularly important if readers are not likely to know the purpose of the subject or it will not be apparent from the description of parts or composition. Thus a description of a stomach pump may include an explanation of the function of each valve and tube so that readers can understand how the parts work together.

Chronological.   The chronological pattern describes features of a subject in the order they were produced or put together. This information may be central to a description of, for example, a Gothic church that took two centuries to build or an anthropological dig where layers of sediments containing primitive tools have been deposited over two million years.

In all cases, consider your readers' knowledge of the subject and the organization that will most help them use the information effectively. A general reader of a description of a Gothic church may want a chronological description that focuses on the historical changes in exterior and interior design. A structural engineer, however, may want a chronological description that focuses on changes in materials and construction techniques.

Sections of a Technical Description

Model 8-1 presents a typical outline for a technical description of an object or mechanism. As this outline illustrates, a technical description has three main sections: an introduction, a description of the parts, and a description of the cycle of operations.

Introduction

The introduction to a technical description orients readers to the subject and gives them general information that will help them understand the details in the body of the description. Follow these guidelines:

1. Write a formal sentence definition of the complete mechanism or object to ensure that your readers understand the subject. If the item is a very

I. Introduction
   A. Definition of the object
   B. Purpose of the object
   C. Overall description of the object—size, color, weight, etc.
   D. List of main parts

II. Description of Main Parts
   A. Main part 1
      1. Definition of main part 1
      2. Purpose of main part 1
      3. Details of main part 1—color, shape, measurements, etc.
      4. Connection to main part 2 or list of minor parts of main part 1
      5. Minor part 1 (if relevant)
         (a) Definition of minor part 1
         (b) Purpose of minor part 1
         (c) Details of minor part 1—color, shape, measurements, etc.
      6. Minor part 2 (if relevant)
         ⋮
   B. Main part 2
      ⋮

III. Cycle of Operation
   A. How parts work together
   B. How object operates
   C. Limitations

MODEL 8-1   Model Outline of Technical Description of a Mechanism

common one, however, you may omit the formal definition unless company policy calls for it.

2. Clarify the purpose if it is not obvious from the definition. In some cases, how the object or mechanism functions may be most significant to your readers, so explain this in the introduction.

3. Describe the overall appearance so that readers have a sense of size, shape, and color. For general readers, include extra details that may be helpful, such as a comparison with an ordinary object. Also include, if possible, a graphic illustration of the object or mechanism.

4. List the main parts in the order you plan to describe them.

Description of Parts

The body of a technical description includes a formal definition and the physical details of each major and minor part presented in a specific organizational pattern, such as spatial or chronological. Include as many details as your readers need to understand what the parts look like and how they are connected. If your readers plan to construct the object or mechanism, they will need to know every bolt and clamp. General readers, on the other band, are usually interested only in major parts and important minor parts. Graphic illustrations of the individual parts or exploded drawings are helpful to readers in this section.

Cycle of Operation

Technical descriptions for in-house use or for expert readers seldom have conclusions. General readers, however, may need conclusions that explain how the parts work together and what a typical cycle of operation is like. If the description will be included in sales literature, the conclusion often stresses the special features or advantages of the product.

Sample Technical Descriptions

Model 8-2 is a technical description of a specific model of a toaster written by a student as a section of a consumer manual that includes a description, operating instructions, and maintenance guidelines. Because this description is of a particular model, the writer describes the parts and their locations in detail. The organization is spatial, moving from the lowest part, the base, to the cord, which enters the housing above the base, and then to the housing. Because the housing is so large, the writer partitions it, describing the outer casing first, the heating wells second, and then the control levers. The writer ends with a brief description of the operating cycle. Notice that this description contains (1) formal sentence definitions of the toaster and each main part, (2) headings to direct readers to specific topics, and (3) specific measurements for each part.

Model 8-3 is a NASA Web site description of a space phenomenon: a comet. The writer begins with an explanation of a comet's origin. The organization of the description is spatial, covering first the comet head and then moving to the tail. Because the writer cannot study a comet at close range, the qualities described are based on scientific evaluations. The writer, therefore, uses phrases, such as "probably" or "scientists think." The words here in boldface represent links to other NASA Web sites.

I. **Introduction**

The Kitchen King toaster, Model 49D, is an electric appliance that browns bread between electric coils inside a metal body. The toaster also heats and browns frozen and packaged foods designed especially to fit in the vertical heating wells of a toaster. The Kitchen King Model 49D is $6\frac{3}{4}$ in. high, $4\frac{1}{2}$ in. wide, $8\frac{3}{4}$ in. long, and weighs 2 lb. There are three main parts: the base, the cord, and the housing.

II. **Main Parts**

The Base

The base is a flat stainless steel plate, $4\frac{1}{2}$ in. wide and $8\frac{3}{4}$ in. long. It supports the housing of the toaster and is nailed to it at all four corners. The base rests on four round, black, plastic feet, each $\frac{1}{2}$ in. high and $\frac{3}{4}$ in. in diameter. The feet are attached to the base $\frac{1}{2}$ in. inside the four corners. The front and back of the base ($2\frac{1}{2}$ in. wide) are edged in black plastic strips that protrude $\frac{3}{4}$ in. past the base. A removable stainless steel plate, $3\frac{1}{2}$ in. wide and $5\frac{1}{4}$ in. long, called the crumb tray, is centered in the base. One of the shorter sides of the crumb tray is hinged. The opposite side has a catch that allows the hinged plate to swing open for removal of trapped crumbs.

The Cord

The cord is an insulated cable that conducts electric current to the heating mechanism inside the body of the toaster. It is 32 in. long and $\frac{1}{8}$ in. in diameter. Attached to the base of the toaster at the back, it enters the housing through an opening just large enough for the cable. At the other end of the cord is a two-terminal plug, measuring 1 in. long, $\frac{3}{4}$ in. wide, and $\frac{1}{2}$ in. thick. The two prongs are $\frac{1}{2}$ in. apart and are each $\frac{5}{8}$ in. long, $\frac{1}{4}$ in. wide, and $\frac{1}{16}$ in. thick. The plug must be attached to an electrical outlet before the toaster is operable.

Housing

The housing is a stainless steel boxlike cover that contains the electric heating mechanism and in which the toasting process takes

MODEL 8-2   Technical Description: Kitchen King Toaster, Model 49D

place. The housing is $8\frac{3}{4}$ in. long, $6\frac{1}{4}$ in. high, and $4\frac{1}{2}$ in. wide. The front and back are edged at the top with black plastic strips that protrude past the housing $\frac{3}{4}$ in. The housing also contains two heating wells and two control levers.

Heating Wells. The heating wells are vertical compartments, $5\frac{1}{2}$ in. long, $1\frac{1}{4}$ in. wide, $5\frac{3}{4}$ in. deep. The wells are lined with electric coils that brown the bread or toaster food when the mechanism is activated. Inside each heating well is a platform on which the toast rests and which moves up and down the vertical length of the well.

Control Levers. The control levers are square pieces of black plastic attached to springs that regulate the heating and the degree of browning. The levers are $6\frac{1}{2}$ in. square and are on the front of the toaster.

Heat Control Lever. The heat control lever is centered 1 in. from the top of the housing and is attached to the platforms inside both heating wells. When the lever is pushed down, it moves along a vertical slot to the base of the toaster, lowering the platforms inside the heating wells. This movement also triggers the heating coils.

Browning Lever. The browning lever is located in the lower right corner on the front of the toaster. The browning lever moves horizontally along a 2-in. slot. The slot is marked with three positions: dark, medium, and light. This lever controls the length of time the heating mechanism is in operation and, therefore, the degree of brownness that will result.

III. Conclusion

The user must insert the cord into a 120-volt AC electrical outlet to begin the operating cycle. Next, the user inserts one or two pieces of bread or toaster food into the heating wells, moves the browning lever to the desired setting, and lowers the heat control lever until it catches and activates the heating mechanism. The toaster will turn off automatically when the heating cycle is complete, and the platforms in the heating wells will automatically raise the bread or toasted food, so the user can remove it easily.

MODEL 8-2   *continued*

COMETS

The name *comet* comes from the Latin word *cometa,* meaning "long haired." Scientists believe that comets are the debris left from the solar **nebula,** which condensed to form the Sun and planets in our **solar system.**

Most comets probably originate in a huge cloud called the **Oort Cloud.** The Oort Cloud is believed to surround our solar system and reach over halfway to the nearest star, Alpha Centauri, 150,000 astronomical units away. Scientists think that about 100 million comets **orbit** the Sun. A comet has a distinct center called a nucleus. Most **astronomers** think the nucleus is frozen water and gases mixed with dust and rocky material. Comet nuclei are described as dirty snowballs. A hazy cloud called a coma surrounds the nucleus. The coma and the nucleus together form the comet's head.

Comets follow a regular **orbit** around the Sun. If the comet nucleus is pulled into an orbit that carries it close to the Sun, the solar heat will cause the outer layers of the icy nucleus to evaporate. During this process, dust and gases that form the coma, around the nucleus are released. As the comet gets closer to the Sun, the coma grows. The **solar winds** push the dust and gas away from the coma, causing them to stream off into space to form the comet's tail, which points away from the Sun. The tails of comets can reach 150 million **kilometers** in length. Each time the comet passes close to the Sun, it loses some of its material. Over time, the comet will break up and disappear completely. A comet has no light of its own. We see it because the Sun's light reflects off the comet and because gas molecules in the coma release energy absorbed from the Sun's rays.

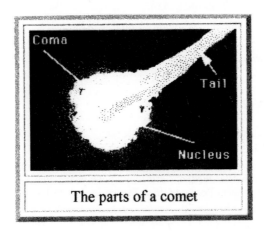

The parts of a comet

MODEL 8-3   Technical Description of Comets

CHAPTER SUMMARY

This chapter discusses writing technical descriptions. Remember:

- Descriptions provide readers with precise details about the physical features, appearance, or composition of a subject.

- In planning a description, writers consider what subjects readers need described, the kinds of information readers need, appropriate detail and language, and helpful graphic aids.

- Subjects for descriptions may include mechanisms, locations, organisms, substances, objects, and conditions.

- Descriptions should include precise details about purpose, measurements, parts, textures, model numbers, operation cycles, and special conditions when appropriate for readers.

- The amount of detail and degree of technical language in a description depends on the readers' purpose and their technical knowledge.

- Graphic aids are essential in descriptions to help readers develop a mental picture of the subject.

- Most descriptions are organized spatially or chronologically.

SUPPLEMENTAL READINGS IN PART 2

Benson, P. J. "Writing Visually: Design Considerations in Technical Publications," *Technical Communication,* p. 454.

"Six Graphics Guidelines," *Simply Stated,* p. 535.

White, J. V. "Color: The Newest Tool for Technical Communicators," *Technical Communication,* p. 551.

ENDNOTES

1. From G. Kohlmaier and B. von Sartory, *Houses of Glass, A Nineteenth-Century Building Type* (Cambridge, MA: The MIT Press, 1991), pp. 87–88.

2. From U.S. Department of Housing and Urban Development, *Comprehensive and Workable Plan for the Abatement of Lead-Based Paint in Privately Owned Housing* (Washington, DC: U.S. Government Printing Office, December 7, 1990), pp. 2–3.

3. From R. D. Mathewson III, *Treasure of the Atocha* (New York: E. P. Dutton, 1986), p. 67.

4. From R. Jastrow, *Red Giants and White Dwarfs* (New York: W. W. Norton, 1979), p. 27.

5. From *The LPTV Report* 4 (October 1989), p. 42. Reprinted with permission of Kompas/Biel Associates, Inc.

MODEL 8-4   Commentary

This model shows the description of a wood-burning stove from a Heatilator, Inc., product brochure. The design here draws the reader's eye across the page, as the description begins with a color photograph on the extreme left followed by three columns of information to the right. The text describes special features of the stove, consumer-oriented options, and specific measurements.

Discussion

1. Consider the three columns of information. Discuss why the writer probably put special features in the first column, options in the second column, and measurements in the third column.

2. Identify the specific language the writer used to appeal to the readers.

3. Compare this model with Models 5-21 and 5-22. All these descriptions are intended for consumers. What differences in style do you find? What differences in emphasis do you find? Discuss why these differences might be relevant to the products and likely purchasers.

4. In groups, prepare a product description following the style in this model. Use a small consumer product that is readily available in your group, such as a wristwatch, eye glasses, or pocket calculator.

S P E C I F I C S

Heating Capacity*: up to 1,500 sq ft

Btu per hour: ....20,000 to 30,000
(natural gas or LP)

Efficiency Rating: Avg. overall heating
efficiency up to 77%

Venting: ....Direct vent,
horizontal or vertical

Height: ....29 1/2"

Width: ....22 3/4"

Depth: ....14 3/4"

Weight: ....220 pounds

Clearances:.........6" from side of stove
4" from back of stove

O P T I O N S

• Lustrous porcelain finish in four
colors: Jersey Creme, French Blue,
Bavarian Green & Puritan Black

• Decorative and functional warming
shelves

• Shelf brackets and mitten rods in
24 carat gold finish or black

• 24 carat gold, or black, door trim

• Convenient remote with thermo-
static control

• 150 CFM fan kit to help circulate
warmed air in room

F E A T U R E S

• Durable cast iron body with
ceramic viewing glass, finished
in matte black metallic paint

• Direct vent system for highest
fuel efficiency and installation
versatility

• Dovre Flame Technology features
ceramic fiber logs molded to look
like real wood, and golden, flick-
ering flames

• Standing pilot generates its own
millivolt power supply to ensure
operation even during a power
outage.

• Convenient on/off switch controls
the variable input, or use our
optional remote control

• Approved as a heater, so you can
add an optional wall thermostat

• Five-year limited warranty

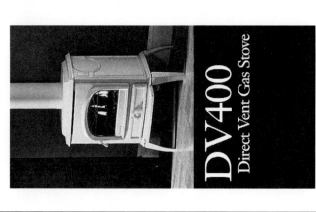

DV400
Direct Vent Gas Stove

These pages are from a 52-page product description manual written by a professional technical writer at Diebold, Inc. The manual describes the structure and function of a specific series of automatic teller machines (ATMs) and includes line drawings of the entire machines and of specific parts of the machines. This detailed description serves as a record of the product features and as a guide to bank administrators who are interested in installing the ATMs. This manual took nearly nine months to complete, as the writer drafted and redrafted in response to reviews by engineers, technicians, and managers.

Discussion

1. Discuss how the organization and format elements help the reader understand the information easily.

2. Review the description and discuss whether the language is strictly objective or contains some sales appeal. Cite specific places in the text to support your opinion.

3. Compare this model with Model 8-4. Both documents are intended for potential customers. Discuss the differences in format and amount of detail provided. In what ways is each model appropriate for its readers?

2.2 Consumer Interface Panel

The Consumer Interface Panel guides the consumer through transactions and allows the consumer to request transactions and enter data. Also, the Consumer Interface Panel can perform important consumer education and advertising functions.

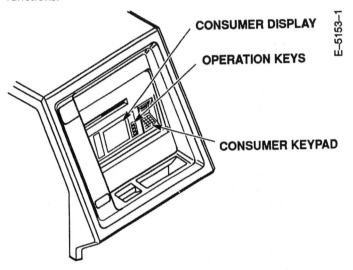

Figure 2-2 Consumer Interface Panel Components (Secure Interior ATM)

Consumer Display

Besides welcoming consumers and showing the instructions that permit transaction processing, the Consumer Display performs two important functions: it can attract new consumers to the ATM, and it can communicate with the user through pictures, words, or both. Pictorial icons or programmable non-English character sets allow the terminal to communicate with people of any nationality.

Two Consumer Displays are available: monochrome and color

Monochrome Monitor

The enhanced brightness, monochrome Consumer Display adjusts for surrounding lighting conditions. This enhances readability (even in direct sunlight), reduces the chance of CRT burn-in, and prolongs the CRT's operational life. This monitor is standard on the *is* terminals.

Color Monitor (ATP only)

The nine-inch (22.9 cm), high-resolution color monitor supports graphics in 16 colors). The color monitor has a resolution of 640 × 240 pixels (horizontal × vertical). The color monitor can show a series of still color images in rapid succession to give the impression of screen animation (see Appendix B).

Both monitors are capable of displaying 20 lines of 40 characters. Additionally, they can show the same 32 × 16 right-justified grid used by the TABS 9000 terminals, a 32 × 16 left-justified grid, or a 32 × 16 center-justified grid.

The Consumer Display has the following additional capabilities:

- Backspacing
- Blinking characters
- Inverse video (40 × 20 grid only)
- Delayed character display
- Graphics

Both Consumer Displays can show the 5 × 9, dot matrix standard and alternate character sets in Appendix A.

Privacy Screen

An optional Privacy Screen attaches to the Consumer Display. Louvers embedded in the Privacy Screen create a Venetian blind effect, so that only a consumer positioned directly in front of the Consumer Display can read the screen.

Consumer Keypad

The Consumer Keypad allows the consumer to enter data into the terminal. On all terminals except the Drive-up and the Island, the Consumer Keypad is recessed for consumer privacy.

Two Consumer Keypads are available; an 11-key keypad and a 16-key keypad. The 11-key keypad has ten numeric keys (0 through 9) and a CANCEL key. The 16-key keypad has ten numeric keys (0 through 9), a CANCEL key, and five additional operational keys. Each keypad provides audible and tactile response to each keystroke and, in the U.S., is equipped with braille key caps.

Operation Keys

To initiate transactions, the consumer evaluates the choices shown on the Consumer Display and presses the appropriate operation key.

Each *i* Series terminal, except the CCD and CTT, is equipped with eight operation keys. These operation keys are installed on both sides of the Consumer Display.

2.3 DISPLAY GRAPHICS

The *i* Series terminals support two kinds of software-driven graphics options for the Consumer Display.

- The Enhanced Monochrome Graphics (EMG) allows fonts and icons to be shown on a monochrome monitor.

- The Color Graphics Feature (CGF) allows 16-color, high-resolution graphics to be shown on a color monitor.

Enhanced Monochrome Graphics (EMG)

The EMG feature allows you to use the prepackaged fonts, icons, and character sets; or you can create your own.

The standard EMG PROM stores the prepackaged library of default fonts and icons (Appendix B) on STP-equipped terminals. On ATP-equipped terminals, these default fonts and icons are stored on disk. You can use these fonts and icons without changing them, or you can customize them for your purposes.

In addition, you can create monochrome graphics on a personal computer using the Diebold Design Utility (DDU). After creating the graphics, you install them at the controller or host for down-line loading to the *i* Series terminal.

Color Graphics Feature (CGF)

Using a PC graphics package, you can create color icons. Or instead of creating new graphics, you can use a hand scanner to electronically scan existing graphics.

The output of the file you create or scan must be in the industry-standard PCX format. Next, you run the Diebold Design Utility (DDU) on a personal computer to convert the PCX file to a format compatible with the *i* Series terminal. The resulting DDU files are stored on the hard drive on an ATP.

The Color Graphics Feature (CGF) offers the same default library of fonts and icons as EMG (Appendix B). However, unlike the EMG where the graphic library is stored on PROM, the default CGF graphics library is stored on disk. For more details on the Color Graphics Feature, refer to the *Color Graphics Feature Programming Manual,* TP-799344-000A and the *MDS Enhanced Graphics Product Description,* TP-799345-000A.

2.4 CONSUMER PRINTERS

All *i* Series terminals provide the consumer with a printed verification of transactions. Two types of Consumer Printers are available:

- A 35-column Consumer Printer
- An 80-column Consumer Printer

35-column Consumer Printer

InterBold's 35-column, dot matrix Consumer Printer is recommended for most general printing applications. This printer incorporates the latest printer technology such as an automated self-loading feature. Operators can change ink ribbon cartridges without removing the paper.

The printer uses 2.75-inch paper (either blank, rolled stock or rolled stock with pre-printed top-of-form marks). A ten-inch supply roll (1,900 linear feet) yields 7,600 three-inch forms or 3,800 six-inch forms.

Control characters in the network-supplied printer text activate special features like selectable horizontal and vertical pitch and graphics printing. At the standard horizontal pitch of 12 characters per inch (CPI), the Consumer Printer prints 25 columns. You can also select a 16 CPI horizontal pitch and print 35 columns. The printer has the following features:

- Bi-directional
- Print rate: 4.3 lines per second
- Character sets: Standard and alternate (Appendix A)
- Form length: 3 to 6 inches
- Horizontal pitch: 10, 12, or 16 CPI
- Vertical pitch: 6 to 8 lines per inch
- Double-width printing
- Double-density printing
- Graphics printing

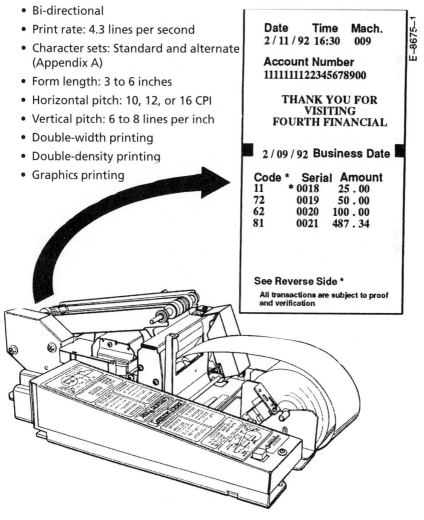

Figure 2-3 35-column Consumer Printer

MODEL 8-6   Commentary

This portion of a police accident report is the required narrative after routine identifications, license numbers, date, and times have been recorded. The readers of police reports include district attorneys, defense lawyers, police, social workers, judges, insurance investigators, and anyone who may have a legal involvement in the case. For consistency, the sections in all such reports are always in the same order.

Each section provides specific details about locations, conditions, and physical damage. The officer includes estimates of distances and notes the paths of the vehicles so that skid marks can be checked later for vehicle speed and direction. In addition, the officer identifies the ambulance service, hospital, and paramedics and lists other police reports that relate to the same case. This information will help readers who need to see all the documents in the case or who may need to interview medical personnel about injuries.

Discussion

1. Discuss the kinds of information included in each section of this report. How would this information help the district attorney prosecuting the case?

2. Assume that an accident has occurred at an intersection you know well. Write a description of the intersection that would be appropriate for the "Description of Scene" section of this type of police report.

3. In groups, assume that an accident has taken place in the classroom you are in. Your group members are witnesses and must write a description of the classroom for the insurance investigator. Compare your description with the ones written by other groups.

SUPPLEMENTAL COLLISION NARRATIVE	Date of Incident: 1/7/99
Location: Newbury Blvd. and Downer Ave. Shorewood, WI	Citation: MM36-T40
Subject: Coronal Primary Collision Report 99-07-42	Officer ID: 455
	Time: 19:25

Description of Scene: Newbury Boulevard is an east-west roadway of asphalt construction with two lanes of traffic in either direction and divided by a grassy median 10 ft wide. All lanes are 14 ft wide. A curb approximately 6 in. high is on the periphery of the East 2 and West 2 lanes. This is a residential street with no business district. Downer Avenue is a north-south roadway of asphalt construction with two lanes of traffic in either direction separated by a broken yellow line. All lanes are 12 ft wide. A curb approximately 6 in. high is on the periphery of the North 2 and South 2 lanes. At the intersection with Newbury Boulevard, Downer Avenue is a residential street. A business district exists four blocks south. The speed on both streets is posted at 30 mph. The roadways are unobstructed at the intersection. Both roadways are straight at this point, and the intersection is perpendicular. At the time of the accident, weather was clear, temperature about 12°F, and the pavements were dry, without ice. Ice was present along the curb lanes extending about 4 in. from the curbs into the East 2, West 2 lanes of Newbury Boulevard.

Description of Vehicle: The Ford Taurus was found at rest in a westerly direction on Newbury Boulevard. The midrear of the vehicle was jammed into the street light pole at the curb of lane West 2 of Newbury Boulevard. Pole number is S-456-03. The vehicle was upright, all four wheels inflated, brakes functional, speedometer on zero, and bucket front seats pressed forward against the dashboard. The front of the vehicle showed heavy damage from rollover. The grillwork was pushed back into the radiator, which, in turn, was pushed into the fan and block. The driver's door was open, but the passenger door was wedged closed. The vehicle rear wheels were on the curb, the front wheels in lane West 2 of Newbury. The windshield was shattered, but still within the frame. Oil and radiator coolant were evident on the roadway from the curb to approximately 6 ft into lane West 2 of Newbury, directly in front of the vehicle.

Driver: Driver Coronal was standing on the curb upon my arrival. After detecting the distant odor of alcohol on his breath and clothes and noting his red, watery eyes and general unsteadiness, I administered a field sobriety test, which Coronal failed. (See Arrest Report 99-07-16.)

Passenger: Passenger Throckmorton was in the passenger seat of the vehicle, pinned between the bucket seat and the dashboard. He was in obvious pain and complained of numbness in his right leg. Passenger was removed from the vehicle and stabilized at the scene by paramedics from Station 104 and transported to Columbia Hospital by Lakeside Ambulance Service.

Physical Evidence: A skid mark approximately 432 ft long began at the center line of Downer Avenue and traveled westerly in an arc into lane West 2 of Newbury Boulevard, ending at the vehicle position on the curb. Gouge marks began in the grassy devil's strip between the curb and the sidewalk. The gouge marks ended at the light pole under the rear wheels of the vehicle. A radio antenna was located 29 ft from the curb, lying on the grassy median of Newbury Boulevard. The antenna fits the antenna base stub on the Ford Taurus.

Other reports: Arrest 99-07-16
                  Blood Alcohol Test 99-07-28
                  Coefficient of Friction Test 99-07-16
                  Hospital Report on Throckmorton

Chapter 8   Exercises

1. Write a technical description of one of the following mechanisms or objects. Assume your description will appear in a consumer booklet about the product. (Or, if your instructor prefers, select a mechanism or object in your field.)

camera	shoe
bicycle	football
blender	broom
electric can opener	badminton racquet
telephone	coffee carafe
stapler	computer disk
lamp	ice skate
microwave oven	wine rack

2. Write a technical description of one of the following organisms or substances. Assume your description will appear in an information leaflet available at a science museum. (Or, if your instructor prefers, select an organism or substance related to your field.)

tree leaf	peanut butter
flower	milk
cat	aspirin
thumb	clay
dog	antifreeze
shrub	gasoline
ladybug	breakfast cereal

3. Select an object or mechanism in your field and find a description of it in a specialized handbook or encyclopedia, such as the *Encyclopedia of Biological Science* or the *Encyclopedia of Computer Science and Technology*. Rewrite the description for two readers: (1) an adult nonexpert interested in the topic and (2) a seventh-grade student. Attach a copy of the original description to your two new versions.

4. Select a building on campus or in your community. Assume that a committee (campus committee or community action committee) wants a three-panel brochure (front and back) that can be folded to fit into a standard business envelope. The brochure will describe the building so that newcomers can become acquainted with the purpose and history of the building. For example, if you choose a museum, assume that you want to interest newcomers in visiting the museum. If you choose a campus building, assume that your readers are new students who want to learn about the campus. Your brochure should include a description of

the building, a description of the location, the history and/or purpose of the build-ing, and related information, such as student services available, hours open to the public, tour information, or other special features. Consider graphics—line draw-ings, maps, floor plans, photographs. If you do not have access to computer soft-ware that can create a three-panel brochure, design a two-page flyer, front and back, with the same information.

5. Assume that you have just taken out a special insurance policy on your room against destruction of the contents and the interior. The insurance com-pany has asked you to prepare a full description of the room and its contents to keep on file as a record of what was insured in case of loss and claim for dam-ages. Write such a description.

6. In groups, write a description of a movable classroom desk chair with attached writing surface. Begin the description with a formal sentence defini-tion. Compare your group's draft with the drafts of other groups. Discuss how the descriptions differ and how each draft is appropriate for the specific reader and purpose.

CHAPTER 9

Instructions, Procedures, and Process Explanations

UNDERSTANDING INSTRUCTIONS, PROCEDURES, AND PROCESS EXPLANATIONS

This chapter discusses three related but distinct strategies for explaining the stages or steps in a specific course of action. Instructions, procedures, and process explanations all inform readers about the correct sequence of steps in an action or how to handle certain materials, but readers and purpose differ.

Instructions

Instructions provide a set of steps that readers can follow to perform a specific action, such as operate a fork lift or build a sundeck. Readers of instructions are concerned with performing each step themselves to complete the action successfully.

Procedures

Procedures in business and industry provide guidelines for three possible situations: (1) steps in a system to be followed by one employee, (2) steps in a system to be followed by several employees, and (3) standards and rules for handling specific equipment or work systems. Readers of procedures include (1) those who must perform the actions, (2) those who supervise employees performing the actions, and (3) people, such as upper management, legal staff, and government inspectors, who need to understand the procedures in order to make decisions and perform their own jobs.

Process Explanations

Process explanations describe the stages of an action or system either in general (how photosynthesis occurs) or in a specific situation (how an experiment was conducted). Readers of a process explanation do not intend to perform the action themselves, but they need to understand it for a variety of reasons.

In some situations, these three methods of presenting information about systems may overlap, but in order to adequately serve your readers, consider each strategy separately when writing a document. Because so many people rely on instructions and procedures and companies may be liable legally for injuries or damage that results from unclear documents, directions of any sort are among the most important documents a company produces.

Graphic Aids

Instructions, procedures, and process explanations all benefit greatly from graphic aids illustrating significant aspects of the subject or those aspects that readers find difficult to visualize. Readers need such graphic aids as (1) line drawings showing where parts are located, (2) exploded drawings showing how parts fit together, (3) flowcharts illustrating the stages of a process, and (4) drawings or photographs showing how actions should be performed or how a finished product should look.

Do not, however, rely on graphic aids alone to guide readers. Companies have been liable for damages because instructions or procedures did not contain enough written text to adequately guide readers through the steps. Visual perceptions vary, and all readers may not view a drawing or diagram the same way. Written text, therefore, must cover every step and every necessary detail.

STRATEGIES—Typeface

- Avoid blocks of text in italics, boldface, or all capitals because they are hard to read in a long passage.
- Do not select a typeface that calls attention to itself and de-emphasizes the text.
- Limit type styles to two per document. Too many variations confuse and distract readers.

WRITING INSTRUCTIONS

To write effective instructions, consider (1) your readers and their knowledge of the subject, (2) an organizational pattern that helps readers perform the action, and (3) appropriate details and language. In addition to the initial instructions, readers may need troubleshooting instructions that tell them what to do if, after performing the action, the mechanism fails to work properly or the expected results do not appear.

Readers

As you do before writing anything, consider who your readers will be. People read instructions in one of three ways. Some, but only a few, read instructions all the way through before beginning to follow any of the steps. Others read and perform each step without looking ahead to the next. And still others begin a task without reading any instructions and turn to them only when difficulties arise. Since you have no way to control this third group, assume that you are writing for readers who will read and perform each step without looking ahead. Therefore, all instructions must be in strict chronological order.

Everyone is a reader of instructions at some point, whether on the job or in private. Generally, readers fall into one of two categories:

1. *People on the job who use instructions to perform a work-related task.* Employees have various specialties and levels of technical knowledge, but all employees use instructions at some time to guide them in doing a job. Design your instructions for on-the-job tasks for the specific groups that will use them. Research chemists in the laboratory, crane operators, maintenance workers, and clerks all need instructions that match their needs and capabilities.

2. *Consumers.*   Consumers frequently use instructions when they (a) install a new product in their homes, such as a VCR or a light fixture, (b) put an object together, such as a toy or a piece of furniture, and (c) perform an activity, such as cook a meal or refinish a table.

Consumers, unlike employees assigned to a particular task, represent a diverse audience in capabilities and situations.

Varied capabilities.   A consumer audience usually includes people of different ages, education, knowledge, and skills. Readers of a pamphlet about how to operate a new gasoline lawn mower may be 12 years old or 80, may have elementary education only or postgraduate degrees, may be skilled amateur gardeners, or may have no experience with a lawn mower. When writing for such a large audience, aim your instructions at the level of those with the least education and experience, because they need your help most. Include what may seem like overly obvious directions, such as, "Make sure you plug in the television set," or obvious warnings, such as, "Do not put your fingers in the turning blades."

Varied situations.   Consider the circumstances under which consumers are likely to use your instructions. A person building a bookcase in the basement is probably relaxed, has time to study the steps, and may appreciate additional information about options and variations. In contrast, someone in a coffee shop trying to follow the instructions on the wall for the Heimlich maneuver to rescue a choking victim is probably nervous and has time only for a quick glance at the instructions.

In all cases, assume that your readers do not know how to perform the action in question and that they need guidance for every step in the sequence.

Organization

Readers have come to expect consistency in all instructions they use—strict chronological order and numbered steps. Model 9-1 presents a typical outline

I. Introduction
   A. Purpose of instructions
   B. Audience
   C. List of parts
   D. List of materials/tools/conditions needed
   E. Overview of the chronological steps
   F. Description of the mechanism or object, if needed
   G. Definitions of terms, if needed
   H. Warnings, cautions, notes, if needed
II. Sequential Steps
   A. Step 1
      1. Purpose
      2. Warning or caution, if needed
      3. Instruction in imperative mood
      4. Note on condition or result
   B. Step 2
      ⋮
III. Conclusion
   A. Expected result
   B. When or how to use

MODEL 9-1   Model Outline for Instructions

for a set of instructions for either consumers or employees. As the outline illustrates, instructions generally have a descriptive title and three main sections.

Title

Use a specific title that accurately names the action covered in the instructions.

Poor:	Snow Removal
Better:	Using Your Acme Snow Blower
Poor:	Good Practices
Better:	Welding on Pipelines

Introduction

Depending on how much information your readers need to get started, your introduction may be as brief as a sentence or as long as a page or more. If appropriate for your readers, include these elements:

Purpose and Audience.   Explain the purpose of the instructions unless it is obvious. The purpose of a coffee maker, for instance, is evident from the name of the product. In other cases, a statement of purpose and audience might be helpful to readers:

> This manual provides instructions for mechanics who install Birkins fine-wire spark plugs.
>
> These instructions are for nurses who must inject dye into a vein through a balloon-tipped catheter.
>
> This safe practices booklet is for employees who operate cranes, riggers, and hookers.

Lists of Parts, Materials, Tools, and Conditions.   If readers need to gather items in order to follow the instructions, put lists of those items in the introduction. *Parts* are the components needed, for example, to assemble and finish a table, such as legs, screws, and frame. *Materials* are the items needed to perform the task, such as sandpaper, shellac, and glue. *Tools* are the implements needed, such as a screwdriver, pliers, and a small paintbrush. Do not combine these items into one list unless the items are simple and the list is very short. If the lists are long, you may place them after the introduction for emphasis. *Conditions* are special circumstances that are important for completing the task successfully, such as using a dry, well-ventilated room. Be specific in listing items, such as

- One $\frac{3}{4}$-in. videotape

- One Phillips screwdriver

- Three pieces of fine sandpaper

- Five 9-volt batteries

- Maintain a 70° to 80°F temperature

Overview of Steps.   If the instructions are complicated and involve many steps, summarize them for the reader:

> The following sections cover installation, operation, start-up and adjustment, maintenance, and overhaul of the Trendometer DR-33 motors.

Description of the Mechanism.   A complete operating manual often includes a technical description of the equipment so that readers can locate specific parts and understand their function. Chapter 8 explains how to prepare technical descriptions.

Definitions.   If you use any terms your readers may not understand, define them. Chapter 7 explains how to prepare formal and informal definitions.

Warnings, Cautions, and Notes.   Readers must be alerted to potential danger or damage before they begin following instructions. If the potential danger or damage pertains to the whole set of instructions, place these in the introduction. When only one particular step is involved, place the warning or caution *before* the step.

Both *Danger* and *Warning* refer to potential injury of a person. *Danger* means that a serious injury or death *will definitely* occur if a hazard is not avoided:

> DANGER: The compressed gas will EXPLODE if the valve is unsealed. DO NOT open the valve.

A *Warning* means that a serious injury or death *may* occur if a hazard is not avoided:

> WARNING: To prevent electrical shock, do not use this unit in water.

Caution refers to possible damage to equipment:

> CAUTION: Failure to latch servicing tray completely may damage the printer.

Notes give readers extra information about choices or conditions:

> *Note:* A 12-in. cord is included with your automatic slicer. An extension cord may be used if it is 120 volt, 10 amp.

In addition to these written alerts, use an appropriate symbol or graphic aid to give the reader a clear understanding of the hazard or condition. Use capital letters or boldface type to highlight key words.

Sequential Steps

Explain the steps in the exact sequence readers must perform them, and number each step. Explain only one step per number. If two steps must be performed simultaneously, explain the proper sequence:

> While pushing the button, release the lever slowly.

Include the reason for a particular action if you believe readers need it for more efficient use of the instructions:

> Tighten the belt. *Note:* A taut belt will prevent a shift in balance.

Use headings to separate the steps into categories. Identify the primary stages, if appropriate:

- Separating
- Mixing
- Applying

Identify the primary areas, if appropriate:

- Top drawer
- Side panel
- Third level

Refer readers to other steps when necessary:

> If the valve sticks, go to Step 12.

Then tell readers whether to go on from Step 12 or go back to a previous step:

> When the valve is clear, go back to Step 6.

For regular maintenance instructions, indicate the suggested frequency of performing certain steps:

Once a month:	• Check tire pressure • Check lights • Check hoses
Once a year:	• Inspect brakes • Change fuel filter • Clean choke

In some cases, writers use a *narrative* format for instructions. A narrative format presents the steps for instructions in sentences in a paragraph. Model 9-9 shows a narrative format for instructions. Because most readers find this format more difficult to follow than numbered steps, use this style only if your readers are experienced, the steps are simple, and you need no more than 100 words for the entire action.

Conclusion

If you include a conclusion, tell readers what to expect after following the instructions and suggest other uses and options if appropriate:

> Your food will be hot, but not as brown as if heated in the oven rather than in the microwave. A few minutes of standing time will complete the cooking cycle and distribute the heat uniformly.

Model 9-2 shows instructions for shutting down a boiler. The step-by-step instructions are numbered, and each step is below a line drawing that illustrates the action or location in the step. Readers are experienced workers who understand the technical terms.

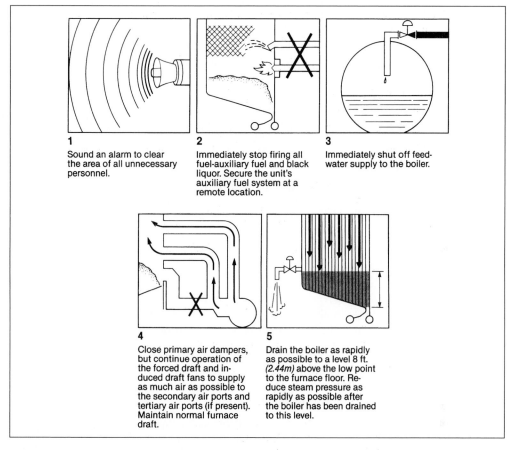

1
Sound an alarm to clear the area of all unnecessary personnel.

2
Immediately stop firing all fuel-auxiliary fuel and black liquor. Secure the unit's auxiliary fuel system at a remote location.

3
Immediately shut off feed-water supply to the boiler.

4
Close primary air dampers, but continue operation of the forced draft and induced draft fans to supply as much air as possible to the secondary air ports and tertiary air ports (if present). Maintain normal furnace draft.

5
Drain the boiler as rapidly as possible to a level 8 ft. (2.44m) above the low point to the furnace floor. Reduce steam pressure as rapidly as possible after the boiler has been drained to this level.

MODEL 9-2   Instructions for Emergency Shutdown of an Operating Recovery Boiler

Details and Language

Whether you are writing for consumers or for highly trained technicians, follow these guidelines:

1. Keep parallel structure in lists. Be sure that each item in a list is in the same grammatical form.

   Nonparallel: This warranty does not cover:
   a. Brakes
   b. Battery
   c. Using too much oil

This list is not parallel because the first two items are names of things (nouns) and the last item is an action (verbal phrase). Rewrite so that all items fit the same pattern.

Parallel: This warranty does not cover:
          a. Brakes
          b. Battery
          c. Excess oil consumption

In this revision, all items are things—brakes, battery, and consumption. Lists can confuse readers if the listed items do not all fit the same category. Here is an example:

Poor: Parts Included for Assembly:
          End frames
          Caster inserts
          Casters
          Screwdriver
          Sleeve screws
          Detachable side handles

The screwdriver is not a part included in the assembly package, but the consumer might think it is and waste time looking for it. List the screwdriver in a different category, such as "Tools Needed."

2. Maintain the same terminology for each part throughout the instructions, and be sure the part is labeled similarly in illustrations. Do not refer to "Control Button," "Program Button," and "On/Off Button" when you mean the same control.

3. Use headings to help readers find specific information. Identify sections of the instructions with descriptive headings:

Assembly Kit Contents
Materials Needed
Preparation
Removing the Cover
Checking the Fuel Filter

4. Use the imperative mood for sequential steps. Readers understand instruction steps better when each is a command:

Adjust the lever.
Turn the handle.
Clean the seal.

5. Never use passive voice in instructions. The passive voice does not make clear who is to perform the action in the step.

Poor: The shellac should be applied.

Better: Apply the shellac.

6. State specific details. Use precise language in all sections.

Poor: Turn the lever to the right.

Better: Turn the lever clockwise one full revolution.

Poor: Keep the mixture relatively cool.

Better: Keep the mixture at 50°F or less.

Poor: Place the pan near the tube.

Better: Place the pan 1 in. from the bottom of the tube.

Poor: Attach the wire to the terminal.

Better: Attach the green wire to the AUDIO OUT terminal.

7. Write complete sentences. Long sentences in instructions can be confusing, but do not write fragments or clip out articles and write "telegrams."

Poor: Repairs excluded.

Better: The warranty does not cover repairs to the electronic engine controls.

Poor: Adjust time filter PS.

Better: Adjust the time filter to the PS position.

8. Do not use *should* and *would* to mean *must* and *is*.

Poor: The gauge should be on empty.

Better: The gauge must be on empty.

Poor: The seal would be unbroken.

Better: The seal is unbroken.

Both *should* and *would* are less direct than *must* and *is* and may be interpreted as representing possible conditions rather than absolute situations. A reader may interpret the first sentence as saying, "The gauge should be on empty, although it might not be." Always state facts definitely.

Troubleshooting Instructions

Troubleshooting instructions tell readers what to do if the mechanism fails to work properly or results do not match expectations. Model 9-3 shows a typical three-part table for troubleshooting instructions. These troubleshooting instructions (1) describe the problem, (2) suggest a cause, and (3) offer a solution. Readers find the problem in the left column and then read across to the suggested solution. Troubleshooting instructions are most helpful when simple adjustments can solve problems.

Problem	Possible Cause	Solution
Snow in picture	Antenna Interference	Check antenna connection Turn off dishwasher, microwave, nearby appliances
Fuzzy picture	Focus pilot	Adjust Sharpness Control clockwise
Multiple images	Antenna Lead-in wire	Check antenna connection Check wire condition
Too much color	Color saturation	Adjust Color Control counterclockwise
Too little color	Color saturation	Adjust Color Control clockwise
Too much one color	Tint level	Adjust Tint Control clockwise

MODEL 9-3   Troubleshooting Guide for a Television Set

WRITING PROCEDURES

Procedures often appear similar to instructions, and people sometimes assume that the terms mean the same thing. However, the term *procedures* most often and most accurately refers to official company guidelines covering three situations: (1) a system with sequential steps that must be completed by one employee, (2) a system with sequential steps that involves several employees interacting and supporting each other, and (3) the standards and methods for handling equipment or events with or without sequential steps.

Because these documents contain the rules and appropriate methods for the proper completion of tasks, they have multiple readers, including (1) employees who perform the procedures, (2) supervisors who must understand the system and oversee employees working within it, (3) company lawyers concerned about liability protection through the use of appropriate warnings, cautions, and guidelines, (4) government inspectors from such agencies as the Occupational Safety and Health Administration who check procedures to see if they comply with government standards, and (5) company management who must be aware of and understand all company policies and guidelines. Although the primary readers of procedures are those who follow them, remember that other readers inside and outside the company also use them as part of their work.

Procedures for One Employee

Procedures for a task that one employee will complete are similar to basic instructions. These procedures are organized, like instructions, in numbered steps following the general outline in Model 9-1. Include the same items in the introduction: purpose, lists of parts and materials, warnings and cautions, and any information that will help readers perform the task more efficiently. Most company procedures include a description of the principles behind the system, such as a company policy or government regulation, research results, or technologic advances. When procedures involve equipment, they often include a technical description in the introduction.

Procedures for one employee also share some basic style elements with instructions:

- Descriptive title

- Precise details

- Complete sentences

- Parallel structure in lists

- Consistent terms for parts

- Headings to guide readers

The steps in the procedure are always in chronological order. Steps may be written as commands, in passive voice, or in indicative mood:

> To prevent movement of highway trucks and trailers while loading or unloading, set brakes and block wheels. (*Command*)

> The brakes should be set and the wheels should be blocked to prevent movement of highway trucks and trailers during loading and unloading. (*Passive voice*)

> To prevent movement of highway trucks and trailers while loading or unloading, the driver sets the brakes and blocks wheels. (*Indicative mood*)

The indicative mood can become monotonous quickly if each step begins with the same words, such as "The driver places . . ." or "The driver then sets. . . ." Commands and passive voice are less repetitious. Do not use the past tense for procedures because readers may interpret this to mean that the procedures are no longer in effect.

Procedures for Several Employees

When procedures involve several employees performing separate but related steps in a sequential system, the *playscript organization* is most effective. This organization is similar to a television script that shows the dialogue in the order the actors speak it. Playscript procedures show the steps in the system and indicate which employee performs each step. The usual pattern is to place the job title on the left and the action on the same line on the right:

Operator:	1. Open flow switch to full setting.
	2. Set remote switch to temperature sensor.
Inspector:	3. Check for water flow to both chiller and boiler.
Operator:	4. Change flow switch to half-setting.
	5. Tighten mounting bolt.
Inspector:	6. Check for water flow to both boiler and chiller.
Operator:	7. Shut off chiller flow.
Inspector:	8. Test boiler flow for volume per second.
	9. Complete test records.
Operator:	10. Return flow switch to appropriate setting.

Generally, the steps are numbered sequentially no matter how many employees are involved. One employee may perform several steps in a row before another employee participates in the sequence. The playscript organization ensures that all employees understand how they fit into the system and how they support other employees also participating in the system. Use job titles to identify employee roles because individuals may come and go, but the tasks remain linked to specific jobs.

Include the same information in the introduction to playscript procedures as you do in step-by-step procedures for a single employee, such as warnings, lists of materials, overview of the procedure, and the principles behind the system. The steps in playscript organization usually are commands, although the indicative mood and passive voice are sometimes used.

Procedures for Handling Equipment and Systems

Procedures for handling equipment and systems include guidelines for (1) repairs, (2) installations, (3) maintenance, (4) assembly, (5) safety practices, and (6) systems for conducting business, such as processing a bank loan or fingerprinting suspected criminals. These procedures include lists of tools, definitions, warnings and cautions, statements of purpose, and the basic principles. They differ from other procedures in an important way: The steps are not always sequential. Often the individual steps may be performed in any order, and they are usually grouped by topic rather than by sequence.

Model 9-4 shows a typical organization for company procedures about safe practices on a construction site. The introduction establishes the purpose of the procedures and warns readers about possible injury if these and other company guidelines are not followed. The individual items are grouped under topic headings. Notice that the items are not numbered because they are not meant to be

---

PROCEDURES FOR SAFE EXCAVATIONS

This safety bulletin specifies correct procedures for all excavation operations. In addition, all Clinton Engineering standards for materials and methods should be strictly observed. Failure to do so could result in injury to workers and to passersby.

PERSONAL PROTECTION:

- Wear safety hard hat at all times.
- Keep away from overhead digging equipment.
- Keep ladders in trenches at all times.

EXCAVATION PROTECTION:

- Protect all sites by substantial board railing or fence at least 48 in. high or standard horse-style barriers.
- Place warning lights at night.

EXCAVATED MATERIALS:

- Do not place excavated materials within 2 ft of a trench or excavation.
- Use toe boards if excavated materials could fall back into a trench.

DIGGING EQUIPMENT:

- Use mats or heavy planking to support digging equipment on soft ground.
- If a shovel or crane is placed on the excavation bank, install shoring and bracing to prevent a cave-in.

MODEL 9-4   A Typical Company Procedures Bulletin Outlining Safe Practices on a Construction Site

sequential. In this sample, the items are written as commands, but, like other procedures, they may be in the passive voice or indicative mood as well.

WRITING PROCESS EXPLANATIONS

A *process explanation* is a description of how a series of actions leads to a specific result. Process explanations differ from instructions and procedures in that they are not intended to guide readers in performing actions, but only in understanding them. As a result, a process explanation is written as a narrative, without listed steps or commands, describing four possible types of actions:

- Actions that occur in nature, such as how diamonds form, how the liver functions, or how a typhoon develops.
- Actions that produce a product, such as how steel, light bulbs, or baseballs are made.

- Actions that make up a particular task, such as how gold is mined, how blood is tested for cholesterol levels, or how a highway is paved.

- Actions in the past, such as how the Romans built their aqueducts or how the Grand Canyon was formed.

Readers

A process explanation may be a separate document, such as a science pamphlet, or a section in a manual or report. Although readers of process explanations do not intend to perform the steps themselves, they do need the information for specific purposes, and one process explanation will not serve all readers.

A general reader reading an explanation in a newspaper of how police officers test drivers for intoxication wants to know the main stages of the process and how a police officer determines if a driver is indeed intoxicated. A student in a criminology class needs more details in order to understand each major and minor stage of the process and to pass a test about those details. An official from the National Highway Traffic Safety Administration may read the narrative to see how closely it matches the agency's official guidelines, while a judge may want to be sure that a driver's rights are not violated by the process. Process explanations for these readers must serve their specific needs as well as describe the sequential stages of the process. Model 9-5 shows how process explanations of sobriety testing may differ for general readers and for students. Notice that the version for students includes more details about what constitutes imbalance and more explanation about the conditions under which the test should or should not be given.

For all process explanations, analyze the intended reader's technical knowledge of the subject and why the reader needs to know about the process. Then decide the number of details, which details, and the appropriate technical terms to include in your narrative.

Organization

Model 9-6 presents a model outline for a process explanation. As the outline illustrates, process explanations have three main sections: an introduction, the stages in the process, and a conclusion.

Introduction

The introduction should include enough details about the process so that readers understand the principles underlying it and the conditions under which it

For a general reader:

THE WALK-AND-TURN TEST

The police officer begins the test by asking the suspect to place the left foot on a straight line and the right foot in front of it. The suspect then takes nine heel-to-toe steps down the line, turns around, and takes nine heel-to-toe steps back. The suspect is given one point each for eight possible behaviors showing imbalance, such as stepping off the line and losing balance while turning. A score of two or more indicates the suspect is probably legally intoxicated.

For a student reader:

The Walk-and-Turn Test

The test is administered on a level, dry surface. People who are over 60 years old, more than 50 pounds overweight, or have physical impairments that interfere with walking are not given this test.

The police officer begins the test by asking the suspect to place the left foot on a straight line and the right foot in front of it. The suspect must maintain balance while listening to the officer's directions for the test and must not begin until the officer so indicates. The suspect then takes nine heel-to-toe steps down the line, keeping hands at the sides, eyes on the feet, and counting aloud. After nine steps, the suspect turns and takes nine heel-to-toe steps back in the same manner. The officer scores one point for each of the following behaviors: failing to keep balance while listening to directions, starting before told to, stopping to regain balance, not touching heel to toe, stepping off the line, using arms to balance, losing balance while turning, and taking more or less than nine steps each way. If the suspect falls or cannot perform the test at all, the officer scores nine points. A suspect who receives two or more points is probably legally intoxicated.

MODEL 9-5   Two Process Explanations of Sobriety Testing

takes place. Depending on your readers' technical expertise and how they intend to use the process explanation, include these elements:

- *Definition.*   If the subject is highly technical or readers are not likely to recognize it, provide a formal definition.

- *Theory behind the process.*   Explain the scientific principles behind the process, particularly if you are describing a research process.

- *Purpose.*   Explain the purpose unless it is obvious from the title or the readers already know it.

I. Introduction
   A. Definition
   B. Theory behind process
   C. Purpose
   D. Historical background, if appropriate
   E. Equipment, materials, special natural conditions
   F. Major stages

II. Stages in the Process
   A. Major stage 1
      1. Definition
      2. Purpose
      3. Special materials or conditions
      4. Description of major stage 1
      5. Minor stage 1
         a. Definition
         b. Purpose
         c. Special materials or conditions
         d. Description of minor stage 1
      6. Minor stage 2
         ⋮
   B. Major stage 2
      ⋮

III. Conclusion
   A. Summary of major stages and results
   B. Significance of process

Model 9-6   Model Outline for a Process Explanation

- *Historical background.*   Readers may need to know the history of a process and how it has changed in order to understand its current form.

- *Equipment, materials, and tools.*   Explain what types of equipment, materials, and tools are essential for proper completion of the process.

- *Major stages.*   Name the major stages of the process so that readers know what to expect.

Stages of the Process

Explain the stages of the process in the exact sequence in which they normally occur. In some cases, one sentence may adequately explain a stage. In other cases, each stage may actually be a separate process that contributes to the whole. In describing each stage, (1) define it, (2) explain how it fits the overall process, (3) note any dangers or special conditions, (4) describe exactly how it occurs, including who or what does the action, and (5) state the results at the end of that particular stage. If a major stage is made up of several minor actions, explain each of these and how they contribute to the major stage. Include the reasons for the actions in each stage:

> The valve is closed before takeoff because. . . .
>
> The technician uses stainless steel implements because. . . .

Conclusion

The conclusion of a process explanation should explain the expected results, what they mean, and how this process influences or interacts with others, if it does. Model 9-7, from the American Heart Association, is a process explanation of the medical condition called *congestive heart failure*. Written for the general public, the text describes the process in a typical patient and includes definitions of two medical terms.

WHAT HAPPENS IN CONGESTIVE HEART FAILURE?

When the heart doesn't pump as efficiently as it should, the blood flow slows down and less blood is pumped. Then blood returning to the heart backs up in the veins. This forces fluid from the blood vessels into tissues of the feet and legs. The swelling that follows is called **edema** of the feet, ankles, and legs. Sometimes the edema involves the wall of the abdomen and liver, too. (Not all edema results from congestive heart failure—only a doctor is qualified to make this diagnosis.)

    The heart's left side receives oxygenated blood from the lungs, then pumps it to the rest of the body. When the heart's left side isn't pumping as well as it should be, blood backs up in the vessels of the lungs. Sometimes fluid is forced out of the lung vessels into the breathing spaces themselves. When this happens, it's called **pulmonary edema;** shortness of breath and a lack of stamina often follow.

MODEL 9-7   Process Outline for Congestive Heart Failure

Reproduced with permission. *Congestive Heart Failure: What You Should Know,* 1995. Copyright American Heart Association.

Details and Language

Process explanations, like instructions, can include these elements:

- Descriptive title
- Precise details
- Complete sentences
- Consistent terms for actions or parts
- Headings in long narratives to guide readers
- Simple comparisons for general readers

In addition, remember these style guidelines:

- Do not use commands. Because readers do not intend to perform the actions, commands are not appropriate.

- Use either passive voice or the indicative mood. Passive voice is usually preferred for process explanations that involve the same person performing each action in order to eliminate the monotony of repeating "The technician" over and over. However, natural processes or processes involving several people are easier to read if they are in the indicative mood (see Model 9-5).

- If you are writing a narrative about a process you were involved in, such as an incident report or a research report, use of the first person is appropriate:

  I arrested the suspect. . . .
  I called for medical attention. . . .
  I spliced both genes. . . .

- Use transition words and phrases to indicate shifts in time, location, or situation in individual stages of the process:

Shifts in time:	then, next, first, second, before
Shifts in location:	above, below, adjacent, top
Shifts in situation:	however, because, in spite of, as a result, therefore

CHAPTER SUMMARY

This chapter discusses writing effective instructions, procedures, and process explanations. Remember:

- Instructions, procedures, and process explanations are related but distinct strategies for explaining the steps in a specific action.

- Instructions provide the steps in an action for readers who intend to perform it, either for a work-related task or for a private-interest task.

- Instructions typically have an introduction that includes purpose; lists of parts, materials, tools, and conditions; overview of the steps; description of a mechanism (if appropriate); and warnings, cautions, and notes.

- The steps in instructions should be in the exact sequence in which a reader will perform them.

- The conclusion in instructions, if included, explains the expected results.

- Instructions should be in the imperative mood and include precise details.

- Troubleshooting instructions explain what to do if problems arise after readers have performed all the steps in an action.

- Procedures are company guidelines for (1) a system with sequential steps that must be completed by one employee, (2) a system with sequential steps that involves several employees, and (3) handling equipment or events with or without sequential steps.

- Procedures for a task that one employee will perform are similar to instructions with numbered steps.

- Procedures for several employees are best written in playscript organization.

- Procedures for handling equipment and systems are often organized topically rather than sequentially because the steps do not have to be performed in a specific order.

- Process explanations describe how a series of actions leads to a specific result.

- The stages of the process are explained in sequence in process explanations, but because readers do not intend to perform the process, the steps are not written as commands.

SUPPLEMENTAL READINGS IN PART 2

Benson, P. J. "Writing Visually: Design Considerations in Technical Publications," *Technical Communication*, p. 454.

Plunka, G. A. "The Editor's Nightmare: Formatting Lists within the Text," *Technical Communication*, p. 515.

"Six Graphics Guidelines," *Simply Stated*, p. 535.

White, J. V. "Color: The Newest Tool for Technical Communicators," *Technical Communication*, p. 551.

These instructions are part of a Ciba Corning reference manual that includes operating instructions for technicians running a computer-operated testing system. The instructions shown here cover filling water bottles and emptying waste bottles—essential procedures. The technical writer who prepared these instructions uses the internationally recognized caution symbol—an exclamation point inside a triangle. The biohazard symbol tells the reader to read an appendix containing precautions for working with biohazardous materials.

Notice that the first step in the instructions is a major one, followed by the six steps necessary to perform the major step. Also notice that the writer directs the reader to other sections in the manual in steps 2 and 5.

Discussion

1. Identify the design elements in these instructions. Discuss how effectively the format serves the reader who must follow the instructions.

2. In groups, write a process explanation for "Preparing the ACS Bottles." Assume your reader is a supervisor who has never performed the process but needs to understand it before attending a meeting with the clinical biology technicians who perform the process daily.

3. Write instructions for cleaning a piece of equipment in your field *or* for cleaning and adjusting a piece of classroom equipment, such as an overly full pencil sharpener or an out-of-focus overhead projector. Identify a specific reader before you begin.

Preparing the ACS Bottles

Use this procedure to fill the ACS water bottle and empty the ACS waste bottle, if required.

If the Extended Operation Module (EOM) is connected to the ACS:180, complete this procedure when you prepare the EOM bottles at the start of each day or shift. Ensure that the EOM is inactive when you prepare the ACS bottles by pressing the EOM button and checking to see that the LED next to the EOM is off. Press the EOM button to activate the EOM when you complete the procedure.

 BIOHAZARD: Refer to Appendix B, *Protecting Yourself from Biohazards,* for recommended precautions when working with biohazardous materials.

 CAUTION: Do not perform this procedure while the system is assaying samples. The system stops the run and the tests in process are not completed.

NOTE: For optimum assay and system performance, fill the ACS water bottle with fresh deionized water at the start of each day or shift.

1. Remove the ACS water bottle and the ACS waste bottle.
    a. Lift the lid above the water bottle until the tubing clears the mouth of the bottle.
    b. Grasp the handle of the water bottle and lift the bottle up and out, and set it aside.
    c. Lift the waste bottle lid until the tubing clears the mouth of the waste bottle.
    d. If the EOM is connected to the ACS:180, disconnect the ACS waste bottle from the waste tubing by pressing the metal latch on the tubing fitting.
    e. Grasp the handle of the waste bottle and lift the bottle up and out.
    f. Gently lower the lid.

2. Empty the contents of the waste bottle into a container or drain approved for biohazardous waste.

    If required, clean the waste bottle as described in Section 2, *Cleaning the ACS Water and the Waste Bottles,* in your *ACS:180 Maintenance and Troubleshooting Manual.*

3. Fill the water bottle with fresh deionized water.

(Continued)

Preparing the ACS Bottles

4. Install the bottles on the system, as shown in Figure 6 – 2.

    a. Lift the waste bottle lid and return the waste bottle to its location.

    b. If the EOM is connected to the ACS:180, connect the waste tubing to the waste bottle by pressing the tubing into the fitting on the bottle, if required.

    c. Lower the waste bottle lid.

    d. Install the water bottle, insert the tubing into the bottle, and lower the water bottle lid.

5. Proceed to Replenishing Supplies, Page 6 – 13.

Figure 6 – 2. Installing the ACS Water and Waste Bottles

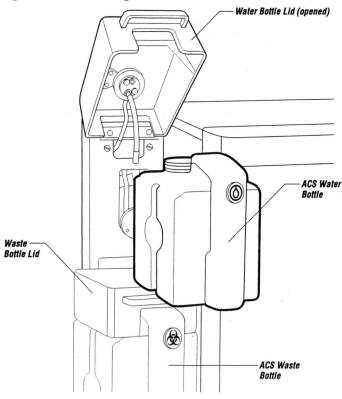

Water Bottle Lid (opened)

ACS Water Bottle

Waste Bottle Lid

ACS Waste Bottle

Model 9-9   Commentary

These instructions are from a Gougeon Brothers manual for readers who are experienced in using epoxy for boat building and repair. This manual, a supplement to the main technical manual for using epoxy on boats, suggests ways the reader can use epoxy for home repairs.

The writer uses a narrative format for the instructions. Notice that the first two paragraphs tell the reader about epoxy use and indicate where it should not be used. The third paragraph covers the simple instructions for the experienced user of this product. Three line drawings illustrate the main steps.

Discussion

1. Identify the language that indicates the reader is an experienced user of this product. Discuss what changes would be needed if the instructions were for a general reader who is not familiar with home repair or this product.

2. In groups, draft instructions in narrative format for one of the following: (1) clocking in with a time card at a job, (2) grilling a hamburger outdoors, (3) using a wall-mounted pencil sharpener, (4) toasting one slice of bread, and (5) parallel parking. Create a graphic aid to accompany your instructions.

Sealing Floors

Epoxy is used on porch decks and under carpeting and wood flooring as a moisture barrier and on concrete garage and shop floors as a finish coating that provides a barrier against grease, oil, and chemicals.

This is not recommended for concrete floors that have serious moisture problems or floors that have been previously sealed or contaminated with grease or oil. All of these conditions inhibit good adhesion. Floors should be clean and dry before coating, which can be difficult on floors below grade. Thorough cleaning with detergents may help to clean some stains enough for epoxy penetration and good adhesion.

To apply a thick coating in one operation, mix a batch of resin and hardener. Add an epoxy pigment (such as 503 Gray Pigment) for a solid color finish. Pour the epoxy on the clean concrete floor, and spread it around evenly with a notched trowel or rubber squeegee. Smooth the coating with a thin foam roller on a long extension handle. Allow the epoxy to cure thoroughly. Wash the cured epoxy with an abrasive pad and water and dry the surface with paper towels before you apply glue or finish coatings.

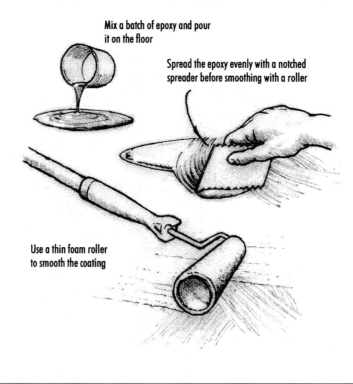

Mix a batch of epoxy and pour it on the floor

Spread the epoxy evenly with a notched spreader before smoothing with a roller

Use a thin foam roller to smooth the coating

This sample from a long troubleshooting guide identifies the computer system error messages that appear on the monitor when the system detects a problem. The messages are listed in alphabetical order in the left-hand column. The instructions for solving the problem appear in the right-hand column. Notice that for some problems the reader is directed to other sections of the manual. If the technician cannot clear up the system error, the last step of the instructions directs him or her to the company's Technical Assistance Center.

Discussion

1. Identify the format elements used here and discuss how helpful they are in guiding the reader through the steps.

2. In groups, select a piece of sports equipment or a household appliance and write a set of troubleshooting instructions to guide someone who has never used the object.

System Error Messages

Message (Alphabetic Order)	Probable Cause and Solution
Dark read data return error: error code **	1. At the Schedule Tests/Review Contents screen, delete the worklist. 2. At the Main Menu, press **F6 Diagnostics and Maintenance.** 3. Press **F4 System Performance Tests.** 4. Press **F5 PMT Test,** then press **START.** 5. Refer to Section 3, *Using the SPTs to Troubleshoot the ACS:180,* Page 3 – 21, to review the test results and take the appropriate action. 6. If the error message appears again, call the Ciba Corning Technical Assistance Center.
Dark read error: error code **	1. At the Schedule Tests/Review Contents screen, delete the worklist. 2. At the Main Menu, press **F6 Diagnostics and Maintenance.** 3. Press **F4 System Performance Tests.** 4. Press **F5 PMT Test,** then press **START.** 5. After the PMT test is finished, schedule and perform the Background

229

System Error Messages

Message (Alphabetic Order)	Probable Cause and Solution
	profile as described in Section 3, *Verifying System Performance.* 6. Refer to Section 3, *Using the SPTs to Troubleshoot the ACS:180,* Page 3 – 21, to review the test results and take the appropriate action. 7. If error message appears again, call the Ciba Corning Technical Assistance Center.
Diskette was removed during operation.	Removing the diskette while the system is reading or writing to the diskette causes the operation to stop and may also damage the diskette. Format the diskette again before using it. ⚠ **CAUTION:** Formatting erases all current files on the diskette. 1. At the System Management/Result Database Operations/Archive Results screen, press **F4 Format Diskette.** 2. Insert a diskette in the diskette drive and press **Y.** 3. If it is a high-density diskette, press **Y;** if not, press **N.**
Due to excessive errors, cuvettes cannot be dispensed.	This message may indicate a jam in the cuvette loading bin. 1. At the Main Menu, press **F6 Diagnostics and Maintenance.** 2. Press **F1 Manual Operations.** 3. Press **F1 Home System.** 4. If needed, home the system again. 5. If needed, clear cuvette jams and track problems at the cuvette loading bin and the cuvette preheater, as described in *Clearing the Cuvette Track,* Page 4–33. 6. If the problem persists, call the Ciba Corning Technical Assistance Center.
Due to excessive errors, reagent probe 1, 2, or 3 has been taken off-line.	1. At the Main Menu, press **F6 Diagnostics and Maintenance.** 2. Press **F1 Manual Operations.** 3. Press **F1 Home System.** 4. If needed, home the system again. 5. Press **STATUS.** 6. Review the errors for reagent probe 1, 2, or 3 at the System Status/Probe Status: Reagent Probe screen, and take the appropriate action. 7. If the problem persists, call the Ciba Corning Technical Assistance Center.

Model 9-11 Commentary

These procedures were written by a student in a technical writing class. The student uses the playscript format to present the steps for handling the company tuition-refund program.

Notice that the writer uses headings to divide the procedures into three stages. Each step is written as a command, and the steps are numbered sequentially from the beginning of the procedure to its conclusion. The introduction explains the company policy on tuition refunds and describes who is eligible for the program.

Discussion

1. Discuss the effectiveness of the playscript format in this situation. For which of the three people involved is the playscript format most useful?

2. Discuss the writer's decision to divide the steps into three stages marked by headings. How do the headings help the three employees involved?

3. In groups, draft procedures in playscript organization for a procedure on campus, such as registering for courses, running for office in student government, or applying for financial aid or a campus job.

PROCEDURES FOR EMPLOYEE TUITION-REFUND PROGRAM

The Barkley Corporation offers an employee tuition-refund program to encourage employees to continue their technical training or complete advanced degrees. All full-time employees who have worked at Barkley for one year may apply for full reimbursement for courses taken for academic credit at fully accredited technical schools, colleges, or universities.

Before Registration

Supervisor:

1. Send a memo to all employees on August 1, December 1, and May 1, informing them of the company tuition program and inviting them to discuss education plans with you.

Employee:

2. See your supervisor at least two weeks before the start of classes to allow time to approve your courses for the tuition-refund program.

Supervisor:

3. Discuss the employee's education plans and explain the application form.

Employee:

4. Complete the application form.

5. Submit the application form to your supervisor.

Supervisor:

6. Review the application form for completeness and send it to the Human Resources Clerk.

Human Resources Clerk:

7. Check the application for compliance with company regulations.

8. Approve or deny the application and return it to the supervisor with comments.

Supervisor:

9. Inform the employee of the decision.

10. If the decision is favorable, sign the Tuition-refund Contract with the employee and send it to the Human Resources Clerk.

11. Be sure the employee knows the required grade and employment status for a full refund.

After Registration

Employee:

12. Submit the fee invoice form to your supervisor after paying tuition so that your record is in order for reimbursement.

Supervisor:

13. Send the employee's fee invoice to the Human Resources Clerk with Form 26A.

Human Resources Clerk:

14. Record the fee invoice as a potential tuition refund in the employee's file.

Supervisor:

15. Meet informally with the employee once a month to determine progress in the course.

16. If the employee is having difficulty with the course, suggest a meeting with the Training Director to discuss study approaches.

After Course Completion

Employee:

17. Upon completion of the course, with a grade of at least B–, submit your final grade report to your supervisor.

Supervisor:

18. Send the employee's final grade report with Form 26B to the Human Resources Clerk.

Human Resources Clerk:

19. Check the course identification and status and prepare a reimbursement check for the full course fee.

Supervisor:

20. Present the check to the employee and offer company congratulations.

MODEL 9-12   Commentary

This model is from an industrial guide. The process explanation covers a specific type of boiler and how it functions. The text is divided into numbered stages. The line drawing of the boiler includes numbers keyed to these stages and arrows that indicate the movements of various elements. Thus, the drawing is also a flowchart showing how the process works within the boiler. Readers are experienced workers who understand the language used.

Discussion

1. Discuss the effectiveness of separating the process explanation into numbered stages.

2. Discuss how the text guides readers through the flowchart. How does the flowchart aid readers?

3. In groups, draft a process explanation for one of the following. Create a flowchart to accompany your process explanation.

    a. Checking a book out of your school library

    b. Ordering and getting food in a fast-food restaurant

    c. Making a photocopy on a copy machine in your school library

    d. Using the spell-check feature in a word processing program

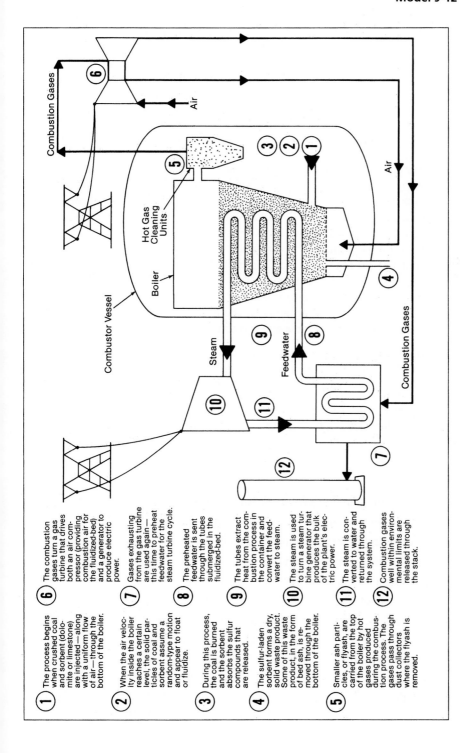

Combined Cycle PFBC

1. The process begins when crushed coal and sorbent (dolomite or limestone) are injected—along with a uniform flow of air—through the bottom of the boiler.

2. When the air velocity inside the boiler reaches a certain level, the solid particles of coal and sorbent assume a random-type motion and appear to float or fluidize.

3. During this process, the coal is burned and the sorbent absorbs the sulfur compounds that are released.

4. The sulfur-laden sorbent forms a dry, solid waste product. Some of this waste product, in the form of bed ash, is removed through the bottom of the boiler.

5. Smaller ash particles, or flyash, are carried from the top of the boiler by hot gases produced during the combustion process. The gases pass through dust collectors where the flyash is removed.

6. The combustion gases turn a gas turbine that drives both an air compressor (providing combustion air for the fluidized-bed) and a generator to produce electric power.

7. Gases exhausting from the gas turbine are used again—this time to preheat feedwater for the steam turbine cycle.

8. The preheated feedwater is sent through the tubes submerged in the fluidized-bed.

9. The tubes extract heat from the combustion process in the container and convert the feedwater to steam.

10. The steam is used to turn a steam turbine generator that produces the bulk of the plant's electric power.

11. The steam is converted to water and returned through the system.

12. Combustion gases well within environmental limits are released through the stack.

1. Rewrite the following into an appropriate set of instructions for a general reader who wants to try some home repair. Add a title, headings, and a useful graphic aid.

> When there is a crack between the bathtub and wall, it should be filled to keep the water out. The crack also catches dirt. Choose either waterproof grout or plastic sealer. Grout comes as powder and must be mixed with water in the amount you need. Plastic sealer comes in a tube. The surface should be prepared by removing the old crack filler, washing and then drying the surface. A small amount of grout in a bowl should be mixed with water until there is a thick paste. This mixture should be pressed into the crack with a putty knife. Press to fill in the crack and smooth the surface. Leftover grout should not be emptied down the drain. Bowls and tools should be washed before grout dries on them. Plastic sealer can be squeezed directly from the tube to the crack. Use a putty knife to press down and fill the crack. Then smooth the surface. The plastic sealer should be capped whenever you are not using it.

2. Write a set of instructions for one of the following activities. Identify your reader and purpose before you begin. Include appropriate warnings and cautions and develop at least one graphic aid, illustrating some aspect of your instructions.

- Driving from campus to two points of interest in your community and then driving back to campus
- Correctly handling a specific piece of sports equipment
- Performing routine maintenance on an automobile, bicycle, or other vehicle
- Performing an outdoor household chore
- Performing an indoor household chore
- Cooking and serving a specific food
- Performing a specific laboratory test or activity in your field
- Safely handling a specific piece of equipment at your job
- Performing a hobby

3. Using the process explanations of the "Walk-and-Turn Test" in Model 9-5, write a set of instructions for a rookie police officer who is administering the test for the first time.

4. The following are some Sandrunne Medical Laboratory safety guidelines for technicians who handle biohazards on the job. Using this list, write a formal set of procedures for safe handling of biohazards in the laboratory. *Note:* These rules are not sequential steps.

- Cover all superficial wounds or cuts before starting work.
- Work area should be kept disinfected.
- All technicians should wear protective clothing, such as lab coats or aprons, when working with possible biohazard contaminants.
- Major sources of contamination are hand-to-mouth contact, hand-to-eye contact, splashes or aerosol contact with eyes or skin, and direct contact with open wounds or cuts or other skin conditions that permit absorption.
- Wear gloves while handling parts of the instrument that have contact with body fluids, such as serum, plasma, urine, or whole blood.
- Technicians should not eat, drink, smoke, or apply cosmetics while in the laboratory.
- To prevent injury, needles should not be recapped, removed from disposable syringes, or otherwise manipulated by hand.
- Contaminated materials should be disposed of according to the laboratory biohazard control procedures.
- Wash your hands before going from a contaminated area to a noncontaminated area or whenever gloves are removed or changed.
- Biohazardous conditions are defined as situations involving infectious agents, such as the hepatitis B virus, the human immunodeficiency virus (HIV), or the tuberculosis bacterium.
- Wear facial protection when splatter or aerosol formation is possible.
- Procedures should be performed carefully to minimize aerosol formation.
- Keep your hands away from your face.
- Tools or other items should not be placed in the mouth.
- Technicians should not use the biohazard sink for washing hands, rinsing coffee cups, or other personal cleaning.
- Disinfect tools and other items with Y2 Bleach.
- Do not transfer any liquid by mouth.

5. Write a set of procedures, using playscript organization, for a system involving several employees at your job. These procedures will be included in the new company procedures manual.

6. Write a process explanation for a test or system that you use in your major, *or* write a process explanation for a procedure used at your job. Identify a reader and purpose. Include one graphic aid.

CHAPTER 10

Formal Report Elements

SELECTING FORMAL REPORT ELEMENTS

Most in-house reports, whatever their purpose, are in memo format, as illustrated in Chapter 11. Long reports, however, whether internal or external, more often include the formal report elements discussed in this chapter.

Management or company policy usually dictates when formal report elements are appropriate. In some companies, certain report types, such as proposals or feasibility studies, always include formal report elements. In addition, long reports addressed to multiple readers often require formal report elements, such as glossaries and appendixes, to effectively serve all reader purposes.

The formal report is distinguished from the informal report by the inclusion of some or all of the special elements described in this chapter.

WRITING FRONT MATTER

Front matter includes all the elements that precede the text of a report. Front-matter elements help a reader (1) locate specific information and (2) become familiar with the general content and organization of the report.

Title Page

A *title page* records the report title, writer, reader, and date. It is usually the first page of a long formal report. In some companies, the format is standard. If it is not, include these items:

- Title of the report, centered in the top third of the page
- Name, title, and company of the primary reader or readers, centered in the middle of the page
- Name, title, and company of the writer, centered in the bottom third of the page
- Date of the report, centered directly below the writer's name

The title should accurately reflect the contents of the report. Use key words that identify the subject quickly and inform readers about the purpose of the report.

Title:	Parking
Revision:	Feasibility Study of Expanding Parking Facilities
Title:	Office Equipment
Revision:	Proposal for Computer Purchases

Transmittal Letter or Memo

A *transmittal letter* or *memo* sends the report to the reader. In addition to establishing the title and purpose of the report, the transmittal letter provides a place for the writer to add comments about procedures, recommendations, or other matters that do not fit easily into the report itself. Here, too, the writer may offer to do further work or credit others who assisted with the report. Place the transmittal letter either immediately after the title page or immediately before it, as company custom dictates. In some companies, writers use a transmittal memo, but the content and placement are the same as for a transmittal letter. If the transmittal letter simply sends the report, it often is before the title page. However, if the transmittal letter contains supplementary information about the report or recommends more study or action, some writers place it immediately after the title page, where it functions as a part of the report. In your transmittal letter,

- State the report title, and indicate that the report is attached.
- Establish the purpose of the report.
- Explain why, when, and by whom the report was authorized.
- Summarize briefly the main subject of the report.
- Point out especially relevant facts or details.
- Explain any unusual features or organization.
- Acknowledge those who offered valuable assistance in gathering information, preparing appendixes, and so on.
- Mention any planned future reports.
- Thank readers for the opportunity to prepare the report, or offer to do more study on the subject.
- Recommend further action, if needed.

Table of Contents

The *table of contents* alerts the reader to (1) pages that contain specific topics, (2) the overall organization and content of the report, and (3) specific and supplemental materials, such as appendixes. Place the table of contents directly after the transmittal letter or title page, if that is after the transmittal letter, and before all other elements. The title page is not listed in the table of contents, but it is counted as page i. All front matter for a report is numbered in small Roman numerals. The first page of the report proper is page 1 in Arabic numbers, and all pages after that have Arabic numbers. In your table of contents,

- List all major headings with the same wording used in the report.
- List subsections, indented under major headings, if the subheadings contain topics that readers are likely to need.

- List all formal report elements, such as the abstract and appendixes, except for the title page.

- Include the titles of appendixes, for example:

  APPENDIX A: PROJECTED COSTS

- Do not underline headings in the table of contents even if they are underlined in the text.

List of Figures

Any graphic aid, such as a bar graph, map, or flowchart that is not a table with numbers or words in columns, is called a *figure*. The list of figures follows the table of contents. List each figure by both number and title, and indicate page numbers:

Figure 1. Map of Mining Surveys 6

Figure 2. Wall Excavation 8

Figure 3. Light Diffusion..9

List of Tables

The list of tables appears directly after the list of figures. List each table by number and title, and indicate page numbers:

Table 1. Equipment Downtime...3

Table 2. Production by Region 5

If your report contains only two or three figures and tables, you may combine them into one "List of Illustrations." In this case, list figures first and then tables.

Abstract and Executive Summary

An *abstract* is a synopsis of the most important points in a report and provides readers with a preview of the full contents. An abstract, which can be either descriptive or informative, is usually one paragraph of no more than 200 words. An *executive summary* is a longer synopsis of one to two pages that provides a more comprehensive overview than the abstract does. An executive summary covers a report's main points, conclusions, recommendations, and the impact of the subject on company planning. In some cases, readers may rely completely on such a synopsis, as, for instance, when a nonexpert reader must read a report written for experts. In other cases, readers use these synopses to orient themselves to the main topics in a report before reading it completely.

The abstract or executive summary in a formal report usually follows the list of tables, if there is one. In some companies, the style is to place an abstract on the title page or immediately after the title page. Whether you decide to include the longer executive summary or the shorter abstract depends on company custom and the expectations of your readers. In some companies, executives prefer to see both an abstract and an executive summary with long reports. If a report is very long, an executive summary allows a fuller synopsis and provides readers with a better understanding of the report contents and importance than an abstract will. Even though they are all synopses, the two types of abstracts and the executive summary provide readers with different emphases.

Descriptive Abstract

A *descriptive abstract* names the topics covered in a report without revealing details about these topics. Here is a descriptive abstract for a proposal to modify and redecorate a hotel restaurant:

> This proposal recommends a complete redesign of the Bronze Room in the Ambassador Hotel to increase our appeal to hotel guests and local customers. A description of the suggested changes, as well as costs, suggested contractors, and management reorganization, is included.

Because a descriptive abstract does not include details, readers must read the full report to learn about specifics, such as cost and planned decor. Descriptive abstracts have become less popular in recent years because they do not provide enough information for busy readers who do not want to read full reports.

Informative Abstract

An *informative abstract*, the one frequently used for formal reports and technical articles, describes the major subjects in a report and summarizes the conclusions and recommendations. This informative abstract is for the same report covered by the preceding descriptive abstract:

> This proposal recommends converting the Bronze Room of the Ambassador Hotel into a nineteenth-century supper club. This style has been successful in hotels in comparable markets, and research shows that it creates an up-scale atmosphere for the entire hotel. The construction and decorating will take about 10 weeks and cost $245,000. The conversion is expected to halt a 5-year decline in local customer traffic and occupancy rates. This redesign of the Bronze Room should put the hotel in a favorable position to compete for convention groups interested in history and the arts.

This informative abstract includes more details and gives a more complete synopsis of the report contents than the descriptive abstract does.

Executive Summary

An *executive summary* includes (1) background of the situation, (2) major topics, (3) significant details, (4) major conclusions or results, (5) recommendations, and (6) a discussion of how the subject can affect the company. Writers often use headings in executive summaries to guide readers to information. Here is an executive summary of the hotel proposal:

> This proposal recommends complete redecoration of the Bronze Room from its present style into a late nineteenth-century supper club.
>
> **Problem**
>
> The Ambassador Hotel has experienced declining occupancy rates and declining local customer traffic for the past 5 years. Three new hotels, all part of well-known chains, have opened within one mile of the Ambassador. The Ambassador's image of elegant sophistication has been eroded by the competition of larger, more modern hotels.
>
> **Comparable Markets**
>
> Research indicates that the image of the main dining room in a hotel has a direct impact on marketing the hotel. A late nineteenth-century style for a hotel main dining room has been successful in Saint Louis, Milwaukee, and Cleveland. These markets are comparable to ours. A survey by Hathaway Associates indicated that local customers would be interested in a dining atmosphere that reflects old-time sophistication and elegance. Beryl Whitman, president of Whitman Design Studio, has prepared a proposal for specific design changes and suggestions for a new name for the Bronze Room.
>
> **Advantages**
>
> - A late nineteenth-century style will create an upscale sophisticated atmosphere that contrasts with the ultramodern look of the competing hotels.
> - Our distinction will come from a perceived return to gracious and efficient hotel service of the past.
> - Other hotel facilities will be undisturbed.
> - Renovation will take 10 weeks and can be completed by November 1, in time for the holiday season.

- Projected cost of $245,000 can be regained within 18 months if we attract convention groups interested in history, such as the North Central Historians Association.
- We can expect an immediate 20% increase in local customers.

The recommendation is to redesign the Bronze Room with a target completion date of November 1.

Abstracts and executive summaries, important elements in formal reports, are difficult to write because they require summarizing in a few words what a report covers in many pages. Remember that an informative abstract or executive summary should stand alone for readers who do not intend to read the full report immediately. In preparing abstracts and executive summaries, follow these guidelines:

1. Write the abstract or executive summary after you complete the report.
2. Identify which topics are essential to a synopsis of the report by checking major headings and subheadings.
3. Rewrite the original sentences into a coherent summary. Simply linking sentences taken out of the original report will not produce a smooth style.
4. Write full sentences, and include articles *a, an,* and *the.*
5. Avoid overly technical language or complicated statistics, which should be in the data sections or an appendix.
6. Do not refer readers to tables or other sections of the original report.
7. If conclusions are tentative, indicate this clearly.
8. Do not add information or opinions not in the original report.
9. Edit the final draft for clarity and coherence.

WRITING BACK MATTER

Back matter includes supplemental elements that some readers need to understand the report information or that provide additional specialized information for some readers.

References

A *reference list* records the sources of information in the report and follows the final section of the report body. Preparation of a reference list is explained later in this chapter under "Documenting Sources."

Glossary/List of Symbols

A *glossary* defines technical terms, such as *volumetric efficiency*, and a *list of symbols* defines scientific symbols, such as *Au*. Include a glossary or list of symbols in a long report if your readers are not familiar with the terms and symbols you use in the report. Also include informal definitions of key terms or symbols in the text to aid readers who do not want to flip pages back and forth looking for definitions with every sentence. If you do use a glossary or list of symbols, say so in the introduction of the report to alert readers to it. The glossary or list of symbols usually follows the references. In some companies, however, custom may dictate that the two lists follow the table of contents. In either case, remember these guidelines:

- Arrange the glossary or list of symbols alphabetically.

- Do not number the terms or symbols.

- Include also any terms or symbols that you are using in a nonstandard or limited way.

- List the terms or symbols on the left side of the page, and put the definition on the right side on the same line:

bugseed	an annual herb in northern temperate regions
Pt	platinum

Appendixes

Appendixes contain supplemental information that is too detailed and technical to fit well into the body of the report or information that some readers need and others do not. Appendixes can include documents, interviews, statistical results, case histories, lists of pertinent items, specifications, or lists of legal references. The recent trend in formal reports has been to place highly technical or statistical information in appendixes for those readers who are interested in such material. Remember these guidelines:

- Label appendixes with letters, such as "Appendix A" and "Appendix B," if you have more than one.

- Provide a title for each appendix, such as "Appendix A. Questionnaire Sample."

- Indicate in the body of the report that an appendix provides supplemental information on a particular topic, such as "See Appendix C for cost figures."

STRATEGIES—Contractions and Clipped Words

Avoid using contractions, such as **can't** or **don't** in formal documents.

No: The plywood sheets **don't** fit.

Yes: The plywood sheets **do not** fit.

Also avoid using clipped words, such as **lab** or **rep**, in formal documents.

No: The **lab** results were inconclusive.

Yes: The **laboratory** results were inconclusive.

DOCUMENTING SOURCES

Documenting sources refers to the practice of citing original sources of information used in formal reports, journal articles, books, or any document that includes evidence from published works. Cite your information sources for the following reasons:

- Readers can locate the original sources and read them if they want.

- You are not personally responsible for every fact in the document.

- You will avoid charges of plagiarism. *Plagiarism* is the unacknowledged use of information discovered and reported by others or the use of their exact words, copied verbatim.

In writing a report that relies somewhat on material from other sources, remember to document information when you are doing either of the following:

- Using a direct quotation from another source

- Paraphrasing information from another source

If, however, the information you are presenting is generally known and readily available in general reference sources, such as dictionaries and encyclopedias, you need not document it. You would not have to document a statement that water is made up of two parts hydrogen and one part oxygen or that it boils at 212°F and freezes at 32°F. In addition, if your readers are experts in a particular field, you need not document basic facts or theories that all such specialists would know.

The documentation system frequently used in the natural sciences, social sciences, and technical fields is the *American Psychological Association (APA) system,* also called the *author-date system.* Another system often used in the sciences or technical fields is the *number-reference system.* Although all documentation systems are designed to help readers find original sources, the systems do vary slightly.

The following is a list of style guides for particular associations or fields.

American National Standard for Bibliographic References

CBE Style Manual: A Guide for Authors, Editors, and Publishers in the Biological Sciences

The Chicago Manual of Style

Guide for Preparation of Air Force Publications

Handbook for Authors of Papers in the Journals of the American Chemical Society

A Manual for Authors of Mathematical Papers

MLA Handbook for Writers of Research Papers

NASA Publications Manual

Publication Manual of the American Psychological Association

Style Manual for Engineering Authors and Editors

Uniform Requirements for Manuscripts Submitted to Biomedical Journals

APA System: Citations in the Text

In the APA system, when you refer to a source in the text, include the author and the date of publication. This paragraph from a psychologist's report illustrates in-text citation:

> Television's portrayal of women has been called "the best of recent years" (Steenland, 1986, p. 17). Since reader-response theory (Allen, 1987) suggests that viewers interpret images individually, research is now focusing on testing viewer perceptions. Atwood, Zahn, and Webber (1986) used random telephone dialing to test viewer response to women on television and found no differences between male and female viewers. A British study (Gunter & Wober, 1982) found that heavy viewers of crime action shows had lowered perceptions of women as traditionally feminine. Durkin (1983) provides a comprehensive survey of all relevant studies of audience perception involving children. A recent study (Howard et al., 1998) reported significant differences in the ratings of female television characters based on the gender of the viewer. Howard et al. also provided comparisons within and among groups of male and female viewers.

Notice these conventions of the APA citation system:

1. If an author's name begins a sentence, place the date of the work in parentheses immediately after.

2. If an author is not referred to directly in a sentence, place both the author's last name and the year of publication, separated by a comma, in parentheses.

3. If there are multiple authors, cite all the names up to six. If there are more than six authors, cite only the first author and follow with et al.:

   Jones et al. (1999) reported. . . .

4. If multiple authors are cited in parentheses, separate names with commas, and use an ampersand (&) between the last two names.

5. If an author is referred to more than once in a single paragraph, do not repeat the year in parentheses as long as the second reference clearly refers to the same author and date as in the first reference.

6. If you are using a direct quotation, state the page numbers immediately after the quotation:

   ". . . further research" (Jackson, 1995, p. 46).

   Jackson (1995) found ". . . further research" (p. 46).

7. If you are citing two works by the same author, give the year of publication of both works:

   Young (1979, 1984) disagrees. . . .

8. If you are citing two works by the same author, published in the same year, distinguish them by *a, b, c,* and so on:

   Lucas (1987a, 1987b) refers to. . . .

9. If you are citing several works by different authors in the same parentheses, list the works alphabetically by first author:

   Several studies tested for side effects but found no significant results (Bowman & Johnson, 1990; Mullins, 1979; Roberts & Allen, 1975; Townsend, 1988).

10. Use last names only unless two authors have the same surname; then include initials to avoid confusion:

    W. S. Caldwell (1993) and R. D. Caldwell (1988) reported varied effects. . . .

    Heightened effects were noted (R. D. Caldwell, 1988; W. S. Caldwell, 1993).

11. Use an *ellipsis* (three spaced periods) to indicate omissions from direct quotations:

    Bagwell (1998) commented, "This handbook will not fulfill most needs of a statistician, but . . . model formulas are excellent."

12. If the omission in a quotation comes at the end of the sentence, use four periods to close the quotation:

    According to Martin (1994), "Researchers should inquire further into effects of repeated exposure. . . ."

13. Use brackets to enclose any information you insert into a quotation:

    Krueger (1997) cited "continued criticism from the NCWW [National Commission on Working Women] regarding salary differences between the sexes" (p. 12).

14. If you are citing personal communication, such as e-mail, telephone conversations, letters, or messages on an electronic bulletin board, state initials and last name of the sender and the date:

    K. J. Kohls said the sales reports were unavailable (personal communication, January 7, 1997).

    The sales reports were unavailable (K. J. Kohls, personal communication, January 7, 1997).

APA System: List of References

This list of references for a report on the job or college paper includes each source cited in the document. Follow these conventions for business reports and college papers:

1. Do not number the list.
2. Indent the second line of the reference three spaces.
3. List items alphabetically according to the last name of the first author.
4. If there is no author, alphabetize by the title, excluding *a*, *an*, and *the*.
5. Alphabetize letter by letter.

   Bach, J. K.
   Bachman, D. F.
   DeJong, R. T.
   DuVerme, S. C.
   MacArthur, K. O.
   Martin, M. R.
   McDouglas, T. P.
   Realm of the Incas
   Sebastian, J. K.
   St. John, D. R.
   Szartzar, P. Y.

6. Place single-author works ahead of multiple-author works if the first author is the same:

   Fromming, W. R.
   Fromming, W. R., Brown, P. K., & Smith, S. J.

7. Alphabetize by the last name of the second author if the first author is the same in several references:

Coles, T. L., James, R. E., & Wilson, R. P.
Coles, T. L., Wilson, R. P., & Allen, D. R.

8. List several works by one author according to the year of publication. Repeat the author's name in each reference. If two works have the same publication date, distinguish them by using *a, b, c,* and so on, and alphabetize by title:

Deland, M. W. (1983).
Deland, M. W. (1989a). Major differences . . .
Deland, M. W. (1989b). Separate testing . . .

Remember that each reference should include author, year of publication, title, and publication data. Here are some sample references for typical situations:

1. *Journal article—one author:*

    Taylor, H. (1995). Vanishing wildlife. *Modern Science, 36,* 356–367.

    Note:

    • Use initials, not first names, for authors.
    • Capitalize only the first word in a title, except for proper names.
    • Underline or italicize journal names and volume numbers.

2. *Journal article—two authors:*

    Hawkins, R. P., & Pingree, S. (1981). Uniform messages and habitual viewing: Unnecessary assumptions in social reality effects. *Human Communication Research, 7,* 291–301.

    Note:

    • Use a comma and ampersand between author names.
    • Capitalize the first word after a colon in an article title.
    • Capitalize all important words in journal names.

3. *Journal article—more than two authors:*

    Geis, F. L., Brown, V., Jennings, J., & Corrado-Taylor, D. (1984). Sex vs. status in sex-associated stereotypes. *Sex Roles, 11,* 771–785.

    Note:

    • Use an ampersand between the names of the last two authors.
    • List all authors even if *et al.* was used in text references.

4. *Journal article—issues separately paginated:*

    Battison, J. (1988). Using effective antenna height to determine coverage. *The LPTV Report, 3*(1), 11.

    Note: If each issue begins on page 1, place the issue number in parentheses directly after the volume number without a space between them.

5. *Magazine article:*

Lamana, D. (1995, August). Tossed at sea. *Cinescape, 1,* 18–23.

Note:

- Include the volume number.
- Include day, month, and year for weekly publications.

6. *Newspaper article—no author:*

Proposed diversion of Great Lakes. (1999, December 7). *Cleveland Plain Dealer,* pp. C14–15.

Note:

- If an article has no author, alphabetize by the first word of the title, excluding *a, an,* and *the.*
- If a newspaper has several sections, include the section identification as well as page numbers.
- Use pp. before page numbers for newspapers.
- Capitalize all proper names in a title.

7. *Newspaper article—author:*

Sydney, J. H. (1996, August 12). Microcomputer graphics for water pollution control data. *The Chicago Tribune,* pp. D6, 12.

Note: If an article appears on nonconsecutive pages, cite all page numbers, separated by commas.

8. *Article in an edited collection—one editor:*

Allen, R. C. (1987). Reader-oriented criticism and television. In R. C. Allen (Ed.), *Channels of discourse* (pp. 74–112). Chapel Hill, NC: Univ. of North Carolina Press.

Note:

- Capitalize only the first word in a book title, except for proper names.
- Underline or italicize book titles.
- Use initials and the last name of the editor in standard order.
- Use *pp.* with page numbers of the article in parentheses after the book title.
- Use the Postal Service ZIP code abbreviations for states in the publication information.

9. *Article in an edited collection—two or more editors:*

Zappen, J. P. (1983). A rhetoric for research in sciences and technologies. In P. V. Anderson, R. J. Brockmann, & C. R. Miller (Eds.), *New essays in technical and scientific communications: Research theory, practice* (pp. 123–138). Farmingdale, NY: Baywood.

Note:

- List all editors' names in standard order.
- Use *Eds.* in parentheses if there is more than one editor.

10. *One book—one author:*

Sagan, C. (1980). *Cosmos.* New York: Random House.

Note: Do not include the state or country if the city of publication is well known for publishing, such as New York, Chicago, London, or Tokyo.

11. *Book—more than one author:*

Johanson, D. C., & Edey, M. A. (1981). *Lucy: The beginnings of humankind.* New York: Simon and Schuster.

Note: Capitalize the first word after a colon in a book title.

12. *Edited book:*

Hunt, J. D., & Willis, P. (Eds.). (1990). *The genius of the place: The English landscape garden 1620–1820.* Cambridge, MA: MIT Press.

Note:

- Place a period after *Eds.* in parentheses.
- Include the state if the city is not well known or could be confused with another city by the same name (e.g., Cambridge, England).

13. *Book edition after first edition:*

Mills, G. H., & Walter, J. A. (1986). *Technical writing* (5th ed.). New York: Holt, Rinehart and Winston.

Note: Do not place a period between the title and the edition in parentheses.

14. *Article in a proceedings:*

Pickett, S. J. (1995). Editing for an international audience. *Proceedings of the Midwest Conference on Multicultural Communication, 12,* 72–86.

Note: If the proceedings are published annually with a volume number, treat them the same as a journal.

15. *Unpublished conference paper:*

Dieken, D. S. (1999, May). *The legal aspects of writing job descriptions.* Paper presented at the meeting of the Southwest Association for Business Communication, San Antonio, TX.

Note: Include the month of the meeting if available.

16. Report in a document deposit service:

Cooper, J. F. (1995). *Clinical practice in nursing education* (Report No. CNC-95-6). Nashville, TN: Council for Nursing Curriculum. (ERIC Document Reproduction Service No. ED 262 116)

Note: Include document number at the end of reference in parentheses.

17. *Report—corporate author, author as publisher:*

American Association of Junior Colleges. (1999). *Extending campus resources: Guide to selecting clinical facilities for health technology programs* (Rep. No. 67). Washington, DC: Author.

Note:

- If the report has a number, insert it between the title of the report and the city of publication, in parentheses, followed by a period.
- If the report was written by a department staff, use that as the author, such as "Staff of Accounting Unit." Then give the corporation or association in full as the publisher.

18. *Dissertation—obtained on microfilm:*

Jones, D. J. (1986). Programming as theory foundation: Microprocessing and microprogramming. *Dissertation Abstracts International, 46,* 4785B–4786B. (University Microfilms No. 86-08, 134)

Note: Include the microfilm number in parentheses at the end of the reference.

19. *Dissertation—obtained from a university:*

Heintz, P. D. (1985). Television and psychology: Testing for frequency effects on children (Doctoral Dissertation, The University of Akron, 1985). *Dissertation Abstracts International, 45,* 4644A.

Note: When using the printed copy of a dissertation, include the degree-granting university and the year of dissertation in parentheses after the title.

20. *Review of Books, Films, and Television Programs:*

Kelves, D. J. (1995, July 30). The race to Armageddon [Review of the book *Dark sun*]. *The New York Times Book Review,* 9.

Jones, S. W. (1994, November 18). The big bite [Review of the film *Interview with the vampire*]. *Entertainment Weekly, 5,* 51–52.

Mason, S. B. (1995, August 12). [Review of television program *Justice Files*]. *Television Commentary, 16,* 36.

Note:

- Identify the book, film, or television program in brackets.
- When the review has no title, retain the brackets around the material identifying the book, film, or television program.

21. *Films and Television Programs:*

Reynolds, K. (Director). (1995). *Waterworld* [Film]. Los Angeles: Universal City Studios, Inc.

Golden, R. S. (Producer). (1997). *Sherlock Holmes mysteries.* New York: Arts & Entertainment Network.

O'Hara, S. C. (1995, June 4). The heist. (P. Corbett, Director). In W. Brown (Producer), *Matlock*. New York: American Broadcasting Corp.

Note:

- For a film, cite the director, considered the primary creative contributor.
- Identify the title as a film in brackets before the period.
- Cite the studio and the city where it has headquarters.
- For a small independent film or an industrial film, give the full address of the distributor or owner in parentheses.
- For a television series, cite the producer and the network that broadcast the series.
- For an individual television program, cite the writer first, the date of broadcast, with the title of the episode followed by the director in parentheses. Then cite the producer of the series and the series name.
- If the names of television writers, directors, or producers are not available, cite the title of the episode or the series name first as you would an article without an author.

22. *Computer Software or Program:*

    Lippard, G. L. (1998). Torsion analysis and design of steel beams [Computer software]. Astoria, NY: Structural Design Software, Inc. (AX-P34-57)

    Note:

    - Identify the title as computer program or software in brackets following the title without any punctuation between the brackets and the title.
    - Cite the city and producer of the software or program.
    - If the item has an identification number, place it in parentheses following the name of the software producer.

23. *Information on CD-ROM:*

    Mitchell, R. N. (1995, July 12). World mining trends [CD-ROM]. *Foreign economic projections*. U.S. Department of Commerce.

    Brown, P. K. (1995). Investment banking in Norway [CD-ROM]. *Business Today, 23*(5), 16–18. Abstract from: ABI/INFORM: 12560.00

    Note:

    - Cite *CD-ROM* in brackets immediately after the title, followed by a period.
    - Give source and retrieval number if possible.
    - Do not put a period after a retrieval number because it may appear to be part of the electronic address.

24. *On-line Databases:*

    Fatal workplace injuries (1993, June) [On-line database]. Washington, DC: U.S. Dept. of Labor, Occupational Safety & Health Administration. Available: http://www.osha.gov/oshstats/transtbl.html [1998, July 6].

Note:

- Cite the author first. If there is no author, cite the title first, followed by the date of the material in parentheses.
- Place *On-line database* in brackets after the date of the material, followed by a period.
- Cite the full electronic address, including secondary pages.
- Provide the date you accessed the material in brackets at the end of the citation.

25. *World Wide Web Home Pages:*

David Clark Company, Incorporated. [On-line]. Available: http://www. davidclark.com/headsets.html [1998, July 10].

Note:

- Cite the full name of the company, organization, or individual followed by a period.
- Put *On-line* in brackets followed by a period.

26. *On-line Newspapers:*

Smith, J. (1998, June 6). Women in banking. *USA Today* [On-line]. Available: http://www.usatoday.com/money.html [1998, June 6].

New rules for tennis rankings. (1998, June 10). *USA Today* [On-line]. Available: http://www.usatoday.com/sports/tennis.html [1998, June 10].

Note:

- Cite the author first if available. If no author is given, begin with the title, followed by a period.
- Place the date of the item in parentheses directly after the author if available or after the title.
- Spell out the full name of the newspaper and underline or italicize.
- Place *On-line* in brackets immediately after the name of the newspaper followed by a period.
- Give the date you accessed the information in brackets at the end of the citation even if it is the same date as the newspaper material.

27. *E-mail Communication:*

Smith, J. (smith@aol.com). (1998, September 16). Suggestions for conference. E-mail to D. C. Reep (dreep@uakron.edu).

Note:

- Although the current APA guide advises against including e-mail in a reference list, most writers now are including citations for e-mail. Consult your instructor.
- Cite the sender's name first, followed by his or her e-mail address in parentheses, followed by a period.

- Cite the date the e-mail was sent in parentheses, followed by a period.
- State the subject if there is one.
- Cite the receiver's name and give his or her e-mail address in parentheses.

Information available on-line may change or disappear immediately after you access it. Always use a print source if you can. Standards for citing electronic documents have not been completely developed, and the most recent APA guide does not cover most electronic sources. Items 24 through 27 here are logical formats based on usual APA style.[1]

Number-Reference System

In the number-reference system, the references are written as shown above, but the reference list is numbered. The list may be organized in one of two ways:

1. List the items alphabetically by last name of author.

2. List the items in the order they are cited in the text.

The in-text citations use only the number of the reference in parentheses. Following is the same paragraph shown in APA style earlier to illustrate in-text citations. Here the number-reference system is used; the reference list is in the order the references appear in the text.

> Television's portrayal of women has been called "the best of recent years" (1:17). Since reader-response theory (2) suggests that viewers interpret images individually, research is now focusing on testing viewer perceptions. Reference 3 used random telephone dialing to test viewer response to women on television and found no differences between male and female viewers. A British study (4) found that heavy viewers of crime action shows had lowered perceptions of women as traditionally feminine. A comprehensive survey (5) of all relevant studies of audience perception involving children was completed in 1985. A recent study (6) reported significant differences in the ratings of female television characters based on the gender of the viewer. The same study also provided comparisons within and among groups of male and female viewers.

Notice these conventions for the number-reference system:

1. Page numbers are included in the parentheses, separated from the reference number by a colon.

2. Sentences may begin with "Reference 6 states. . . ." However, for readability, rewrite as often as possible to include the reference later in the sentence.

For some readers, the APA system is easier to use because dates and the names of authors appear in the text. The number-reference system requires readers to flip back and forth to the reference list to find dates and authors. Whichever system you use, be consistent throughout your report.

CHAPTER SUMMARY

This chapter explains how to prepare front and back matter for formal reports and how to document sources of information. Remember:

- Front matter consists of elements that help readers locate specific information and become familiar with report organization and content before reading the text. Included are the title page, transmittal letter or memo, table of contents, list of figures, list of tables, abstract, and executive summary.

- Back matter consists of elements that some readers need to understand the report information or that provide additional information for readers. Included are a glossary, list of symbols, and appendixes.

- Documenting sources is the practice of citing the original sources of information used in formal reports and other documents.

- Sources of information should be documented whenever a direct quotation is used or whenever information is paraphrased and used.

- The APA system of documentation is used frequently in the natural sciences, social sciences, and technical fields for citations in the text and for references.

- The number-reference system, similar to APA style, is also used in the sciences and technical fields.

SUPPLEMENTAL READINGS IN PART 2

Benson, P. J. "Writing Visually: Design Considerations in Technical Publications," *Technical Communication*, p. 454.

"Six Graphics Guidelines," *Simply Stated*, p. 535.

Tarutz, J. H. "Editing for an International Audience," *Technical Editing*, p. 551.

ENDNOTE

1. Mary Ellen Guffey, "Formats for the Citation of Electronic Sources in Business Writing," *Business Communication Quarterly* 60.1 (March 1997): 59–76.

The following samples of front matter are from the same formal report—a feasibility study prepared by an outside consultant. The writer has evaluated three possible solutions to the company's need for more space and presents his findings along with his recommendation.

- The title page reflects the contents and purpose of the report with a descriptive title.
- The transmittal letter presents the report to the client, identifies the subject and purpose, and includes the recommendation. The writer also credits two company managers who assisted him. In a goodwill closing, the consultant also comments favorably on his working relationship with the client and offers to consult further.
- The table of contents shows the main sections of the report. Notice that the writer uses all capitals for main headings and capitals and lowercase letters for subheadings. The pagination is in small Roman numerals for front matter and in Arabic numbers for the report body and back matter.
- The list of illustrations includes both figures and tables. Notice that tables are listed second even though they appear in the report ahead of the figures.
- The executive summary for this report identifies the purpose, briefly describes the problem, reviews the main elements for each alternative solution, and states the recommendation. This report probably will have several secondary readers before company officers make a decision on relocation. The executive summary provides more detail for these readers than an abstract would. Notice that the page includes the report title and the words *executive summary*. The Roman numeral pagination is centered at the bottom of the page.

Discussion

1. Compare this transmittal letter with those that appear in Models 11-7 and 12-6. Discuss which elements in each are meant to help the reader use the report.

2. Discuss the visual aspects of the table of contents. What features help guide the reader to specific information?

3. Based on the information in the executive summary, draft an informative abstract for this report. Discuss which information you can cut out, and compare drafts with your classmates.

FEASIBILITY STUDY OF OFFICE EXPANSION
FOR UNITED COMPUTER TECHNOLOGIES, INC.

Prepared for
Joanne R. Galloway
Senior Vice President
United Computer Technologies, Inc.

By
William D. Santiago
Senior Partner
PRT Management Consultants, Inc.

March 3, 1999

PRT MANAGEMENT CONSULTANTS, INC.
10 City Center Square
Sherwood Hills, Ontario N5A 6X8

(519) 555-3000   Fax (519) 555-3002

March 3, 1999

Ms. Joanne R. Galloway
Senior Vice President
United Computer Technologies, Inc.
616 Erie Street
Sherwood Hills, Ontario N5A 2R4

Dear Ms. Galloway:

Enclosed is the feasibility study PRT has prepared at your request. The report analyzes the options United Computer Technologies has in expanding the present physical space.

As we discussed in our February 2 meeting, our firm investigated three reasonable options—redesigning your current facilities, renovating the Wallhaven Complex and moving your offices there, or leasing space in the Huron Circle Building. Our staff researched these possibilities and consulted with the two managers you suggested, Daniel Kaffee in Design Technology and Paul Weinberger in Marketing Systems. We also obtained data from the central office of Retail Facilities, Inc., in Toronto.

Although each option has merit, our report concludes that leasing space in the Huron Circle building is the best choice for your company at this time. The attached report reviews all three options.

Working with you and your staff has been a pleasure. If you have any questions after reading the report or would like to discuss our conclusions, please call me at 555-3000.

Sincerely,

William D. Santiago

William D. Santiago
Senior Partner

WDS:sd

TABLE OF CONTENTS

LIST OF ILLUSTRATIONS

Figures

Tables

EXECUTIVE SUMMARY

**Feasibility Study of Office Expansion
for United Computer Technologies, Inc.**

This report evaluates three options for expanding the office space of United Computer Technologies, Inc. At present, the company has 640 full-time employees and 46 regular part-time employees in office space designed to accommodate 600 people. Also, the company's client traffic has increased 14% in the past year, creating a need for at least three more conference rooms.

Options were evaluated on the basis of cost, time constraints, office layout, location, and appropriateness for the client base.

- **Redesign of the current offices**—Redesign to accommodate present needs would be extensive, requiring wall removal and other major construction. Cost is estimated at $350,000. Clients would have to visit amid noise and debris for the 4 to 5 months of construction.

- **Renovating and moving to the Wallhaven Complex**—The Wallhaven Complex would require some renovation, such as painting, redecorating interior offices, and creating conference rooms. Cost is estimated at $200,000 with a time estimate of 6 weeks until the company could move in. A major drawback is the location near a busy landfill. The area might deter clients.

- **Leasing offices in the Huron Office Building**—This building has adequate space and its location is easy to reach from a major freeway. Some redesign would be needed here, but the building is only 12 years old, so no major construction is necessary. Cost is estimated at $60,000.

Based on the estimated costs and the desire of United Computer Technologies to expand as soon as possible, the recommendation is to lease offices in the Huron Office Building.

v

This model contains samples of back matter.

- The reference list is from a student research report on ancient Celtic weapons. The writer uses the APA documentation style. Notice that the header at upper right includes the writer's name and the page number.

- The glossary is from a long technical report to multiple readers. The writer knows that at least half the readers are not experts in the technical subject and includes the glossary to help readers understand the information.

- The sample appendix is from a company reference manual and lists the specifications for a technical procedure. Notice that a brief description of the particular features or capacity of each component is included.

Discussion

1. Discuss the visual design of the glossary and the appendix. What features help readers who need this information?

2. As a self-test, identify the type of source (i.e., article, book chapter, etc.) in each item of the reference list. Compare your results with a classmate. If you disagree about an item, compare it to the documentation samples in this chapter and identify the type of source.

Drake-16

REFERENCE LIST

Albers, G. T. (1994, March 3). Celtic chariots at Telemon. Historic Trails, 12, 23–26, 87.

The Battersea shield. (1994, June 23). Boston Globe, p. B8.

Buford, J. G., & Longstreet, J. R. (1994). Celtic excavations in 1990. Journal of the Ancient World, 42(3), 25–41.

Cunliffe, B. R. (1992). Pits, preconceptions and propitiation in the British Iron Age. Oxford Journal of Archaeology, 11, 69–83.

Dukes, J. T. (Director). (1994). Iron Age hillfort [Film]. (Available from History Cinema, 62 South Street, Chicago, IL 60610)

Hancock, G. H., Lee, R. T., & Berenger, T. N. (1995). The Celtic longboat. Proceedings of the Northeast Association of Historians, 16, 43–49.

Merriman, N. (1987). Value and motivation in prehistory: The evidence for Celtic spirit. In I. Hodder (Ed.), The archaeology of Celtic meanings (pp. 111–116). Cambridge, England: Cambridge Univ. Press.

Niblett, R. T. (1992). A chieftain's burial from St. Albans. Antiquity, 66, 917–929.

Pleiner, R. (1993). The Celtic sword. Oxford: Oxford Univ. Press.

Rigby, V. (1986). The iron age: Continuity or invasion? In P. Longworth & C. J. Cherry (Eds.), Archaeology in Britain since 1945 (pp. 52–72). London: British Museum.

Searching for Celtic weapons. (1997, April 3). USA Today [On-line]. Available: http://www.usatoday.com/life.html [1997, April 3].

GLOSSARY

Accelerometer ....An electrical device that measures vibration and converts the signal to electrical output.

Air/Fuel Mixture........................A ratio of the amount of air mixed with fuel before it is burned in the combustion chamber.

Ammeter..................................An electric meter that measures current.

Amplitude ....The maximum rise or fall of a voltage signal from 0 volts.

Battery-Hot ....Circuit fed directly from the starter relay terminal. Voltage is available whenever the battery is charged.

Blown ....A melted fuse filament caused by overload.

Capacitor ....A device for holding or storing an electric charge.

DVOM
   (Digital Volt-Ohmmeter) ....A meter that measures voltage and resistance and displays them on a liquid crystal display.

ECA (Electronic Control
   Assembly) ....See Processor

Fuse..A device containing soft metal that melts and breaks the circuit when it is overloaded.

Induced Current ....The current generated in a conductor as a magnetic field moves across the conductor.

Oscillograph ....A device for recording the waveforms of changing currents or voltages.

APPENDIX D: ACS:180 SPECIFICATIONS

This section summarizes the ACS:180 specifications. The ACS:180 design meets the requirements of the following agencies:

- UL

- CSA

- IEC

- JIS

- FCC Class A

- VDE Class A

Component Specifications

Cuvette	disposable reaction vessel with a 1.0-mL maximum fill volume
Cuvette Loading Bin	holds 250 cuvettes and automatically feeds the cuvettes into the track
Cuvette Preheater	regulated at a temperature of 37.0°C (+/−0.5°C) to heat the cuvettes
Cuvette Track	aluminum track, thermostatically controlled by four thermal electric devices (TEDs) to maintain the present temperature of 37.0°C (+/−0.5°C)
Cuvette Waste Bin	autoclavable collection bin fitted with a disposable, biohazard liner that holds up to 250 used cuvettes
Heating Bath	static fluid bath that contains a specially conditioned circulating fluid; fluid temperature is regulated at 37.5°C (+/−1.0°C)
Waste Bottle	removable container that holds approximately 2.8 liters (capacity of 200 tests) of waste fluid
Water Bottle	removable container that holds approximately 2.6 liters (capacity for 200 tests) of deionized water at temperatures between 15.0° and 37.0°C

1. The following abstract of a two-page product description is intended for use in a catalog of exercise equipment. Because of space limitations, the abstracts must be no longer than 50 words. Revise this abstract to retain the information and meet the word limitations.

> The Hercules Treadmill is unusually quiet, easy to operate, and easily adjustable to your personal preferences. The graphic control panel displays real time, speed, and distance. The innovative panel allows the user to program elevation and end time as well as calculate calories and heart rate. Speed, up to 8 mph, and incline, from 0% to 15%, can be adjusted with the touch of a button. The Hercules Treadmill accommodates people up to 375 lb and has a comfortable 20 in. by 64 in. shock-absorbing running deck. The Hercules Treadmill also offers forward and reverse belt movement.

2. Prepare a glossary of five key terms in your field. Exchange glossaries with a classmate in another field and review the entries for clarity.

3. Your boss, Gerald Althorp, is speaking to a high school class about preparing for careers. Read "What Skills Will You Need to Succeed?" by Graham in Part 2, and write an informative abstract. Then write a transmittal memo to accompany the abstract and explain why you think your boss will find the information helpful in his talk at the high school.

4. Here is an informative abstract of the article "Prepare, Listen, Follow Up," by Messmer in Part 2. Read the article and then evaluate how well this abstract represents the article. In groups, write a new informative abstract of the article.

> When looking for a job, arranging an informational interview with someone in the field may help. For a good informational interview, prepare your questions, stick to the time limit, and get names of other people you can contact.

5. If you are writing a long report for one of your classes, write an appropriate transmittal memo to your instructor.

CHAPTER 11

Short and Long Reports

UNDERSTANDING REPORTS

Next to correspondence, reports are the most frequently written documents on the job. Reports usually have several purposes, most commonly these:

- To inform readers about company activities, problems, and plans so that readers are up to date on the current status and can make decisions—for example, a progress report on the construction of an office building or a report outlining mining costs.

- To record events for future reference in decision making—for example, a report about events that occurred during an inspection trip or a report on the agreements made at a conference.

- To recommend specific actions—for example, a report analyzing two production systems and recommending adoption of one of them or a report suggesting a change in a procedure.

- To justify and persuade readers about the need for action in controversial situations—for example, a report arguing the need to sell off certain company holdings or a report analyzing company operations that are hazardous to the environment and urging corrective action.

Reports may vary in length from one page to several hundred, and they may be informal memos, formal bound manuscripts, rigidly defined form reports, such as an accident report at a particular company, or documents for which neither reader nor writer has any preconceived notion of format and organization. Reports may have only one reader or, more frequently, multiple readers with very different purposes.

Whether a report is short or long depends on how much information the reader needs for the specific purpose in the specific situation, not on the subject or the format of the report. Busy people on the job do not want to read reports any longer than necessary to meet their needs. Long reports are usually necessary in the following situations:

- Scientists report results of experiments and investigations.

- Consultants evaluate company operations and recommend changes.

- Company analysts predict future trends in the industry.

- Writers report on complex industry or company developments.

For all reports, analyze reader and purpose before writing, as discussed in Chapter 3, and organize your information, as outlined in Chapter 4. In addition, use the guidelines for planning, gathering information, taking notes, interpreting data, and drafting discussed later in this chapter. Reports for specific purposes are discussed in Chapter 12. The rest of this chapter focuses on the general structure of short and long reports and on ways to develop long reports that deal with complex subjects and require information from many sources.

DEVELOPING SHORT REPORTS

Most short reports within an organization are written as memos. Short reports written to people outside the organization may be formal reports, with the elements described in Chapter 10, or letters, as shown in Models 4-6 and 11-6. Because short reports provide so much of the information needed to conduct daily business and because readers on the job are always pressed for time, most short reports, whatever their format, are organized in the opening-summary, or front-loaded, pattern. The delayed-summary pattern is used primarily when readers are expected to be hostile to the report's subject or conclusions.

Opening-summary Organization

The *opening-summary organization* is often called *front-loaded* because this pattern supplies the reader with the most important information—the conclusions or results—before the specific details that lead to these results or conclusions. The pattern has two or three main sections, depending on the writer's intent to emphasize certain points.

Opening Summary

The opening is a summary of the essential points covered in the report. Through this summary, the reader has an immediate overall grasp of the situation and understands the main point of the report. Include these elements:

- The subject or purpose of the report
- Special circumstances, such as deadlines or cost constraints
- Special sources of information, such as an expert in the subject
- Main issues central to the subject
- Conclusions, results, recommendations

Readers who are not directly involved in the subject often rely solely on the opening summary to keep them informed about the situation. Readers who are directly involved prefer the opening-summary pattern because it previews the report for them so that, when they read the data sections, they already know how the information is related to the report conclusions. Here is an opening from a short report sent by a supervisor of a company testing laboratory to his boss:

> The D120 laboratory conducted a full temperature range test on the 972-K alternator. The test specifications came from the vendor and the Society of Automotive Engineers and are designed to check durability while the alternator is functioning normally. Results indicate that the alternator is acceptable, based on temperature ranges, response times, and pressure loads.

In this opening summary, the supervisor identifies the test he is reporting, cites the standards on which the test is based, and reports the general result—the alternator is acceptable. The reader who needs to know only whether the alternator passed the test does not have to read further.

Data Sections

The middle sections of a short report provide the specific facts relevant to the conclusions or recommendations announced in the opening. The data sections for the report about the alternator would provide figures and specific details about the three tested elements—temperature ranges, response times, and pressure loads—for readers who need this information.

Closing

Reports written in the opening-summary pattern often do not have closings because the reader knows the conclusions from the beginning and reads the data sections for details, making any further conclusions unnecessary. However, in some cases you may want to reemphasize results or recommendations by repeating them in a brief closing. Depending on the needs of your readers, your closing should:

- Repeat significant results/recommendations/conclusions
- Stress the importance of the matter
- Suggest future actions
- Offer assistance or ask for a decision

Here is the closing paragraph from the short report written by the supervisor in the testing laboratory:

> In conclusion, the 972-K alternator fits our needs and does not require a high initial cost. The quality meets our standards as well as those set by the Society of Automotive Engineers. Because we

need to increase our production to meet end-of-the-year demands, we should make a purchase decision by November 10. May I order the 972-K for a production run starting November 20?

In this closing, the supervisor repeats the test results—that the alternator meets company standards. He also reminds his reader about production deadlines and asks for a decision about purchasing the alternators. Because of a pressing deadline, the supervisor believes he needs a closing that urges the reader to reach a quick decision.

Model 11-1 presents a short report in the opening-summary pattern. The writer was told to research the dangers and physical discomfort involved in long-term use of video display terminals. Because employees had been complaining about pain, the writer focuses on solutions to their concerns. The opening summary identifies the problems employees have raised and explains where the writer got her information. She also states her general conclusion—there is no danger to employees and there are ways to increase employee comfort.

The middle sections cover the danger issue first because it is the most serious. Other sections focus on various discomfort issues and offer suggestions. The conclusion briefly recommends the changes and includes an offer to speak on the topic at an upcoming meeting.

Delayed-summary Organization

The *delayed-summary organization,* as its name suggests, does not reveal the main point or result in the opening. This organizational pattern slows down rather than speeds up the reader's understanding of the situation and the details. Use the delayed-summary pattern when you believe that your reader is not likely to agree with your conclusions readily and that reading these conclusions at the start of the report will trigger resistance to the information rather than acceptance. In some cases, too, you may know that your reader usually prefers to read the data before the conclusions or recommendations or that your reader needs to understand the data in order to understand your conclusions or recommendations. The delayed-summary organization has three main sections.

Introductory Paragraph

The introductory paragraph provides the same information as the opening summary, except that it does not include conclusions, results, or recommendations.

Data Sections

The data sections cover details relative to the main subject just as the data sections in the opening-summary pattern do.

To: Michael O'Toole   October 12, 1999
         Director of Human Resources

From: Leila Bracco *LB*
         Division II Supervisor

Re: Problems with Video Display Terminals

As you know, employees who spend most of their day word processing or entering data have been complaining about safety concerns, eye fatigue, and general physical discomfort in using video display terminals (VDTs). Following your suggestion, I researched safety and comfort issues. Since Electric Power, Inc., has a work situation similar to ours, I consulted with Beth Reinhold, Assistant Director of Human Resources, and I obtained an OSHA fact sheet on safety issues (#95-24, January 1, 1995). Overall, I believe we can assure our employees there are no safety concerns in working with VDTs. I also have suggestions for simple modifications to help ease fatigue.

Employee Safety Concerns

The central concern of employees is possible exposure to radiation. I found that the National Institute for Occupational Safety and Health (NIOSH) and the U.S. Army Environmental Hygiene Agency have measured radiation emitted by VDTs. Tests show that levels for all types of radiation are below those allowed in current standards. Employees, therefore, appear to be in no danger from excess radiation.

Although OSHA has no data that any birth defects have resulted from working with VDTs, I suggest we assign employees to other duties during pregnancy to minimize their concerns. We need to encourage employees to report pregnancy at once.

Employee Discomfort

Employees have a variety of complaints about discomfort, including (1) eye fatigue and headaches, (2) pain or stiffness in back, shoulders, or neck, and (3) hand and wrist pain. All of these can be minimized with some adjustments or relatively inexpensive new equipment.

Eye Fatigue. Eye fatigue and headaches can result from glare off the screen and poor lighting. I suggest three changes:

- Consult each employee for preferences in placing the VDT to avoid window glare or reflections. There is no work-related

MODEL 11-1   A Short Report Organized in an Opening-summary Pattern

Mr. Michael O'Toole   -2-   October 12, 1999

reason to have all computers located on the left side of the station as they are now.

- Supplement the current lighting with individual "task" lighting as selected by each employee. We may find that some additional desk lighting will reduce eye strain.

- Purchase viewers to magnify the screen. A new Bausch & Lomb PC Magni-Viewer magnifies the screen text 175% and is easy to attach to a monitor. Cost is about $250 each, and the viewers can be easily moved from computer to computer. Electric Power has purchased these, and employees are quite pleased.

Pain or Stiffness. Pain and stiffness can usually be corrected by adjusting the physical environment of the employee. Work stations should allow flexibility in movement. I suggest we have the vendor for our office furniture make the following adjustments to each employee's specifications:

- Seat and backrest of the employee's chair should support comfortable posture.

- Chair height should allow the entire sole of the foot to rest on the floor.

- Computer screen and document holder should be the same distance from the eye and close together to avoid strain as the employee looks back and forth.

Wrist and Hand Pain. This pain comes from repetitive movement. I suggest the following:

- Regular five-minute breaks should be scheduled so employees can perform simple hand exercises. Our company nurse, Cathy Powell, tells me she has a set of recommended exercises, which takes only 3 to 4 minutes to perform.

- Keyboards should be movable and at a height that allows the hands to be in a reasonably straight line with the forearm.

Conclusion

I suggest we make these simple changes in the work environment by December 1. We should assure employees at once that they are in no danger from excess radiation. I would be happy to make a brief report on this topic at the October 20 meeting of the section supervisors.

MODEL 11-1   *continued*

Closing Summary

Because the introductory paragraph does not include results, conclusions, or recommendations, a closing that summarizes the main points, results, general observations, and recommendations is essential. The closing also may include offers of assistance, reminders about deadlines or other constraints, and requests for meetings or decisions.

The short report in Model 11-2 shows the delayed-summary pattern. The writer is asking for expensive equipment, and he probably suspects that the reader will be resistant to his recommendation. The writer uses the delayed-summary organization so that he can present his rationale, supported by data, before his request. In his closing, the writer stresses the need for the new equipment and suggests a meeting to discuss the matter. In this situation, the opening-summary organization could trigger immediate rejection by the reader, who might not even read the data. Also, depending on the relationship between writer and reader, the opening-summary might seem inappropriately demanding.

STRATEGIES—International Trade Information

These sources are from the Department of Commerce, International Trade Association publication *Export Programs Guide: A Business Guide to Federal Export Assistance*. The guide is free and can be ordered by calling 1-800-USA-TRADE.

Office of Trade and Economic Analysis (OTEA) (www.ita.doc.gov/ tradestats): U.S. foreign trade data by major export categories and foreign markets.

International Data Base (www.census.gov/ipc/www/idbnew.html): Up-to-date global demographic and social information.

DEVELOPING LONG REPORTS

Long reports (over five pages) may be written as memos or letters, but frequently they are written as formal documents with such elements as appendixes and a table of contents, as explained in Chapter 10. Long reports tend to deal with complex subjects that involve large amounts of data, such as an analysis of how well a company's 12 branch offices are performing with recommendations for shutting down or merging some offices. In addition to dealing with complicated information, a long report nearly always has multiple readers who are concerned with different aspects of the subject and have different purposes for using the information in the report.

TO: T. R. Lougani   January 16, 1999
        Vice President, Support Services

FROM: C. S. Chen   *CSC*
        Asst. Director of Radiology

SUBJECT: **Ultrasound Equipment**

Since ultrasound is a noninvasive procedure and presents no radiation
risk to the patient, it has become increasingly popular with most
physicians. In our department, ultrasound use over the past five years
has increased 32%. In 1995, we performed 1479 procedures, and last
year we performed 2186 procedures. We expect this increased demand
to continue. To prepare for the demand on our equipment (estimated
2297 this year), we need to consider ways to increase our capability.

Updating Current Equipment.   One possibility is to update the current
ultrasound unit with new software. Costs for updating the present
equipment are as follows:

Current unit update	$28,000
Maintenance contract	8,500
(first year)	————
Total	$36,500

The maintenance contracts will increase slightly in each succeeding year.
The maintenance charge is rather high because, as the equipment ages,
more replacement parts will be needed. The basic hardware is now
seven years old. Although updating the present equipment will improve
the performance of the equipment, it will only marginally increase the
number of procedures that can be performed over a 24-hour period. We
cannot reasonably expect to make up the cost of updating our equipment
because our volume will not increase significantly.

Purchasing New Equipment.   Purchasing new ultrasound equipment
will provide Columbia Hospital with the ability to keep up with the
expected growth in requests for the procedure. A new unit with
increased capability will allow us to expand by 15% in the first year. The
unit alone will enable this expansion; we will not need new staff or floor
space. Increased capability will also increase our patient referrals. At an
average cost of $120 per examination, an additional $41,000 will result

MODEL 11-2   A Short Report Organized in a Delayed-summary Pattern

T. R. Lougani　　　　　　　　　　-2-　　　　　　　　January 16, 1999

in the first year, and the full cost of equipment should be recovered within the first two years. Patients may also use other services at the hospital once they come here for ultrasound, resulting in further income. Cost of new equipment is as follows:

New unit	$74,000
Maintenance contract	0
Total	$74,000

Conclusion.　Updating old equipment is merely a holding technique, even though such a decision would save money initially. To increase our capability and provide the latest technology for our patients, I recommend that we purchase a new unit to coincide with the opening of the new community clinic on our ground floor, March 1. I would appreciate the opportunity to discuss this matter further. If you wish to see sales and service literature, I can supply it.

MODEL 11-2　*continued*

Planning Long Reports

Consider these questions when you begin planning a long report:

- *What is the central issue?* In clarifying the main subject of a long report, consider the questions your readers need answered: (1) Which choices are best? (2) What is the status of the situation, and how does it affect the company's future? (3) What changes must we make and why? (4) What results will various actions produce? (5) What are the solutions to certain problems? (6) How well or how badly does something work? Not all your readers are seeking answers to the same questions, so in planning a long report you should consider all possible aspects that might concern your readers.

- *Who are your readers, and what are their different purposes?* Because long reports tend to have multiple readers, such reports usually cover several aspects of a subject. You must consider your readers' purposes and how to effectively provide enough information for each purpose. Remember that long reports generally need to include more background information than short reports because (1) multiple readers rarely have an identical understanding of the subject and (2) long reports may remain in company files for years and serve as an information source to future employees dealing with a similar situation. Chapter 3 explains specific strategies for identifying readers' purposes.

- *How much information do I need to include in this report?* The relevant data for all readers and all purposes sometimes constitute masses of information. Determine what kinds of facts you need before you begin to gather information so that you are sure to cover all areas.

Gathering Information

When you gather information for a long report, consult secondary and primary sources for relevant facts.

Secondary Sources

Secondary sources of information consist of documents or materials already prepared in print, on tape, or on film. For a long project, consult secondary sources first because they are readily available and easy to use. Also, the information in secondary sources reflects the work of others on the same subject and may help direct your plans for further research or trigger ideas about types of information your readers need to know.

Unless you have a specific author or title of an article in mind when you use these secondary sources, you must search for information by subject. For effective searches, check under other key topics as well as the main subject. If you are looking for information about diamonds, check under the key word *diamond*, as well as under such topics as mining, precious gems, minerals, South Africa, and carbon. Major secondary sources are as follows.

Library Catalog. Nearly all libraries now use an on-line catalog that lists all books, films, tapes, disks, periodicals, and any materials on microfilm or microfiche in the library. The catalog information will tell you the call number of each item and where it is located. The catalog also usually indicates whether the item is currently available or is checked out and due back on a certain date.

Periodical Indexes. Published articles about science, technology, and business topics are listed in periodical indexes. Your library may have these available in print, on-line, or on CD-ROM. Your librarian can help you get started using an index that is likely to cover the topic you are researching. The most useful indexes for people in professional areas include *ABI/Inform* (available only electronically), *Engineering Index, Applied Science and Technology Index, Business Periodicals Index,* and *General Science Index.* Most indexes cover several fields, but no one index covers all the relevant journals in a particular field.

Newspaper Indexes. The two newspaper indexes available in most college libraries are *The New York Times Index* and *The Wall Street Journal Index.* Some periodical indexes include these newspapers and others, such as *The Financial Times of Canada.*

Abstract Indexes. Abstract indexes provide summaries of published articles about science, technology, and business. Read the abstract to decide whether the article contains the kinds of information you need. If it does, look for the article in the journal listed. Specialized abstract indexes include *Biology Digest, Chemical Abstracts, Computer and Control Abstracts, Electrical and Electronic Abstracts, Geological Abstracts, Mathematical Reviews, Microbiology Abstracts, Nuclear Science Abstracts,* and *Water Resources Abstracts.*

Company Documents. Libraries often collect the annual reports of *Fortune* 500 companies as well as those of local companies. The reports cover financial information for the previous year. Most companies now have Web sites that offer varying kinds of information, such as product catalogs, company statistics, names of officers, and telephone numbers of specific divisions.

Government Documents. The federal government maintains Web sites for all departments, such as the Department of Commerce. From these sites, you can retrieve information sheets, statistics, technical reports, and newsletters. These are updated regularly, so your information will be the latest available. Your library may have the *Monthly Catalog of United States Government Documents,* which lists unclassified reports and brochures available to the public.

Encyclopedias, Directories, and Almanacs.   College research requires specialized encyclopedias and directories, such as *Meteorology Source Book, Encyclopedia of Energy,* and *McGraw-Hill Encyclopedia of Science and Technology.* Almanacs give specific dates and facts about past events.

Internet.   The Internet might provide both secondary and primary sources. A document written by a scientist who conducted an environmental test for the Department of the Interior is a primary source. A consumer Web site that discusses the test is a secondary source. Use the Internet wisely. Anyone can put anything on the Internet, so consider whether the source of the information is an established authority on the subject. John Doe's ideas about the environment expressed in a chat room are not a legitimate source of information, nor is his personal Web page.

Currently, there are over 300 million Web sites. To use the Internet effectively, you must use a search engine to sort through available data. Search engines are relatively easy to use. Follow the directions on the screen. The search may give you thousands of sites, but the ones listed first are usually the most important and relevant. Just click on an address that looks as though it contains the type of information you want. The following search engines, each indexing millions of Web pages, are most helpful for research in science, technology, and business:

> **Alta Vista** (http://www.altavista.digital.com)
>
> **Infoseek** (http://www.infoseek.com)
>
> **HotBot** (http://www.hotbot.com)
>
> **Yahoo** (http://www.search.yahoo.com)
>
> **Lycos Pro** (http://lycospro.lycos.com)
>
> **Excite** (http://www.excite.com)
>
> **Webcrawler** (http://www.webcrawler.com)
>
> **Dogpile** (http://www.dogpile.com)

Primary Sources

Primary sources of information involve research strategies to gather unpublished or unrecorded facts. Scientific research reports, for example, are usually based on original experiments, a primary source. A marketing research report may be based on a consumer survey, also a primary source. Secondary sources can provide background, but they cannot constitute a full research project. Only primary sources can provide new information to influence decision making and scientific advances. The major primary sources of information follow.

Personal Knowledge.   When you are assigned to a report project on the job, it is usually because you are already deeply involved in the subject. Therefore, much of the information needed for the report may be in your head. Do not rely on remembering everything you need, however—make notes. Writing down what you know about a subject will clarify in your own mind whether you know enough about a particular aspect of the subject or need to gather more facts.

Observation.   Gathering information through personal observation is time consuming, but it can be essential for some subjects. Experienced writers collect information from other sources before conducting observations so that they know which aspects they want to focus on in observation. Scientists use observation to check, for example, how bacteria are growing under certain controlled conditions. Social scientists may use observation to assess how people interact or respond to certain stimuli. Technology experts may use observation to check on how well machinery performs after certain adjustments. Do not interfere with or assist in any process you are observing. Observation is useful only when the observer remains on the sidelines, watching but not participating.

Interviews.   Interviews with experts in a subject can yield valuable information for long reports. Writers usually gather information from other sources first and then prepare themselves for an interview by listing the questions they need answered. Know exactly what you need from the person you are interviewing so that you can cover pertinent information without wasting time. Use the guidelines for conducting interviews in Chapter 3.

Tests.   Tests can be useful in yielding information about new theories, systems, or equipment. A scientist, for example, must test a new drug to see its effects. A market researcher may test consumer reaction to new products.

Surveys.   Surveys collect responses from individuals who represent groups of people. Results can be analyzed in various ways, based on demographic data and responses to specific questions. A social scientist who wants to find out about voting patterns for people in a specific geographic area may select a sample of the population that represents all voting age groups, men and women, income groups, and any other categories thought to be significant. Internet surveys may seem an easy way to gather responses from a large number of people because of the speed and ease of sending and receiving messages. The disadvantages are that respondents are not anonymous, the sample is limited to Internet users, and computer problems could destroy data. Designing an effective questionnaire is complicated because questions must be tested for reliability. If you are not trained in survey research, consult survey research handbooks and ask the advice of experts before attempting even an informal survey on the job.

Taking Notes

Taking useful notes from the multiple sources you consult for a long report is necessary if you are to write a well-developed report. No one can remember all the facts gathered from multiple sources, so whenever you find relevant information, take notes.

Although putting notes in a spiral notebook may seem more convenient than shuffling note cards while you are gathering information, notes in a notebook will be more difficult to use when you start to write. Because such notes reflect the order in which you found the information and not necessarily the order relevant to the final report organization, the information will seem "fixed" and nearly impossible to rearrange easily, thus interfering with effective organization for the reader. You would have to flip pages back and forth, wasting time searching for particular facts as you try to organize and write.

A more efficient way to record facts is to use note cards because such cards are easy to rearrange in any order and are durable enough to stand up to frequent handling. Some people prefer to put notes on computers. If you do that, record the same information that would be on a note card. Keep one note per page. Make a backup file every time you add notes. Follow these guidelines for using notes on cards or on a computer to keep track of the information you gather for a long report:

- Fill out a separate note card for each source of information. For printed material, record complete bibliographic data, including the library call number. For film or television material, record the producer, director, title, studio or network, and the date. For interviews, record the name, date, subject discussed, and any other identifying material. For electronic sources, record author, date, title, database, date you accessed the material, and electronic address. Keep these cards or computer file as your bibliography.

- For information notes, record the source name in a top corner, page number for written material, and date of access for electronic material. For convenience in sorting, also record a key word in the opposite corner identifying the topic, such as "Travel Costs."

- Put only one item of information from one source on each card. If you mingle notes on cards, you will end up with the same unorganized information you would have had in a spiral notebook.

- If you write down the exact words from the original source, use quotation marks.

- Condense and paraphrase information for notes, but do not change the meaning. If the original source states, "Consumer reports appear to indicate . . . ," do not condense as "Consumer reports indicate. . . ." The original sentence implied uncertainty with the word *appear.* Keep the meaning of the original clear in your notes.

- Record exact figures and dates, and doublecheck before leaving the source.
- Record enough facts so you can recall the full meaning of the original. One or two key words are not usually enough to help you remember detailed information.

Interpreting Data

Readers need the facts you present in a long report, but they also need help in interpreting those facts, particularly as to how the information affects their decision making and company projects. When you report information, tell readers what it means. Explain why the information is relevant to the central issue and how it supports, alters, or dismisses previous decisions or how it calls for new directions. Your objective in interpreting data for readers is to help them use the facts efficiently. Whatever your personal bias about the subject, be as objective as you can, and remember that several interpretations of any set of facts may be possible. Alert your readers to all major possibilities. Declining sales trends in a company's southwest sales region may indicate that the company's marketing efforts are inadequate in the region, but the trends also may indicate that consumers are dissatisfied with the products or that the products are not suitable for the geographic region because of other factors. Give the readers all the options when you interpret facts. After you have gathered information for your report and before you write, ask yourself these questions:

- Which facts are most significant for which of my readers?
- How do these facts answer my readers' questions?
- What decisions do these facts support?
- What changes do these facts indicate are needed?
- What option seems the best, based on these facts?
- What trends that affect the company do these facts reveal?
- What solutions to problems do these facts support?
- What actions may be necessary because of these facts?
- What conditions do these facts reveal?
- What changes will be useful to the company, based on these facts?
- How does one set of facts affect another set?
- When facts have several interpretations, which interpretations are the most logical and most useful for the situation?
- Is any information needed to further clarify my understanding of these facts?

Presenting data is one step, and interpreting their meaning is the second step in helping readers. If you report to your readers that a certain drainage system has two-sided flow channels, tell them whether this fact makes the system appropriate or inappropriate for the company project. Your report should include the answers to questions relevant to your subject and to your readers' purposes.

Drafting Long Reports

Long reports usually include the formal report elements discussed in Chapter 10. Like short reports, long reports may be organized in either the opening-summary or delayed-summary pattern, depending on your analysis of your readers' probable attitudes toward the subject. Whatever the pattern, long reports generally have three major sections.

Introductory Section

The introductory section in a long report usually contains several types of information. If this information is lengthy, it may appear as subsections of the introduction or even as independent sections. Depending on your subject and your readers, these elements may be appropriate in your introduction:

Purpose.   Define the purpose of your report—for example, to analyze results of a marketing test of two colognes in Chicago. Include any secondary purposes—for example, to recommend marketing strategies for the colognes or to define the target consumer groups for each cologne. For a report on a scientific research project, tell your readers what questions the research was intended to answer. Also clarify in this section why you are writing the report. Did someone assign the writing task to you or is the report subject your usual responsibility? Be sure to say if one person told you to write the report and address it to a third person.

Methods.   Explain the methods you used to obtain information for your report. In a research report, the methods section is essential for readers who may want to duplicate the research and for readers who need to understand the methods in order to understand the results. Include in this section specific types of tests used, who or what was tested, the length of time involved, and the test conditions. If appropriate, also describe how you conducted observations, interviews, or surveys to gather information and under what circumstances and with which people. You need not explain going to the library or searching through company files for information.

Background.   If the report is about a subject with a long history, summarize the background for your readers. The background may include past research on the same subject, previous decisions, or historical trends and developments. Some readers may know nothing about the history of the subject; others may know only one aspect of the situation. To effectively use the report information, readers need to know about previous discussions and decisions.

Report Limitations.   If the information in the report is limited by what was available from specific sources or by certain time frames or conditions, clarify this for your readers so that they understand the scope of the information and do not assume that you neglected some subject areas.

Report Contents.   For long reports, include a section telling readers the specific topics covered in the report. Some readers will be interested only in certain information and can look for that at once. Other readers will want to know what is ahead before they begin reading the data. Indicate also why these topics are included in the report and why they are presented in the way they are to help your readers anticipate information.

Recommendations/Results/Conclusions.   If you are using the opening-summary pattern of organization, include a section in which you provide an overview of the report conclusions, research results, or recommendations for action.

Data Sections

The data sections include the facts you have gathered and your interpretations of what they mean relative to your readers. Present the facts in ways best suited to helping your readers use the information. The patterns of organization explained in Chapter 4 will help you present information effectively. Chapter 12 explains data sections in specific types of reports. For a report of a research study, the data sections cover all the results obtained from the research.

Concluding Section

Long reports generally have a concluding section even if there is an opening summary because some readers prefer to rely on introductory and concluding sections. If the report is in the opening-summary pattern, the concluding section should summarize the facts presented in the report and the major conclusions stemming from these facts. Also explain recommendations based on the conclusions. Some readers prefer that recommendations always appear in a separate section, and if you have a number of recommendations, a separate section will help readers find and remember them.

If the report is in the delayed-summary pattern, the concluding section is important because your readers need to understand how the facts lead to specific conclusions. Present conclusions first; then present any recommendations that stem from these conclusions. Include any suggestions for future studies of the subject or future consideration of the subject. Do not, however, as you may do in short reports, include specific requests for meetings or remind readers about deadlines.

The multiple readers of a long report and the usual formal presentation of long reports make these remarks inappropriate. You may include such matters in the transmittal letter that accompanies your long report, as explained in Chapter 10.

CHAPTER SUMMARY

This chapter discusses the usual organization of short and long reports and provides guidelines for report planning, information gathering, note taking, data interpretation, and drafting. Remember:

- Reports generally have one or more of these purposes: to inform, to record, to recommend, to justify, and to persuade.

- Most short internal reports are written as memos, and most short external reports are written as letters or as formal documents.

- Most short reports are organized in the opening-summary pattern.

- Long reports may be in the opening-summary pattern or the delayed-summary pattern and are usually written as formal documents.

- Planning reports includes identifying the central issue, analyzing readers and purpose, and deciding how much information is necessary for your readers.

- Writers gather information for reports from both primary and secondary sources.

- Notes are best collected on note cards, one item per card.

- For effective reports, writers must interpret the data for their readers.

- Long reports usually have three major divisions: an introduction, information sections, and a concluding section.

SUPPLEMENTAL READINGS IN PART 2

Benson, P. J. "Writing Visually: Design Considerations in Technical Publications," *Technical Communication*, p. 454.

"Six Graphics Guidelines," *Simply Stated*, p. 535.

Tarutz, J. H. "Editing for an International Audience," *Technical Editing*, p. 545.

White, J. V. "Color: The Newest Tool for Technical Communicators," *Technical Communication*, p. 551.

MODEL 11-3   Commentary

This short report in memo format is organized in the opening-summary pattern. The writer is presenting information about new computer software. Notice that the writer does not offer a recommendation in the opening. He knows that the reader is interested only in information at this point. In the closing, the writer offers to provide printed materials and suggests arranging a demonstration of the software for supervisors who will be involved in the decision-making process.

Discussion

1. Discuss the writer's choice of headings and how helpful they are to the reader.

2. Compare the opening summary in this model and the one in Model 11-1. How useful are they in introducing the reader to the topic and clarifying the main points?

3. Discuss what other kinds of information the reader may want before reaching a decision. Draft a memo to the writer and ask him to get this information.

4. In groups, select one of the following topics and assume you are writing an information report. Decide what kinds of information you would need to include in such a report.

- A comparison of two locations for a new pet store
- A comparison of two models of sports equipment for use in a high school
- A comparison of two word-processing programs for someone just beginning to use a computer

To: Yvette Hernandez
        Vice President—Communication Systems

From: Rick Wilder *RW*
        Operations Manager

Date: May 6, 1999

Re: Voice Recognition Software

As we discussed over a year ago, I have been monitoring developments
in voice recognition software. Significant advances have occurred, and
we might want to consider investing in at least one program on a test
basis. I personally investigated the most recent versions of three new
programs: Meade Systems, SpeakEase; Komar, Inc. VoiceNow; and Bierce
Co., Fast Voice. Following is a comparison of some major features that
are relevant to our work situation. As you will notice, all three
programs have advantages.

Required Hardware

All three programs require PCs with Pentium central processing units;
16-bit sound card and a CD-ROM drive for installation; speakers for
playback and audio testing; and sufficient hard drive space and speed.
All but one section has this hardware now, and we are upgrading that
section this year.

Each program also requires the user to wear a headset (included) to
cancel outside noise.

Setup

Although setup takes some time, it is not overly difficult and should
present no problems. One of our specialists can install any of the three
programs in 2 to 3 hours with assistance from the vendor. The employee
who will use the program must also be involved. Steps include
(1) plugging in the headset, (2) installing software from a CD-ROM, and
(3) setting up the microphone and sound card. Available help materials
include print manuals, on-screen tutorials, and company Web sites.

All three programs require the potential user to "enroll" and "train" the
system. The user must read 200 to 300 lines of dictation before getting
any recognition from the program.

Y. Hernandez   -2-   May 6, 1999

Dictation

The user must speak into a microphone located close to the mouth.
Dictation must include all the words and all the necessary punctuation.
For instance, the user must dictate "I am glad to collect those figures
period when do you want the report question mark." All the programs
also allow dictating numbers, such as dates or money, but only Fast
Voice recognizes "twelve dollars and sixty-two cents." The others require
the user to say each figure separately.

Vocabulary size also varies. VoiceNow starts at 26,000 words and can
grow to 68,000 words. SpeakEase and Fast Voice start at 40,000 words
and can grow to about 200,000. The user must "train" the program to
recognize new words.

All three programs allow the user to move the cursor, select text, and
set point size, boldface, underlining, and italics. All three programs also
make occasional mistakes and treat commands as dictation.

Conclusion

It took me about six hours to become used to the dictation process. If we
try one of these programs, we should assign an experienced staffer to
test it so as to cut down on the inevitable frustrations that arise when
using new computer programs. These programs will certainly change as
new versions are developed, but I think they are at a level that might
prove useful in our operation. I have printed information about the
three programs that I would be glad to give you. Or, if you prefer, I can
arrange a demonstration for the section heads.

MODEL 11-4 Commentary

This letter report was written in the delayed-summary organization. The president of the student senate chose to write her report as a letter because she felt uncomfortable sending a memo to the director of student services. Although both reader and writer are connected to the same organization, they are not both employees, and the writer preferred the slightly more formal letter format for her report. She begins by thanking the reader for his past assistance, then explains the survey she conducted, describes the results, and concludes by recommending the renovation (possibly costly) of a room in the student center.

Discussion

1. Discuss why the writer chose to present her report in the delayed-summary pattern. What kinds of difficulties might the opening-summary pattern have created in this situation?

2. Discuss the writer's opening paragraph. What impression is she trying to create?

3. How effectively does the writer present her results? How well do the details support her conclusions? Discuss whether she should have included cost figures for renovating the Hilltop.

4. In groups or alone, as your instructor prefers, draft a letter to the director of student services on your campus and ask for renovations of a specific room. Explain why the renovations are needed and discuss your proposed changes in detail.

South Central University
University Park, Georgia 30638

Office of Student Government
(912) 555–1100

April 21, 1999

Mr. Patrick R. Sheehan
Director, Student Services
South Central University
University Park, GA 30638

Dear Mr. Sheehan:

I appreciate your assistance in coordinating student organization events this year and your efforts to expand services in Jacobs Student Center. During our meeting in February, you suggested that I survey students regarding the services in the Student Center and develop a five-year agenda for issues and projects. I took your advice and conducted a survey of students on several topics, and I can now report the results and highlight the area of most interest.

Survey

With the assistance of my fellow officers, Carlos Vega, vice president, and Marylee Knox, secretary, I surveyed 100 students in the Jacobs Student Center, April 2–6, 1999. We interviewed only those students who had at least two more semesters to complete at South Central. The students surveyed were as follows: males 47% and females 53%; freshmen 29%, sophomores 32%, juniors 39%.

Each student filled out a written questionnaire about number of hours spent weekly in the Student Center, eating and recreation time in the Center, study time in the Center, and preferences in rooms. An open-ended question asked students to suggest changes in the room they used most often. We interviewed students at the main entrance to Jacobs Student Center.

Results

Overall, students spend an average of 12 hours a week in the Center. Study time averaged 5 hours, and eating/recreation time averaged 7

Mr. Patrick R. Sheehan   -2-   April 21, 1999

hours. There were wide variations in these figures from individual students. The student who spent the least amount of time reported only 1 hour, and the student who spent the most time reported 20 hours. Most students report both study time and eating/recreation time in the Center. Student responses included every public room in the Center—the first-floor food court, bowling alley, billiard room, Hilltop Cafeteria, lounge areas on every floor, and video game room. We were surprised to discover that the most frequently used room was the Hilltop Cafeteria. Students (73%) reported using the Hilltop Cafeteria for both study and eating/recreation at least 50% of the hours they were in the Student Center. Because 79% of the suggestions for changes focused on the Hilltop Cafeteria, I will concentrate on those in this report.

Proposed Changes for Hilltop Cafeteria

Students said they used Hilltop Cafeteria for studying, eating, and meeting with friends, and they had specific criticisms about the facility. As Hilltop also serves as a banquet hall and dance floor for special events, I believe the student concerns merit attention. Comments were primarily about the furniture, lighting, decor, temperature, and atmosphere.

Furniture.   Students reported that many of the tables and chairs are in disrepair. Recently, a table collapsed while students were eating lunch, and chair backs often snap if leaned on. In addition, the tables and chairs are scarred, with chipped tabletops and cracks in the chair seats.

Lighting.   The current lighting is both unattractive and too dim for efficient study. Part of the problem may be the wide spacing between light fixtures. Students requested more lights and higher power.

Decor.   The dull green wall color was cited as making the room look "institutional." Also, the walls near the entrances are dirty from fingerprints, scrapes from chairs, and people brushing against them. Fresh paint in a soft color or muted white was suggested. Because the Hilltop has no windows, there is extensive wall space. Several students suggested wall decorations, such as photographs showing the university's history or student paintings.

Temperature.   Students reported that Hilltop was frequently too warm for comfort. Stacks of cafeteria trays left over from lunch produce an

Mr. Patrick R. Sheehan   -3-   April 21, 1999

unpleasant aroma, making the room unappealing. One suggestion was to install several ceiling fans to circulate air more effectively. Also, the trays could be removed promptly at the end of the main lunch period.

Atmosphere.   Students mentioned that the food court is usually noisy with heavy traffic, and the lounge areas with couches are more suited for socializing than for studying. They prefer the Hilltop if they plan to eat and study. Several suggestions focused on providing classical music in the background, played at a low level. Rearrangement of tables and chairs could create study areas distinct from the eating areas, while still allowing students the option of having soft drinks and snacks while studying.

Conclusions

Based on these student responses to our survey, I believe the first priority for the Office of Student Services should be improvements in the Jacobs Student Center, specifically renovation of the Hilltop Cafeteria. Renovation would include painting the room, installing improved lighting, installing ceiling fans, purchasing new tables and chairs, and installing a music system. I have not obtained any cost figures for these suggested improvements. Student suggestions for improving the Hilltop were so numerous I believe this issue should be discussed. I would be happy to meet with you and provide copies of the questionnaires used in our survey, so you can see the results in greater detail. The officers of the Student Senate are interested in working with you in evaluating student interests and needs on the South Central campus.

Sincerely,

Judith L. Piechowski

Judith L. Piechowski
President
Student Senate

JP:mk

MODEL 11-5   Commentary

This formal report is a feasibility study in which the writer compares two technical systems and recommends which is best for the company. The writer begins his report by explaining the expected benefits of installing this type of system and establishes the criteria he used in his evaluation. He then reviews in detail the qualities and costs of each system and concludes with his recommendation.

The report uses the opening-summary pattern because the reader has asked for the study and expects a recommendation. The writer discusses the features of each system in detail and includes a table showing cost comparisons.

The abstract for this report appears on the title page because that format is customary at this company. Although this is an internal report, the writer uses a transmittal letter rather than a memo.

Discussion

1. Discuss the headings in this report. How helpful are they for the reader who must make a decision based on this information?

2. The writer compares the two systems by topic. Discuss how helpful this organization is for the reader.

3. Discuss why the writer probably chose to write a transmittal letter rather than a memo.

4. In this chapter, Models 11-2 through 11-5 all make recommendations. Discuss the differences in reader, purpose, and writing situation that probably helped to determine the kinds of information included in the reports.

FEASIBILITY STUDY OF SYSTEMS FOR SLAG DETECTION FOR THE CONTINUOUS CASTER AT ALLIED STEEL WORKS

Prepared for
Edward P. Magnus
General Manager

Submitted by
Brian Fedor
Quality Manager

November 16, 1999

Abstract

Research conducted over a 30-day period determined the best slag detection system for the continuous caster at Allied Steel Works. The RVX Vibration and the Balid were compared for cost, installation, compatibility with current procedures, performance, reliability, and system maintenance. Although both systems exceeded our performance and minimum maintenance requirements, the RVX Vibration system is recommended because of its lower cost, ease of installation, fewer changes in operating procedure, and reliability.

ALLIED STEEL WORKS
1000 Industrial Parkway
Milwaukee, Wisconsin 53209

(414) 555–6000

November 16, 1999

Mr. Edward P. Magnus
General Manager
Allied Steel Works
1000 Industrial Parkway
Milwaukee, Wisconsin 53209

Dear Mr. Magnus:

Here is the feasibility study that you asked for concerning an effective
slag detection system for Allied Steel Works. Over the last month, I have
researched and compared slag detection systems. The only two systems
used in the steel industry are the RVX Vibration and the Balid systems.

Even though both systems are capable of meeting the high performance
and minimum maintenance requirements of the caster, I recommend the
RVX Vibration system as the best one for Allied because of its lower
cost, ease of installation, fewer changes in operating procedures, and
reliability.

I'll be glad to discuss this research with you in detail before you present
this report to the Executive Board.

Sincerely,

Brian Fedor

Brian Fedor
Quality Manager

BF:kk

Feasibility Study
of Systems for Slag Detection for
the Continuous Caster at Allied Steel Works

Introduction

This study compares two slag detection systems for use at Allied Steel Works. The two systems researched are the RVX Vibration and Balid. After reviewing the data sent by both companies as well as information from companies with continuous casters similar to ours, I recommend the RVX Vibration system.

Background

The need for a slag detection system has become necessary since the start-up of the ladle metallurgical facility (LMF). Before the start-up of the LMF our quality index of 91% could not get better due to a lack of slag treatment at the basic oxygen furnace (BOF). Therefore, the present method of the ladleman closing the ladle when slag appears is sufficient. This reaction method can only allow us a maximum quality index of 94%. With the LMF now on line, we are supplied with 99.9% slag-free steel. This 99.9% slag-free steel means that our present 91% quality index reading can theoretically be raised to 99.9%. However, the only way we will obtain a quality index close to 99.9% is through the use of a slag detection system.

System Criteria

The system criteria were established by our operating staff. The two systems were judged on the following criteria in order of importance: cost, installation, compatibility with operating practices, performance, reliability, and maintenance.

Possible Alternatives

The RVX Vibration and the Balid systems are the only two systems on the market. Both are used throughout the steel industry. Even though they are used by several casters, I only considered data supplied by our sister casters at British Steel's Newcastle Works and Defasco's Erie Works. Like ours, the two casters listed are both built by Mannesmann-Demag and are rated at the same tonnage per year.

The two systems operate on different scientific principles. The RVX system uses an accelerometer to measure change in the vibration of the ladle as the steel stream changes from liquid steel to liquid steel and slag.

The Balid system uses electromagnetic signals to detect a change in steel density as the steel stream changes from steel to a steel–slag mix.

Comparison of Systems

Cost

Cost was determined to be the most important criteria because of the decline in sales we experienced in 1998. Due to the decline in sales, our capital improvements account has been limited to a balance of $170,000. If we spend over $170,000, the corporate finance office will deduct the excess from our general purchase fund. We cannot afford that because the general purchase fund is used to buy everyday operating supplies such as oil and grease.

The RVX system is considerably less expensive than the Balid system. The cost of each unit is as follows:

	RVX Vibration	Balid
Direct Labor*	$ 24,600	$ 33,628
Labor Overhead*	36,055	39,560
Initial Installation Parts	48,102	77,828
Spare Parts	17,480	22,000
Shipping	1,200	600
	$127,437	$173,616

*Direct labor is the cost of our mechanics installing the system, and labor overhead is the cost of training our staff and consultation fees.

The actual difference in cost between the two systems is $46,179. This difference makes the RVX system a better buy for the money.

Installation

Installation was considered the second most important aspect for three reasons. First, the slag detection system must be compact so that it does not crowd the limited work space on the ladle deck. Second, no extra downtime can be used to install the system. This requirement means that the system we choose must be installed during one repair turn. Finally, the installation must be done by our technicians. This requirement is in the union contract.

3

The RVX system is preferable in this category because it is the most compact unit of the two. The RVX unit is installed conveniently on the side of the ladle manipulator, and the signal cable runs under the tundish car floor to the ladle deck pulpit. The unit measures 1 foot in height, 2 feet in length, and 6 inches in width. The RVX unit will fit under the fire protection shroud on the manipulator. Since the cable runs under the tundish car floor, there is no danger of tripping. This unit can be installed in a 12-hour repair turn.

The Balid system requires that the unit be mounted on the side of each ladle and a cable plugged into that unit on every ladle turnaround. This cable cannot be buried under the tundish car floor because the ladle sizes are different and the cable must be placed in different areas. This requirement means that the cable must be free to move, and the work area on the ladle deck would be decreased by 2 feet. Also, this unit would require a 16-hour repair turnaround for our technicians.

The RVX system best fills our needs because of its compact size and quick installation. Another added plus is that the RVX system can be quickly installed by our technicians.

Compatibility with Operating Practices

This area is important for three reasons. First, the union contract does not allow this system to displace any workers. Second, the new system must not add a significant amount of time to ladle turnarounds because of possible breakouts while waiting for the ladle to open. Finally, the system must be able to operate on all grades of steel because of our vast product mix.

The RVX system will not displace any workers. Also, the RVX unit will save us time during ladle turnarounds due to its automatic ladle shutoff feature. This time-saving feature is a positive factor that will help make our process more efficient. Finally, the RVX system can be used on all grades of steel.

The Balid unit also will not eliminate any jobs. One drawback to the Balid system, however, is that it requires a ladleman to plug and unplug the sensor. This activity adds an average of 5 seconds to a ladle turnaround. This extra 5 seconds would put us dangerously close to

4

the maximum 40-second ladle turnaround time. Like the RVX unit, the Balid unit can be used on all grades of steel.

The RVX unit is the clear choice in this category not only because it can be used on all grades of steel and satisfies the union contract agreement, but also because it will speed up ladle turnarounds.

Performance

This category is important for a number of reasons. First, the use of a slag detection unit will improve our quality index. Second, our tonnage yield will increase. Third, tundish life will increase due to reduced tundish wear (a side effect of slag in the tundish). Finally, the potential for breakouts will lessen due to less slag in the tundish. The performance results were obtained from British Steel's Newcastle caster and Defasco's Erie Works caster, both of which are identical to our caster. We could not actually test the slag detection units in our plant without purchasing them.

The RVX system had an average response time of 4 seconds faster than the ladleman response method used at our caster. This faster response resulted in a reduction of slag in the tundish from 15% to 7.5%, which extended the tundish life one heat. Increased yield while the system was in use was an extra 5 tons a heat. This increase was due to fewer inclusion-rejected slabs. Tundish-to-mold yield also increased an average of 5 tons. Detected vortexing improved quality 0.01%, or one slab a heat. This vortex detection improvement would result in an extra 3000 slabs produced a year.

The Balid system had an average response time of 2 seconds faster than our ladleman reaction method. Slag in the tundish was reduced on average from 15% to 9.7%. This reduction in tundish slag extended the tundish life half a heat. Increased yield was 5 tons a heat. This increase was due to fewer inclusion-rejected steel slabs. Tundish-to-mold yield increased 7 tons. However, this system cannot detect vortexing. Therefore, no extra slabs would be produced because of vortex detection.

Although both systems increase yield, the RVX unit performs the best because of its ability to detect vortexing and extend tundish life longer.

5

Reliability and Maintenance

Reliability and maintenance were combined as a topic by the operating staff because they are interdependent.

For example, the reliability will depend on routine maintenance procedures like calibration. Another factor that could affect the reliability of the units is the amount of maintenance that will have to be done on the units by departments other than ours.

The RVX unit needs to be calibrated twice a year by the RVX representative at a cost of $750 a visit. Routine maintenance must be performed every week to check for possible damage due to overheating or wire shorts due to steel splashing. The unit is self-contained on the ladle deck, so no other maintenance departments are involved in maintaining the system.

The Balid system needs to be calibrated once a year by a factory representative at a cost of $1000 a visit. Routine maintenance must be performed twice a week to check for wire and sensor damage. Since the plug and sensor are on the ladle, the BOF shop maintenance department must be relied upon to adequately maintain those delicate parts. Another area of concern with respect to reliability is that, with so many parts, the accuracy of the sensor will suffer as the ladle is used.

The advantages of selecting the RVX unit over the Balid are the fewer parts to maintain, and the RVX unit can be serviced by our technicians. With fewer parts to break down and all the maintenance work done by our staff, we will have a reliable, low maintenance slag detection unit.

Conclusions and Recommendation

A slag detection unit is necessary if Allied Steel Works is to remain a world-class quality supplier of steel slabs. Both the RVX system and the Balid system are quite capable of improving our quality with minimal maintenance well into the 21st century. However, the RVX Vibration system is considerably less expensive than the Balid while providing better performance, more reliability, and low maintenance. Therefore, I recommend the RVX Vibration system over the Balid.

1. Assume you are writing a report on the current state of U.S. coastal wetlands for a geography class. You find the following paragraph in a U.S. Geological Survey fact sheet. Read the paragraph and take notes for a report that focuses on one of the following topics: (1) reasons for the loss of wetlands, (2) rate of loss of wetlands, or (3) Louisiana's problems with wetlands. Compare your notes with those taken by your classmates.

> Approximately half the Nation's original wetland habitats have been lost over the past 200 years. In part, this has been a result of natural evolutionary processes, but human activities, such as dredging wetlands for canals or draining and filling for agriculture, grazing, or development, share a large part of the responsibility for marsh habitat alteration and destruction. Louisiana's wetlands today represent about 40 percent of the wetlands of the continental United States, but about 80 percent of the losses. The State's wetlands extend as much as 130 kilometers inland and along the coast for about 300 kilometers. Not all the wetlands are receding; in fact, some wetlands are stable, and others are growing. But, at the present net rate of wetlands loss, Louisiana will have lost this crucial habitat in about 200 years. Considerable effort has been expended, and will continue to be expended, on understanding the processes that control wetlands evolution.

2. You are a summer intern at Kramden-Gleason Securities, Inc. Your supervisor, Carlos Blanco, wants to create a handy list of Web sites for financial information of interest to his clients—individual investors in the stock market. He tells you to find five Web sites. Write an opening-summary report to Mr. Blanco in which you identify five sites and explain why these sites would be useful to individual investors.

3. You are the assistant to Wilma Bonney, Communication Director at Universal Insurance Company. The annual sales meeting is coming up, and you are expecting 900 agents, at least half of whom will bring their spouses with them. Ms. Bonney is creating an information packet about activities for spouses. She wants you to recommend a museum or historical site that would interest out-of-town visitors. Visit a local museum or historical site (e.g., building, house, battlefield) and write a recommendation report to Ms. Bonney in which you describe the arrangement and displays (for a museum) or the physical appearance and importance (for a historical site) and recommend that the museum or site be included in the information packet for visitors. Attach a brochure from the museum or historical site to your report. Use the opening-summary organization pattern. You are aware that Ms. Bonney will probably use some of your description in the information packet, so you will include details that would interest visitors.

4. Assume you are employed in your field. Austin Everitt Chancellor, the president of your company, plans to attend a high-level meeting of industry leaders. His assistant, Tiffini Mortenson, asks you to research one of the recent developments affecting your field and write a documented report that will bring Mr. Chancellor up to date on the subject. Topics such as new banking regulations, new technology, the impact of an emerging social or medical problem, foreign competition, mandatory drug testing, waste disposal, new government regulations, or public demands for safety, service, or conservation would be appropriate. You were told that Mr. Chancellor wants current information and is particularly interested in knowing how this subject is expected to affect your industry.

Write a formal report with a title page, letter of transmittal, abstract, and reference list. Depending on your subject, you may need other formal elements or graphic aids. To be up to date, you need to use library sources or reliable Internet sources from the last three years for the report. Review Chapter 10 for formal report elements and for instructions on documenting sources within the text and creating a reference list. Decide whether to use an opening-summary or delayed-summary organization pattern. Your instructor may want you to prepare a 5- or 10-minute oral presentation of your subject for your class. If so, review Chapter 14 and read the oral presentation articles in Part 2.

CHAPTER 12

Types of Reports

UNDERSTANDING CONVENTIONAL REPORT TYPES

Over the years, in industry, government, and business, writers have developed conventional organizational patterns for the most frequently written types of reports. Just as tables of contents and glossaries have recognizable formats, so too have such common reports as progress reports and trip reports. Some companies, in fact, have strict guidelines about content, organization, and format for report types that are used frequently. Conventional organizational patterns for specific types of reports also represent what readers have found most useful over the years. For every report, you should analyze reader, purpose, and situation and plan your document to serve your readers' need for useful information. You will also want to be knowledgeable about the conventional structures writers use for common report types.

This chapter explains the purposes and organizational patterns of six of the most common reports. Depending on reader, purpose, situation, and company custom, these reports may be written as informal memos, letters, or formal documents that include all the elements discussed in Chapter 10.

WRITING A FEASIBILITY STUDY

A *feasibility study* provides information to decision makers about the practicality and potential success of several alternative solutions to a problem.

Purpose

Executives often ask for feasibility studies before they consider a proposal for a project because they want a thorough analysis of the situation and all the alternatives. The writer of a feasibility study identifies all reasonable options and prepares a report that evaluates them according to features important to the situation, such as cost, reliability, time constraints, and company or organization goals. Readers expect a feasibility study to provide the information necessary for them to make an informed choice among alternatives. The alternatives may represent choices among products or actions, such as the choice among four types of heating systems, or a choice between one action and doing nothing, such as the decision to merge with another company or not to merge. When you write a feasibility study, provide a full analysis of every alternative, even if one seems clearly more appropriate than the others.

Organization

Model 12-1 shows a feasibility study written by an executive to the president of the company. The company management has already discussed relocation to a new city and the need for this study. In her report, the writer presents information she has gathered about two possible sites, evaluates them both as to how well they match the company's requirements, and recommends one of them. Feasibility studies usually include four sections.

Introduction

The introduction of a feasibility study provides an overview of the situation. Readers may rely heavily on the introduction to orient them to the situation before they read the detailed analyses of the situation and the possible alternatives. Follow these guidelines:

- Describe the situation or problem.

- Establish the need for decision making.

- Identify those who participated in the study or the outside companies that provided information.

- Identify the alternatives the report will consider, and explain why you selected these alternatives, if you did.

- Explain any previous study of the situation or preliminary testing of alternatives.

- Explain any constraints on the study or on the selection of alternatives, such as time, cost, size, or capacity.

- Define terms or concepts essential to the study.

- Identify the key factors by which you evaluated the alternatives.

In Model 12-1, the writer opens with a short statement that includes the report purpose and her recommendation of which location is best.

Comparison of Alternatives

The comparison section focuses equally on presenting information about the alternatives and analyzing that information in terms of advantages and disadvantages for the company. Organize your comparison by topic or by complete subject. For feasibility reports, readers often prefer to read a comparison by key topics because they regard some topics as more important than others and they can study the details more easily if they do not have to move back and forth between major sections. Whether comparing by topic or by complete subject, discuss the alternatives in the same order under each topic, or discuss the topics in the same order under each alternative. Follow these guidelines:

- Describe the main features of each alternative.

- Rank the key topics for comparison by using either descending or ascending order of importance.

- Discuss the advantages of each alternative in terms of each key topic.

- Point out the significance of any differences among alternatives.

The writer in Model 12-1 compares the two possible sites by topic, using subheadings to help readers find specific types of information. The subheadings represent the established criteria for evaluating the locations.

Conclusions

The conclusions section summarizes the most important advantages and disadvantages of each alternative. If you recommend one alternative, do so in the conclusions section or in a separate section if you have several recommendations. State conclusions first, because they are the basis for any recommendations. If you believe some advantages or disadvantages are not important, explain why. Follow these guidelines:

- Separate conclusions adequately so that readers can digest one at a time.

- Explain the relative importance to the company of specific advantages or disadvantages.

- Include conclusions for each key factor presented in the comparison.

Recommendations

The recommendations section, if separate from the conclusions, focuses entirely on the choice of alternative. Your recommendations should follow logically from your conclusions. Any deviations will confuse readers and cast doubt on the thoroughness of your analysis. Follow these guidelines:

- Describe your recommendations fully.

- Provide enough details about implementing the recommendations so that your reader can visualize how they will be an effective solution to the problem.

- Indicate a possible schedule for implementation.

In Model 12-1, the writer combines her conclusions and recommendation. She reviews the company's decision to relocate, and she next explains that both sites are acceptable. Because Randolph Center involves less cost and will be ready for occupancy ahead of the company's deadline, she recommends that site.

WRITING AN INCIDENT REPORT

An *incident report* provides information about accidents, equipment break-downs, or any disruptive occurrence.

Purpose

An incident report is an important record of an event because government agencies, insurance companies, and equipment manufacturers may use the report in legal actions if injury or damage has occurred. In addition, managers need such reports to help them determine how to prevent future accidents or disruptions. An incident report thoroughly describes the event, analyzes the probable causes, and recommends actions that will prevent repetition of such events. If you are responsible for an incident report, gather as many facts about the situation as possible and carefully distinguish between fact and speculation.

Organization

Model 12-2 is an incident report about a fatal accident while workers were putting in sewer pipe. Although the writer was not present when the accident occurred, he gathers information from those who were and inspects the site.

Most large companies have standard forms for reporting incidents during working hours. If there is no standard form, an incident report should include the following sections.

Description of the Incident

The description of the incident includes all available details about events before, during, and immediately after the incident in chronological order. Since all interested parties will read this section of the report and may use it in legal action, be complete, use nonjudgmental language, and make note of any details that are not available. Follow these guidelines:

- State the exact times and dates of each stage of the incident.
- Describe the incident chronologically.
- Name the parties involved.
- State the exact location of the accident or the equipment that malfunctioned. If several locations are relevant, name each at the appropriate place in the chronological description.
- Identify the equipment, by model number, if possible, involved in a breakdown.

- Identify any continuing conditions resulting from the incident, such as the inability to use a piece of equipment.

- Identify anyone who received medical treatment after an accident.

- Name hospitals, ambulance services, and doctors who attended accident victims.

- Name any witnesses to the incident.

- Report witness statements with direct quotations or by paraphrasing statements and citing the source.

- Explain any follow-up actions taken, such as repairs or changes in scheduling.

- Note any details not yet available, such as the full extent of injuries.

The writer of Model 12-2 provides a chronological description of the accident, including time, date, and place. He also identifies the employees involved and reports the conditions and resulting injuries.

Causes

This section includes both direct and indirect causes for the incident. Be careful to indicate when you are speculating about causes without absolute proof. Follow these guidelines:

- Identify each separate cause leading to the incident under discussion.

- Analyze separately how each stage in the incident led to the next stage.

- If you are merely speculating about causes, use words such as *appears, probably,* and *seems.*

- Point out the clear relationship between the causes and the effects of the incident.

In analyzing the cave-in, the writer of Model 12-2 cites the obvious cause: no shoring. He also cites lack of training for trench work and the heavy vibrations from passing traffic.

Recommendations

This section offers specific suggestions keyed to the causes of the incident. Focus your recommendations on prevention measures rather than on punishing those connected with the incident. Follow these guidelines:

- Include a recommendation for each major cause of the incident.

- List recommendations if there are more than one or two.

- Describe each recommendation fully.

- Relate each recommendation to the specific cause it is designed to prevent.

- Suggest further investigation if warranted.

The recommendations in Model 12-2 include training sessions for trench work and three specific requirements for trenches 4 ft or more deep.

WRITING AN INVESTIGATIVE REPORT

An *investigative report* analyzes data and seeks answers to why something happens, how it happens, or what would happen under certain conditions.

Purpose

An investigative report summarizes the relevant data, analyzes the meaning of the data, and assesses the potential impact that the results will have on the company or on specific research questions. The sources of the data for investigative reports can include field studies, surveys, observation, and tests of products, people, opinions, or events both inside and outside the laboratory. Investigations can include a variety of circumstances. An inspector at the site of an airplane crash, a laboratory technician testing blood samples, a chemist comparing paints, a mining engineer checking the effects of various sealants, and a researcher studying the effect of air pollution on children are all conducting investigations, and all will probably write reports on what they find. Remember that readers of an investigative report need to know not only what the data are, but also what the data mean in relation to what has been found earlier and what may occur in the future.

Organization

Model 12-3 is an investigative report based on the results of a survey. In such reports, the writer usually examines a research question or problem, discusses the need to find answers, describes the method of investigation, and then analyzes the results from that investigation. The conclusions often point out what questions remain unanswered and the kinds of future research needed. The report in Model 12-3 is an investigation of the percentage of U.S. homes that have lead-based paint. Results are based on a survey of a random sample of dwellings across the United States. Scientific investigation reports are often published in journals or by research centers and agencies. They generally include an abstract as the report in Model 12-3 does. Most investigative reports include the following sections.

Introduction

The introduction of an investigative report describes the problem or research question that is the focus of the report. Since investigative reports may be used as a form of evidence in future decision making, include a detailed description of the situation and explain why the investigation is needed. Readers will be interested in how the situation affects company operations or how the research will answer their questions. Follow these guidelines:

- Describe specifically the research question or problem that is the focus of the investigation. Avoid vague generalities, such as "to check on operations" or "to gather employee reactions." State the purpose in terms of the specific questions the investigation will answer.

- Provide background information on how long the situation has existed, previous studies of the subject by others or by you, or previous decisions concerning it. If a laboratory test is the focus of the report, provide information about previous tests involving the same subject.

- Explain your reasons if you are duplicating earlier investigations to see if results remain consistent.

- Point out any limits of the investigation in terms of time, cost, facilities, or personnel.

The report in Model 12-3 explains that past research on the incidence of lead-based paint has been inconclusive and, therefore, a need for an accurate estimate exists. The introduction also discusses the hazard of lead-based paint. In some cases, specific objectives for a research study appear in a separate section, but, in this report, the writer includes a list of objectives in the introduction.

Method

This section should describe in detail how you gathered the information for your investigative report. Include the details your readers will be interested in. For original scientific research, your testing method is a significant factor in achieving meaningful results, and readers will want to know about every step of the research procedure. For field investigations, summarize your method of gathering information, but include enough specific details to show how, where, and under what conditions you collected data. Follow these guidelines, where appropriate, for your research method:

- Explain how and why you chose the test materials or specific tests.

- Describe any limits in the test materials, such as quantities, textures, types, or sizes, or in test conditions, such as length of time or options.

- List test procedures sequentially so that readers understand how the experiment progressed.

- Identify by category the people interviewed, such as employees, witnesses, and suppliers. If you quote an expert, identify the person by name.

- If appropriate, include demographic information, such as age, sex, race, physical qualities, and so on, for the people used in your study.

- Explain where and when observation took place.

- Identify what you observed, and why.

- Mention any special circumstances and what impact they had on results.

- Explain the questions people were asked or the tests they took. If you write the questions yourself, attach the full questionnaire as an appendix. If you use previously validated tests, cite the source of the tests.

The method section in Model 12-3 (1) identifies the type of housing surveyed for the study, (2) explains the coding system used in the survey, (3) describes how the sample of dwellings was chosen, and (4) explains the interview system used.

Results

This section presents the information gathered during the investigation and interprets the data for readers. Do not rely on the readers to see the same significance in statistics or other information that you do. Explain which facts are most significant for your investigation. Follow these guidelines:

- Group the data into subtopics, covering one aspect at a time.

- Explain in detail the full results from your investigation.

- Cite specific figures, test results, and statistical formulas, or use quotations from interviewees.

- Differentiate between fact and opinion when necessary. Use such words as *appears* and *probably* if the results indicate but do not prove a conclusion.

- If you are reporting statistical results, indicate (1) means or standard deviations, (2) statistical significance, (3) probability, (4) degrees of freedom, and (5) value.

- Point out highlights. Alert readers to important patterns, similarities to or differences from previous research, cause and effect, and expected and unexpected results.

The results section in Model 12-3 provides percentages of homes that have lead-based paint. In an appendix, the writer provides a table with results of the survey, but he also discusses the table in the results section and draws the reader's attention to specific figures. The results section also includes other survey results not shown on the table.

Discussion

This section interprets the results and their implications for readers. Explain how the results may affect company decisions or what changes may be needed because of your investigation. Show how the investigation answered your original research questions about the problem being investigated. If your results do not satisfactorily answer the original questions, clearly state this. Follow these guidelines where appropriate for your type of investigation:

- Explain what the overall results mean in relation to the problem or research question.

- Analyze how specific results answer specific questions or how they do not answer questions.

- Discuss the impact of the results on company plans or on research areas.

- Suggest specific topics for further study, if needed.

- Recommend actions based on the results. Detailed recommendations, if included, usually appear in a separate recommendations section.

Conclusion

When a research investigation is highly technical, the conclusion summarizes the problem or research question, the overall results, and what they mean in relation to future decisions or research. Nontechnical readers usually rely on the conclusion for an overview of the study and results. Follow these guidelines:

- Summarize the original problem or research question.

- Summarize the major results.

- Identify the most significant research result or feature uncovered in the investigation.

- Explain the report's implications for future planning or research.

- Point out the need for any action.

In Model 12-3, the conclusion section summarizes the overall results. The writer also discusses the high cost of removing the lead-based paint and the need to evaluate available removal methods. Finally, the writer calls for increased public awareness of the hazard and a comprehensive plan to deal with the problem.

WRITING A PROGRESS REPORT

A *progress report* (also called a *status report*) informs readers about a project that is not yet completed.

Purpose

The number of progress reports for any project usually is established at the outset, but more might be called for as the project continues. Progress reports are often required in construction or research projects so that decision makers can assess costs and the potential for successful completion by established deadlines. Although a progress report may contain recommendations, its main focus is to provide information, and it records the project events for readers who are not involved in day-to-day operations. The progress reports for a particular project make up a series, so keep your organization consistent from report to report to aid readers who are following one particular aspect of the project.

Organization

Model 12-4 is a progress report written by the on-site engineer in charge of a dam repair project. The report is one in a series of progress reports for management at the engineering company headquarters. The writer addresses the report to one vice president, but copies go to four other managers with varying interests in the project. The writer knows, therefore, that she is actually preparing a report that will be used by at least five readers. Progress reports include the following sections.

Introduction

The introduction reminds readers about progress to date. Explain the scope and purpose of the project, and identify it by specific title if there is one. Follow these guidelines:

- State the precise dates covered by this particular report.

- Define important technical terms for nonexpert readers.

- Identify the major stages of the project, if appropriate.

- Summarize the previous progress achieved (after the first report in the series) so that regular readers can recall the situation and new readers can become acquainted with the project.

- Review any changes in the scope of the project since it began.

The writer in Model 12-4 numbers her report and names the project in her subject line to help readers identify where this report fits in the series. In her introduction, she establishes the dates covered in this report and summarizes the dam repairs she discussed in previous reports. She also indicates that the project is close to schedule, but that the expected costs have risen because another subcontractor had to be hired.

Work Completed

This section describes the work completed since the preceding report and can be organized in two ways: You can organize your discussion by tasks and describe the progress of each chronologically, or you can organize the discussion entirely by chronology and describe events according to a succession of dates and times. Choose the organization that best fits what your readers will find useful, and use subheadings to guide them to specific topics. If your readers are interested primarily in certain segments of the project, task-oriented organization is appropriate. If your readers are interested only in the overall progress of the project, strict chronological organization is probably better. Follow these guidelines:

- Describe the tasks that have been completed in the time covered by the report.

- Give the dates relevant to each task.

- Describe any equipment changes.

- Explain special costs or personnel charges involved in the work completed.

- Explain any problems or delays.

- Explain why changes from the original plans were made.

- Indicate whether the schedule dates were met.

The engineer in Model 12-4 organizes her work-completed section according to the repair stages and then lists them in chronological order. She also includes the date on which each event occurred or each stage was completed.

Work Remaining

The section covering work remaining includes both the next immediate steps and those in the future. Place the most emphasis on the tasks that will be covered in your next progress report. Avoid overly optimistic promises. Follow these guidelines:

- Describe the major tasks that will be covered in the next report.

- State the expected dates of completion for each task.

- Mention briefly those tasks that are further in the future.

The work-remaining section in Model 12-4 describes the upcoming stage of the repair work and states the expected completion date.

Adjustments/Problems

This section covers issues that have changed the original plan or time frame of the project since the last progress report. If the project is proceeding on schedule with no changes, this section is not needed. If it is necessary, follow these guidelines:

- Describe major obstacles that have arisen since the last progress report. (Do not discuss minor daily irritations.)

- Explain needed changes in schedules.

- Explain needed changes in the scope of the project or in specific tasks.

- Explain problems in meeting original cost estimates.

The writer in Model 12-4 includes an adjustments section in her report to explain unexpected costs and a short delay because of the deteriorating condition of the dam area.

Conclusion

The conclusion of a progress report summarizes the status of the project and forecasts future progress. If your readers are not experts in the technical aspects of the project, they may rely heavily on the conclusion to provide them with an overall view of the project. Follow these guidelines:

- Report any progress on current stages.

- Report any lack of progress on current stages.

- Evaluate the overall progress so far.

- Recommend any needed changes in minor areas of scheduling or planning.

- State whether the project is worth continuing and is still expected to yield results.

The engineer's conclusion in Model 12-4 assures her readers that, although she is three days behind schedule, she expects no further delays. She also identifies the final stage of the dam repairs and the expected completion date.

STRATEGIES—Voice Mail

Do identify yourself and your subject immediately.

Do be specific and organized in your message.

Do state the time and date of your call if relevant.

Do close by indicating what kind of response you want.

Do not put confidential information or bad news on voice mail.

Do not shout, mumble, or speak too rapidly.

Do not use up time with small talk or gossip.

Do not use voice mail to avoid talking to someone directly.

WRITING A TRIP REPORT

A *trip report* provides a record of a business trip or visit to the field.

Purpose

A trip report is a useful record both for the person who made the trip and for the decision makers who need information about the subjects discussed during the trip. The trip report records all significant information gathered either from meetings or from direct observation.

Organization

Model 12-5 is a trip report written in the opening-summary organization pattern described in Chapter 11. The writer has visited another company to learn about a training system for a new, complicated software package. The report covers a brief description of the training system and what she learned from the trainers at the other company. Trip reports should contain the following sections.

Introductory Section

Use the subject line of your trip report to identify the date and location of the trip. Begin your report with an opening summary that explains the purpose of the trip and any major agreements or observations you made. Identify all the major events and the people with whom you talked. Follow these guidelines:

- Describe the purpose of the trip.

- Mention special circumstances connected to the trip's purpose.

- If the trip location is not in the subject line, state the dates and the locations you visited.

- State the overall results of the trip or any agreements you made.

- Name the important topics covered in the report.

The opening summary in Model 12-5 states the reason for the trip and includes the writer's recommendation that her company adopt the other company's training system.

Information Sections

The information sections of your trip report should highlight specific topics with informative headings. Consider which topics are important to your readers, and group the information accordingly. Follow these guidelines:

- State the names and titles of people you consulted for specific information.

- Indicate places and dates of specific meetings or site visits.

- Describe in detail any agreements made and with whom.

- Explain what you observed and your opinion of it.

- Give specific details about equipment, materials, or systems relevant to company interests.

The writer in Model 12-5 divides her information into two sections—one describing the training system and the other describing her talks with the company trainers.

Conclusions and Recommendations

In your final section, summarize the significant results of your trip, whether positive or negative, and state any recommendations you believe are appropriate. Follow these guidelines:

- Mention the most significant information resulting from the trip.
- State whether the trip was successful or worthwhile.
- Make recommendations based on information gathered during the trip.
- Mention any plans for another trip or further meetings.

In Model 12-5, the writer uses the final section to repeat her recommendation. She also mentions other materials she has from the trip and an offer of help from the trainer at the other company.

WRITING A PROPOSAL

Proposals suggest new ways to respond to specific company or organization situations, or they suggest specific solutions to identified problems. A proposal may be internal (written by an employee to readers within the company) or external (written from one company to another or from an individual to an organization).

Purpose

Proposals vary a great deal, and some, such as a bid for a highway construction job on a printed form designed by the state transportation department, do not look like reports at all. In addition, conventional format varies according to the type of proposal and the situation. Proposals usually are needed in these circumstances:

1. A writer, either inside or outside a company, suggests changes or new directions for company goals or practices in response to shifts in customer needs, company growth or decline, market developments, or needed organizational improvements.

2. A company solicits business through sales proposals that offer goods or services to potential customers. The sales proposal, sometimes called a *contract bid,* identifies specific goods or services the company will provide at set prices within set time frames.

3. Researchers request funds to pay for scientific studies. The research proposal may be internal (if an organization maintains its own research and development division) or external (if the researcher seeks funding from government agencies or private foundations).

Proposal content and organization usually vary depending on the purpose and reader-imposed requirements. External proposals, in particular, often must follow specific formats devised by the reader. This chapter discusses the conventional structure for a proposal that is written to suggest a solution to a company problem—the most common proposal type.

In general, this type of proposal persuades readers that the suggested plan is practical, efficient, and cost effective and suits company or research goals. Readers are decision makers who will accept or reject the suggested plan. Therefore, a successful proposal must present adequate information for decision making and stress advantages in the plan as they relate to the established company needs. In a high-cost, complicated situation, a proposal usually has many readers, all of whom are involved with some aspect of the situation.

Proposals are either solicited or nonsolicited. If you have not been asked to submit a proposal for a specific problem, you must consider whether the reader is likely to agree with you that a problem exists. You may need to persuade the reader that the company has a problem requiring a solution before presenting your suggested plan.

Organization

Model 12-6 is an unsolicited proposal written by a manager of a city water treatment plant to his superior. The writer identifies a serious safety problem resulting from the current method of installing portable generators during rain storms. His proposal suggests changes to eliminate the safety hazard.

The writer of this formal proposal includes an informative abstract on the title page. His transmittal letter stresses the seriousness of the problem and notes the attached supplementary reports. He also requests authority to proceed with the project and offers to discuss the matter further. The body of the proposal represents the traditional organization for such a document.

Problem

The introductory section of a proposal describes the central problem. Even if you know that the primary reader is aware of the situation, define and describe the extent of the problem for any secondary readers and for the record, and also explain why change is necessary. If the reader is not aware of the problem, you may need to convince him or her that the situation is serious enough to require changes. The first section of the proposal also briefly describes the recommended solution. Include these elements:

- A description of the problem in detail. Do not, for instance, simply mention "inadequate power." Explain in detail what is inadequate about the generator.

- An explanation of how the situation affects company operations or costs. Be specific.

- An explanation of why the problem requires a solution.

- The background of the situation. If a problem is an old one, point out when it began and mention any previous attempts to solve it.

- Deadlines for solving the problem if time is a crucial factor.

- An indication that the purpose of the proposal is to offer recommendations to solve the problem.

- Your sources of data—surveys, tests, interviews, and so on.

- A brief summary of the major proposed solution, for example, to build a new parking deck. Do not attempt to explain details, but alert the reader to the plan you will describe fully in the following sections.

- The types of information covered in the proposal—methods, costs, timetables, and so on.

The writer in Model 12-6 begins by stating that there is a safety problem in the current method of installing portable generators and then describes the method in detail, pointing out where the hazards occur. He also warns the reader that the department is in violation of the Occupational Safety and Health Administration regulations.

Proposed Solution

This section should explain your suggestions in detail. The reader must be able to understand and visualize your plan. If your proposal includes several distinct actions or changes, discuss each separately for clarity. Follow these guidelines:

- Describe new procedures or changes in systems sequentially, according to the way they would work if implemented.

- Explain any methods or special techniques that will be used in the suggested plan.

- Identify employees who will be involved in the proposal, either in implementing it or in working with new systems or new equipment.

- Describe changes in equipment by citing specific manufacturers, models, and options.

- Mention research that supports your suggestions.

- Identify other companies that have already used this plan or a similar one successfully.

- Explain the plan details under specific subheadings relating to schedules, new equipment or personnel, costs, and evaluation methods in an order appropriate to your proposal.

The writer in Model 12-6 proposes four new installations—all designed to simplify the current method of installing portable generators. He uses subheadings to direct the reader to specific information about the schedule, costs, and coordination of the project.

Needed Equipment/Personnel

Identify any necessary equipment purchases or new personnel required by your proposal. Follow these guidelines:

- Indicate specific pieces of equipment needed by model numbers and brand names.

- Identify new employee positions that will have to be filled. Describe the qualifications people will need in these positions.

- Describe how employee duties will change under the proposed plan and how these shifts will affect current and future employees.

Schedules

This section is especially important if your proposal depends on meeting certain deadlines. In addition, time may be an important element if, for instance, your company must solve this problem in order to proceed with another scheduled project. Follow these guidelines if they are appropriate to your topic:

- Explain how the proposed plan will be phased in over time or on what date your plan should begin.

- Mention company deadlines for dealing with the problem or outside deadlines, such as those set by the IRS.

- Indicate when all the stages of the project will be completed.

The proposed changes in Model 12-6 will require the department to call for bids by contractors, obtain city permits, and review the design. Because of these requirements, the writer describes the necessary schedule in detail. For the reader's convenience, the writer separates the process into four stages.

Budget

The budget section of a proposal is highly important to a decision maker. If your plan is costly relative to the expected company benefits, the reader will need to see compelling reasons to accept your proposal despite its high cost. Provide as realistic and complete a budget projection as possible. Follow these guidelines:

- Break down costs by category, such as personnel, equipment, and travel.
- Provide a total cost.
- Mention indirect costs, such as training or overhead.
- Project costs for a typical cycle or time period, if appropriate.

In Model 12-6, the writer includes a table to supplement the cost section. Because government units operate under budgets established by legislative bodies, the writer also explains how to cover the costs of this proposal under current budget allocations.

Evaluation System

You may want to suggest ways to measure progress toward the objectives stated in your proposal and for checking the results of individual parts of the plan. Evaluation methods can include progress reports, outside consultants, testing, statistical analyses, or feedback from employees. Follow these guidelines:

- Describe suggested evaluation systems, such as spot checks, surveys, or tests.
- Provide a timetable for evaluating the plan, including both periodic and final evaluations.
- Suggest who should analyze the progress of the plan.
- Assign responsibility for writing progress reports.

The writer in Model 12-6 offers to accept the responsibility of directing this project. As part of this responsibility, he will train employees in the new system, write monthly progress reports, obtain necessary permits, and monitor compliance with building regulations.

Expected Benefits

Sometimes writers highlight the expected benefits of a proposal in a separate section for emphasis. If you have such a section, mention both immediate and long-range benefits. Follow these guidelines:

- Describe one advantage at a time for emphasis.

- Show how each aspect of the problem will be solved by your proposal.

- Illustrate how the recommended solution will produce advantages for the company.

- Cite specific savings in costs or time.

Because this proposal involves a safety hazard, the writer in Model 12-6 uses the benefits section to emphasize how the proposed changes will solve the problem and bring the plant into compliance with existing safety regulations.

Summary/Conclusions

The final section of your proposal is one of the most important because readers tend to rely on the final section in most reports and, in a proposal, this section gives you a chance to emphasize the suitability of your plan as a solution to the company problem. Follow these guidelines:

- Summarize the seriousness of the problem.

- Restate your recommendations without the procedural details.

- Remind the reader of the important expected benefits.

- Mention any necessary deadlines.

The writer in Model 12-6 uses his conclusion to emphasize the safety hazard and stress the need for changes.

CHAPTER SUMMARY

This chapter discusses the conventional content and structure for the six types of reports most commonly written on the job. Remember:

- A feasibility study analyzes the alternatives available in a given situation.

- An incident report records information about accidents or other disruptive events.

- An investigative report explains how a particular question or problem was studied and the results of that study.

- A progress report provides information about an ongoing project.

- A trip report provides a record of events that occurred during a visit to another location.

- A proposal suggests solutions to a particular problem.

SUPPLEMENTAL READINGS IN PART 2

Benson, P. J. "Writing Visually: Design Considerations in Technical Publications," *Technical Communication,* p. 451.

Munter, M. "Meeting Technology: From Low-Tech to High-Tech," *Business Communication Quarterly,* p. 508.

"Six Graphics Guidelines," *Simply Stated,* p. 535.

Tarutz, J. H. "Editing for an International Audience," *Technical Editing,* p. 545.

White, J. V. "Color: The Newest Tool for Technical Communicators," *Technical Communication,* p. 551.

This feasibility study provides information to top executives who must select a site for the company headquarters in a new city. The report evaluates two available sites for their suitability for company operations and recommends one of them.

Discussion

1. The president of the company is the primary reader of this report, but other executives get copies. Officers of the company have already discussed moving to a new city, and the president is expecting this report. Review the "Introduction" section. What kinds of information would the writer have had to include if readers had never considered the possibility of moving the company to a new city?

2. Discuss the headings used in this report. How useful are they to a reader seeking specific information? What changes or additions might help the reader locate specific facts?

3. Discuss the overall organization in this report. How effective is it to discuss the Randolph Center ahead of the Lincoln Industrial Park in every section under the heading "Alternative Locations"?

4. Discuss how effectively the writer presents a case for choosing Randolph Center as the new location. Are there any points you would emphasize more than the writer does? What other kinds of information might support the writer's recommendation of Randolph Center?

To: Samuel P. Irving
           President

From: Isobel S. Archer
           Vice President—Administration

Date: April 16, 1999

Subject: Feasibility Study of Sites for Kansas City Offices

Introduction

This report assesses two available locations in greater Kansas City as possible sites for the new corporate offices of Sandrunne Enterprises. After reviewing the background, company needs, and features of the two available sites, I recommend we buy a building and lot in the Randolph Center.

Background

Sandrunne Enterprises has been considering moving the corporate headquarters to Kansas City from Springfield for about two years. Due to streamlining operations and expanding services, the current building in Springfield no longer fits the Company needs. Further, location in Kansas City will enhance our transportation connections and improve our ability to meet schedules. As you know, the Board of Directors has set strict parameters regarding the potential location for Sandrunne. The building/land must be large enough to accommodate our current requirements with enough room for reasonable expansion over the next five years, but overall acreage should not exceed two acres. The building/land must be in excellent condition, located in the greater Kansas City area in Missouri, and readily accessible to transportation carriers. Project cost should not exceed $600,000, and relocation should be completed by February 2000, when our current lease expires.

Possible Alternatives

I have surveyed the available building and land combinations with the assistance of Martin Realty Company, and the two locations that seem most appropriate are Randolph Center, a complex in North Kansas City, and Lincoln Industrial Park, also in North Kansas City. The two alternatives were chosen based on space suitability, condition of the

S. P. Irving   -2-   April 16, 1999

building/land, transportation accessibility, cost, and availability within
our time frame. Information for this study was obtained through
meetings with William Martin, president of Martin Realty, Tracey
Manchester, Director of Kansas City Regional Development Board,
and John Blackthorn, Real Estate Administrator for the Department
of Planning and Urban Development of Kansas City. I made two trips
to each site, accompanied by Rafael Mendez, from our transportation
planning division.

Alternative Locations

Space Suitability

The Randolph Center building is on 1.2 acres of land and fits the basic
corporate office/warehouse specifications required by the Board of
Directors. Although the acreage is less than two acres, the office
building, warehouse facility, and truck docks fit our exact requirements.
Only minor modifications to the office building and the warehouse would
be needed at Randolph Center. The warehouse space is actually 2,000
square feet over our current requirement and, therefore, allows for
future expansion.

The Lincoln Industrial Park site is 2.4 acres. Most industrial parks are
already plotted with specified acreage per plot, and the 2.4 plot available
was one of the smaller locations close to our two-acre ideal.

Condition of Building/Land

The Randolph Center location contains a brick building built in 1985
and in excellent condition with well-landscaped grounds. We would need
inspections before purchase, but the current condition of the building
seems in good repair. The offices have oak paneling, new carpeting,
skylights in the reception area, windows and crown molding in every
office, six-panel doors, and tiled bathrooms. Overall, the offices have
a professional appearance in keeping with Sandrunne's image. The
warehouse is equally well built with cement blocks throughout, and
the layout, including the two dock areas, would fit Sandrunne's
activities nicely.

The Lincoln Industrial Park location is newer (1990), and we would
have to landscape the area as well as build offices. The land is flat and

S. P. Irving   -3-   April 16, 1999

dry, making construction fairly straightforward. Paved roads to the site are complete, and other existing buildings are of high quality. Sandrunne would have to break ground for construction, but, of course, we could design the building exactly the way we want it.

Location and Transportation Accessibility

Since all of Sandrunne product is transported by truck, we must have access to a highway system and a layout and docking area in which the truckers can maneuver relatively easily. Both locations are within the general area we had chosen as appropriate. Both have adequate trucking access, and employees could reach either one via a four-lane highway system. Rafael Mendez assured me that the truckers would be pleased with the docking areas in Randolph Center. The basic docking areas at Lincoln Industrial Park are excellent too, and our new building could be constructed with the warehouse and docking facilities suitable for our operation.

Cost

Only minor modifications are needed at the Randolph Center location. At the Lincoln Industrial Park location, construction and landscaping will be required. Total estimated cost for the two locations is as follows:

Randolph Center

Office Modifications	$ 14,000
Warehouse Modifications	55,600
Total Improvements	$ 69,600
Purchase Price	$400,000
Total Randolph Center Cost	$469,600

Lincoln Industrial Park

Office Construction	$200,000
Warehouse Construction	400,000
Land Purchase	60,000
Total Lincoln Costs	$660,000

Note: Cost estimates are from Gramm, Weismann, and McCall, Associates, construction consultants

S. P. Irving   -4-   April 16, 1999

The Lincoln Industrial Park location would be $60,000 over the
established limit. Both location costs are estimated, and construction
overruns could add considerably to the total cost for the Lincoln location.
Costs could also be higher at the Randolph Center, but the risk is less.

Feasible Relocation Date

According to the realtors, the Randolph Center building is currently used
for storage by the owners and could be vacated quickly upon closing. The
closing time would be about 60 days, and an additional 60 days would be
needed for modifications and cleaning. Sandrunne could probably move
into the Randolph Center offices by September 1, 1999, well ahead of
our February 2000 deadline.

The Lincoln Industrial Park location has more variables. The timetable
must include design plans, site preparation, general contractor bids,
license permits, and landscaping; therefore, completion is harder to
predict. John Blackthorn estimates that Sandrunne could move in
by January 1, 2000, but the risk of not making that deadline is
somewhat high.

Conclusion and Recommendations

Sandrunne Enterprises has reached the point of moving to Kansas City
to solidify its corporate position and expand its operation further. Both
the alternative sites I investigated in North Kansas City have long-range
advantages and meet the Company criteria. However, Lincoln Industrial
Park involves a greater risk that both cost and deadline limits will be
exceeded. Considering our need to move without hindrance, I recommend
Randolph Center as our best choice. The location is excellent, the project
cost is under budget, and the deadline can be met easily.

I have reports from our consultants that I would like to discuss further
with you. My secretary will make an appointment for a discussion time.

IA:sd
c: M.L. Wilding
   M.P. Todd
   E.T. Fishman
   R.D. Micelli
   J.J. Warner

This incident report, written by a construction project manager, describes an accident resulting in a death. The writer includes information he collected from witnesses, personal inspection of the site, and hospital reports on the two men involved in the accident. In the description section, the writer gives a chronological account of the accident. The causes section covers the obvious reasons for the accident. The writer's recommendations focus on steps that would prevent such an accident in the future.

Discussion

1. Consider the "Recommendations" section of this report, and assume you decide to write a memo to all construction crews warning them about proper procedures. In groups, draft such a memo and compare your version with that of other groups.

2. Consider accidents you may have seen at work or on campus. Write an incident report based on your knowledge of the accident. Discuss in class whether you lack some relevant information.

3. Read several newspapers in your campus library and notice the reports of industrial accidents. Select one accident and write an incident report based on the information in the newspaper story.

To: Will Brady, Vice President

From: Ed Consuelos *EC*

Date: July 14, 1999

Re: Accident Report—Cave-in

Description of the Incident

On July 13, 1999, at 2:45 p.m., Mike Koziak and Steve Medina were laying sewer pipe in a trench about 15 ft deep on the northwest corner of the intersection of Clay and Hardy streets. Traffic was heavy at that time. According to Jason Rafter, another crew member, both Mr. Koziak and Mr. Medina were attempting to climb out of the trench when a small cave-in occurred, covering Mr. Medina in sand to his ankles. Mr. Koziak, who was farther up the back wall, turned back to lend a hand, and another cave-in occurred, covering Mr. Medina to his waist. Mr. Rafter saw the second cave-in and called the fourth crew member, Ray Gutierrez, to assist in rescuing the men. The two men at the top of the trench managed to pull up Mr. Koziak, but they had to call 911 for assistance in extracting Mr. Medina, who was covered in sand and gravel up to his shoulders before being pulled out. He died from a ruptured right ventricle of his heart on the way to St. Vincent's Hospital. Mr. Koziak was unhurt.

Causes

After inspecting the scene and interviewing the surviving crew members, I have determined that the sides of the trench were not shored to prevent a cave-in. To exit the trench, the men had to climb up the backfill, thus causing the gravel to give way. In addition, the heavy traffic, particularly the loaded school buses that had just driven past, probably caused vibrations that loosened the soil. None of the four men on the job site had had a training session on shoring or sloping trenches.

Recommendations

I recommend a mandatory training program for all workers in recognizing hazardous conditions and safety in preparation of trenches. I also recommend the following:

- Trenches 5 ft or more deep must be shored or braced to prevent cave-ins.

- Excavations close to highway traffic must have extra shoring.

- All trenches 4 ft or more deep must include ladders.

This investigative report, adapted from a book-length report to Congress, gives the results of a survey to estimate the number of housing units with lead-based paint in the United States.

In research reports published in scientific journals or issued by research and government agencies, the abstract often appears on the first page between the title and the introduction, as shown here. A table showing partial results appears at the end of the report in an appendix.

Discussion

1. Discuss the "Method" section. How helpful is it for a reader who wants to know how the survey was conducted but does not intend to duplicate the survey? If the reader wants to duplicate the survey, what kinds of information about the method should be added?

2. Discuss the "Introduction." If a reader knows nothing about the lead-based paint hazard, how does the introduction help prepare the reader to understand the study?

3. Notice that the "Results" section contains some of the data available in the table at the end of the report. Discuss why the writer would repeat information from the table in the "Results" section.

4. The "Conclusion" section repeats the major results. As this information also appears in the "Results" section and in the appendix, why would a writer include it in the "Conclusion" section?

5. The investigative report format is designed for readers who are researchers particularly interested in the method of investigation. Such readers prefer to know results before conclusions. Discuss what format general readers probably prefer. In groups and using the information in this report, write a bulletin for general readers to alert them to the hazard of lead-based paint in homes.

SURVEY OF LEAD-BASED PAINT
IN U.S. HOUSING

Abstract

This report focuses on a 1989–90 survey conducted to estimate the number of housing units in the United States that contain lead-based paint. The survey centered on private single and multifamily dwelling units and public housing. In-person visits and interviews with a systematic random sample of houses were conducted. Overall results indicate that 74 percent of all homes built before 1980 have some lead-based paint, and 71 percent of the homes with lead-based paint have children under age seven in them. The survey also indicates that there is no difference in the incidence of lead-based paint based on income, home value, or rent. Methods for removing lead-based paint should be evaluated, and public awareness of the hazard should be increased.

Introduction

Medical research during the past decade has found that childhood lead poisoning is more widespread and has more serious consequences than previously thought. Published research has found strong connections between prenatal lead exposure and deficiencies in infant development. Such consequences indicate lead-based paint in houses poses a serious health hazard. Yet, the cost of removing lead-based paint is very high, and the removal process may increase the hazard by creating lead dust.

The 1987 amendments to the Lead-Based Paint Poisoning Prevention Act call for an estimate of the extent of lead-based paint hazard in the United States. Because there are no accurate estimates of the number of U.S. houses with lead-based paint, the Department of Housing and Urban Development sponsored the first national survey of lead-based paint in housing to provide estimates. The survey was conducted in 1989–90, and the objective was to obtain data for estimating the following:

- The number of housing units (private, single family, private multifamily, and public housing) with lead-based paint, by year of construction.

- The extent or surface area of lead-based paint in housing, to develop an estimate of national abatement costs.

- The condition of the paint.

-2-

- The incidence of lead in dust and in soil around the residential structure.

- The characteristics of housing with varying levels of potential hazard, to examine possible priorities for abatement.

Method

The study focused on housing constructed in the United States before 1980 and centered on private housing because data on public housing was too small to generalize. Newer houses were presumed to be lead free because, in 1978, the Consumer Product Safety Commission banned the sale of lead-based paint to consumers and the use of such paint in residences. Housing excluded from the study included housing exclusively for the elderly, group quarters such as nursing homes and dormitories, homes in Alaska and Hawaii, and military housing.

Private housing was grouped into (1) private single family houses, defined as one to four dwelling units, and (2) private multifamily houses, defined as five or more dwelling units. Dates of houses were coded as (1) built before 1940, (2) built between 1940 and 1959, and (3) built between 1960 and 1979.

The objectives of the study required in-person visits to the dwelling units. A sample of 30 counties in the United States was selected, and within these counties, five geographic areas were chosen by random systematic selection. Samples of individual dwelling units were selected also by systematic random sampling. A field interviewer visited each unit and talked with an adult occupant to collect basic information. Inspection visits then were scheduled with residents who were willing to complete a full interview. Each resident who cooperated was paid a $50 incentive. Total sample size was 284 dwelling units. Because of disproportionate sampling of housing types, sampling weights were applied to each completed case, and initial weights were adjusted to balance differences in nonresponse and noncoverage.

Results

Table 1 (see Appendix) shows the results of coding homes for lead-based paint. An estimated 74 percent of all homes built before 1980 contain lead-based paint, and 71 percent of the homes with lead-based

-3-

paint are occupied by children under age seven. Older homes are more likely to have lead-based paint than newer homes. An estimated 90 percent of homes built before 1940 have lead-based paint in the interior or on the exterior, while 62 percent of homes built between 1960 and 1970 have lead-based paint in the interior or on the exterior. The age of the home was the only distinguishing feature.

Based on the interviews, there are no significant differences in the incidence of lead-based paint relative to the income of the household, the value of the home, or the rent. There is also no significant difference between single family homes and multifamily homes. Lead-based paint is found in the South (58%) less often than in other regions because the South was significantly less urban than other regions until the 1970s, and its housing, on the average, was built more recently.

The survey also provides information about the location of lead-based paint in the home. While most public policy discussions have been concerned with lead-based paint on interior walls and in dust inside the dwelling unit, the survey shows that lead-based paint is more common on the outside of dwelling units. An estimated 23 percent of homes have lead-based paint only on the exterior; 14 percent have it only on the interior; 37 percent have it on both the interior and exterior.

Conclusions

This national survey tends to confirm earlier research about the incidence of lead-based paint: (1) housing built before 1940 is most likely to have lead-based paint; (2) about 74 percent of all housing built before 1980 has some lead-based paint; (3) about 71 percent of the housing with lead-based paint is occupied by children under age seven; (4) lead-based paint appears to contribute to lead in dust.

This survey also provides new information about the problem of lead-based paint: (1) lead-based paint occurs as often in the homes of the wealthy as of the poor; (2) lead-based paint is more commonly found on the exterior than the interior; (3) lead dust is found more frequently around the windows than on the floors, and the dust comes from both the interior and the exterior.

The cost of lead-based paint abatement in American homes is potentially very large (from $2100 to $8900 per home, depending on the method), and the long-range effectiveness of any abatement method

-4-

is uncertain. The traditional abatement methods focus on peeling paint or interior paint to a height of five feet, and these methods contain a risk from the lead dust remaining after cleanup. Evaluation of possible alternative ways to clean up lead dust should be undertaken immediately.

Except in cases of actual lead poisoning, little is being done to reduce the hazard in homes, even among the wealthy. Public awareness must increase. However, industry lacks the capacity to perform testing and abatement work. The nation requires a comprehensive plan to address the hazards of lead-based paint.

-5-

APPENDIX

Table 1
Estimated Number of Privately Owned
Housing Units with Lead-Based Paint

Characteristic	Housing w/Lead-based Paint	No. of Units
Year:		
1960–1979	62%	120
1940–1959	80%	87
Before 1940	90%	77
Housing Type:		
Single Family	74%	227
Multifamily	73%	57
Children under Age 7	71%	90
Region:		
Northeast	93%	53
Midwest	76%	69
South	58%	116
West	80%	46
Value of Owner-occupied Home:		
Less than $40,000	79%	39
$40,000–$79,000	53%	46
$80,000–$149,000	65%	45
Over $150,000	87%	42
Rent:		
Less than $400	69%	59
Over $400	87%	40
Household Income:		
Less than $30,000	76%	156
Over $30,000	72%	107

This progress report, written by an on-site engineer, is one of a series of reports on a specific company project—dam repairs. The report will be added to the others in the series and kept in a three-ring binder at the company headquarters for future reference when the company has another contract for a similar job.

The writer addresses the report to a company vice-president, but four other readers are listed as receiving copies.

Discussion

1. The writer knows that her readers are familiar with the technical terms she uses. If this report were needed by a nontechnical reader at the company, which terms would the writer have to define?

2. Discuss the information in the introduction and how effectively it supports the writer's assertion that work on the dam is progressing satisfactorily.

3. Discuss how the writer's organization and use of format devices support her report of satisfactory progress. Why did she list items under "Work Completed" but not under "Work Remaining"?

TO: Mark Zerelli   October 16,1999
            Vice-President
            Balmer Company

FROM: Tracey Atkins *TA*
            Project Manager

SUBJECT: Progress Report #3–Rockmont Canyon Dam

Introduction

This report covers the progress on the Rockmont Canyon Dam repairs
from September 15 to October 15 as reported previously. Repairs to the
damaged right and left spillways have been close to the original
schedule. Balmer engineers prepared hydraulic analyses and design
studies to size and locate the aeration slots. These slots allowed Balmer
to relax tolerances normally required for concrete surfaces subjected to
high-velocity flows. Phillips, Inc., the general contractor, demolished and
removed the damaged structures. To expedite repairs, construction
crews worked on both spillways simultaneously. Construction time was
further reduced by hiring another demolition company, Rigby, Inc. The
project costs rose during the first month when Phillips, Inc., had to build
batching facilities for the concrete because the dam site had no facilities.

Work Completed

Since the last progress report, three stages of work have been
completed:

1. On September 18, aggregate for the concrete mix was hauled
230 miles from Wadsworth, Oregon. The formwork for the tunnel linings
arrived from San Antonio, Texas, on September 20.

2. Phillips developed hoist-controlled work platforms and man-cars
to lower workers, equipment, and materials down the spillways.
Platforms and man-cars were completed on September 22.

3. Phillips drove two 20-foot-diameter modified-horseshoe-shaped
tunnels through the sandstone canyon walls to repair horizontal
portions of the tunnel spillways. A roadheader continuous-mining
machine with a rotary diamond-studded bit excavated the tunnels in
three weeks, half the time standard drill and blast techniques would
have taken. The tunnels were completed on October 15.

Mark Zerelli   -2-   October 16, 1999

Work Remaining

The next stage of the project is to control flowing water from gate leakage. Phillips will caulk the radial gates first. If that is not successful in controlling the flow, Phillips will try French drains and ditches. After tunnels are complete, both spillways will be checked for vibration tolerance, and the aeration slot design will be compared with Balmer's hydraulic model. Full completion of repairs is expected by November 15.

Adjustments

Some adjustments have been made since the last progress report. During construction work on both spillways, over 50 people and 200 pieces of equipment were on the site. Heavily traveled surfaces had to be covered with plywood sheets topped with a blanket of gravel. This procedure added $3500 to the construction costs and delayed work for half a day.

Conclusion

The current work is progressing as expected. The overall project has fallen three days behind estimated timetables, but no further delays should occur. The final stage of the project will require measurements at several areas within both spillways to be sure they can handle future flood increases with a peak inflow of at least 125,000 cfs. Balmer expects to make the final checks by November 25.

TA:ss
c: Robert Barr
    Mitchell Lawrence
    Mark Bailey
    Joseph Novak

This trip report describes a visit to another company to observe an in-house training system for new computer software. The writer addresses the vice-president she reports to and recommends that they adopt the training system.

Discussion

1. The writer of this report includes two information sections—one describing the training system and the other describing what the trainers at the other company told her about an alternative system. Discuss the headings for these sections. Why would the writer decide to emphasize her meeting with trainers in the heading rather than emphasize the alternative system? Her opening identifies Mr. Golden as the Bretton training coordinator. What is her purpose for identifying two more trainers later in the report?

2. Discuss how effective the opening summary is for the reader who needs to make a decision about training employees on the new software.

3. Discuss whether the report could—or should—be longer with additional information included. What kinds of information might be added?

To: Timothy O'Banyon, Vice President   *MT*   Date: May 6, 1999
From: Melissa Thacker, Training Director
Re: Trip to Bretton Technology, Houston, Texas, May 1–2

Summary

To prepare for our conversion to the MIRA-32 integrated software package, I spent two days at Bretton Technology, observing the training system Bretton is using during its conversion to the software. Richard Golden, the training coordinator, met me and explained the training system, why it was chosen, and why it has proved effective. Based on my observation and the information from Mr. Golden, I recommend that we adopt the Bretton training system for our employees during our conversion to MIRA-32.

User Training

The Bretton system requires a minimum of 40 days of user practice in the company training room, using actual company records and dummy data files. Thus, employees learn the system while working with familiar files. Full implementation of the 15 modules in the MIRA-32 takes about 18 months, and training should begin on each module one week before it is implemented. This schedule allows employees to move smoothly from the dummy files to the real ones as the modules enter the system.

Meeting with Bretton Trainers

In addition to Mr. Golden, I met with Sara Wyman and Tyrone Parms, both experienced software trainers. Mr. Parms said Bretton had begun a "train the trainer" system for MIRA-32 with the idea of having the trainers monitor employees as they used the software on the job. However, immediate problems developed in coordinating training sessions with the vendor schedule for implementing the system. In addition, employees did not have time to practice on the software, and this training system did not create employee confidence about handling the MIRA-32. All three trainers at Bretton recommend the 40-day training schedule with hands-on practice.

Conclusion and Recommendation

I believe we should duplicate the training system used at Bretton Technology. Bretton's organization is similar to ours, and we can learn from the experience there. I have copies of the Bretton training outlines, and Mr. Golden has offered to consult with us via videoconference when we set up our training room and schedule.

This unsolicited proposal identifies a hazardous situation at a city water treatment plant. The writer prepares a formal proposal in this instance because he expects the reader to show it to others, and he knows that requests for significant extra expenditures traditionally are presented in a formal report style in the city government offices.

The writer begins by describing the problem in detail so that the reader can understand the inherent dangers in the current situation. He then suggests a specific set of changes to eliminate the hazard to employees. In this case, the suggested changes are relatively uncomplicated, but the process of soliciting bids and getting permits has specific stages, and the writer outlines these in a timetable.

Discussion

1. The reader of this proposal has not asked for it and may not be aware of the problem. Discuss how effectively the writer makes his point that a serious situation exists and must be resolved.

2. Discuss how effectively the writer presents the benefits section of his proposal.

3. The suggested timetable and projected costs are presented within the report. Discuss whether, as a reader, you would prefer these details in an appendix.

4. In groups, identify a campus problem that affects a large number of students. Draft a description of the problem that could be an opening section of a proposal for changes.

PROPOSAL FOR STANDBY POWER IMPROVEMENTS
AT WATER TREATMENT PLANT

Prepared for
Richard T. Sutton
Director of Operations

Submitted by
Michael J. Novachek
Water Department Manager

November 16, 1999

Abstract

Since 1994, the City Water Treatment Plant (WTP) has used two generators to operate high-service pumps during electrical power failures. One of these generators creates a dangerous safety condition because electricians have to stand outside during rain storms to make connections. The proposal is to install exterior outlets under shelter so standby power can be safely connected.

CHESTERTON WATER DEPARTMENT
65 Portage Road
Chesterton, TN 38322

(423) 555-1000   Fax (423) 555-1100

November 16, 1999

Mr. Richard T. Sutton
Director of Operations
City of Chesterton
111 Civic Plaza
Chesterton, TN 38303

Dear Mr. Sutton:

I am attaching a proposal for installation of new electrical outlets and
outside shelter at the Water Treatment Plant to correct a current safety
problem. Our method for connecting standby power equipment during
rain storms is in violation of OSHA regulations and should be addressed
at once.

The recommended improvements are relatively minor. I am attaching a
report from Raymond and Burnside Engineering Associates, outlining
specifications and design features of the suggested improvements. Our
procedures for soliciting and reviewing construction bids will take about
seven months, so I would like to begin this project at once. May I have your
authorization to proceed?

Please call me at Ext. 5522 if you would like to discuss this matter in
greater detail.

Sincerely,

M. J. Novachek

Michael J. Novachek
Water Department Manager

MJN:sd
Attachment

PROPOSAL FOR STANDBY POWER IMPROVEMENTS AT WATER TREATMENT PLANT

Safety Problem with Standby Power

The WTP uses four high-service pumps, which provide treated water to our customers. Three of the pumps have a rated capacity of 2 million gallons per day (MGD). The fourth pump has a rated capacity of 3 MGD. The average and peak daily demands at the WTP are 5 MGD and 7 MGD, respectively. Therefore, we typically run a combination of the pumps to meet our demand.

When an electrical failure occurs, we develop an unsafe situation for our electricians. The plant was originally designed and constructed to provide standby power only to the largest pump. The standby power came from the diesel-powered generator located alongside, and directly tied to, the 3-MGD pump. Therefore, when a power failure occurs, the power supply to the 3-MGD pumps can be switched from the standard supply to the generator. Under normal conditions, the plant is required to operate a 2-MGD pump along with the 3-MGD pump to meet customer demand. During power failures, we temporarily connect a portable standby power generator to one of the 2-MGD pumps. This temporary generator installation creates an unsafe condition.

The portable standby generator is stored on a trailer at Pump Station No. 11. During power failures, two electricians transport the portable generator to the WTP. The portable generator is parked outside, next to the doors of the pump room. The electricians run power cables from the generator to the Motor Control Center (MCC) of the pump, which is located in the pump room. Since power failures usually result from a severe storm, the electricians often make the generator connections while standing in the rain. The doors to the pump room remain open to provide an opening for the power cables to run from the generator, along the pump room floor, to the MCC. This setup exposes plant personnel to a live power cable and wet floor conditions and is in violation of Occupational Safety and Health Administration (OSHA) regulations. These conditions could create an enormous liability to the City if they result in an accident to an electrician or plant operator.

-2-

Proposed Solution

To eliminate hazardous conditions connected with installing the portable generators, I recommend the following:

- Install a male adapter plug to the portable standby generator
- Install a female wall outlet at the exterior south wall of the pump room
- Install an awning at the exterior south wall of the pump room
- Install permanent wire and conduit from the outlet to the MCC of the pumps

During a power failure, plant personnel can transport the portable standby power generator to a covered area located at the south exterior wall of the pump room. Personnel can connect standby power to the pump by inserting the generator plug into the permanent outlet. The awning covers the generator and wall outlet and keeps this area relatively dry. The pump room doors could be kept closed. No live electrical connections are required. Finally, no power cables are strewn along the floor.

Schedule

In order to incorporate the recommended improvements, the project will require four phases.

The design phase will require the services of a consultant engineer. I have discussed the project with engineers at Raymond and Burnside Associates, the company that designed the plant 15 years ago. The engineers assured me that the project is feasible and can be completed within the budgetary and time constraints set herein. The consultant will be responsible for the preparation of plans, specifications, and bid documents, as well as permits required by the Environmental Protection Agency. I recommend that Raymond and Burnside Associates handle the design services for this project since we have an existing agreement and they are familiar with the plant.

The bid phase will require the services of a consultant, as well as the City law director, to review the bids and recommend a contractor.

-3-

The construction phase will require an electrical contractor to perform the work. I recommend we use Raymond and Burnside Associates to verify that the work is being performed in accordance with the design plans and specifications.

The implementation phase comes after the improvements are completed. Once the system is in place, the two electricians on standby duty will be replaced by one on-duty plant maintenance worker.

I suggest the following schedule for the installation of the improvements:

Item	Completion Date
Service director approval to proceed	December 1, 1999
Procure agreement with engineer	December 14, 1999
Complete plans, specifications, and bid documents	January 3, 2000
City review of plans, specifications, and bid documents	January 17, 2000
Submit permits and plans to Ohio EPA	February 1, 2000
Ohio EPA review	April 1, 2000
Advertisement for bid	April 14, 2000
Bid opening	May 1, 2000
Award bid	June 1, 2000
Start construction	July 1, 2000
Complete construction	August 1, 2000

Cost

The estimated project cost to install a new standby power system improvement is $27,615. This cost includes engineering, construction, and contingencies as shown in Table 1.

Table 1
Probable Project Cost

Engineering

Design	$ 8,000
Services During Construction	4,000
Total Engineering Cost	$12,000

-4-

Construction

Awning	$ 2,500
Electrical Adapter	500
Electrical Outlet	500
Wire and Conduit	7,000
MCC Switches	3,800
Total Construction Cost	$14,300
Total Project Cost	$26,300
With 5% Contingency	$27,615

The engineering fee includes design, preparation of plans, specifications and bid documents, review of bid, and services during construction. Construction costs include all labor and materials required to construct the improvements. A contingency fee of 5 percent of the total engineering and construction costs is included to cover costs not foreseen at this time.

The expected 2000 annual operation costs with these improvements is $400. Without the improvements, cost is $2,500. This higher cost comes from the additional employees required to provide the service necessary to achieve the standby power.

The project probably can be funded out of the water fund. We had $20,000 left from last year's budget. A line item of $7,000 could be allotted from this year's budget. The combination of funds will cover the total cost.

Coordination

The improvements will require the coordination and cooperation of City forces to construct and operate the system. As Manager of the Water Department, I will take full responsibility for the following:

1. Instruct the employees regarding the new operation procedures once the improvements are installed.

2. Provide monthly progress reports to the Mayor, and the Directors of Service, Law, and Finance.

-5-

3. Ensure that proper Ohio EPA and building permits are obtained.

4. Ensure that all City regulations involving capital improvements are followed.

5. Obtain proper approvals from the City Planning Commission and City Council.

Benefits

The main benefit of the proposed improvement is safety. As City leaders, we are responsible for the safety of our employees. The existing condition is unsafe and violates OSHA regulations. Also, the current permanent standby power system does not meet today's design standards. After improvements we will be in full compliance with all safety regulations. The expected initial cost is reasonable given the seriousness of the situation, and the proposed improvements will lower personnel costs in the future.

Conclusion

Currently, the City water treatment plant operates its standby power system in an unsafe manner, thereby risking the health and safety of plant electricians and operators. With the installations proposed, these unsafe conditions can be eliminated. In addition, these improvements will bring our operation up to current design standards.

1. You have been hired as a management consultant to the JJ Health Club, owned by Jennifer Jasper. The health club is not affiliated with a national chain and is currently located in Pilgrim Plaza, a strip mall in your community. Ms. Jasper is not happy with her current location because of limited customer parking and no space to add a steam room as she would like to. Select two potential new locations for JJ Health Club, and write a formal feasibility report to Ms. Jasper. Analyze the locations for how well they would serve customers and help the business. *Next,* select one option and write a formal proposal to Ms. Jasper for that option.

2. Assume you are the computer consultant to McAdams Realty Company. The company is owned by partners Benjamin Paine and Janella Marting. They have 17 full-time and 6 part-time real estate agents, all working on commission. Three secretaries are employed in the office. The partners want to upgrade their out-of-date computer system, hardware and software. Write a formal feasibility report to the partners, assessing two computer systems (hardware and software) for the office. *Next,* write a formal proposal for one option to the partners.

3. Assume you are the project manager on a construction site. This morning you were called to the site because a fatal accident occurred. Two workers were trying to adjust the brakes on a backhoe. One man, who had been on the job only 3 hours, told the backhoe operator, who had been on the job 4 days, to raise the wheels off the ground with the front bucket and the outriggers. The operator did so and put the backhoe in idle while stepping on the brakes. The site was near a major highway with heavy truck traffic. The backhoe operator had a portable radio turned on during the incident. The victim crawled under the machine to adjust the brakes. About 5 minutes later, a third worker noticed the victim lying limp in the 36-in. space between the ground and the drive shaft. The victim's neck had been broken. His jacket hood had wrapped around the backhoe drive shaft. The accident surprises you because everyone knows that a backhoe should be shut off before any adjustments are made. You gather the facts, interview the witnesses, and write an incident report to the president of M. K. Construction, Inc. Add any details you believe should be in the report.

4. Assume you are a supervisor at the Holden Ceramics plant. Yesterday, a worker was injured when he opened a furnace door to load ceramic materials for firing. The furnace was in a narrow pit. The door fell off its hinges and pinned the worker in the pit. Police were called to the scene. The door weighs 3 tons, and the furnace heats to 2300 degrees. When you examine the door, you notice that the bolts securing the hinge have sheared off the furnace. A witness working 3–4 ft above the victim saw the accident and said the victim attempted to evade the door but could not get out of the pit. The injured worker was taken to General Medical Center. Doctors report he has second-degree burns on his legs, a crushed pelvis, and internal injuries. Full recovery will take a year

or more. Add any details you believe are necessary, and write an incident report to the vice-president of the company.

5. Research current job prospects in your field in the location where you would like to work. Use at least five sources, including an interview with someone already in the field, even if not at the location you want. Write an investigative report on job prospects in general and in that specific location. Consider variations in your field, such as types of accounting jobs or public and private security work. Address the informal report to the director of your campus placement service. Assume that the director has asked for this report so counselors can give students practical advice on this topic.

6. This assignment requires a visual inspection of one public room on your campus. You select the room. Observation or inspection requires that you examine the area under *existing* conditions. Make no attempt to control or manipulate the situation. The purpose of your study is to investigate conditions in one room *after 10 a.m. or after the public has been using it for at least 2 hours.* Record what you see, smell, hear, and so on. You must interview at least one person, either someone using the room or someone responsible for maintenance, and include that person's comments in your report. You should inspect the following: light fixtures, doors/entrances, windows, walls/floors, and special features of the room, such as sinks, desks, blinds, and so on. Make notes on needed repair or replacement. *Also* observe how many people are using the room during your inspection and record any need for more supplies, more furniture, and so on. You *will not* make any specific recommendations in this report, but you can conclude that the room needs attention in some ways. Address your report to Tom Ortega, director of physical facilities. Assume that you are a member of a team of students who have been hired to inspect campus facilities from the student perspective. If your instructor wants you to write a formal report, follow the guidelines in Chapter 10.

7. Based on the investigative report you wrote for Exercise 6, write a short informal proposal for one specific improvement in the room you observed. Address your proposal to Tom Ortega, director of physical facilities.

8. Assume that you are a member of the student government at your school and are writing a proposal on behalf of the officers. You want to establish a permanent student committee to investigate student inquiries or complaints about the *campus physical facilities* and to make recommendations for changes. You will have to consider such questions as the following: How will the committee members be selected? How big will the committee be? Will supplies or office space be needed? What are the costs involved? How will the committee process student complaints? Other questions must also be covered in your proposal. Remember, a proposal is a persuasive report. Convince the reader that this idea will be beneficial to your school. Address your report to the campus director of student services.

9. Study a problem at the company where you work. The problem should be a situation that requires a change in procedures or new equipment. Investigate at least two alternative solutions to this problem. Then write a feasibility study in which you evaluate all the solutions and recommend one of them. Address the report to the appropriate person at your company, and assume that this person asked you to write the report. If your instructor wants you to prepare a formal report, use the guidelines in Chapter 10.

10. Write a progress report for a project you are doing in a science or technology class. Report your progress as of the midpoint of your project. Address the report to the instructor of the science or technology class and say that you will submit another progress report when the project is nearly finished.

11. Write a proposal for a change at your job to your supervisor or the appropriate person. The change you propose may include equipment purchases, reorganizing work duties, a new system, new parking arrangements, and so on. If you do not have a current job, propose a change on campus, such as increased food services or reorganization in the bookstore. Address the director of student services. Assume that your supervisor or the director of student services did not ask you for this proposal, so you need to make a persuasive case that a problem exists and needs to be solved. If your instructor wants you to write a formal proposal, use the guidelines in Chapter 10.

CHAPTER **13**

Correspondence

UNDERSTANDING LETTERS, MEMOS, AND E-MAIL

Correspondence includes letters, memos, and e-mail. Although these frequently are addressed to one person, they often have multiple readers because the original reader passes along the correspondence to others, or the writer sends copies to everyone involved in the topic.

Give the same careful attention to reader, purpose, and situation in correspondence that you do in all writing. Because of its person-to-person style, however, correspondence may create emotional responses in readers that other technical documents do not. A reader may react positively to a bulletin in a company manual, but a memo from a supervisor on the same subject may strike the reader as dictatorial. Consider tone and organizational strategy from the perspective of how your readers will respond emotionally, as well as logically, to the message.

Letters

Letters are written primarily to people outside an organization and cover a variety of situations, such as (1) requests, (2) claims, (3) adjustments, (4) orders, (5) sales, (6) credit, (7) collections, (8) goodwill messages, (9) announcements, (10) records of agreements, (11) follow-ups to telephone conversations, (12) transmittals of other technical documents, and (13) job applications.

Memos

Memos are written primarily to people inside an organization. With the exception of job applications, memos cover the same topics as letters. In addition, many internal reports, such as trip reports, progress reports, and short proposals, may be in memo form.

E-Mail

E-mail (electronic mail) allows transmission of letters, memos, and other documents from one computer to another through a series of computer networks. Millions of people now use e-mail daily because of the speedy transmission and the convenience, especially for short messages between people who have an established subject or who are communicating about routine matters. E-mail has many clear advantages, such as the following:

- Managers can reach dozen of employees quickly.
- Team members working on projects can communicate easily on small points without meeting.

- People can avoid playing "telephone tag," which is frustrating and time consuming.
- People can communicate over long distances without regard to time zone differences.
- Companies can save postage and paper costs.

E-mail, however, must be used with caution. Because e-mail does not pass through human hands and receivers use a password to access their e-mail, senders often assume it is private. E-mail is not private.

By pressing one button, a receiver can send your message to thousands of people. The consequences can be serious. Only hours after Air Force pilot Scott O'Grady, shot down in Bosnia, was rescued by other U.S. pilots, one of the pilots sent a long detailed message about the rescue to a few friends. The message included pilot code names, weapons loads, radio frequencies, and other classified information. Within minutes of reading the message, the pilot's friends forwarded it to other friends, who also passed it on. Finally the message was posted on bulletin boards available to millions of people. The classified information was now in the hands of anyone interested in U.S. military operations.[1]

There are other dangers in casual use of e-mail. Companies and individuals can be liable for messages sent on e-mail. Lawsuits for sexual harassment, age discrimination, product liability, and other matters have resulted from e-mail messages.[2] A receiver or a hacker can alter a message and send it under your name. Many people do not realize that employers have the right to monitor e-mail that is sent on a system paid for by the employer. Some computer systems save all e-mail even if the receiver deletes it, and computer experts can find files that were "deleted" months before. People have been fired as a result of information they have revealed in e-mail messages. Consider carefully the way you use e-mail, and do not send messages that could embarrass you, get you fired, cost you money, or send you to jail.

DEVELOPING EFFECTIVE TONE

Tone refers to the feelings created by the words in a message. Business correspondence should have a tone that sounds natural and conveys cooperation, mutual respect, sincerity, and courtesy. Tone of this kind establishes open communication and reflects favorably on both the writer and the company. Because words on paper cannot be softened with a smile or a gesture, take special care in word choice to avoid sounding harsh or accusing. Remarks that were intended to be objective may strike your reader as overly strong commands or tactless insinuations, especially if the subject is at all controversial. Remember the following principles for creating a pleasant and cooperative tone in your correspondence.

Natural Language

Use clear, natural language, and avoid falling into the habit of using old-fashioned phrases that sound artificial. A reader who has to struggle through a letter filled with out-of-date expressions probably will become annoyed with both you and your message, resulting in poor communication. This sentence is full of out-of-date language:

> Per yours of the tenth, please find enclosed the warranty.

No one really talks this way, and no one should write this way. Here is a revision in more natural language:

> I am enclosing the warranty you requested in your letter of March 10.

Keep your language simple and to the point. This list shows some stale business expressions that should be replaced by simpler, more natural phrases:

Old-Fashioned	*Natural*
Attached hereto . . .	Attached is . . .
We beg to advise . . .	We can say that . . .
Hoping for the favor of a reply . . .	I hope to hear from you . . .
As per your request . . .	As you requested . . .
It has come to my attention . . .	I understand that . . .
Prior to receipt of . . .	Before we received . . .
Pursuant to . . .	In regard to . . .
The undersigned will . . .	I will . . .

If you use such out-of-date expressions, your readers may believe you are as out of date in your information as you are in your language.

Positive Language

Keep the emphasis on positive rather than negative images. Avoid writing when you are angry, and never let anger creep into your writing. In addition, avoid using words that emphasize the negative aspects of a situation; emphasize the positive whenever you can, or at least choose neutral language. Shown below are sentences that contain words that emphasize a negative rather than a positive or neutral viewpoint. The revisions show how to eliminate the negative words.

> *Negative:*   When I received your complaint, I checked our records.
> *Positive:*   When I received your letter, I checked our records.

Negative: To avoid further misunderstanding and confusion, our sales representative will visit your office and try to straighten out your order.

Positive: To ensure that your order is handled properly, our sales representative will visit your office.

Negative: I am sending a replacement for the faulty coil.

Positive: I am sending a new coil that is guaranteed for one year.

Negative: The delay in your shipment because we lost your order should not be longer than four days.

Positive: Your complete order should reach you by September 20.

In these examples, a simple substitution of positive-sounding words for negative-sounding words improves the overall tone of each sentence, whereas the information in each sentence and its purpose remain the same.

No matter what your opinion of your reader, do not use language that implies that the reader is dishonest or stupid. Notice how the following revisions eliminate the accusing and insulting tone of the original sentences.

Insulting: Because you failed to connect the cable, the picture was blurred.

Neutral: The picture was blurred because the V-2 cable was not connected to the terminal.

Insulting: You claimed that the engine stalled.

Neutral: Your letter said that the engine stalled.

Insulting: Don't let carelessness cause accidents in the testing laboratory.

Neutral: Please be careful when handling explosive compounds.

Negative language, either about a situation or about your reader, will interfere with the cooperation you need from your reader. The emphasis in correspondence should be on solutions rather than on negative events.

You-Attitude

The *you-attitude* refers to the point of view a writer takes when looking at a situation as the reader would. In all correspondence, try to convey an appreciation of your reader's position. To do this, present information from the standpoint of how it will affect or interest your reader. In these sample sentences, the emphasis is shifted from the writer's point of view to the reader's by focusing on the benefits to the reader in the situation:

Writer emphasis: We are shipping your order on Friday.

Reader emphasis: You will receive your order by Monday, October 10.

| *Writer emphasis:* | To reduce our costs, we are changing the billing system. |
| *Reader emphasis:* | To provide you with clear records, we are changing our billing system. |

| *Writer emphasis:* | I was pleased to hear that the project was completed. |
| *Reader emphasis:* | Congratulations on successfully completing the project! |

By stressing your reader's point of view and the benefits to your reader in a situation, you can create a friendly, helpful tone in correspondence. Of course, readers will see through excessive praise or insincere compliments, but they will respond favorably to genuine concern about their opinions and needs. Here are guidelines for establishing the you-attitude in your correspondence:

1. Put yourself in your reader's place, and look at the situation from his or her point of view.

2. Emphasize your reader's actions or benefits in a situation.

3. Present information as pleasantly as possible.

4. Offer a helpful suggestion or appreciative comment when possible.

5. Choose words that do not insult or accuse your reader.

6. Choose words that are clear and natural, and avoid old-fashioned or legal-sounding phrases.

Tone is often a serious problem in e-mail messages. Because so much e-mail consists of short messages, senders often do not realize how abrupt or harsh they may sound. Check your messages carefully for appropriate tone and word choice before pushing the "send" button.

ORGANIZING LETTERS AND MEMOS

Most correspondence is best organized in either a *direct* or an *indirect pattern,* depending on how the reader is likely to react emotionally to the message. If the news is good, or if the reader does not have an emotional stake in the subject, use the direct pattern with the main idea in the opening. If, however, the news is bad, the indirect pattern with the main idea after the explanation is often most effective because a reader may not read the explanation of the situation if the bad news appears in the opening. Most business correspondence uses the direct pattern. The indirect pattern, however, is an important strategy whenever a writer has to announce bad news in a sensitive situation and wants to retain as much goodwill from the reader as possible. A third pattern is the *persuasive pattern,* which also places the main idea in the middle portion or even the closing of a message. Writers use this pattern for sales messages and when the reader needs to be convinced about the importance of a situation before taking action.

Memos present a special writing challenge in that very often they have mixed purposes. A memo announcing the installation of new telephone equipment is a message to inform, but if the memo also contains instructions for using the equipment, the purpose is both to announce and to direct. Moreover, a memo can be either good or bad news, and if the memo is addressed to a group of employees, it can contain *both* good and bad news, depending on each individual's reaction to the topic. A memo announcing a plant relocation can be good news because of the expanded production area and more modern facility; however, it also can be bad news because employees will have to uproot their lives and move to the new location. You will have to judge each situation carefully to determine the most effective approach and pattern to use.

Avoid presenting bad news through e-mail if possible. E-mail messages tend to be too short for well-developed negative messages. Bad news is best presented in letters or memos, which allow you to offer a detailed explanation of the situation.

Direct Organization

Model 13-1 shows a letter that conveys good news and is written in the direct pattern. In this situation, a customer has complained about excessive wear on the tile installed in a hospital lobby. Because the tile was guaranteed by the company that sold and installed it, the customer wants the tile replaced. The company will stand behind its guarantee, so the direct pattern is appropriate in this letter because the message to the customer is good news. The direct pattern generally has three sections:

1. The opening establishes the reason for writing the letter and presents the main idea.

2. The middle paragraphs explain all relevant details about the situation.

3. The closing reminds the reader of deadlines, calls for an action, or looks to future interaction between the reader and the writer.

In Model 13-1, the opening contains the main point, that is, the good news that the company will grant the customer's request for new tile. The middle paragraph reaffirms the guarantee, describes the tile, and explains why the replacement tile should be satisfactory. In the closing, the manager tells the customer to expect a call from the sales representative and also thanks the customer for her information about the previous tile order. The writer uses a pleasant, cooperative tone and avoids repeating any negative words that may have appeared in the customer's original request; therefore, the letter establishes goodwill and helps maintain friendly relations with the reader.

PRESCOTT TILE COMPANY
444 N. Main Street
Ottumwa, Iowa 52555–2773

April 13, 1999

Ms. Sonia Smithfield
General Manager
City Hospital
62 Prairie Road
Fort Madison, IA 52666–1356

Dear Ms. Smithfield:

We will be more than happy to replace the Durafinish tile in front of the
elevators and in the lobby area of City Hospital as you requested in your
letter of April 6.

When we installed the tile—model 672—in August 1998, we guaranteed
the nonfade finish. The tile you selected is imported from Paloma
Ceramic Products in Italy and is one of our best-selling tiles. Recently,
the manufacturer added a special sealing compound to the tile, making it
more durable. This extrahard finish should withstand even the busy
traffic in a hospital lobby.

Our sales representative, Mary Atwood, will call on you in the next few
days to inspect the tile and make arrangements for replacement at no
cost to you. I appreciate your calling this situation to my attention
because I always want to know how our products are performing. We
guarantee our customers' satisfaction.

Sincerely yours,

Michael Allen

Michael Allen
Product Installation Manager

MA:tk

c: Mary Atwood

MODEL 13-1   A Sample Letter Using Direct Organization (in Semiblock Style)

Indirect Organization

The basic situation in the letter in Model 13-2 is the same as in Model 13-1, but in this case the letter is a refusal because the guarantee does not apply. Therefore, indirect organization is used.

The indirect pattern generally contains these elements:

1. The opening is a "buffer" paragraph that establishes a friendly, positive tone and introduces the general topic in a way that will later support the refusal or negative information and help the reader understand it. Use these strategies when appropriate:

   - Agree with the reader in some way:

     You are right when you say that. . . .

   - State appreciation for past efforts or business:

     Thank you for all your help in the recent. . . .

   - State good news if there is any:

     The photographs you asked for were shipped this morning under separate cover.

   - Assure the reader the situation has been considered carefully:

     When I received your letter, I immediately checked. . . .

   - Express a sincere compliment:

     Your work at the Curative Workshop for the Handicapped has been outstanding.

   - Indicate understanding of the reader's position:

     We understand your concern about the Barnet paint shipment.

   - Anticipate a pleasant future:

     The prospects for your new business venture in Center City look excellent.

   Do not use negative words in the buffer or remind your reader about the unpleasantness of the situation. Buffers should establish a pleasant tone and a spirit of cooperation, but do not give the reader the impression that the request will be granted or that the main point of the message is good news.

2. The middle section carefully explains the background of the situation, reminding the reader of all the details that are important to the main point.

3. The bad news follows immediately after the explanation and in the same paragraph. Do not emphasize bad news by placing it in a separate paragraph.

PRESCOTT TILE COMPANY
444 N. Main Street
Ottumwa, Iowa 52555–2773

April 13, 1999

Ms. Sonia Smithfield
General Manager
City Hospital
62 Prairie Road
Fort Madison, IA 52666–1356

Dear Ms. Smithfield:

You are certainly correct that we guarantee our tile for 20 years after installation. We always stand behind our products when they are used according to the manufacturer's recommendations and the recommendations of our design consultant.

When I received your letter, I immediately got out your sales contract and checked the reports of the design consultant. Our records indicate that the consultant did explain on March 6, 1998, that the Paloma tile—model 672—was not recommended for heavy traffic. Although another tile was suggested, you preferred to order the Paloma tile, and you signed a waiver of guarantee. For your information, I'm enclosing a copy of that page of the contract. Because our recommendation was to use another tile, our usual 20-year guarantee is not in force in this situation.

For your needs, we do recommend the Watermark tile, which is specially sealed to withstand heavy traffic. The Watermark tile is available in a design that would complement the Paloma tile already in place. Our design consultant, Trisha Lyndon, would be happy to visit City Hospital and recommend a floor pattern that could incorporate new Watermark tile without sacrificing the Paloma tile that does not show wear. Enclosed is a brochure showing the Watermark designs. Ms. Lyndon will call you for an appointment this week, and because you are a past customer, we will be happy to schedule rush service for you.

Sincerely,

Michael Allen
Product Installation Manager

MA/dc
Encs.: Watermark brochure
        contract page
c: Ms. Trisha Lyndon

MODEL 13-2   A Sample Letter Using Indirect Organization (in Full-Block Style)

4. The closing maintains a pleasant tone and, if appropriate, may suggest alternatives for the reader, resell the value of the product or service, or indicate that the situation can be reconsidered in the future.

The emphasis in an indirect pattern for bad news should be to assure the reader that the negative answer results from careful consideration of the issue and from facts that cannot be altered by the writer. As the writer of a bad news letter, you do not want to sound arbitrary and unreasonable.

In Model 13-2, the opening "buffer" paragraph does confirm the guarantee but mentions restrictions. In the next section the manager carefully explains the original order and reminds the customer that she did not follow the company's recommendation—thus the guarantee is not in effect. The manager encloses a copy of the waiver that the customer signed. The refusal sentence comes as a natural result of the events that the manager has already described. The final section represents a movement away from the bad news and suggests a possible solution—ordering different tile. The manager also suggests how some of the original tile can be saved. The final sentences look to the future by promising a call from the design consultant and noting the enclosure of a brochure that illustrates the suggested new tile. In this letter the manager does not use such phrases as "I deeply regret" or "We are sorry for the inconvenience" because these expressions may imply some fault on the company's part, where there is none. Instead, the manager emphasizes the facts and maintains a pleasant tone through his suggestion for a replacement tile and his offer to find a way to save some of the old tile.

Because you cannot give readers good news if there is none, use the indirect pattern of organization to help your readers understand the reasons behind bad news, and emphasize goodwill by suggesting possible alternatives.

Persuasive Organization

Model 13-3 shows a letter written in the persuasive pattern of sales messages. This letter was sent to company trainers who conduct seminars for employees on a variety of topics. The trainers are urged to give up traditional chalkboards and purchase porcelain marker boards for their training sessions.

The persuasive pattern generally includes these elements:

1. The opening in a persuasive letter catches the reader's attention through one of these strategies:

   • A startling or interesting fact:

     Every night, over 2000 children in our city go to bed hungry.

   • A solution to a problem:

     At last, a health insurance plan that fits your needs!

SPEAKERS' SUPPLIES, INC.
1642 Ludlow Road
Portland, Oregon 97207-6123

Dear Trainer:

Would you like to eliminate irritating chalk dust and messy, hard-to-read chalkboards from your training sessions?

Let us introduce you to Magna Dry-Erase Boards. These heavy-duty, high-quality marker boards use special dry-erase color markers that glide smoothly over the porcelain-on-steel boards. One wipe of the special eraser, and you have a spotless surface on which to write again. If you prefer to use washable crayons or water-soluble markers, you can erase easily with a damp cloth. In addition, these versatile boards accommodate magnets, so you can easily display visuals, such as maps or charts, without extra equipment cluttering up your presentation area.

The Magna Dry-Erase Boards are suitable for a variety of training situations. Notice these special features:

- sizes from 2 ft × 3 ft to 4 ft × 12 ft
- beige, white, or silver-gray surface
- frames of natural oak or satin-anodized aluminum
- full-length tray to hold markers and eraser
- markers (red, blue, green, black) and eraser included
- hanging hardware included
- special board cleaner included

The enclosed brochure shows the beauty and usefulness of these durable boards—guaranteed for 20 years! Please call 1-800-555-3131 today and talk to one of our sales consultants, who will answer your questions and arrange for a local dealer to contact you. Or call one of the dealers in your area listed on the enclosed directory and ask about Magna Dry-Erase Boards. Get rid of that chalk dust forever!

Sincerely,

Nicole Fontaine

Nicole Fontaine
Sales Manager

NF:bp

P.S. Place an order for two 4 ft × 12 ft boards and get one of any other size at half price.

MODEL 13-3   A Sample Letter Using Persuasive Organization (in Full-Block Style)

- A story:

    Our company was founded 100 years ago when Mrs. Clementine Smith began baking. . . .

- An intriguing question:

    Would you like to enjoy a ski weekend at a fabulous resort for only a few dollars?

- A special product feature:

    Our whirlpool bath has a unique power jet system.

- A sample:

    The sandpaper you are holding is our latest. . . .

2. The middle paragraphs of a persuasive letter build the reader's interest by describing the product, service, or situation. Use these strategies when appropriate:

    - Describe the physical details of the product or service to impress the reader with its usefulness and quality.

    - Explain why the reader needs this product or service both from a practical standpoint and from an enjoyment standpoint.

    - Explain why the situation is important to the reader.

    - Describe the benefits to the reader that will result from this product or service or from handling the situation or problem.

3. After arousing the reader's interest or concern, request action, such as purchasing the product, using the service, or responding favorably to the persuasive request.

4. The closing reminds the reader of the special benefits to be gained from responding as requested and urges action immediately or by a relevant deadline.

In Model 13-3, the first paragraph asks a question that probably will elicit a yes answer from the reader. The next paragraph describes the marker boards, pointing out how convenient and versatile they are. The list of special features highlights items that will appeal to the reader. The closing refers to the enclosed brochure and urges the reader to call a toll-free number and discuss a purchase. The final sentence returns to the topic in the first sentence and promises a solution to the chalk dust problems. Notice that a persuasive sales letter may differ from other letters in these ways:

- It may not be dated. Companies often use the same sales letters for several months, so the date of an individual sales letter is not significant.

- It may be a form letter without a personal salutation. The sales letter for marker boards is addressed to "Dear Trainer," identifying the job of the reader.

- It may include a P.S. In most letters, using a P.S. implies that the writer neglected to organize the information before writing. In persuasive sales letters, however, the P.S. is often used to urge the reader to immediate action or to offer a new incentive for action. The P.S. in the sales letter in Model 13-3 offers a special price on a third marker board if the reader buys two of the largest size.

- It may not include prices if other enclosed materials explain the costs. Sometimes the product cost is one of its exciting features and appears in the opening or in the product description. Usually, however, price is not a particularly strong selling feature. For example, the sales letter in Model 13-3 does not mention prices because they are listed in the enclosed brochure, and the writer wants the reader to see the color photographs before learning the cost. Most sales letters, such as those for industrial products, magazine subscriptions, or mail-order items, include supplemental materials that list the prices.

Persuasive memos rarely follow this persuasive sales pattern completely, but they often do begin with an opening designed to arouse reader interest, such as

> With a little extra effort from all of us, South Atlantic Realty
> will have the biggest sales quarter in the history of the company.

WRITING MEMOS AS A MANAGER

A mutually cooperative communication atmosphere is just as important between managers and employees as it is between employees and people outside a company. The tone and managerial attitude in a manager's memos often have a major impact on employee morale. Messages with a harsh, demanding tone that do little more than give orders and disregard the reader's emotional response will produce an atmosphere of distrust and hostility within a company. For this reason, as a manager, you need to remember these principles when writing memos:

1. *Provide adequate information.*   Do not assume that everyone in your company has the same knowledge about a subject. Explain procedures fully, and be very specific about details.

2. *Explain the causes of problems or reasons for changes.*   Readers want more than a bare-bones announcement. They want to know *why* something is happening, so be sure to include enough explanation to make the situation clear.

3. *Be clear.*   Use natural language, and avoid loading a memo with jargon. Often employees in different divisions of the same company do not understand the same jargon. If your memo is going beyond your unit, be sure to fully identify people, equipment, products, and locations.

4. *Be pleasant.*   Avoid blunt commands or implications of employee incompetence. A pleasant tone will go a long way toward creating a cooperative environment on the job.

5. *Motivate rather than order.*   When writing to subordinates, remember to explain how a change in procedure will benefit them in their work, or discuss how an event will affect department goals. Employees are more likely to cooperate if they understand the expected benefits and implications of a situation.

6. *Ask for feedback.*   Be sure to ask the reader for suggestions or responses to your memo. No one person has all the answers; other employees can often make valuable suggestions.

Here is a short memo sent by a supervisor in a testing laboratory. The memo violates nearly every principle of effective communication.

> Every Friday afternoon there will be a department cleanup beginning this Friday. <u>All</u> employees must participate. This means cleaning your own area and then cleaning the complete department. Thank you for your cooperation.

The tone of this memo indicates that the supervisor distrusts the employees, and the underlying implication is that the employees may try to get out of doing this new task. The final sentence seems to be an attempt to create a good working relationship, but the overall tone is already so negative that most employees will not respond positively. The final sentence is also a cliché closing because so many writers put it at the end of letters and memos, whether it is appropriate or not. Although the memo's purpose is to inform readers about a new policy, the supervisor does not explain the reason for the policy and does not provide adequate instructions. Employees will not know exactly what to do on Friday afternoon. Finally, the memo does not ask for feedback, implying that the employees' opinions are not important. Here is a revision:

> As many of you know, we have had some minor accidents recently because the laboratory equipment was left out on the benches overnight and chemicals were not stored in sealed containers. Preventing such accidents is important to all of us, and, therefore, a few minutes every Friday afternoon will be set aside for cleanup and storage.
>
> Beginning on Friday, October 14, and every Friday thereafter, we'll take time at 4:00 p.m. to clean equipment, store chemicals, and straighten up the work areas. If we all pitch in and help each other, the department should be in good order within a half-hour. Please let me know if you have any ideas about what needs special attention or how to handle the cleanup.

This memo, in the direct organizational pattern, explains the reason for the new policy, outlines specifically what the cleanup will include, mentions safety as a reader benefit, and concludes by asking for suggestions. The overall tone emphasizes mutual cooperation. This memo is more likely to get a positive response from employees than the first version is. Since a manager's success is closely linked to employee morale and cooperation, it is important to take the time to write memos that will promote a cooperative, tension-free environment.

SELECTING LETTER FORMAT

The two most common letter formats are illustrated in Model 13-1, the semiblock style, and Model 13-2, the full-block style. In the *full-block style,* every line—date, address, salutation, text, close, signature block, and notations— begins at the left margin. In the *semiblock style,* however, the date, close, and signature block start just to the right of the center of the page. Business letters have several conventions in format that most companies follow.

Date Line

Since most company stationery includes an address, or letterhead, the date line consists only of the date of the letter. Place the date two lines below the company letterhead. If company letterhead is not used, put your address directly above the date:

```
1612 W. Fairway Street
Dayton, OH 45444-2443
May 12, 2001
```

Spell out words such as *street, avenue,* and *boulevard* in addresses.

Inside Address

Place the reader's full name, title, company, and address two to eight lines below the date and flush with the left margin. Spell out the city name, but use the Postal Service two-letter abbreviations for states. Put one space between the state and the ZIP code. The number of lines between the date and the inside address varies so that the letter can be attractively centered on the page.

Salutation

The salutation, or greeting, appears two lines below the inside address and flush with the left margin. In business letters, the salutation is always followed by a colon. Address men as Mr. and women as Ms., unless a woman specifically indicates that she prefers Miss or Mrs. Professional titles, such as Dr., Judge, or Colonel, may be used as well. Here are some strategies to use if you are unsure exactly who your reader is.

Use Titles

When writing to a group or to a particular company position, use descriptive titles in the salutations:

Dear Members of Com-Action:

Dear Project Director:

Dear Customer:

Dear Contributor:

Use Attention Lines

When writing to a company department, use an attention line with no salutation. Begin the letter two lines below the attention line:

Standard Electric Corporation
Plaza Tower
Oshkosh, WI 54911–2855

Attention: Marketing Department

According to our records for 1999. . . .

Use an attention line also if the reader has not been identified as a man or a woman:

Standard Electric Corporation
Plaza Tower
Oshkosh, WI 54911–2855

Attention: J. Hunter

According to our records for 1999. . . .

Model 13-4 shows a letter that uses an attention line. The company is sending this form letter to all its suppliers; therefore, the attention line identifies the department or type of department that should respond to this inquiry.

YORK FOOD PRODUCTS, INC.
Harper Plaza
Windsor, Pennsylvania 15802-2600

January 23, 1999

Cabell Salt Company
400 Eastern Boulevard
Lexington, Kentucky 40503-1906

Attention: Product Control

As you know, the State of California has adopted the "Safe Drinking Water and Toxic Enforcement Act," also referred to as Proposition 65. The California Health and Welfare Agency, which administers Proposition 65, maintains a list of the chemical substances the State of California has declared cause cancer, birth defects, or other reproductive harm (see attached). The presence of any of these chemicals requires a warning on the label of the product.

Since the attached list is a revision, dated January 10, 1999, we are writing to ask if any of the chemicals listed are present in any products you supply to our company. If any are present, please (1) identify the specific chemical, (2) state its concentration level, and (3) state its form in the product. We are relying on your reports to us to determine whether warning labels are required on our products. Therefore, please respond within thirty days of the date of this letter.

When the Proposition 65 list is modified, we would also appreciate continuing information on whether any of the listed chemicals are present in any products supplied to our company.

Sincerely,

Ryan H. Grant

Ryan H. Grant
Vice President-Purchasing

RG/sd

Enc.

MODEL 13-4   A Sample Letter Using an Attention Line (in Full-Block Style)

Omit Salutations

When writing to a company without directing the letter to a particular person or position, omit the salutation and begin the letter three lines below the inside address:

> Standard Electric Corporation
> Plaza Tower
> Oshkosh, WI 54911–2855
>
> According to our records for 1999. . . .

General salutations, such as "Dear Sir" or "Gentlemen," are not used anymore because they might imply an old-fashioned, sexist attitude.

Use Subject Lines

Some writers prefer to use subject lines in letters to identify the main topic immediately. A subject line may also include specific identification, such as an invoice number, date of previous correspondence, or a shipping code. The subject line may appear in several different places, depending on the preference of the writer or on company style. First, the subject line may appear in the upper right-hand corner, spaced between the date line and the inside address:

> September 24, 2000
>
> Subject: Policy #66432–A6
>
> Ms. Victoria Hudson
> Marketing Analyst
> Mutual Insurance Company
> 12 Main Street
> Watertown, IL 60018–1658

Second, the subject line may appear flush with the left margin, two lines below the salutation and two lines above the first line of the letter:

> Dear Ms. Valdez:
>
> Subject: International Expo 2001
>
> As you know, when the first contracts were. . . .

Third, some writers center the subject line between the salutation and the first line of the letter:

Dear Ms. Valdez:

Subject: International Expo 2001

As you know, when the first contracts were. . . .

The subject line may be underlined or typed in all capitals to help the reader see it quickly and to distinguish it from the first paragraph of the letter. Wherever you place a subject line, keep it brief, and use key terms or specific codes to help the reader easily identify the topic of the letter.

Body

The body of a letter is typed single-spaced and double-spaced between paragraphs. Although computers can justify (end the lines evenly) the right margins, most people are used to seeing correspondence with an uneven right margin. Justified margins imply a mass printing and mailing, while unjustified margins imply an individual message to a specific person.

Close

The close appears two lines below the last sentence of the body and consists of a standard expression of goodwill. In semiblock style, the close appears just to the right of the center of the page (see Model 13-1). In full block style, the close is at the left margin (see Model 13-2). The most common closing expressions are "Very truly yours," "Sincerely," and "Sincerely yours." As shown in Model 13-1, the first word of the close is capitalized, but the second word is not. The close is always followed by a comma.

Signature Block

The signature block begins four lines below the close and consists of the writer's name with any title directly underneath. The signature appears in the four-line space between the close and the signature block.

Notations

Notations begin two lines below the signature block and flush with the left margin. In Model 13-1, the capital initials "MA" represent the writer, and the lowercase initials "tk" represent the typist. A colon or slash always appears between the two sets of initials.

If materials are enclosed with the letter, indicate this with either the abbreviation *Enc.* or the word *Enclosure.* Some writers show only the number of enclosures as "Encs. (3)"; others list the items separately, as shown in Model 13-2.

If other people receive copies of the letter, be sure to indicate this. Use *c* or *copy* to signal the reader that other people received copies of this correspondence (see Models 13-1 and 13-2). For copy notations, use full names alone (see Model 13-1) or include courtesy titles (see Model 13-2). List people receiving copies according to company rank, the highest first. If space permits, type the copy notation two lines below any other notations, as shown in Model 13-1. If the letter is long, the copy notation should follow other notations without the extra line, as in Model 13-2.

Second Page

If your letter has a second page, type the name of the addressee, page number, and date across the top of the page:

Ms. Sonia Smithfield   2   April 13, 1999

This heading may also be typed in the upper left-hand corner:

Ms. Sonia Smithfield
page 2
April 13, 1999

Envelope

Post-office scanning equipment can process envelopes most rapidly when the address is typed (1) with a straight left margin, (2) in all capitals, (3) without punctuation, (4) with an extra space between all words or number groups:

DR RONALD BROWNING
1234 N SPRINGDALE LANE
AKRON OH 44313-1906

This format is not appropriate for the inside address of the letter.

SELECTING MEMO FORMAT

Many companies have printed forms so that all internal messages have a consistent format. If there is no printed form, the memo format shown in Model 13-9 is often used.

Subject Line.   The subject line should be brief but should clearly indicate a specific topic. Use key words, so readers can recognize the subject and the memo can be filed easily. Capitalize the main words.

Close.   Memos do not have a closing signature block as letters do. Write your initials next to your name in the opening or write your name at the bottom of the page. The writer's and typist's initials appear two lines below the last line of the memo, followed by enclosure or copy notations.

Second Page.   Format the second page of a memo like the second page of a letter with receiver's name, page number, and date at the top of the page.

SELECTING E-MAIL FORMAT

Your software will format the mechanical elements of your e-mail messages. You should add elements that create a business message appropriate for your reader and situation.

Subject Line.   Put key words in your subject line so the reader can identify the content quickly. When you respond to an e-mail, be sure to check that the subject line is still accurate. Using an old subject line with a new message on a different topic is a common error.

Salutation.   Begin the message portion of your e-mail with a formal salutation, such as "Dear Professor Jones:." If you normally use the reader's first name, use that in the salutation, such as "Dear Heather:." Some people prefer to drop the "dear" and begin with the receiver's name only, as in "Professor Jones:" or "Heather:." Notice that all the salutations end in a colon. If you are uncertain, the formal salutation is always a safe choice. The e-mail message in Model 13-5 uses the formal salutation because the writer is contacting a stranger in another workplace.

Style.   Be concise and direct. Readers do not like to scroll through several screens to read a long message. Because readers cannot glance back over a long message on e-mail as easily as they can over a printed memo, they will have to print out complicated or detailed messages anyway. Keep your e-mail to one screen whenever possible.

Subject: Guest Lecture

Date: Thu 17 Sep 1999 11:38:20

From: Dana Kerr <dana9@uig.com>

To: skortze@hot1ph.com

Dear Mr. Kortze:

I am the program director for the annual July sales meeting held by Universal Insurance General. We are currently considering hotels for our 2003 meeting and are interested in the Phoenix Conference Center. We generally expect about 1000 sales representatives and 500 guests at the 4-day conference. I would appreciate receiving information on your hotel and conference facilities as well as menu selections for a banquet. Any materials you have that would help us make a decision about a conference site would be appreciated.

Sincerely,

Dana Kerr
Public Relations
Universal Insurance General
100 Eagle Plaza
Oklahoma City, OK 73112–0387
405.555.2611
Fax 405.555.2688
<dana9@uig.com>

MODEL 13-5   Sample E-mail Message

Close.   Because e-mail addresses often do not reveal the company name or other details, use a full signature block for your closing, including (1) your full name, (2) your title or department, (3) the company name, (4) street address, (5) telephone number, and (6) fax number or e-mail address. Model 13-5 shows a closing that gives the receiver useful information.

USING THE FAX

Most companies now have fax (facsimile) machines to receive and transmit copies of correspondence and graphics to readers inside and outside the organization. The fax uses telephone lines and, therefore, arrives much faster than correspondence sent through the mail or even through interoffice mail in large institutions, such as a university.

Standard cover sheets usually are available to use when you send a fax. Be sure to include your company name, address, telephone and fax numbers as well as your name, department, and telephone extension. Clearly write the name and title of the person receiving the correspondence along with the number of pages you are sending. Because the quality of fax machines varies and lines may experience interference, many people who fax correspondence in the interests of speed also send a printed copy through the mails, so the reader receives a high-quality document.

Be aware that using the fax machine prevents confidentiality. You rarely can be certain who is standing at the receiving fax machine when you send a letter or memo. Faxed correspondence arrives unsealed as loose sheets. Marking the cover sheet confidential will not necessarily create any privacy. Fax machines are usually in high-traffic areas, and many people have access to them. If your correspondence is confidential or potentially damaging to someone's interests, do not send a fax, or call the receiver and ask permission to send a confidential fax.

WRITING JOB-APPLICATION LETTERS

One of the most important letters you will write is a letter applying for a job. The application letter functions not only as a request for an interview, but also as the first demonstration to a potential employer of your communication skills. An application letter should do three things:

1. *Identify what you want.* In the opening paragraph, identify specifically the position you are applying for and how you heard about it—through an advertisement or someone you know. In some cases, you may write an application letter without knowing if the company has an opening. Use the first paragraph to state what kind of position you are qualified for and why you are interested in that particular company.

2. *Explain why you are qualified for the position.* Do not repeat your résumé line for line, but do summarize your work experience or education and point out the specific items especially relevant to the position you are applying for. In discussing your education, mention significant courses or special projects that have enhanced your preparation for

the position you want. If you have extracurricular activities that show leadership qualities or are related to your education, mention these in this section. Explain how your work experience is related to the position for which you are applying.

3. *Ask for an interview.* Offer to come for an interview at the employer's convenience; however, you also may suggest a time that may be suitable. Tell the reader how to reach you easily by giving a telephone number or specifying the time of the day you are available.

In Model 13-10, the writer begins her application letter by explaining how she heard about the position, and she identifies her connection with the person who told her to apply for the job. In discussing her education, she points out her training in computers and mentions her laboratory duties that gave her relevant experience in product chemistry. Her work experience has been in research laboratories, so she explains the kind of testing she has done. In closing, she suggests a convenient time for an interview and includes a phone number for certain daytime hours. Overall, the letter emphasizes the writer's qualifications in chemistry and points out that the company could use her experience (reader benefits). An application letter should be more than a brief cover letter accompanying a résumé; it should be a fully developed message that provides enough information to help the reader make a decision about offering an interview.

STRATEGIES—Job Interviews

- Answer questions with specific examples of your skills, qualities, or experiences.

- If asked to solve a hypothetical workplace problem, do not give a quick, simple answer. Consider the situation and suggest alternatives depending on conditions.

- Research the company and prepare several questions about the job and the industry.

- Never say anything negative about former employers, professors, or fellow students.

WRITING RÉSUMÉS

The résumé for a new college graduate is usually one page long and summarizes the applicant's career objective, education, work experience, and activities. Model 13-11 shows the résumé that would accompany the application letter in Model 13-10. Remember that anyone reading a résumé wants to find information easily and quickly, so the headings that direct the reader to specific information should stand out clearly. Because the résumé in Model 13-11 is for a new college graduate, education has a prominent position. There are many résumé styles; this one is a basic chronological format:

Heading.   Put your name, address, and telephone number at the top of your résumé. You may include a business telephone number and e-mail address.

Objective.   List a specific position that matches your education and experience, because employers want to see a clear, practical objective. Avoid vague descriptions, such as, "I am looking for a challenging position where I can use my skills." Availability to travel is important in some companies, so the phrase "willing to travel" can be used under the objective. If you are not willing to travel, say nothing.

Education.   List education in reverse chronological order, your most recent degree first. Once you have a college degree, you can omit high school. Be sure to list any special certificates or short-term training done in addition to college work. Include courses or skills that are especially important to the type of position for which you are applying. List your grade-point average if it is significantly high, and indicate the grade-point scale. Some people list their grade-point average in their majors only, since this is likely to be higher than the overall average.

Work Experience.   List your past jobs in reverse chronological order. Include the job title, the name of the company, the city, and the state. Describe your responsibilities for each job, particularly those that provided practical experience connected with your career goals. In describing responsibilities, use action words, such as *coordinated, directed, prepared, supervised,* and *developed.* Dates of employment need not include month and day. Terms such as *vacation* or *summer* with the relevant years are sufficient.

Honors and Awards.   List scholarships, prizes, and awards received in college. Include any community honors or professional prizes as well. If there is only one honor, list it under "Activities."

Activities.   In this section list recent activities, primarily those in college. Be sure to indicate any leadership positions, such as president or chairperson of a group. Hobbies, if included, should indicate both group and individual interests.

References.   Model 13-11 shows the most common way to mention references. If you do list references, include the person's business address and telephone number. Be sure to ask permission before listing someone as a reference.

It is best to omit personal information about age, height, weight, marital status, and religion. Employers are not allowed to consider such information in the employment process, and most prefer that it not appear on a résumé.

Model 13-13 shows a résumé for a job applicant who is more advanced in his chemistry career than the applicant in Model 13-11. This résumé lists experience first, in the most prominent position. Other significant differences from the résumé for the new college graduate include the following:

Major Qualifications.   Instead of an objective, this applicant wants to highlight his experience, so he uses the *capsule résumé* technique to call attention to his years of experience and his specialty. He can discuss his specific career goals in his application letter.

Professional Experience.   This applicant has had more than one position with the same employer because he has been promoted within the company. The applicant highlights his experience by stacking his responsibilities into impressive-looking lists.

Education.   This applicant includes his date of graduation but does not emphasize it, and he omits his grade-point average because his experience is now more important than his college work. He lists his computer knowledge because such knowledge is useful in his work.

Activities and Memberships.   After several years of full-time work, most people no longer list college activities. Instead, they stress community and professional service. This applicant lists his professional membership in the American Chemical Society to indicate that he is keeping current in his field.

Model 13-14 shows another résumé style. This job applicant is also advanced in his career, and he wants to emphasize the skills he has developed on the job as well as highlight his successes. His actual dates of employment or of college graduation are less important than the types of projects he has worked on. This résumé style is used most by experienced job applicants who want to change the focus of their careers or who have been out of the job market for a while and are now reentering it. New college graduates with activities and part-time work experience that developed skills relative to their career goals may also find this style useful. In addition, the job applicant using this résumé style may revise the lists of accomplishments and skills to emphasize different areas for different positions. This résumé does list employment and education but it differs from Models 13-11 and Model 13-13 in two important areas:

- *Accomplishments.*   Rather than beginning with his work record, the applicant lists significant achievements and honors to draw the reader's attention to a pattern of success. Many people are in sales. The applicant here emphasizes his out-of-the-ordinary performance.

- *Special Skills.*   The applicant identifies the types of skills he has developed and lists them under a specific heading. In this case, the applicant is interested in a management position, and he knows that communication and organization skills are crucial for effective managers. Other types of special skills might include researching, public speaking, writing, counseling, analyzing, managing, or designing. This applicant's record of employment supports his list of accomplishments and skills. Do not list skills so vague you cannot provide specific details to support your assertion. Saying that you are "good with people" without any specific accomplishments to demonstrate your claim will not strengthen your résumé.

PREPARING SCANNABLE RÉSUMÉS

Many large companies use computers to scan and store résumé information. When employers want to interview prospective employees for a position, they screen every résumé in their electronic files for key qualifications. For employers, the advantages of electronic screening are that it (1) eliminates the difficulty of handling thousands of résumés in a fair manner, (2) quickly identifies candidates who have the primary job qualifications, and (3) processes more applications at less cost.

Electronic screening requires a special résumé style. After writing your traditional résumé, rewrite it in appropriate electronic style so you have both available. If you are applying to a company that uses electronic screening, you can inquire about a preferred format. If you cannot easily find out what the company prefers, send both a traditional and a scannable résumé, and state in your application letter that you are sending both as a convenience to the employer. Following are guidelines for developing a scannable résumé.

Name and Address.   Your name should be the first line of your résumé. Put your address, telephone numbers, and e-mail in a stacked list.

Key Words.   Immediately after your opening information, list key words that identify such items as your previous job titles, job-related experience, skills, or special knowledge, degrees, certifications, and colleges attended. Be sure to use the terms listed in a job advertisement because these are the terms the scanner is seeking. For example, if the advertisement asks for "public speaking," use that term rather than "oral presentations." Some companies scan only a portion of a résumé, so you must be sure that your key words appear near the top of the page.

Single Columns.   Scanners read across every line from left to right. Do not use double columns to list information because it will look like gibberish in the computer files.

Paper and Typeface.   Computers prefer clean and simple résumés. Use only smooth white paper with black ink and 12- or 14-point type. Do not use italics, underlining, boxes, shading, or unusual typeface. Capitals and boldface are acceptable as long as the letters do not touch each other.

Abbreviations.   Use abbreviations sparingly. Scanners can miss information if they are programmed to search for a whole word.

Folding and Stapling.   Do not staple or fold a scannable résumé. The scanner may have trouble finding words that are in the creases or that cover staple holes.

White Space.   Organize with lots of white space, so the scanner does not overlook key words.

Model 13-12 shows the electronic version of the résumé in Model 13-11. Notice that some information, such as activities and references, is omitted. For a comprehensive job search, you will need both the traditional and the electronic résumés.

The purpose of the application letter and résumé is to present an interest-attracting package that will result in an interview. Because the letter and résumé are often the first contact a new college graduate has with a potential employer, the initial impression from these documents may have a decisive impact on career opportunities.

WRITING OTHER JOB-SEARCH LETTERS

The article by Boe in Part 2 gives advice about preparing for the job interview. The first interview, however, may be only one step in the job application process. Many employers conduct several interviews with the top candidates before filling a position. The first interview may be brief, perhaps a half-hour, allowing the interviewer to eliminate some candidates. Longer interviews then follow with the remaining candidates until the company offers the position to someone. If, after your first interview, you are very interested in the position, write a brief follow-up letter to remind the interviewer who you are and what special qualifications you have for the position. Because most job applicants do not take the time to write follow-up letters, you can make a stronger impression on the interviewer by doing so.

Write your follow-up letter within three to four days after your interview. The letter should be short but include the following:

1. Express appreciation for the opportunity to discuss the position.
2. Refer specifically to the date of the interview and the position you applied for.
3. Mention something that happened during the interview (e.g., a tour of the plant) or refer to a subject you discussed (e.g., a new product being developed).
4. Remind the interviewer about your qualifications or mention something you forgot to bring up in the interview.
5. Express your continuing interest in the company.

Here is a sample follow-up letter that covers these points:

> I appreciated the opportunity to talk to you on September 3 about the position in cost accounting. During my tour of your offices, Ms. McNamara gave me a thorough introduction to the accounting operation at HG Logan Associates, and I remain very interested in your company.
>
> After hearing the details about the position, I believe my course work in cost accounting computer systems would be an asset in your organization.
>
> Thank you for your consideration of my application, and I look forward to hearing from you soon.

If you have another interview, write another follow-up letter to express your continuing interest.

If you receive a job offer and want to accept it, do so promptly and in writing. Use the letter to establish your eagerness to begin work and to confirm the details mentioned in the company's offer. Here is a sample acceptance letter:

> I am pleased to accept your offer of a position as financial analyst at Brady, Horton and Smythe at a salary of $42,000. As you suggested, I will stop in the Human Resources Office this week to get a packet of benefit enrollment forms.
>
> I am eager to join the people I met during my visit to the Investment Sales Department and look forward to beginning work on June 15.

If you receive a job offer, but you have decided not to accept it, write promptly and decline. Express your gratitude for the offer. You may or may not give a specific reason for your decision. Here is a sample letter declining a job offer:

> Thank you for your offer of a position in the engineering division at Hughes Manufacturing. I was very impressed with the dynamic people I met during my visit, and I carefully considered your offer. Because of my interest in relocating to the Southwest, however, I have decided to accept a position with a company in New Mexico.
>
> I appreciate your time and consideration.

You may receive a job offer but be uncertain about whether you want to accept it because you have other interviews pending, and you want to complete those before making a decision. If so, write a letter asking for more time to respond to the company's offer. Express your interest in the position and explain that you need a short extension of their deadline in order to be sure of your decision. Here is a sample letter asking for a delay in responding to a job offer:

> I appreciate your offer of a nursing position in your clinic. Your facilities and staff made a strong impression on me, and I know that working at Family Health Care would be an exciting challenge.
>
> Because I do have two interviews scheduled at hospitals in the city, I would appreciate your giving me until March 1 to respond to your offer. The extra ten days will allow me the opportunity to evaluate my career options and make the decision that is right for me and for my employer.
>
> If you need my answer immediately, I, of course, will give it. If you can allow me the extra time to make a decision, I would be grateful. Please let me know.

All these letters may be part of your job-search process. Writing them carefully shows the company that you take the position seriously and are professional in your approach to your career.

CHAPTER SUMMARY

This chapter discusses how to write effective letters, memos, job-application letters, and résumés. Remember:

- Letters are written primarily to people outside an organization, and memos are written primarily to people inside an organization.
- Effective tone in letters and memos requires natural language, positive language, and the you-attitude.
- E-mail transmits messages rapidly but lacks confidentiality.
- Correspondence can be organized in the direct, indirect, or persuasive pattern.
- Direct organization presents the main idea in the opening.
- Indirect organization delays the main idea until details have been explained.
- Persuasive organization begins with an attention-getting opening.
- Managers need to create a cooperative atmosphere in their memos to employees.
- The fax machine transmits messages rapidly, but is not confidential.
- The two most common letter formats are full block style and semiblock style.

- A job-application letter presents a writer's qualifications for a position and requests an interview.

- Résumés list a writer's most significant achievements relative to a position.

- A follow-up letter after a job interview will remind the interviewer about your qualifications.

SUPPLEMENTAL READINGS IN PART 2

Boe, E. "The Art of the Interview," *Microwaves and RF,* p. 465.

Graham, J. R. "What Skills Will You Need to Succeed?" *Manager's Magazine* , p. 487.

Hartman, D. B., and Nantz, K. S. "Send the Right Messages about E-Mail," *Training & Development,* p. 489.

Humphries, A. C. "Business Manners," *Business & Economic Review,* p. 497.

Messmer, M. "Prepare, Listen, Follow up," *Management Accounting,* p. 506.

Nielsen, J. "Be Succinct! (Writing for the Web)," *Alertbox,* p. 513.

"The Practical Writer," *The Royal Bank of Canada,* p. 524.

ENDNOTES

1. Brigid Schulte, "Pilot's Computer Note Reveals Military Secrets," *Akron Beacon Journal* (July 12, 1995): A2.
2. Stephanie Stahl, "Dangerous E-Mail," *Informationweek* (September 12, 1994): 12.

This model shows a claim letter for defective screw tubes in a recent shipment. The writer addresses the reader by his first name because of the long business relationship they have had. Notice that the writer clearly states the order date and number in his opening sentence.

Discussion

1. Identify the organizational pattern used in this letter and discuss why the writer would use this organization.

2. Why does the writer describe the problem in detail? Why not just state that the screw tubes are defective?

3. Discuss the tone in the letter. Does the writer seem angry? How effective do you think the closing paragraph will be in getting action?

4. Assume you are William Ruggles and write a response to this claim. You will ship a new batch of screw tubes as soon as you finish checking production quality, and you are glad he sent the two samples. Your 15-year business relationship with this company is important, and you want to do everything possible to keep your customers happy. You estimate that it will take two days to match the new screw tubes against the specifications Brett Howard sent.

MARLEY ASSEMBLIES, INC.
1600 Spike Road
Mechanicsburg, PA 17066-4260
(412) 555-1313   FAX (412) 555-1300

March 15 1999

Mr. William Ruggles
Production Manager
Acme Tubing, Inc.
750 Mull Road
Toledo, OH 43607–1389

Dear Bill:

I appreciate your promptness in getting our March 1, 1999, order
#A9968 to us within five days. The screw tubes #0867 were your usual
high quality, but screw tubes #0183 do not fit our assemblies properly.

I am enclosing two sample screw tubes #0183 from the order and a copy
of our specifications and line drawings. The problem with the screw
tubes is that the 20° bend is really 25°-27°, and the slot is not full length
as indicated on the specs. You will also notice that the two samples do
not measure the same width on the spring. Neither width is an exact fit
for our pans, which require the 3/16-in. width marked on the drawing.

I will keep the defective screws until you tell me what you want done
with them. In the meantime, we want a new shipment of screw tubes
#0183 after you have inspected them for conformity to our
specifications. I understand that these variations happen, and I know
you will want to take care of replacements immediately.

Sincerely,

Brett Howard

Brett Howard
Product Supervisor

BH:sd

Enc.

This model shows a form letter sent to all savings customers of a large bank. Although envelopes will be individually addressed and the letter is dated, there is no inside address. The writer is announcing a change that will affect all the bank's savings customers, so no references to specific accounts are included in the letter.

Discussion

1. Identify the specific organization pattern used in this letter and discuss why the writer chose that pattern.

2. In what ways does the writer imply the change is not a significant one?

3. In groups, draft a letter to all students at your school to announce a $50 increase in "special fees" beginning next term. This increase will cover the cost of periodical subscriptions in the library. Without the money from the special fee, the library will have to cancel over 200 periodical subscriptions.

CONTINENTAL BANK AND TRUST COMPANY
1000 Central Plaza
San Antonio, Texas 78205-1104

January 6, 2000

Dear Savings Customer:

Thank you for choosing Continental as your full-service banking institution. We are committed to providing superior banking services that match today's needs and conditions.

As you no doubt are aware, today's economy is characterized by low inflation and declining interest rates. This low inflation rate has enabled our customers to experience a consistent return on their savings or even an increase in "real" returns compared to years of skyrocketing inflation. The lower interest rates have spurred economic growth and investment and allowed customers to purchase new homes and new cars. Both low inflation and lower interest rates have had an impact on all the financial plans available at our institution. Rates based on yesterday's economy do not reflect today's conditions. Therefore, effective January 15, 2000, the annual interest rate on the passbook savings account and the Money Market Deposit account will be reduced by 1 percent. No other features of your accounts will be affected.

Your personal banker will be happy to review the variety of services available for savings and investments to meet your financial needs. For example, our "supersaver" Certificate of Deposit offers an interest rate of 4.5% with a maturity of three years. All our savings plans, of course, are backed by the safety and security of FDIC insurance and Continental's 72 years of banking experience. Please call your personal banker at 555-7899 if you have any questions. We appreciate the opportunity to serve your financial needs now and in the future.

Sincerely,

LaShandra Perkins
Vice President

LP:sd

This persuasive letter is individually addressed, but is actually a form letter that The Construction Specifications Institute sends to people who have contacted the Institute for technical information. The purpose of this letter is to persuade the reader to become a member.

Discussion

1. Discuss how this letter fits the persuasive organization pattern discussed in this chapter.

2. Identify the persuasive appeals used in this letter. How does the writer imply that membership in the Institute is essential for anyone in any area of construction?

3. Identify the format elements used in this letter. How do these elements serve the writer's purpose of persuading the reader to join the Institute?

4. In groups, draft a persuasive letter that could be sent to students on your campus to encourage them to join a particular campus group or activity. You may write a letter suitable for a specific group of students, such as freshmen or engineering majors.

THE CONSTRUCTION SPECIFICATIONS INSTITUTE
601 Madison Street
Alexandria, Virginia 22314
(703) 684–0300

August 3, 1999

Mr. Hunter Matthison
Randall Construction Company
1200 Union Drive
Memphis, TN 38104

Dear Mr. Matthison:

Thank you for your interest in The Construction Specifications Institute. I hope the information you received has served your purpose and that you will continue to consider CSI as a vital source of information in the future.

CSI has nearly 19,000 members who are dedicated to advancing construction technology through communication, education, research, and service. These members also enjoy:

- **Diverse membership**—CSI membership is open to everyone in the construction industry, including architects, engineers, specifiers, contractors, manufacturers' representatives, and product distributors, providing a diversity that makes networking with individuals from all phases of the construction process easy.

- **Subscriptions** to The Construction Specifier, the industry's leading monthly magazine, and Newsdigest, CSI's monthly newsletter, keep you informed about industry and association news.

- **Technical documents** standardizing the preparation of construction documents is the mainstay of CSI. Members receive substantial discounts.

- **Seminars** on timely and career-oriented topics are presented nationwide. Registration fees are discounted for members.

- **CSI's annual convention** is the largest exhibit of nonresidential construction products, materials, and services in the country, featuring more than 1,000 exhibit booths.

Mr. Hunter Matthison   -2-   August 3, 1999

- **Certification programs**—Certified Construction Specifier (CCS) and
  Construction Documents Technologist (CDT) programs elevate the
  skills and status of knowledgeable individuals.

Why not join the thousands of construction professionals who have
found membership in CSI professionally rewarding? Simply fill out the
enclosed application and return it with your dues payment to CSI. If you
have any questions, call CSI's Membership Department at (703)
684–0300. Or fax your questions or requests to (703) 684–0465.

Sincerely,

Mary H. Bailey

Mary H. Bailey
Manager, Membership Programs

MHB/sd
Enclosure

MODEL 13-9   Commentary

This memo is from a supervisor to a division head, asking for maintenance support.

Discussion

1. Identify the organizational strategies the writer uses, and discuss why the writer probably chose these strategies.

2. Consider the tone of this memo. How does the writer place blame for the situation? How does the writer convey the seriousness of the problems?

3. In what ways does the writer show the reader that there are benefits in solving these problems? Is there any advantage to addressing the reader by name in the memo?

4. Write a brief memo to D. P. Paget from T. L. Coles announcing that R. Fleming, the maintenance supervisor, has been told to report on the problems within two days. Assure Paget that the problems are being taken seriously.

October 3, 1999

To: T. L. Coles, Division Chief

From: D. P. Paget, Supervisor

Subject: Problems in Cost Center 22, Paint Line

As I've discussed with Bill Martling, our department has had problems with proper maintenance for six weeks. Although the technicians in the Maintenance Department respond promptly to our calls, they do not seem to be able to solve the problems. As a result, our maintenance calls focus on the same three problems week after week. I've listed below the areas we need to deal with.

Temperature.   For the past two weeks, our heat control has not consistently reached the correct temperature for the different mixes. The Maintenance technician made six visits in an attempt to provide consistent temperature ranges. R. Fleming investigated and decided that the gas mixture was not operating properly. He did not indicate when we might get complete repairs. In the last ten working days, we've experienced nearly five hours of total downtime.

Soap.   The soap material we currently use in the waterfall booth does not break up the paint mixtures and, as a result, the cleanup crew cannot remove all the excess paint. Without a complete cleanup every twenty-four hours, the booth malfunctions. Again, we have downtime. We need to investigate a different soap composition for the waterfall booth.

Parking Lever.   The parking lever control has not been in full operation since January 14. Technicians manage to fix the lever for only short periods before it breaks down again. I asked for a replacement, but was told it wasn't malfunctioning enough to warrant being replaced. This lever is crucial to the operation because, when it isn't functioning, the specified range slips and paint literally goes down the drain. As a result, we use more paint than necessary and still some parts are not coated correctly.

I'd appreciate your help in getting these problems handled, Tom, because our cost overruns are threatening to become serious. Since all maintenance operations come under your jurisdiction, perhaps you could consider options and let me know what we can do. I'd be glad to discuss the problems with you in more detail.

Models 13-10 through 13-15   Commentary

These models demonstrate application materials.

- Model 13-10 is a job application letter from a recent college graduate. The writer reviews her qualifications and emphasizes her strengths.
- Model 13-11 is the résumé that accompanies the application letter in Model 13-10. The résumé uses the traditional chronological format.
- Model 13-12 shows the electronic-style résumé of the same job applicant. Notice the differences between this style and the traditional style in Model 13-11.
- Model 13-13 is the résumé of a job applicant who has extensive professional experience. Notice he has had several positions with one employer, and the format stresses his experience rather than his education.
- Model 13-14 is a functional-style résumé that emphasizes the job applicant's special accomplishments and skills.
- Model 13-15 is the résumé of a job applicant who interrupted her education to marry and have children. She uses the functional style to emphasize the experience gained from both her jobs and her education. She is now working full time and taking classes part time. Notice that she lists her degree as expected at a future date and uses the term "general studies" to describe her one year of college work in Texas.

Discussion

1. Discuss how the writer in Model 13-10 manages to put persuasive appeal in her application letter.

2. Compare these résumés and discuss the effectiveness of the differences in format.

3. Assume you were going to write an electronic-style résumé for Models 13-13 and 13-14. Identify key words you would use in each case.

4. In groups, write an application letter to accompany the résumé in Model 13-15. Assume that Felicia Cummings is writing to the Museum of New England History in Albany, New York, and she hopes the museum has a suitable opening for her.

1766 Wildwood Drive
Chicago, Illinois 60666
July 12, 1999

Mr. Eric Blackmore
Senior Vice President
Alden-Chandler Industries, Inc.
72 Plaza Drive
Milwaukee, WI 53211-2901

Dear Mr. Blackmore:

Professor Julia Hedwig suggested that I write to you about an opening
for a product chemist in your chemical division. Professor Hedwig was
my senior adviser this past year.

I have just completed my B.S. in chemistry at Midwest University with a
3.9 GPA in my major. In addition to chemistry courses, I took three
courses in computer applications and developed a computer program on
chemical compounds. As a laboratory assistant to Professor Hedwig, I
entered and ran the analyses of her research data. My senior project,
which I completed under Professor Hedwig's guidance, was an analysis
of retardant film products. The project was given the Senior Chemistry
Award, granted by a panel of chemistry faculty.

My work experience would be especially appropriate for Alden-Chandler
Industries. My internship in my senior year was at Pickett Laboratory,
which does extensive analyses for the Lake County Sheriff's office. My
work involved writing laboratory reports daily. At both Ryan Laboratories
and Century Concrete Corporation, I have worked extensively in
compound analysis, and I am familiar with standard test procedures.

I would appreciate the opportunity to discuss my qualifications for the
position of product chemist. I am available for an interview every
afternoon after three o'clock, but I could arrange to drive to Milwaukee
any time convenient to you. My telephone number during the day
between 10:00 a.m. and 3:00 p.m. is (312) 555-1212.

Sincerely,

Kimberly J. Oliver

Kimberly J. Oliver

Enc.

Kimberly J. Oliver
1766 Wildwood Drive
Chicago, Illinois 60666
(312) 555-6644

OBJECTIVE: Chemist with responsibility in product development and production. Willing to travel.

EDUCATION

Midwest University, Chicago, Illinois
B.S. in Chemistry; GPA: 3.6 (4.0 scale), June 1999

Computer Languages: Lotus 1-2-3, HTML, Minitab

WORK EXPERIENCE

Century Concrete Corp., Chicago, Illinois, 1997–present

Research Assistant: Set up chemical laboratories, including purchasing equipment and materials. Perform ingredient/compound analysis. Produce experimental samples according to quality standards. (part-time)

Pickett Laboratory, Chicago, Illinois, Summer 1998

Research Intern: Set up testing compounds. Wrote laboratory test reports for compound analysis.

Ryan Laboratories, Chicago, Illinois, Summers 1996–1997

Laboratory Assistant: Assisted in testing compounds. Prepared standard test solutions; recorded test data; operated standard laboratory equipment; wrote operating procedures.

HONORS AND AWARDS

Chemical Society of Illinois Four-Year Scholarship, 1995–1999
Senior Chemistry Award, Midwest University, 1999
Outstanding Chemistry Major, Midwest University, 1998

ACTIVITIES

Member, American Chemistry Association, 1997–present
President, American Chemistry Association (student chapter), 1997–1998
Member, Toastmaster Association, 1995–1998
Council Member, Women in Science Student Association, 1997–1999
Hobbies: sailing, piano, tennis

REFERENCES AVAILABLE ON REQUEST.

Kimberly J. Oliver
1766 Wildwood Drive
Chicago, Illinois 60666
(312) 555-6644

Key Words: Product chemistry. Bachelor's degree. Laboratory internship. Compound analysis. Laboratory test reports. Midwest University. Chemical Society of Illinois Scholarship. Written and oral communication skills. Lotus 1-2-3, HTML, Minitab.

Objective: Chemist in product development and testing.

Education

Midwest University, Chicago, Illinois June 1999
B.S. in Chemistry; GPA 3.6 on 4-point scale

Computer Languages: Lotus 1-2-3, HTML, Minitab

Work Experience

Century Concrete Corp., Chicago, Illinois, 1997–present

Research Assistant: Set up chemical laboratories, including purchasing equipment and materials. Perform ingredient/compound analysis. Produce experimental samples according to quality standards. (part-time)

Pickett Laboratory, Chicago, Illinois, Summer 1998

Research Intern: Set up testing compounds. Wrote laboratory test reports for compound analysis.

Ryan Laboratories, Chicago, Illinois, Summers 1996–1997

Laboratory Assistant: Assisted in testing compounds. Prepared standard test solutions; recorded test data; operated standard laboratory equipment; wrote operating procedures.

Honors and Awards

Chemical Society of Illinois Four-Year Scholarship, 1995–1999
Senior Chemistry Award, Midwest University, 1999
Outstanding Chemistry Major, Midwest University, 1998

Jack E. Montgomery
21 Camelot Court, Skokie, IL 60622
(312) 555-5620 <jmont6@cdnrt.com>

Major Qualifications: 15 years in product development chemistry.
Specialty: Adhesives

PROFESSIONAL EXPERIENCE

CDX TIRE AND RUBBER CORPORATION, Chicago, IL

Formulation Chemist, 1987–present
- Develop new hot-melt adhesives, pressure sensitives, and sealants
- Perform analysis of competitors' compounds
- Determine new product specification
- Calculate raw materials pricing
- Conduct laboratory programs for product improvement

Analytical Chemist, 1985–1987
- Performed ingredient/compound analysis
- Developed and tested compounds (cured/uncured)
- Wrote standard operating procedures
- Developed improved mixing design
- Supervised processing technicians

STERLING ANALYTICAL LABORATORIES, Pittsburgh, PA

Research Laboratory Assistant, 1983–1985 (part time)
- Prepared solutions
- Drafted laboratory reports
- Supervised students during testing procedures

EDUCATION

B.S.—Chemistry, Minor—Biology. University of Pittsburgh, 1985

COMPUTER SKILLS

PASCAL, Lotus 1-2-3, Minitab, Sigmastat

ACTIVITIES AND MEMBERSHIPS

District Chairman, United Way Campaign, 1995
Member, Illinois Consumer Protection Commission, 1987–1991
Member, American Chemical Society, 1985–present

References furnished on request.

Jeffrey L. Hirsch
1630 W. Lynd Drive
Mount Troy, MI 44882
(517) 555-2327
jlhirsch@hallm.com

Objective: Marketing and Sales Management

Qualifications: Ten Years in retail marketing; MBA in Management

Accomplishments:
- Exceeded district objectives in 23 accounts, $2.6 million sales.
- Increased territory volume by 17%.
- Managed sales team of 12 people.
- Negotiated improved leases for retailers.
- Earned district, regional, and national awards for high performance including Market Development Award 1997, National R.B. Hall Award 1998, and Sales Development Professional of the Year 1998.
- Published marketing advice in *Sales World* and district newsletters.

Organizational and Communication Skills:
- Coordinated 1996 National Sales Meeting—Chicago.
- Developed regional sales programs and seminars.
- Presented district seminars for retailers.
- Conducted training seminars for new salespeople.
- Presented career seminars for high school programs.

Employment History:
    Hallmark Marketing Corporation, Hallmark Cards, Inc.
        District Sales Representative, 1992–present.
        Retail Sales Coordinator, 1990–1992.

Education:
    MBA, emphasis in Management, University of Illinois, 1994.
    BBA in Marketing, Illinois State University, 1990.

Professional Memberships:
    Michigan Sales Associates, Program Coordinator, 1995.
    Metropolitan Business Association.
    Retail Business Association High School Mentor Program.

References: Available on request.

Felicia Cummings
4236 N. Ryan Road
Port William, NY 10011
(216) 555-8457 (home)
(216) 555-1212 (business)

Objective: Museum Display/Historical Artifacts Displays

Qualifications: Six Years' Experience in Museum and Collectible Displays

Display Experience:
- Developed Southwest Artifacts Display for Museum
- Designed collectibles display for advertising photography
- Organized historical weaponry display for public exhibition
- Coordinated university displays of student art history research projects

Communication Skills:
- Wrote lectures and led museum tours for community groups
- Wrote brochures for museum fund-raising committee
- Use PowerPoint, Pagemaker, Microsoft Front Page

Research Experience:
- Catalogued historical collectibles and replications for artifacts dealer
- Organized research notes and wrote reports for archeology expedition to the Yucatan.

Employment History:
Assistant Manager, PW Antiques, Port William, NY, 1996–present
Assistant to curator, Museum of Indian Art, El Paso, TX, Summers, 1988–1989

Education:
B.A. in Art History, Port William College (expected June 2002)
General Studies, University of Texas-El Paso (1988–1989)

Professional Membership:
American Art History Association

References are available on request.

1. The following e-mail message was sent to all employees at a large consumer products company housed in a two-building complex. Many of the 900 employees, especially women, became upset both at the news and at the tone of the message. Readers said the message was "inadequate" and "insensitive." Discuss the problems in this e-mail, and rewrite for better tone and you-attitude.

> ALL EMPLOYEES:
>
> Several rumors are circulating about an alleged series of assaults on women in both our buildings. The rumors have prompted numerous phone calls to the president's office and are a gross exaggeration causing undue concern. The latest rumor links the assault on Tuesday afternoon in the women's restroom off the Mason Street lobby with one on Wednesday morning in the parking lot on Dixon Avenue. The woman who was assaulted in the restroom gave police a description, and police do not think this suspect is connected to the parking lot assault nor to the assault last week in the first floor stairwell off the Mason Street lobby. Rumors create unnecessary panic. Please do not repeat rumors and cause confusion.

2. As Executive Manager of the Caribbean Deluxe Resort in St. Thomas, you have been told that the water lines serving the resort need immediate repair. Thus, all water must be shut off at 9:00 A.M. tomorrow until at least 5:00 P.M., perhaps longer. The 500-room resort is full. You must tell the guests that they cannot use the bathrooms or the poolside showers, and no food will be available after 9:00 A.M. tomorrow. You are arranging for deliveries of bottled water by 10:00 A.M., so you can set up a lobby bar to dispense water for drinking. Unfortunately, this problem developed so quickly, you are not able to give much notice, and you expect some people to awaken after 9:00 A.M. and discover that they cannot shower or brush their teeth. You will have to write a form letter that will be slipped under every guest's door as soon as it is ready. It is now 5:15 P.M.

3. As the shipping director of PACGO Equipment Company, you discover maintenance costs are rising on the fleet of trucks. The diesel engines need major overhauling much sooner than they should. An overhaul can cost up to $2,000. In discussing the situation with several drivers and the loading supervisor, you conclude that the drivers' practice of idling for long periods is having a negative effect on engine longevity. The extensive idling increases the rate of wear on the engine components. Also, the mileage is not changed through idling, but the oil is being used, and oil changes are not occurring at proper intervals. On the other hand, the practice of starting a cold engine and trying to drive away immediately also is wearing out engine components. Write a memo to the drivers directing them to stop excessive idling while they wait for pickups and to warm up a cold engine before driving. When starting cold engines, drivers should reach normal oil pressure before pulling away.

4. As the head of clinical pathology at St. Elizabeth's Hospital, you receive a letter from an irate patient. The patient says that she arrived at the hospital for her regular quarterly blood tests, glycosylated albumin and hemogram. The outpatient technician tried to give her a different blood test. The patient's letter states that she knew what test she needed, but she had to argue with three outpatient technicians before one agreed to doublecheck her files. A technician checked the records and agreed that the patient was correct. The technician also wrote the name of the correct test on an index card and gave it to the patient. After returning to her office, the patient looked at the card and realized that the other side had another patient's name and test information on it. The information should be confidential, and the patient returned the card with her letter. You call in the laboratory operations manager and discuss the situation. She agrees that there is no excuse for such a lapse, but does comment that the laboratory was particularly busy that week with twice the usual patient traffic. You tell her to hold a staff review of procedures at once. Now you will write a letter to the patient, thanking her for bringing up the matter and for returning the card. You will try to restore her confidence in the hospital. Also, write a memo to the technicians in the laboratory and tell them you are arranging for a staff review of procedures. Tell them why the review is needed. Add any details you wish.

5. As director of the Hamilton County Social Services Division, you have decided to offer a retirement planning workshop to employees to be held next month one evening after the office closes. Ms. Vonda Watkins, a financial planner from the Sentry Bank headquarters in Atlanta, will present the workshop. Employees will be welcome to bring their spouses. Add any details you wish, and write an e-mail message for all employees.

6. You are an assistant to the communication director of your state's Recreation Bureau. Your office prepares all the printed materials about state parks, historical sites, and recreation activities (e.g., boating and fishing). These materials are written for tourists and other visitors. Delbert Hutchins writes to your office from a neighboring state. He is planning a vacation in your area and wants information. Select one location or activity in your state, and write a letter to Mr. Hutchins that both informs him and persuades him to visit. *Or*, if your instructor prefers, develop a one-page flyer on the location or activity and write a letter to accompany the flyer.

7. Courtland Electronics has been experimenting with a 4-day work week for the past six months. Employees work 10-hour days 4 days a week and have Fridays or Mondays off. After evaluating the results, management has decided to return to the traditional 8-hour day, 5 days a week. Overall production has dropped during the experiment, and dealers have complained they cannot reach the people they need. You believe the 10-hour day creates too much fatigue in employees. You notice that people stand around drinking coffee for nearly an hour before beginning work, and complaints from assembly workers about carpal tunnel syndrome have increased. Other employees have had trouble getting children off to school before they begin work at 7 A.M.; still others have had babysitting problems; and an accountant told you he gained 15 lb from eating fast food at the office instead of having a well-balanced evening meal. However, many employees like the long weekends and the chance to schedule personal appointments. Write a memo to all employees telling them that the company will return to a 5-day week 8 hours a day in six weeks. You want them to have time to make new family arrangements if needed. Present this mixed good and bad news message so the employees will understand and accept the decision.

8. Find an advertisement for a technical product. Assume the product is a new development that few people have heard of. Consider what type of people would be potential customers, and write a sales letter for the new product to that group.

9. You are marketing director for Geneva Software, Inc. Because of a fire in one warehouse and the business failure of two printing companies you used, you are going to have to ship software and manuals separately from two locations for about four months until you can arrange to ship materials together. For now, you cannot guarantee that software and manuals will arrive at the same time or even in the same week. Write a form letter to your dealers and regular business customers explaining the situation and asking for patience on their part. Add any details you wish.

10. Select a "real world" memo or letter of at least one page. Make enough copies for class members. Present a critique of the memo or letter to the class, pointing out both effective and ineffective aspects of the sample. *In addition,* submit a revision of the sample. The revision should reflect your ideas about how to improve the original memo or letter for greatest effectiveness. Do not change the original situation in the writing sample. Your job is to improve and develop the message. You may add any logical material to your revision in order to improve it.

11. Prepare a résumé based on the formats in this chapter. Select a company in your area, and apply for a summer job (or a part-time job during the semester) in your career area. Graduating seniors should apply for a full-time job in their career area. Write an application letter that realistically discusses your interest in and qualifications for a position based on your *present* situation. Key your remarks to your résumé, and attach your résumé to the letter.

CHAPTER 14

Oral Presentations

UNDERSTANDING ORAL PRESENTATIONS

Although most people hate to speak in front of a group, you must be prepared to handle oral presentations gracefully. One study indicates that 30 million business presentations take place each day, and the 725 managers surveyed ranked the ability to communicate in front of an audience as the number one skill needed for career advancement.[1] Oral presentations can be internal, i.e., for management or staff, or external, i.e., for clients, prospective customers, or colleagues at scientific conferences. Most presentations are face to face, but videoconferencing, involving two or more groups at separate sites, is increasing in frequency and importance.

Purpose

Like written documents, oral presentations often have mixed purposes. A scientist speaking at a conference about a research study is informing listeners as well as persuading them that the results of the study are significant. Oral presentations generally serve these purposes, separately or in combination:

- *To inform.* The speaker presents facts and analyzes data to help listeners understand the information. Such presentations cover the status of a current project, results of research or investigations, company changes, or performance quality of new systems and equipment.

- *To persuade.* The speaker presents information and urges listeners to take a specific action or reach a specific conclusion. Persuasive presentations involve sales proposals to potential customers, internal company proposals, or external grant proposals.

- *To instruct.* The speaker describes how to do a specific task. Presentations that offer instruction include training sessions for groups of employees and demonstrations for procedures or proper handling of equipment.

Advantages

Oral presentations have these advantages over written documents:

- The speaker can explain a procedure and demonstrate it at the same time.

- The speaker controls what is emphasized in the presentation and can keep listeners focused on specific topics.

- A speaker's personality can create enthusiasm in listeners during sales presentations and inspire confidence during informative presentations.

- Speakers can get immediate feedback from listeners and answer questions on the spot.

- Listeners can raise new issues immediately.

- If most of the listeners become involved in the presentation—asking questions, nodding agreement—those who may have had negative attitudes may be swept up in the group energy and become less negative.

Disadvantages

Oral presentations are not adequate substitutes for written documents, however, because they have these distinct disadvantages:

- Oral presentations are expensive because listeners may be away from their jobs for a longer time than it would take them to read a written document.

- Listeners, unlike readers, cannot select the topic they are most interested in or proceed through the material at their own pace.

- Listeners can be easily distracted from an oral presentation by outside noises, coughing, uncomfortable seating, and their own wandering thoughts.

- A poor speaker will annoy listeners, who then may reject the information.

- Spoken words vanish as soon as they are said, and listeners remember only a few major points.

- Time limitations require speakers to condense and simplify material, possibly omitting important details.

- Listeners have difficulty following complicated statistical data in oral presentations, even with graphic aids.

- Audience size has to be limited for effective oral presentations unless expensive video/TV equipment is involved.

Types of Oral Presentations

An oral presentation on the job is usually in one of these four styles:

Memorized Speech.   Memorization is useful primarily for short remarks, such as introducing a main speaker at a conference. Unless it is a dramatic reading, a memorized speech has little audience appeal. A speaker reciting a memorized speech is likely to develop a monotone that will soon have the listeners glassy-eyed with boredom. In addition, in such presentations, if the speaker is interrupted by a question, the entire presentation may disappear from memory.

Written Manuscript.   Speakers at large scientific and technical conferences often read from a written manuscript, particularly when reporting a research study or presenting complex technical data. The written manuscript enables the speaker to cover every detail and stay within a set time limit. Unfortunately, written manuscripts, like the memorized speeches, also may encourage speakers to develop a monotone. Usually, too, the speaker who reads from a manuscript has little eye contact or interaction with the audience. Listeners at scientific conferences frequently want copies of the full research report for reference later.

Impromptu Remarks.   Impromptu remarks occur when, without warning, a person is asked to explain something at a meeting. Although others in the meeting realize that the person has had no chance to prepare, they still expect to hear specific information presented in an organized manner. Always come to meetings prepared to explain projects or answer questions about activities under your supervision. Bring notes, current cost figures, and other information that others may ask you for.

Extemporaneous Talk.   Most oral presentations on the job are extemporaneous, that is, the speaker plans and rehearses the presentation and follows a written topic or sentence outline when speaking. Because this type of on-the-job oral presentation is the most common, the rest of this chapter focuses on preparing and delivering extemporaneous talks.

ORGANIZING ORAL PRESENTATIONS

As you do with written documents, analyze your audience and their need for information, as explained in Chapter 3. Consider who your listeners are and what they expect to get from your talk. The key to a successful presentation is knowing what facts your audience will be most interested in. Emphasize these points in your presentation. Oral presentations also must be as carefully organized as written documents are. Even though you are deeply involved in a project, do not rely on your memory alone to support your review of the information or your proposal. Instead, prepare an outline, as discussed in Chapter 4, that covers all the points you want to make. An outline also will be easier to work with than a marked copy of a written report you plan to distribute because you will not have to fumble with sheets of paper.

Use either a topic or a sentence outline—whichever you feel most comfortable with and whichever provides enough information to stir your memory. Remember that topic outlines contain only key words, whereas sentence outlines include more facts:

Topic: Venus—Earth's twin

Sentence: Venus is Earth's twin in size, mass, density, and gravity.

Some people prefer to put an outline on note cards, only one or two topics or sentences per card. Other speakers prefer to use an outline typed on sheets of paper because it is easier to glance ahead to see what is coming next. Oral presentations generally have three sections:

Introduction.   Your introduction should establish (1) the purpose of the oral presentation, (2) why it is relevant to listeners, and (3) the major topics that will be covered. Since listeners, unlike readers, cannot look ahead to check on what is coming, they need a preview of main points in the opening so that they can anticipate and listen for the information relevant to their own work. Your introduction also should define your terms. Even if your audience consists of experts in the topic, do not assume they understand everything you do. Explain the terms you use and check your audience's comprehension before continuing.

Data Sections.   The main sections of your presentation are those that deal with specific facts, arranged in one of the organizational patterns discussed in Chapter 4. Remember these tips when presenting data orally:

- Include specific examples to reinforce your main points.
- Number items as you talk so that listeners know where problem number 2 ends and problem number 3 begins.
- Refer to visual illustrations and explain the content to be sure people understand what they are looking at.
- Cite authorities or give sources for your information, particularly if people in the audience have contributed information for your presentation.
- Simplify statistics for the presentation, and provide the full tables or formulas in handouts.

Conclusion.   Your conclusion should summarize the main points and recommendations to fix them in listeners' minds. In addition, remind listeners about necessary future actions, upcoming deadlines, and other scheduled presentations on the subject. Also ask for questions so that listeners can clarify points immediately.

Model 14-1 is a sentence outline of an oral presentation by the communications manager at a large company. The manager is alerting company officers to the dangers of voice-mail fraud based on information gathered at a seminar on communications security.

As the outline shows, the introduction (1) identifies the main topic, toll fraud and its costs, and (2) identifies the source of the information. Sections II and III explain the risks of voice mail and the methods hackers use to enter the systems. Section IV provides strategies the company can use to protect itself, and the conclusion warns listeners that a company can never be completely safe. To help listeners understand the information, speakers often supplement oral presentations with handouts that highlight specific points or distribute full written reports on the subject of the presentation. Listeners then can check the report later for items they are most interested in, read sections not fully covered in the oral presentation, and confirm their memories of significant details.

The outline in Model 14-1 includes reminders of when to use visual aids, as well as a note to distribute a handout and ask for questions. Such reminders in your outline are important safeguards against your concentrating so much on your speech that you forget your visual aids. Some speakers put extra-wide margins in their outlines to allow room for extra notes.

PREPARING FOR ORAL PRESENTATIONS

Because oral presentations usually have time restrictions, concentrate on the factors that your audience is most interested in, and prepare written materials covering other points that you do not have time to present orally. In addition, for oral presentations, you must check on these physical conditions, if possible:

- *Size of the group.* Is the group so large that you need a microphone to be heard in the back, and will those in the back be able to see your graphic aids? Remember that the larger the group, the more remote the listeners feel from the speaker and the less likely they are to interact and provide feedback.

- *Shape of the room.* Can all the listeners see the speaker, or is the room so narrow that those in the back are blocked from seeing either the speaker or the graphic aids? Does the speaker have to stand in front of a large glass wall through which listeners can watch other office activities? An inability to see or an opportunity to watch outside activities will prevent listeners from concentrating on the presentation.

- *Visual equipment.* Does the room contain built-in visual equipment, such as a movie screen or chalkboard, or will these have to be brought in, thus altering the shape of the speaking area? Will additional equipment in the room crowd the speaker or listeners? Are there enough electrical outlets,

VOICE-MAIL SECURITY REPORT

I. **Toll fraud is a growing problem in corporate telecommunications.**
   A. Information in this report comes from the Society of Information Management seminar, New York, October 1–2, 1997.
   B. Toll fraud costs over one billion dollars annually.
      [Slide I—SIM 5-YEAR TABLE]
      1. Long-distance carriers absorb most of the costs.
      2. All companies with a voice mail system are vulnerable.

II. **Voice-mail systems have increased corporate risk of toll fraud.**
   A. Hackers can browse through systems and use abandoned voice-mail boxes.
   B. Hackers can use voice mail to travel through corporate PBX systems and access a dial tone.
   C. Voice-mail fraud is difficult to trace.
      [Slide II—FLOWCHART OF FRAUD ATTEMPT]

III. **Voice-mail systems have two vulnerable elements.**
   A. Most companies (including ours) have an 800 number for remote access.
   B. Employees overuse default passwords.
      1. Hackers can delete or alter messages.
      2. Hackers can access a remote dial tone.

IV. **Companies must take steps to protect against voice-mail fraud.**
   A. All default passwords must be changed.
   B. Passwords should be no shorter than six digits.
   C. Unused voice-mail boxes must be deleted.
   D. Ability to transfer from voice mail to a remote PBS should be disabled by the vendor.
   E. Billing for voice-mail 800 numbers should be monitored.

V. **No company system can be 100% safe.**
   [DISTRIBUTE TOLL FRAUD CHART AND ASK FOR QUESTIONS]

MODEL 14-1 Sentence Outline for Oral Presentation

or will long extension cords be necessary, thereby creating walking obstacles for the speaker or those entering the room?

- *Seating arrangements.* Are the chairs bolted in place? Is there room for space between chairs, or will people be seated elbow-to-elbow in tight rows? If listeners want to take notes, is there room to write? People hate to be crowded into closely packed rows. An uncomfortable audience is an inattentive one.

- *Lighting.* Is there enough light so that listeners can see to take notes? Can the light be controlled to prevent the room from being so bright that people cannot see slides and transparencies clearly?

- *Temperature.* Is the room too hot or too cold? Heat is usually worse for an audience because it makes people sleepy, especially in the afternoon. If the temperature is too cold, people may concentrate on huddling in jackets and sweaters rather than listening to the presentation. A cool room, however, will heat up once people are seated because of body heat. Good air circulation also helps keep a room from being hot, stuffy, and uncomfortable.

You may not be able to control all these factors, but you can make some adjustments to enhance your presentation. You can adjust the temperature control or change the position of the lectern away from a distracting window, for example.

STRATEGIES—Graphics to Enhance Presentations

- Select a consistent color scheme for background and text.
- Use a 24-point font or larger for text to ensure readability.
- Use bullet points for text—no more than five or six per slide or overhead.
- Use simple, easy-to-read pie graphs, bar graphs, or line graphs to illustrate statistics.
- Distribute complicated spreadsheets or diagrams on handouts.
- Include the corporate logo in the corner of slides, overheads, or handouts when presenting to outside clients.

DELIVERING ORAL PRESENTATIONS

After planning your oral presentation to provide your listeners with the information they need and organizing your talk, you must deliver it. Fairly or unfairly, listeners tend to judge the usefulness of an oral presentation at least partly by the physical delivery of the speaker. Prepare your delivery as carefully as you do your outline.

Rehearsal

Everyone who speaks in front of a group is somewhat nervous. Fortunately, nerves create energy, and you need energy to deliver your talk. Picture yourself performing well beforehand, and remember that no one is there to "catch" you in a mistake. In fact, the audience usually does not know if you reverse the order of transparencies or discuss points out of order. Rehearse your oral presentation aloud so that you know it thoroughly and it fits the allotted time. Rehearsing it will also help you find trouble spots where, for instance, your chronology is out of order. If possible, practice in the room you intend to use so that you can check the speaking area, seating arrangements, and lighting.

If you "go blank" during a presentation, pause and repeat your last point, using slightly different words. This repetition often puts a speaker back on track. Consider speaking in front of a group not as a dreadful ordeal that you must suffer through, but as an essential part of your job, and develop your ability to make an effective presentation.

Notes and Outlines

Have your notes organized before arriving in the room, and number each card or page in case you drop them and have to put them in order quickly. If a lectern is available, place your notes on that. Avoid waving your notes around or making them obvious to your listeners. They want to concentrate on what you are telling them, not on a sheaf of white cards flapping in the air.

Visual Equipment

Practice using any visual equipment before your talk so that you know where the control buttons are and how the machine works. If you know you write slowly on chalkboards and flip charts, put your terms or lists on them before the presentation so that you can simply refer to them at the appropriate time. If you are using VCRs or cassettes, set the tapes to the exact start spot and know which key word or image signals where you want to shut them off. If any equipment breaks during your presentation, continue without it. Trying to manage repairs in the middle of a presentation will result in chaos. No matter what kind of visual equipment you use, be sure that all members of the audience can see the visual part of your presentation adequately.

Voice

If you are nervous, your voice may reveal it more than any mistakes you make. Do not race through your talk on one breath, forcing your audience to listen to an unintelligible monotone, but do not pause after every few words either, creating a stop-and-start style. Avoid a monotone by being interested in your own presentation. Speak clearly, and check the pronunciation of difficult terms or foreign words before your talk. Be sure also to pronounce words separately. For example, say "would have" instead of "wouldof."

Professional Image

When you speak in front of a group, you are in a sense "on stage." Dress conservatively but in the usual office style. Uncomfortable clothes that are too tight or that have unusual, eye-catching decorations are not appropriate for oral presentations. They will distract both you and your audience. Do not hang on the lectern, perch casually on the edge of a table, or sway back and forth on your feet. Be relaxed, but stand straight.

Gestures

Nervous gestures can distract your audience, and artificial "on purpose" gestures look awkward. If you feel clumsy, keep your hands still. Do not fiddle with your note cards, jewelry, tie, hair, or other objects.

Some gestures, however, can help focus the audience's attention on a specific point. If you suggest two solutions for a problem and hold up two fingers to emphasize the choice, the gesture will help your audience remember the number of alternatives you have explained.

Eye Contact

Create the impression that you are speaking to the individuals in the room by establishing eye contact. Although you may not be able to look at each person individually, glance around the room frequently. Do not stare at two or three people to the exclusion of all others, but do not sweep back and forth across the room like a surveillance camera. Eye contact indicates that you are interested in the listener's response, and a smile indicates that you are pleased to be giving this presentation. You should project both attitudes.

Questions

One of the advantages of oral presentations is that listeners can ask questions immediately. Answer as many questions as your time limitations permit. If you do not know the answer to a question, say so and promise to find the answer later. You may ask if anyone else in the audience knows the answer, but do not put someone on the spot by calling his or her name without warning. If there is a reason you cannot answer a question, such as the information being classified, simply say so. If you are not sure what the questioner means, rephrase the question before trying to answer it by saying, "Are you asking whether . . . ?" In all cases, answer a question completely before going on to another.

JOINING A TEAM PRESENTATION

In some instances, such as sales presentations to potential clients or training sessions, a team of people makes the oral presentation, with each person on the team responsible for a unit that reflects that person's speciality. Although each person must plan and deliver an individual talk, some coordination is needed to be sure the overall presentation goes smoothly. Remember these guidelines:

- One person should be in charge of introducing the overall presentation to provide continuity. This person also may present the conclusion, wrapping up the team effort.

- One person should be in charge of all visual equipment so that, for example, two people do not bring overhead projectors.

- If the question period is left to the end of the team presentation, then one person should be in charge of moderating the questions that the team members answer in order to maintain an orderly atmosphere.

- All members should pay close attention to time limits so that they do not infringe on other team members' allotted time.

- All team members should listen to the other speakers as a courtesy and because they may need to refer to each other's talks in answering questions.

FACING INTERNATIONAL AUDIENCES

As companies expand their operations into worldwide markets and become partners with companies in other countries, you may have to make an oral presentation to an international audience. If so, you must consider language barriers. First, determine whether your audience understands English or you will be using a translator. If a translator will be repeating your words in another language after every sentence, your presentation will take twice as long, and you must adjust the length accordingly.

Rather than speak from an outline, write out your speech in detail. You want to be sure that nothing in your speech will offend or confuse your audience. Ask someone who speaks your audience's language to review your speech carefully and cut out all confusing jargon, slang, acronyms, popular culture references, and humor. These elements do not translate well. When you give your speech, keep to the written script to avoid straying into comments that will present problems for the translator. As a courtesy, you might prepare visual aids in the language of your audience.

Even if your audience understands English, you will need to research the appropriate ways to open your presentation, how much time to allot for questions, and how to end without giving offense. For example, American presentation style is to begin by pointing out objectives. However, an Arab speaker may begin by expressing appreciation for hospitality and appealing for harmony. Germans typically do not interact with speakers, and the question session may be short, but Mexicans enjoy a long question-and-answer session. The American closing typically calls for action, but other cultures may close presentations by emphasizing future meetings or group harmony.[2]

It takes time and thought to prepare an appropriate oral presentation for an international audience. To be an effective speaker in such circumstances, you must develop techniques to ensure that your technical information is not changed in translation and your presentation style fulfills your audience's cultural expectations.

CHAPTER SUMMARY

This chapter discusses making oral presentations on the job. Remember:

- Oral presentations may have these purposes, separately or in combination: informing, persuading, instructing.

- Oral presentations have the advantages of allowing the speaker to create enthusiasm through a dynamic personality as well as allowing listeners to ask questions on the spot.

- Oral presentations have disadvantages in that listeners cannot study materials thoroughly and are easily distracted.

- Oral presentations may be (1) a memorized speech, (2) a written manuscript, (3) impromptu remarks, or (4) an extemporaneous talk.

- Speakers usually use topic or sentence outlines for oral presentations.

- If possible before a presentation, speakers should check the room layout, lighting, temperature, and visual equipment.

- Speakers should (1) control nerves by preparing thoroughly, (2) rehearse aloud, (3) speak clearly, (4) dress professionally, (5) keep hand gestures to a minimum, (6) establish eye contact, (7) number notes and outline sheets, (8) practice with equipment, and (9) answer questions fully.

- For a team presentation, one speaker should handle the general introduction and conclusion.

- For international audiences, prepare a written speech.

SUPPLEMENTAL READINGS IN PART 2

Alessi, R. J. "Doing Business in Mexico," *Association Management,* p. 444.

Calabrese, R. "Designing and Delivering Presentations and Workshops," *The Bulletin of the Association for Business Communication,* p. 474.

Graham, J. R. "What Skills Will You Need to Succeed?" *Manager's Magazine,* p. 487.

Hulbert, J. E. "Barriers to Effective Listening," *The Bulletin of the Association for Business Communication,* p. 492.

Martel, M. "Combating Speech Anxiety," *Public Relations Journal,* p. 499.

Munter, M. "Meeting Technology: From Low-Tech to High-Tech," *Business Communication Quarterly,* p. 508.

Smith, T. C. "Listen Up—Tips from the Top on Talks," *Technical Communication,* p. 541.

"Tips, Tricks and Pitfalls to Avoid When Doing Business in the Tough but Lucrative Korean Market," *Business America,* p. 549.

ENDNOTES

1. "Critical Link between Presentation Skills, Upward Mobility," *American Salesman* 36.8 (August 1991): 16–20.

2. Elashmawl, Farid, "Multicultural Business Meeting and Presentations: Tips and Taboos," *Tokyo Business Today* 59.11 (November 1991): 66–68.

Chapter 14   Exercises

1. For panel presentations, your instructor will divide the class into groups, and each group will work on one of the following topics, assigning subtopics to each group member. Read the articles in Part 2 dealing with oral presentations for tips in preparation and delivery. Plan a 5-minute presentation for each group member unless your instructor assigns a different length. Practice your presentation to be sure it fits the required time. Your classmates want information directed at their needs. Tailor your presentation to this audience. After making your oral presentation, submit an executive summary of your talk to your instructor. Write a transmittal memo to accompany the executive summary. Guidelines for these are in Chapter 10.

   a. *Job Interviewing*: Report on typical questions to expect in job interviews and ways to answer them; behavioral interviews; information sources for learning about companies; handling a panel interview; questions to ask the interviewer.

   b. *Body Language and Appearance*: Report on dressing for success; company "casual dress" days; body language turn-ons and turn-offs; accessories and grooming for interviews; items to bring with you to a job interview.

   c. *Job Prospects*: Report on opportunities for new graduates in specific careers that students in your class are interested in; types of positions available; expected entry salaries; promotion possibilities.

   d. *Business Etiquette*: Report on how to take part in a meeting; arranging business lunches; office politics; telephone manners; making introductions.

   e. *International Business Customs*: Each panel member selects a country and reports on customs for conducting meetings, making oral presentations, and negotiating business deals.

2. Prepare a 3- or 4-minute oral presentation to give to your class based on one of your written assignments in this class. Prepare a sentence outline of your oral presentation to submit to your instructor.

Guidelines for Grammar, Punctuation, and Mechanics

These guidelines for grammar, punctuation, and mechanical matters, such as using numbers, will help you revise your writing according to generally accepted conventions for correctness. These guidelines cover the most frequent questions writers have when they edit their final drafts. Your instructor may tell you to read about specific topics before revising. In addition, use this Appendix to check your writing before you submit it to your instructor.

GRAMMAR

Dangling Modifiers

Dangling modifiers are verbal phrases, prepositional phrases, or dependent clauses that do not refer to a subject in the sentence in which they occur. These modifiers are most often at the beginning of a sentence, but they may also appear at the end. Correct by rewriting the sentence to include the subject of the modifier.

Incorrect: Realizing the connections between neutron stars, pulsars, and supernovas, the explanation of the birth and death of stars is complete. (The writer does not indicate *who* realized the connections.)

Correct: Realizing the connection between neutron stars, pulsars, and supernovas, many astronomers believe that the explanation of the birth and death of stars is complete.

Incorrect:	To obtain a slender blade, a cylindrical flint core was chipped into long slivers with a hammerstone. (The writer does not indicate *who* worked to obtain the blade.)
Correct:	To obtain a slender blade, Cro-Magnon man chipped a cylindrical flint core into slivers with a hammerstone.
Incorrect:	Born with cerebral palsy, only minimal mobility was possible. (The writer does not indicate *who* was born with cerebral palsy.)
Correct:	Born with cerebral palsy, the child had only minimal mobility.
Incorrect:	Their sensitivity to prostaglandins remained substantially lowered hours after leaving a smoke-filled room. (The writer does not indicate *who* or *what* left the room.)
Correct:	Their sensitivity to prostaglandins remained substantially lowered hours after the nonsmokers left a smoke-filled room.

Misplaced Modifiers

Misplaced modifiers are words, phrases, or clauses that do not refer logically to the nearest word in the sentence in which they appear. Correct by rewriting the sentence to place the modifier next to the word to which it refers.

Incorrect:	The financial analysts presented statistics to their clients that showed net margins were twice the industry average. (The phrase about *net margins* does not modify *clients.*)
Correct:	The financial analysts presented their clients with statistics that showed net margins were twice the industry average.

Squinting Modifiers

Squinting modifiers are words or phrases that could logically refer to either a preceding or a following word in the sentence in which they appear. Correct by rewriting the sentence so that the modifier refers to only one word in the sentence.

Incorrect:	Physicians who use a nuclear magnetic resonance machine frequently can identify stroke damage in older patients easily. (The word *frequently* could refer to *use* or *identify.*)
Correct:	Physicians who frequently use a nuclear magnetic resonance machine can identify stroke damage in older patients easily.
Correct:	Physicians who use a nuclear magnetic resonance machine can identify stroke damage in older patients frequently and easily.

Parallel Construction

Elements that are equal in a sentence should be expressed in the same grammatical form.

Incorrect:	With professional care, bulimia can be treated and is controllable. (The words *treated* and *controllable* are not parallel.)
Correct:	With professional care, bulimia can be treated and controlled.
Incorrect:	The existence of two types of Neanderthal tool kits indicates that one group was engaged in scraping hides, while the other group carved wood. (The verbal phrases after the word *group* are not parallel.)
Correct:	The existence of two types of Neanderthal tool kits indicates that one group scraped hides, while the other group carved wood.
Incorrect:	The social worker counseled the family about preparing meals, cleaning the house, and gave advice about childcare. (The list of actions should be in parallel phrases.)
Correct:	The social worker counseled the family about preparing meals, cleaning the house, and caring for children.

Elements linked by correlative conjunctions (*either . . . or, neither . . . nor, not only . . . but also*) also should be in parallel structure.

Incorrect:	Such symptoms as rocking and staring vacantly are seen not only in monkeys that are deprived of their babies but also when something frightens mentally disturbed children. (The phrases following *not only* and *but also* are not parallel.)
Correct:	Such symptoms as rocking and staring vacantly are seen not only in monkeys that are deprived of their babies but also in mentally disturbed children who are frightened.

Pronoun Agreement

A pronoun must agree in number, person, and gender with the noun or pronoun to which it refers.

Incorrect:	Each firefighter must record their use of equipment. (The noun *firefighter* is singular, and the pronoun *their* is plural.)
Correct:	Each firefighter must record his or her use of equipment.
Correct:	All firefighters must record their use of equipment.

Incorrect:	Everyone needs carbohydrates in their diet. (*Everyone* is singular, and *their* is plural.)
Correct:	Everyone needs carbohydrates in the diet.
Correct:	Everyone needs to eat carbohydrates.
Correct:	Everyone needs carbohydrates in his or her diet.
Incorrect:	The sales department explained their training methods to a group of college students. (*Sales department* is singular and requires an *it*. Correct by clarifying *who* did the explaining.)
Correct:	The sales manager explained the department training methods to a group of college students.
Correct:	The sales manager explained her training methods to a group of college students.
Incorrect:	The International Microbiologists Association met at their traditional site. (*Association* is singular and requires an *it*.)
Correct:	The International Microbiologists Association met at its traditional site.

Pronoun Reference

A pronoun must clearly refer to only one antecedent.

Incorrect:	Biologists have shown that all living organisms depend on two kinds of molecules—amino acids and nucleotides. They are the building blocks of life. (*They* could refer to either *amino acids*, *nucleotides*, or both.)
Correct:	Biologists have shown that all living organisms depend on two kinds of molecules—amino acids and nucleotides. Both are the building blocks of life.
Incorrect:	Present plans call for a new parking deck, a new entry area, and an addition to the parking garage. It will add $810,000 to the cost. (*It* could refer to any of the new items.)
Correct:	Present plans call for a new parking deck, a new entry area, and an addition to the parking garage. The parking deck will add $810,000 to the cost.

Reflexive Pronouns

A *reflexive pronoun* (ending in *-self* or *-selves*) must refer to the subject of the sentence when the subject also receives the action in the sentence. (Example: She cut herself when the camera lens cracked.) A reflexive pronoun cannot serve instead of *I* or *me* as a subject or an object in a sentence.

Incorrect:	The governor presented the science award to Dr. Yasmin Rashid and myself. (*Myself* cannot serve as the indirect object.)
Correct:	The governor presented the science award to Dr. Yasmin Rashid and me.
Incorrect:	Mark Burnwood, Christina Hayward, and myself conducted the experiment. (*Myself* cannot function as the subject of the sentence.)
Correct:	Mark Burnwood, Christina Hayward, and I conducted the experiment.

Reflexive pronouns are also used to make the antecedent more emphatic:

The patient himself asked for another medication.

Venus itself is covered by a heavy layer of carbon dioxide.

Sentence Faults

Comma Splices

A *comma splice* results when the writer incorrectly joins two independent clauses with a comma. Correct by (1) placing a semicolon between the clauses, (2) adding a coordinating conjunction after the comma, (3) rewriting the sentence, or (4) creating two sentences.

Incorrect:	The zinc coating on galvanized steel gums up a welding gun's electrode, resistance welding, therefore, is not ideal for the steel increasingly used in autos today.
Correct:	The zinc coating on galvanized steel gums up a welding gun's electrode; resistance welding, therefore, is not ideal for the steel increasingly used in autos today.
Correct:	The zinc coating on galvanized steel gums up a welding gun's electrode, so resistance welding, therefore, is not ideal for the steel increasingly used in autos today.
Correct:	Because the zinc coating on galvanized steel gums up a welding gun's electrode, resistance welding is not ideal for the steel increasingly used in autos today.
Correct:	The zinc coating on galvanized steel gums up a welding gun's electrode. Resistance welding, therefore, is not ideal for the steel increasingly used in autos today.

Fragments

A *sentence fragment* is an incomplete sentence because it lacks a subject or a verb or both. Correct by writing a full sentence or by adding the fragment to another sentence.

Incorrect:	As the universe expands and the galaxies fly farther apart, the force of gravity is decreasing everywhere. According to one imaginative theory. (The phrase beginning with *According* is a fragment.)
Correct:	According to one imaginative theory, as the universe expands and the galaxies fly farther apart, the force of gravity is decreasing everywhere.
Incorrect:	Apes are afraid of water when they cannot see the stream bottom. Which prevents them from entering the water and crossing a stream more than 1 ft deep. (The phrase beginning with *which* is a fragment.)
Correct:	Apes are afraid of water when they cannot see the stream bottom. This fear prevents them from entering the water and crossing a stream more than 1 ft deep.

Run-on Sentences

A *run-on sentence* occurs when a writer links two or more sentences together without punctuation between them. Correct by placing a semicolon between the sentences or by writing two separate sentences.

Incorrect:	The galaxy is flattened by its rotating motion into the shape of a disk most of the stars in the galaxy are in this disk.
Correct:	The galaxy is flattened by its rotating motion into the shape of a disk; most of the stars in the galaxy are in this disk.
Correct:	The galaxy is flattened by its rotating motion into the shape of a disk. Most of the stars in the galaxy are in this disk.

Subject/Verb Agreement

The verb in a sentence must agree with its subject in person and number. Correct by rewriting.

Incorrect:	The report of a joint team of Canadian and American geologists suggest that some dormant volcanos on the West Coast may be reawakening. (The subject is *report*, which requires a singular verb.)
Correct:	The report of a joint team of Canadian and American geologists suggests that some dormant volcanos on the West Coast may be reawakening.

Incorrect: The high number of experiments that failed were disappointing. (The subject is *number,* which requires a singular verb.)

Correct: The high number of experiments that failed was disappointing.

Incorrect: Sixteen inches are the deepest we can drill. (The subject is a single unit and requires a singular verb.)

Correct: Sixteen inches is the deepest we can drill.

When compound subjects are joined by *and,* the verb is plural.

Computer-security techniques and plans for evading hackers require large expenditures.

When one of the compound subjects is plural and one is singular, the verb agrees with the nearest subject.

Neither the split casings nor the cracked layer of plywood was to blame.

When a compound subject is preceded by *each* or *every,* the verb is singular.

Every case aide and social worker is scheduled for a training session.

When a compound subject is considered a single unit or person, the verb is singular.

The vice-president and guiding force of the company is meeting with the Nuclear Regulatory Commission.

PUNCTUATION

Apostrophe

An apostrophe shows possession or marks the omission of letters in a word or in dates.

The engineer's analysis of the city's water system shows a high pollution danger from raw sewage.

The extent of the outbreak of measles wasn't known until all area hospitals' medical records were coordinated with those of private physicians.

Chemist Charles Frakes' experiments were funded by the National Institute of Health throughout the '70s.

Do not confuse *its* (possessive) with *it's* (contraction of *it is*).

The animal pricked up its ears before feeding.

Professors Jones, Higgins, and Carlton are examining the ancient terrain at Casper Mountain. It's located on a geologic fault, and the professors hope to study its changes over time.

Colon

The colon introduces explanations or lists. An independent clause must precede the colon.

> The Olympic gymnastic team used three brands of equipment: Acme, Dakota, and Shelby.

Do not place a colon directly after a verb.

> *Incorrect:*   The environmentalists reported finding: decreased oxygen, pollution-tolerant sludgeworms, and high bacteria levels in the lake. (The colon does not have an independent clause preceding it.)
>
> *Correct:*   The environmentalists reported finding decreased oxygen, pollution-tolerant sludgeworms, and high bacteria levels in the lake.

Comma

To Link.   The comma links independent clauses joined by a coordinating conjunction (*and, but, or, for, so, yet,* and *nor*).

> The supervisor stopped the production line, but the damage was done.
>
> Rheumatic fever is controllable once it has been diagnosed, yet continued treatment is often needed for years.

To Enclose.   The comma encloses parenthetical information, simple definitions, or interrupting expressions in a sentence.

> Gloria Anderson, our best technician, submitted the winning suggestion.
>
> The research team, of course, will return to the site after the monsoon season.
>
> The condition stems from the body's inability to produce enough hemoglobin, a component of red blood cells, to carry oxygen to all body tissues.

If the passage is essential to the sentence (restrictive), do not enclose it in commas.

> Acme shipped the toys that have red tags to the African relief center. (The phrase *that have red tags* is essential for identifying which toys were shipped.)

To Separate.   The comma separates introductory phrases or clauses from the rest of the sentence and also separates items in a list.

> Accurate to within 30 seconds a year, the electronic quartz watch is also water resistant.
>
> Because so many patients experienced side effects, the FDA refused to approve the drug.

To calculate the three points, add the static head, friction losses, velocity head, and minor losses. (Retain the final comma in a list for clarity.)

The comma also separates elements in addresses and dates.

The shipment went to Hong Kong on May 29, 1999, but the transfer forms went to Marjorie Howard, District Manager, Transworld Exports, 350 Michigan Avenue, Chicago, Illinois 60616.

Dash

The dash sets off words or phrases that interrupt a sentence or that indicate sharp emphasis. The dash also encloses simple definitions. The dash is a more emphatic punctuation mark than parentheses or commas.

The foundation has only one problem—no funds.

The majority of those surveyed—those who were willing to fill out the questionnaire—named television parents in nuclear families as ideal mother and father images.

Exclamation Point

The exclamation point indicates strong emotion or sharp commands. It is not often used in technical writing, except for warnings or cautions.

Insert the cable into the double outlet.

Warning! Do not allow water to touch the cable.

Hyphen

The hyphen divides a word at the end of a typed line and also forms compound words. If in doubt about where to divide a word or whether to use a hyphen in a compound word, consult a dictionary.

Scientists at the state-sponsored research laboratory are using cross-pollination to produce hybrid grains.

Modifiers of two or three words require hyphens when they precede a noun.

Tycho Brahe, sixteenth-century astronomer, measured the night sky with giant quadrants.

The microwave-antenna system records the differing temperatures coming from Earth and the cooler sky.

Parentheses

Parentheses enclose (1) nonessential information in a sentence or (2) letters and figures that enumerate items in a list.

The striped lobsters (along with solid blue varieties) have been bred from rare red and blue lobsters that occur in nature.

Early television content analyses (from 1950 to 1980) reported that (1) men appeared more often than women, (2) men were more active problem solvers than women, (3) men were older than women, and (4) men were more violent than women.

Parentheses also enclose simple definitions.

The patient suffered from hereditary trichromatic deuteranomaly (red-green color blindness).

Question Mark

The question mark follows direct questions but not indirect questions.

The colonel asked, "Where are the orders for troop deployment?"

The colonel asked whether the orders for troop deployment had arrived.

Place a question mark inside quotation marks if the quotation is a question, as shown above. If the quotation is not a question but is included in a question, place the question mark outside the quotation marks.

Why did the chemist state "The research is unnecessary"?

Quotation Marks

Quotation marks enclose (1) direct quotations and (2) titles of journal articles, book chapters, reports, songs, poems, and individual episodes of radio and television programs.

"Planets are similar to giant petri dishes," stated astrophysicist Miranda Caliban at the Gatewood Research Institute.

"Combat Readiness: Naval Air vs. Air Force" (journal article)

"Science and Politics of Human Differences" (book chapter)

"Feasibility Study of Intrastate Expansion" (report)

"Kariba: The Lake That Made a Dent" (television episode)

Place commas and periods inside quotation marks. Place colons and semi-colons outside quotation marks. See also "Italics" under "Mechanics" in this Appendix.

Semicolon

The semicolon links two independent clauses without a coordinating conjunction or other punctuation.

The defense lawyer suggested that the arsenic could have originated in the embalming fluid; Bateman dismissed this theory.

All the cabinets are wood; however, the countertops are of artificial marble.

The semicolon also separates items in a series if the items contain internal commas.

The most desirable experts for the federal environmental task force are Sophia Timmons, Chief Biologist, Ohio Water Commission; Clinton Buchanan, Professor of Microbiology, Central Missouri State University; and Hugo Wysoki, Director of the California Wildlife Research Institute, San Jose.

Slash

The slash separates choices and parts of dates and numbers.

For information about the property tax deduction, call 555–6323/7697. (The reader can choose between two telephone numbers.)

The crew began digging on 9/28/96 and increased the drill pressure ¾ psi every hour.

MECHANICS

Acronyms and Initialisms

An *acronym* is an abbreviation formed from the first letters of the words in a name or phrase. The acronym is written in all capitals with no periods and is pronounced as a word.

The crew gathered in the NASA conference room.

Some acronyms eventually become words in themselves. For example, *radar* was once an acronym for *radio detecting and ranging.* Now the word *radar* is a noun meaning a system for sensing the presence of objects.

Initialisms are also abbreviations formed from the first letters of the words in a name or phrase; here each letter is pronounced separately. Some initialisms are written in all capital letters; others are written in capital and lowercase letters. Some are written with periods; some are not. If you are uncertain about the conventional form for an initialism, consult a dictionary.

The technician increased the heat by 4 Btu.

The C.P.A. took the tax returns to the IRS office.

When using acronyms or initialisms, spell out the full term the first time it appears in the text and place the acronym or initialism in parentheses immediately after to be sure your readers understand it. In subsequent references, use the acronym or initialism alone.

The Federal Communication Commission (FCC) has authorized several thousand licenses for low-power television (LPTV) stations.

In a few cases, the acronym or initialism may be so well known by your readers that you can use it without stating the full term first.

The experiment took place at 10:15 A.M. with the application of DDT at specified intervals.

Plurals of acronyms and initialisms are formed by adding an *s* without an apostrophe, such as YMCAs, MBAs, COLAs, and EKGs.

Brackets

Brackets enclose words that are inserted into quotations by writers or editors. The inserted words are intended to add information to the quoted material.

"Thank you for the splendid photographic service [to the Navy, 1976–1982] and the very comprehensive collection donated to the library," said Admiral Allen Sumner as he dedicated the new library wing.

Brackets also enclose a phrase or word inserted into a quotation to substitute for a longer, more complicated phrase or clause.

"The surgical procedure," explained Dr. Moreno, "allows [the kidneys] to cleanse the blood and maintain a healthy chemical balance."

Capital Letters

Capital letters mark the first word of a sentence and the first word of a quotation. A full sentence after a colon and full sentences in a numbered list may also begin with capital letters if the writer wishes to emphasize them.

> Many of the photographs were close-ups.
>
> Pilots are concerned about mountain wave turbulence and want a major change: Higher altitude clearance is essential.

Capital letters also mark proper names and initials of people and objects.

> Dr. Jonathan L. Hazzard
>
> Ford Taurus
>
> USS *Fairfax*

In addition, capital letters mark nationalities, religions, tribal affiliations, and linguistic groups.

> British (nationality)
>
> Lutheran (religion)
>
> Cherokee (tribal affiliation)
>
> Celtic (linguistic group)

Capital letters also mark (1) place names, (2) geographical and astronomical areas, (3) organizations, (4) events, (5) historical times, (6) software, and (7) some calendar designations.

> San Diego, California (place)
>
> Great Plains (geographic area)
>
> League of Women Voters (organization)
>
> Robinson Helicopter Company (company)
>
> World Series (event)
>
> Paleocene Epoch (historical time)
>
> WordPerfect (software)
>
> Tuesday, July 12 (calendar designations)

Capital letters also mark brand names but not generic names.

> Tylenol (acetaminophen)

Capital letters mark the first, last, and main words in the titles of (1) books, (2) articles, (3) films, (4) television and radio programs, (5) music, and (6) art objects. Do not capitalize short conjunctions, prepositions, or articles (*a, an, the*) unless they begin the title or follow a colon. *Note:* If you are preparing a reference list, see Chapter 10 for the correct format.

> *The Panda's Thumb* (book)
> "Information Base: On Line with CompuServe" (article)
> *Gunfight at Smokey Ridge* (film)
> "The Search for the Dinosaurs" (television episode)
> *Concerto in D Major, Opus 77, for Violin and Orchestra* (music)
> *The Third of May* (art)

Companies and institutions often use capital letters in specific circumstances not covered in grammar handbooks. If in doubt, check the company or organization style guide.

Ellipsis

An *ellipsis* (three spaced periods) indicates an omission of one or more words in a quotation. When the omission is at the end of a sentence or includes an intervening sentence, the ellipsis follows the final period.

> General Donald Mills stated, "It is appalling that those remarks . . . by someone without technical, military, or intelligence credentials should be published."
>
> At the fund-raising banquet, Chief of Staff Audrey Spaulding commented, "All of the volunteers—more than 600—made this evening very special. . . ."

Italics

Italics set off or emphasize specific words or phrases. If italic type is not available, underline the words or phrases. Italics set off titles of (1) books, (2) periodicals, (3) plays, films, and television and radio programs, (4) long musical works, (5) complete art objects, and (6) ships, planes, trains, and aircraft. The Bible and its books are not italicized.

> *The Cell in Development and Inheritance* (book)
> *Chicago Tribune* (newspaper)
> *Scientific American* (journal)
> *Inherit the Wind* (play)
> *Blade Runner* (film)
> *60 Minutes* (television program)
> *Carmen* (long musical work)

The Thinker (art object)
City of New Orleans (train)
Apollo III (spacecraft)

Italics also set off words and phrases discussed as words and words and phrases in foreign languages or Latin. Scientific terms for plants and animals also are italicized.

The term *mycobacterium* refers to any one of several rod-shaped aerobic bacteria.

These old fossils may be closer to the African *Australopithecus* than to *Homo*.

See also "Quotation Marks" under "Punctuation" in this Appendix.

Measurements

Measurements of physical quantities, sizes, and temperatures are expressed in figures. Use abbreviations for measurements only when also using figures and when your readers are certain to understand them. If the abbreviations are not common, identify them by spelling out the term on first use and placing the abbreviation in parentheses immediately after. Do not use periods with measurement abbreviations unless the abbreviation might be confused with a full word. For example, *inch* abbreviated needs a period to avoid confusion with the word *in*. Use a hyphen when a measurement functions as a compound adjective.

The pressure rose to 12 pounds per square inch (psi).

Workers used 14-in. pipes at the site.

The designer wanted a 4-oz decanter on the sideboard.

Ship 13 lb of feed. (Do not add *s* to make abbreviations plural.)

Ship several pounds of feed. (Do not use abbreviations if no numbers are involved.)

If the measurement involves two numbers, spell out the first or the shorter word.

The supervisor called for three 12-in. rods.

Here are some common abbreviations for measurements:

C	centigrade	kW	kilowatt
cm^3	cubic centimeter	l	liter
cm	centimeter	lb	pound

cps	cycles per second	m	meter
cu ft	cubic foot	mg	milligram
dm	decimeter	ml	milliliter
F	Fahrenheit	mm	millimeter
fl oz	fluid ounce	mph	miles per hour
fpm	feet per minute	oz	ounce
ft	foot	psf	pounds per square foot
g	gram	psi	pounds per square inch
gal	gallon	qt	quart
gpm	gallons per minute	rpm	revolutions per minute
hp	horsepower	rps	revolutions per second
in.	inch	sq	square
kg	kilogram	t	ton
km	kilometer	yd	yard

Numbers

Use figures for all numbers over ten. If a document contains many numbers, use figures for all amounts, even those under ten, so that readers do not overlook them.

The testing procedure required 27 test tubes, 2 covers, and 16 sets of gloves.

Do not begin a sentence with a figure. Rewrite to place the number later in the sentence.

Incorrect:　　42 tests were scheduled.
Correct:　　We scheduled 42 tests.

Write very large numbers in figures and words.

2.3 billion people
$16.5 million

Use figures for references to (1) money, (2) temperatures, (3) decimals and fractions, (4) percentages, (5) addresses, and (6) book parts.

$4230
$.75
72°F
0°C

3.67

¾

12.4%

80%

2555 N. 12th Street

Chapter 7, page 178

Use figures for times of day. Because most people are never certain about P.M. and A.M. in connection with 12 o'clock, indicate noon or midnight in parentheses.

4:15 P.M.

12:00 (noon)

12:00 (midnight)

Add an *s* without an apostrophe to make numbers plural.

4s   1980s   33s

Symbols and Equations

Symbols should appear in parenthetical statistical information but not in the narrative.

Incorrect:	The *M* were 2.64 (Test 1) and 3.19 (Test 2).
Correct:	The means were 2.64 (Test 1) and 3.19 (Test 2).
Incorrect:	The sample population (number = 450) was selected from children in the second grade.
Correct:	The sample population ($N = 450$) was selected from children in the second grade.
Incorrect:	We found a high % of error.
Correct:	We found a high percentage of error.

Do not try to create symbols on a typewriter or computer by combining overlapping characters. Write symbols not on the keyboard by hand in ink.

$$\chi^2 \, (N = 916) = 142.64 \qquad p < 0.001$$

Place simple or short equations in the text by including them in a sentence.

The equation for the required rectangle is $y = a + 2b - x$.

To display (set off on a separate line) equations, start them on a new line after the text and double space twice above and below the equation. Displayed equations must be numbered for reference. The reference number appears in parentheses flush with the right margin. In the text, use the reference number.

$$F(9{,}740) = 2.06 \qquad p < 0.05 \tag{1}$$

If the equation is too long for one line, break it before an operational sign. Place a space between the elements in an equation as if they were words.

$$3v - 5b + 66x$$
$$+ 2x - y = 11.5$$

Very difficult equations that require handwritten symbols should always be displayed for clarity. Highly technical symbols and long equations in documents intended for multiple readers are best placed in appendixes rather than in the main body of the document.

APPENDIX B

Frequently Confused Words

Even careful writers sometimes confuse one word with another that sounds or looks similar. To help you edit your writing, here are definitions for some easily confused words.

affect/effect: The verb **affect** means to influence. The noun **effect** means result; the verb **effect** means to make something happen.

- The strong winds **affected** (influenced) airport traffic.
- The new drugs have a positive **effect** (result) on angina.
- The engineer was able to **effect** (make happen) a transfer of equipment.

a lot: Do not write **a lot** as one word. The nonstandard "alot" is not acceptable.

already/all ready: Use the one word **already** to mean previous to a certain time. Use the two words **all ready** to mean completely prepared.

- The satellite was **already** breaking up when it reentered Earth's atmosphere.
- The sales packets were **all ready** for the meeting.

all right: Do not write **all right** as one word. The nonstandard "alright" is not acceptable.

amount/number: Use **amount** when the quantity is bulk and cannot be counted. Use **number** when the quantity can be separated and counted.

- A large **amount** of snow blocked truck access.
- The new telemedicine link to Mozambique offers a **number** of services.

biweekly/bimonthly: These terms mean twice a week or month and also every other week or month. Because readers will not be sure what you mean, avoid using them.

- The company newsletter appeared **every other week.**

can/may/might: Use **can** to indicate the ability to do something. Use **may** to mean getting permission. **Might** indicates uncertainty or a situation contrary to fact.

- At full speed, the train **can** reach Munich by 2:00 P.M.
- The clerks **may** be able to take a longer lunch hour.
- The tour guide **might** have helped if he had been told of the problem.

continuous/continual: Use **continuous** to mean unceasing without interruption, and use **continual** to mean recurring in rapid succession.

- The **continuous** whine of the drill was annoying.
- The **continual** equipment breakdowns held up production.

e.g./i.e.:   The abbreviation **e.g.** means "for example," and **i.e.** means "that is." Because readers may be confused, avoid both of these abbreviations and use the English words.

flammable/inflammable: These words both mean capable of burning. Safety experts prefer **flammable** because consumers (used to *active* and *inactive*) may think **inflammable** means something that will not burn.

imply/infer: The speaker or writer may **imply** (suggest without stating), but the listener or reader must **infer** (draw a conclusion).

- The CEO **implied** that the new European currency would encourage company mergers.
- The employees **inferred** that more layoffs were coming.

lay/lie: Use **lay** to indicate placing something somewhere. The verb always requires a direct object. Use **lie** to mean to recline or to be situated somewhere.

- She **lay** the report on the supervisor's desk.
- He is **lying** on the sofa.
- Hillsdale **lies** at the junction of two rivers.

oral/verbal: Spoken communication is **oral.**   **Verbal** means consisting of words, either written or spoken. For clarity, use either **oral** or **written.**

- The trainer gave **oral** instructions to the group.
- He prepared **written** guidelines for newcomers.

sight/site/cite: Use **sight** when referring to a view or something that is seen. Use **site** when referring to a specific location. The verb **cite** means to refer to or mention.

- The landfill, neglected for years, was a dreadful **sight.**
- The council selected Center Plaza as the **site** for the Civil War monument.
- The speaker **cited** Thomas Jefferson as an outstanding writer.

than/then: Use **than** to introduce the second item in a comparison. Use **then** to indicate time or sequence.

- The new generator is bigger **than** our old one.
- The game starts at 4:00 P.M.; we will leave **then.**
- The clerk scanned the groceries and **then** put them in a plastic sack.

PART 2

Technical Writing: Advice from the Workplace

Doing Business in Mexico

Russell J. Alessi

Worldwide trading and joint production have created a need for understanding cultural and social customs in other countries. This article provides a view of Mexican customs that can affect business relationships.

Having last visited Mexico nine years earlier, my expectations concerning Mexican sensitivity to travelers' needs were rather low. From the moment I arrived at the Mexico City airport in 1993, however, I knew I'd entered a new Mexico—one that's trying to facilitate and cater to tourism and business travel.

Also evident during my meetings with Mexican government and corporate executives was the need for business travelers to understand the many cultural and social differences between doing business in Mexico and in the United States. Here's an overview of those differences.

Formality. During initial and follow-up meetings, Mexicans normally remain formal and refer to participants on a last-name basis (for example, Señor Alessi). It would be unusual to slide into a first-name basis. Travelers from the United States who say, "Please, call me Joe," during the first meeting as a gesture of friendship and openness may communicate less respect and give Mexican counterparts the perception that the meeting isn't important.

Time Frames. Punctuality isn't as important in Mexico as in the United States. You'll find it perfectly acceptable to arrive 15 or 20 minutes late for a meeting. In fact, tardiness is sometimes seen as a courtesy because it implies a respect for the person's other appointments, which have started late. Several Mexican executives I met with, however, made a point to arrive on time or early to accommodate my schedule and American expectations.

Conducting business around breakfast or a long lunch is quite common in Mexico. But breakfast can be an early break in the work day, say from 9:30–10:30 A.M. Lunch meetings generally start at 2 P.M. and go to 4 P.M. or later.

Personal Information. When establishing a business relationship in Mexico, make sure you spend time exchanging information on family and personal backgrounds. One Mexican businessman told me that he spends at least 30 minutes learning about a client's family and personal interests before discussing business. This is done while maintaining the formal decorum concerning name and title.

Business Cards. Another formal part of Mexico's business environment, business cards usually carry a title such as "Licenciado (Lic.)" or "Ingeniero (Ing.)." The first means that the person is a university graduate, while the latter indicates the person is an engineer.

Mexican business cards show a title, first name, family last name, and mother's last name along with an address, telephone numbers, and other common information.

U.S. Education.   Educational credentials obtained in the United States are highly valued in Mexico. Therefore, your degree and alma mater can serve as an excellent marketing and networking advantage; be sure to exchange this information while discussing personal backgrounds with your colleagues in Mexico.

The American Chamber of Commerce in Mexico City can provide information that will help you understand the cultural differences and important social and business issues in Mexico. The chamber can also help you research key business contacts in Mexico; for example, it identified and set up a meeting with my industry counterparts.

Ethics in Technical Communication

Lori Allen and Dan Voss

This excerpt from the book Ethics in Technical Communication *discusses unethical use of statistics, graphics, and photographs. Ethical communication involves illustrations as well as words. Consider these guidelines when you are preparing graphics.*

LYING WITH STATISTICS

Misuse of numbers for purposes of deception is analogous to misuse of words for deception. Actually changing numbers is commission. Conveniently leaving out numbers that don't serve one's interests is omission. Manipulating numbers to send a distorted message is like using circumlocution or slanted language. All are unethical. Of the myriad opportunities for deception with statistics, three of the most common are invalid survey techniques, misuse of percentages, and misleading use of averages.

Surveys

Surveys are tricky animals. To be valid, they must represent a sufficiently large and representative segment of the population. Questions must be worded to clearly differentiate between opinions, not to deliberately lead respondents down a primrose path to desired responses.

Consider this situation: A group of high school students is asked to survey residents of a wealthy and predominantly elderly community known to oppose tax increases on whether they would support a bond issue for a new football stadium with Astroturf. The students knock on 100 doors. In 95 cases, as soon as the homeowners learn the subject of the survey, they chase the students down the driveway wielding frying pans and broomsticks. In the other five cases, the students find one genuine supporter, one who is adamantly opposed, and three who are opposed but whom the students badger for hours until they finally give in and check "Yes" as the only way to get the students off their property. The result is "Four out of five residents surveyed recommended grassless football stadiums for those high schools that have football stadiums." The other 95? Oh, that's right—they weren't surveyed.

Percentages

Percentages are meaningful only if they are presented along with the base to which they are applied and they can be very misleading. Consider the executive who tells her employees that she will be receiving only a 3 percent raise this year while they all receive 6 percent. That sounds great until you allow for the fact that the executive's raise is 3 percent of $100,000 and the workers' raise is 6 percent of $20,000. Or consider this one: If somebody offered to give you a 50 percent raise this month if you agreed to accept a 40 percent cut the following month, would you take it? Your first impulse might be to say, "Sure." Try it out. Let's say you're making $10 an hour. With a 50 percent raise, you'd be making $15 an hour. Now apply the 40 percent cut. You drop to $11 an hour, so you're still $1 ahead, right? Think again. The 40 percent cut applies to your *new* base salary, not your original base salary and 40 percent of $15 is $6. The net result is: You'd wind up working for $9 an hour, $1 less than you started out with.

Averages

Averages come in three flavors: mean, median, and mode. When most people use the word "average," they are referring to the mean, which is computed by adding all the individual values and dividing by the total number of items. *Mean* gives an honest expression of average when there is a fairly even distribution of values. When the values are clustered at the extremes of the range, the mean presents a distorted picture. *Median* refers to the midpoint among the values: the point at which there are an equal number of items of lesser and greater value. It is more valid than the mean for cases involving extremes; less so for even distributions. *Mode* refers to the individual value that occurs most often. It would be useful if you were trying to present the average height of a class which contained four 6'8" basketball players and one 5'2" cheerleader.

Of the three types of averages, the mean offers the most opportunity for deception. Consider the robber baron who claims that the employees in his dilapidated sweatshop of a factory live in comfort. His promotional brochure boasts: "Our employees work in a climate-controlled environment with an average temperature of 75 degrees." This deception is particularly masterful, because it demonstrates both verbal and statistical persiflage. The factory is, indeed, controlled by the climate. Since it has neither heating nor air conditioning, it is 90 degrees in the summer and 60 degrees in the winter. What is the average? You guessed it—75 degrees!

Or suppose you run into a state trooper on your way back from your bachelor's or bachelorette's party. The conversation might run something like this:

"Gee, officer, I was only averaging 50 miles an hour!"

True statement. Unfortunately, you achieved that average by going from 0 to 100.

LYING WITH GRAPHICS

If one picture is worth a thousand words, then one lie with graphics is worth a thousand lies with words. Examples of deliberate deception with charts and figures abound. Pie charts can lie if the slices do not accurately reflect the percentages (which, of course, are in one-point type). Line graphs can lie by distorting the axes. Organization charts can present a misleading picture of the chain of command.

Figure 4.1a might come from the annual report of an unprincipled charitable organization seeking to raise funds. It differs from an honest depiction of the same data (Figure 4.1b) in two important respects. First, it divides the overhead costs into two subcategories to conceal the amount of expenses unrelated to patient services. Second, it visually distorts the slices to well below the actual 40 percent overhead figure. The real numbers are there to avoid fraud charges, but they're about as legible as the Surgeon General's warning on cigarette packages.

Figure 4.2 "loads the dice" by manipulating the units of measure on the ordinate or Y-axis. At first glance, the reader might conclude that the workers' wages are climbing much more rapidly than those of the executives. Look again. The units

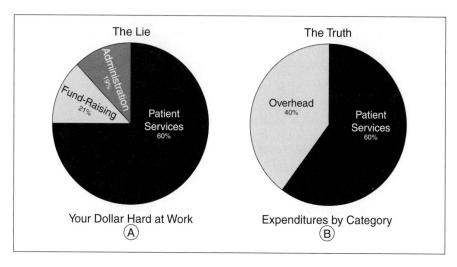

FIGURE 4.1   Pie charts lie when the numbers don't match the slices.

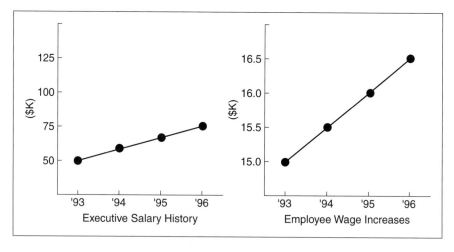

FIGURE 4.2   Who's been getting bigger raises? Look again.

of measure on the vertical axis of the executive pay chart are much larger than they are on the vertical axis of the similar looking employee pay chart, thereby making it appear as if the executives' pay increases are smaller than those of the employees when, in fact, they are much larger.

Figure 4.3 might be the version of the organization chart that Employee B sends out with his or her résumé. It is carefully designed to convey the impression

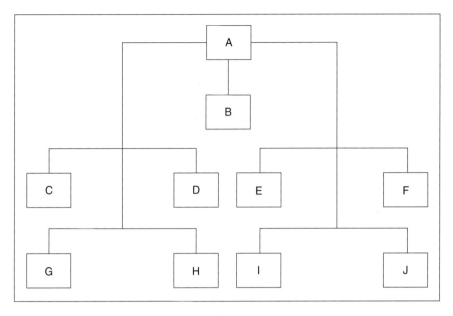

FIGURE 4.3   Who's more important, J or B?

that Employee B is second in command to A. It also tends to imply that Employees C, D, E, and F are below B but above Employees G, H, I, and J in the pecking order—which further reinforces B's "vice-emperor" message. However, if you follow the reporting lines closely, you will find that Employees B through J are actually all equal; all bear the same relationship with the boss.

LYING WITH PHOTOGRAPHS

Nearly everyone in our generation recalls the use of obviously doctored photographs in tabloid newspapers back in the 1950s and 1960s: "Kitten Born with Dog's Head" screamed the headline. To document this noteworthy biological event, under the headline appeared a lurid photograph with a puppy's head clumsily airbrushed onto a kitten's body. Sometimes if you looked closely, you could even discern the traces of the airbrush.

Well, that happens no more. No more clumsiness, that is. In today's world of dizzily onrushing technology, any entry-level illustrator with the appropriate software can, in a matter of minutes, give a kitten a dog's head. Or slap an electronic test set on a piece of equipment where it has never been used before. Or deftly whisk away any telltale plumes of pollution from the smokestacks of a factory when designing the company's environmental awareness brochure.

Given the present shift from optical to digital technology in photography, within a few years nearly all business and technical photography will be computer based. And since any digital file can be subtly—or not so subtly—altered without a trace, it will become almost impossible to know whether a photograph is genuine or retouched.

This technological advance has upped the ethical ante for technical communicators. Increasingly, if our audiences are to trust the integrity of the photographs in the documents and visual presentations we produce, they will have to depend on our honesty.

Consider this scenario. Suppose the manufacturer of a CAT scan imaging system asks a technical illustrator in its publications department to enhance the clarity of its images for a promotional brochure. Suppose, further, that the perception of higher resolution than the product can actually provide sways a hospital purchasing agent to order one of the systems. And suppose, six months later, that a neurosurgeon depends on that equipment to pinpoint a blood clot so she can operate on a child who has been gravely injured in a car–bike accident. The neurosurgeon goes in, the clot isn't where the machine says it was, and before she can get to it, the child dies on the table. What is the ethical responsibility of the technical illustrator to the parents of the child?

How to Avoid Costly Proofreading Errors

Carolyn Boccella Bagin and Jo Van Doren

Proofreading errors cost businesses money. This article tells you how to produce error-free copy. Try finding all the mistakes in the sample copy in the article, and check your results against the corrected version.

Are proofreading errors costing you money? Some organizations have sad stories to tell about the price of overlooked mistakes.

- One insurance firm reported that an employee mailed a check for $2,200 as a settlement for a dental claim. Payment of only $22.00 had been authorized.

- One executive wasted $3 million by not catching a hyphen error when proofreading a business letter. In originally dictating the letter to his secretary, the executive said, "We want 1,000-foot-long radium bars. Send three in cases." The order was typed, "We want 1,000 foot-long radium bars."

- A magazine accidentally ran a cake recipe in which "$\frac{3}{4}$ cup" was printed as "$\frac{1}{4}$ cup." Irate readers sent complaint letters and cancelled their subscriptions.

Your company's image could be marred by unfortunate mistakes that find their way into the documents you produce. Developing good proofreading techniques and systems can save time, money, and embarrassment.

HOW CAN YOU PRODUCE ERROR-FREE COPY?

- Never proofread your own copy by yourself. You'll tire of looking at the document in its different stages of development and you'll miss new errors. (If you must proof your own copy, make a line screen for yourself or roll the paper back in the typewriter so that you view only one line at a time. This will reduce your tendency to skim your material.)

- Read everything in the copy straight through from beginning to end: titles, subtitles, sentences, punctuation, capitalizations, indented items, and page numbers.

- Read your copy backward to catch spelling errors. Reading sentences out of sequence lets you concentrate on individual words.

- Consider having proofreaders initial the copy they check. You might find that your documents will have fewer errors.

- If you have a helper to proof numbers that are in columns, read the figures aloud to your partner, and have your partner mark the corrections and changes on the copy being proofread.

- If time allows, put your material aside for a short break. Proofreading can quickly turn into reading if your document is long. After a break, reread the last few lines to refresh your memory.

451

- Read the pages of a document out of order. Changing the sequence will help you to review each page as a unit.
- List the errors you spot over a month's time. You may find patterns that will catch your attention when you proofread your next document.
- If you can, alter your routine. Don't proofread at the same time every day. Varying your schedule will help you approach your task with a keener eye.
- Not everyone knows and uses traditional proofreading marks. But a simple marking system should be legible and understandable to you and to anyone else working on the copy.

Where Do Errors Usually Hide?

- Mistakes tend to cluster. If you find one typo, look carefully for another one nearby.
- Inspect the beginning of pages, paragraphs, and sections. Some people tend to skim these crucial spots.
- Beware of changes in typeface—especially in headings or titles. If you change to all uppercase letters, italics, boldface, or underlined copy, read those sections again.
- Make sure your titles, subtitles, and page numbers match those in the table of contents.
- Read sequential material carefully. Look for duplications in page numbers or in lettered items in lists or outlines.
- Double-check references such as, "see the chart below." Several drafts later, the chart may be pages away from its original place.
- Examine numbers and totals. Recheck all calculations and look for misplaced commas and decimal points.
- Scrutinize features that come in sets, such as brackets, parentheses, quotation marks, and dashes.

Try Your Hand (and Eye) At This Test

Mark the mistakes and check your corrections with our marked copy on page 453.

It is improtant to look for certain item when proofing a report , letter, or othr document. Aside from spelling errors, the prooffer should check for deviations in format consitent use of punctuation, consistent use of capitol letters, undefined acronyms and correctpage numbers listed in the the Table of contents.

After checking a typed draft againts the original manuscript one should also read the draft for aukward phrasing, syntactical errors, and subject/ verb agreement and grammatical mistakes. paralell structures should be used im listings headed by bullets or numbers: ie, if one item starts with the phrase "to understand the others should start with to plus a verb.

The final step in proofing involves review of the overall appearance on the document. Are the characrters all printed clearly Are all the pages there? Are the pages free of stray marks ? Is the graphics done? Are bullets filled in? All of the above items effect the appearance of the the document and determine whether the document has the desired effect on the reader.

How Did You Do?

Check your markup against ours. (We only show corrections in the copy and not the margin notes that most proofreaders typically use.)

It is imp/otant to look for certain item when proofing a report, letter, or othr document. Aside from spelling errors, the proofer should check for deviations in format, consitent use of punctuation, consistent use of capital letters, undefined acronyms and correct page numbers listed in the the Table of contents.

After checking a typed draft against the original manuscript, one should also read the draft for awkward phrasing, syntactical errors, and subject/verb agreement and grammatical mistakes. parallel structures should be used in listings headed by bullets or numbers; ie, if one item starts with the phrase "to understand," the others should start with "to" plus a verb.

The final step in proofing involves review of the overall appearance on the document. Are the characrters all printed clearly? Are all the pages there? Are the pages free of stray marks ? Is the graphics done? Are bullets filled in? All of the above items effect the appearance of the the document and determine whether the document has the desired effect on the reader.

Writing Visually: Design Considerations in Technical Publications

Philippa J. Benson

Readers find documents most usable when the visual design guides them to the information they need. This article provides guidelines for using visual devices, such as typeface, headings, and graphics, to produce a document your readers can use easily.

Writers and graphic designers are working more closely together as each learns more about how the other approaches the task of planning and structuring a document. The field of document design has developed from this synthesis of the processes of writing and design: writers and designers have come to agree that the most effective documents are those that use both words and design to reveal and reinforce the structure of information in a text.

The synthesis of writing and design is supported not only by the developing bond between writers and designers, but also by the conclusions of applied research. Research in cognitive psychology, instructional design, reading, and graphic design indicates that documents are most usable when the information in them is apparent both visually and syntactically. In particular, the results of usability tests of documents are providing concrete evidence that readers find documents most usable when the visual aspects of a document support the hierarchy of the information in a text.[1-5]

The synthesis of writing and design has also been evolving because computers increasingly put control over typography and page format in the writer's domain. Although many text-formatting programs limit the design decisions that we can make, they do allow us to simultaneously write and design information.

The increasing use of computers has also led to the development of a new concern for document designers: online information. Designers of online documentation should be concerned with many of the same issues as page designers—that is, the legibility and accessibility of information.

UNDERSTANDING CONSTRAINTS ON DESIGNING A DOCUMENT

How effectively writers and designers can work together depends not only on how well they can communicate but also on the practical constraints of their working environment. Before you begin planning a document, find out about the limits of your schedule and budget, and the flexibility of the method you'll be using to produce the end product (printer, typesetter, printing process). Your schedule, budget, and method of printing may limit what you can do with the design of your document. Constraints may affect these aspects of your book:

- Page count, page size
- Packaging (binding, cover, separators, etc.)

- Typeface, type size
- Range of available fonts
- Use of color and graphics
- Number of heading levels available
- Kinds of graphics you can use (tables, flowcharts, illustrations)

If you find that the constraints depart from the principles of good document design, you should consider trying to change them. For example, you may be told you must use a type size of smaller than 8 or 9 points or set a sizable portion of text in uppercase. The research cited in this article provides evidence you can use to convince your managers to change the constraints that would make your document less usable. Once you know your constraints, you can choose design options that are compatible with them.

DESIGNING FOR YOUR AUDIENCE(S) AND THEIR TASKS

A primary step in planning a document is understanding the audience for the document and their purpose in reading it. For example, if you are writing a book about how to service a software product on a computer system, you may have several audiences. Some readers may simply want to know the procedures they need to follow to service the product, while other readers may want to know how these procedures affect the computer system as a whole.

Research indicates that document designers should consider how readers will use the document. In a document with multiple audiences, each with different purposes and tasks in mind, research suggests that you should design the document so that members of each audience can quickly find the specific information they need.[6-8]

Depending on the reading situation, readers come to a technical document with assumptions and expectations about its structure, in terms of both its language and its design. For example, readers of a tutorial manual may expect to see step-by-step procedural instructions, while readers of a reference manual may expect to see lots of definition lists. The tutorial or reference manual you design, however, may be very different from what the reader initially expects. The design options you use can affect the assumptions and expectations readers have when they begin using a book and, in doing so, can affect the way the readers understand and use it. To design a document well, you need to imagine what linguistic and visual organizers will help readers understand how the text is structured.[9,10]

Here are some guidelines you can use to help readers find, understand, use, and remember the information in a document:

Guideline: Provide Readers with Road Maps Through the Document

Think about how you can design the tables of contents, glossaries, indexes, appendixes, and other materials that support the body of text so that readers can quickly find the information they need. One type of road map is a separator between each section of a document, marked with icons, followed by text explaining the information that will be covered in that section.

One type of roadmap is a section
heading with an icon.

Another type of road map is a table that directs readers to specific information. Here is an example of a table road map:

If you want to	Go to
Install product x	Section A
Use product x	Section B
Service product x	Section C

Guideline: Make Your Document Aesthetically Pleasing

Many readers are motivated to use a document that is aesthetically pleasing. Documents should be attractively bound and packaged, have well-balanced page layouts, contain some graphics and illustrations to break up the text, and be legible.

A good and a poor page layout.

Guideline: Be Consistent in the Visual Formats and Prose Styles You Use

Readers can use a document more effectively when it contains consistent visual patterns, such as use of boldface or italic type, and a consistent linguistic style, such as use of the active voice or direct address. Readers use these patterns and styles to help them structure, comprehend, and remember the relationships between different levels and types of information in a text.

DESIGNING THE VISUAL STRUCTURE OF YOUR DOCUMENT

You can think of the structure of a document on several levels: as a whole, as a set of interrelated parts (chapters/sections), as a series of pages, and as text. Because the

audience, purpose, and information for each document are unique, the relationships between these levels are different for each document you produce. Your challenge as a document designer is to choose design options that will support the
document on all levels.

Research on design options suggests guidelines on how to graphically reinforce
the structure of a text and, therefore, how to improve its usability. These guidelines cover

- Serif vs. Sans-Serif Typeface
- Lowercase vs. Uppercase Type
- Type Weight and Font
- Type Size, Line Length, and Leading
- Justification of Lines, Size of Margins, Use of White Space
- Headings
- Graphs, Tables, Flowcharts, and Diagrams

Serif vs. Sans-Serif Typeface.   Guideline: Choose between a serif and sans-
serif typeface according to the visual tone of the document you want. Note: Use a
type size 10 points or larger, 2 or more points of leading between lines, and a moderate line length.

Serif typefaces have small strokes added to the edges of each letter. Serifs reinforce the horizontal flow of letters and make each letter distinct. Letters in sans-
serif typefaces are less distinct from each other not only because they lack the extra,
ornamental strokes of serif type, but also because the widths of the lines that constitute each sans-serif letter are often uniform. Sans-serif typefaces are generally
thought to have a cleaner, more modern look than serif type.

Some studies indicate that readers can read text set in serif typefaces more
quickly than text in sans-serif type. Readers also seem to prefer text set in serif type.

However, research also shows that the legibility of serif and sans-serif typefaces
is approximately the same if the text follows general standards for type size and
leading (10-point or larger type size with 2–4 points of leading). Because the legibility of serif and sans-serif print is so similar when properly designed, many
researchers and typographers suggest that document designers choose a serif or
sans-serif typeface according to what visual texture they want the text to have.[11–13]

Choose a serif or sans-serif
typeface according to the
visual texture you want your
document to have.

Choose a serif or sans-serif
typeface according to the
visual texture you want your
document to have.

Serif and sans-serif typefaces.

Lowercase vs. Uppercase Type.   Guideline: Avoid using all uppercase type.
When you want to emphasize a word or portion of text, use boldface type or italics.

Research supports the conclusion that in printed text words set in lowercase are faster to read than words set in uppercase.[14–17] Text set in lowercase is easier to read than text in uppercase because

1. Lowercase letters take up less space and, therefore, allow readers to take in more words as they scan a line of text.
2. Each lowercase word has a distinct outline that aids recognition and recall of the word.

However, some research does indicate that in some situations, such as when readers are scanning text or reading short informational statements, words set in uppercase are easier for readers to locate and read.[18, 19] Therefore, you can put words in uppercase, like "WARNING!" when it is appropriate.

LOWERCASE WORDS TAKE UP LESS SPACE THAN UPPERCASE WORDS AND ALSO HAVE A DISTINCT OUTLINE.

Lowercase words take up less space than uppercase words and also have a distinct outline.

Text set in all uppercase and mixed upper- and lowercase.

Type Weight and Font.   Guidelines: Use a medium type weight. Use boldface type to emphasize words or short portions of text.

Research suggests that when a text has a logical structure, typographic distinctions such as changes in type weight or typeface may help readers understand the structure. Research specifically indicates that readers notice changes in type weight (heavy, medium, light) more readily than they notice changes in typeface and that readers find very light or very heavy type tiring and difficult to read.[20]

Readers may find large blocks of text set in very heavy or very light type difficult and tiring to read.

Readers may find large blocks of text set in very heavy or very light type difficult and tiring to read.

Text set in a very heavy type and a light type.

Type Size, Line Length, and Leading.   Guidelines: Use 9- to 11-point type for text. Use between 2 and 4 points of leading between lines of text. Use a moderate line length, approximately twice the length of the alphabet of the typeface you use.

Type size, line length, and leading all affect the legibility of print. The actual point size of a typeface does not necessarily reflect the perceived size of a letter. Words set in the same type size may appear larger or smaller because of variations in the height of the lowercase letters.

☐   **And then there was light**

☐   And then there was light

☐   And then there was light

Same type size with different type styles.

However, research supports a conclusion that type sizes larger than 9 points are easier to read than smaller type sizes—when they are set with an appropriate amount of leading, usually 2 to 4 points.[21, 22]

Although researchers have developed some rules of thumb for considering combinations of line length and leading, these rules are not hard and fast.[14, 16, 21, 23] For example, if a text is set in a typeface that appears small, reducing leading between lines may well have no effect on the legibility of the text.

When you consider options of type size, line length, and leading, remember:

- Sans-serif typefaces may be easier to read with slightly more leading.
- Long lines may be easier to read with more leading between them.
- As type size increases, the effect of leading on legibility decreases.

Justification of Lines, Size of Margins, Use of White Space.   Guidelines: Use ragged-right margins (unjustified text). Use white space in margins and between sections.

Unjustified text is less costly to produce and easier to correct than justified text. Also, many readers prefer unjustified text. However, many publications still set text with both left and right justified margins.

Unjustified text is less costly to produce and easier to correct than justified text. Also, many readers prefer unjustified text. However, many publications still set text with both left and right justified margins.

Unjustified and justified text.

Many researchers and typographers advocate the use of ragged-right margins both because research indicates that justified text is more difficult for poor readers to read and comprehend, and because many readers prefer text with ragged-right margins.[24–26] Unjustified text is also less costly to produce and easier to correct than justified text.

Headings.   Guidelines: Use informative headings. Make all headings consistent and parallel in structure.

Research suggests that readers understand and remember text preceded by titles and/or headings better than text with no headings or titles. Poor readers are significantly aided by headings that are full statements or questions.[27]

Clear, active, and specific headings can also alter how readers comprehend a text. Headings can affect both what sections of text readers choose to read and how readers remember the organization of the text.[28–32]

For example, which of the following headings do you find easier to understand and remember?

> Subpart B: Applications and Licensee
>   83.20 Authorization required.
>   83.22 General citizenship requirements.
>   83.24 Eligibility for license.

or

> 2—How to get a license
>   2.1 Do I need a license?
>   2.2 How do I apply for a license?
>   2.3 May I operate my car while my
>   applications are being processed?

Graphs, Tables, Flowcharts, and Diagrams.   Guideline: When you are considering using graphics to convey quantitative or procedural information, you should consider

- The reader
- The amount and kinds of information the graphics must display
- How the reader will use the graphics
- What graphic forms you can use (tables, graphs, charts)

If you decide it is appropriate to use graphics, keep the following guidelines in mind:

1. Reinforce all graphics with supporting text.
2. Use typographic cues (changes in type weight and style) to distinguish between different types of information, such as headings or different kinds of data.
3. Use 8- to 12-point type and adequate spacing between printed items.
4. Include informative labels with all types of graphic devices.
5. Use only those lines, grid patterns, and other ink markings necessary to make the information clear.
6. Whenever possible, arrange items vertically so they can be easily scanned.

Because readers' skills in interpreting graphics vary so widely, and because graphic displays can be designed and used in so many different ways, a tremendous amount of research has been done to explore the most effective ways to present quantitative and procedural information.[33-40]

This research strongly suggests that many readers can understand and use complex information more quickly and accurately when it is presented in well-designed tables, graphs, flowcharts, or diagrams rather than solely in text. However, these graphic devices are even more effective when they are reinforced with explanatory text.[41-44]

Some research suggests that bar charts are easier to understand than line, pie, or surface charts; or text.[36, 45]

(A)

Range (in miles)		Payload (in lbs)
878	100	710
630	200	598
459	300	471
388	400	326

(B)

Range (in miles)	Payload (in lbs)	Payload (in lbs)	Range (in miles)
100	878	100	710
200	630	200	598
300	459	300	471
400	388	400	326

Table B is easier to use than Table A because the columns are explicitly labeled.

WHAT DOES THE RESEARCH SUGGEST TO THE PRACTITIONER?

Although the relationship between writers and designers is often a difficult one to develop, research in document design (and the practical experience of designers and writers) supports the conclusion that to produce good technical documentation, designers and writers must work together from the beginning of the document design process. As you begin to plan a document, you should not only consider who your audience is and how they will use the document, but also how you can use the visual presentation of the text to reinforce the structure of the information.

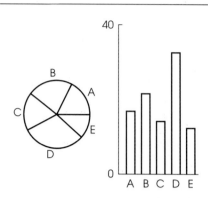

This bar chart reveals the difference in proportions more clearly than the pie chart.

To develop a sound working relationship, writers and designers should make conscious efforts to learn about how the other approaches planning and preparing a document so they can communicate effectively.

REFERENCES

1. J. Hartley, *Designing Instructional Text* (New York: Nichols Publishing Company, 1978).

2. D. H. Jonassen, ed., *The Technology of Text* (Englewood Cliffs, NJ: Educational Technology Publications, 1982).

3. P. Wright, "Usability: The Criterion for Designing Written Information," *Processing Visible Language, Vol. 2,* ed. Koler, Wrolstad, and Bouman (New York: Plenum Press, 1979), pp. 182–205.

4. L. T. Frase, "Reading Performances and Document Design," Bell Laboratories, paper given at Society for Applied Learning Technologies, Washington, DC, June, 1976.

5. R. Waller, "Typographic Access Structures for Educational Texts," *Processing Visible Language, Vol. 1,* ed. Koler, Wrolstad, and Bouman (New York: Plenum Press, 1979), pp. 175–187.

6. E. E. Miller, *Designing Printed Instructional Materials: Content and Format* (Alexandria, VA: Human Resources Research Organization, 1975).

7. W. Diehl and L. Mikulecky, "Making Written Information Fit Workers' Purposes," *IEEE Transactions on Professional Communication* PC-24 (1981).

8. J. Redish, R. Battison, and E. Gold, "Making Information Accessible to Readers," *Research in Non-Academic Settings,* ed. Odell and Goswami (Guilfor Press, in press).

9. P. Carpenter and M. Just, "Reading Comprehension as Eyes See It," *Cognitive Processes in Comprehension,* ed. Just and Carpenter (Hillsdale, NJ: Lawrence Erlbaum Assoc., 1977), pp. 109–139.

10. A. Marcus, "Icon Design Requires Clarity, Consistency," *Computer Graphics Today,* November 1984,

11. R. McLean, *The Thames and Hudson Manual of Typography* (London: Thames and Hudson, Ltd., 1980), pp. 42–48.

12. D. Robinson, M. Abbamonte, and S. Evans, "Why Serifs Are Important," *Visible Language* 4 (1971).

13. R. F. Rehe, *Typography: How to Make It Most Legible* (Carmel, IN: Design Research International, 1981), p. 32.

14. A. Seigel, *Designing Readable Documents: State of the Art* (New York: Seigel and Gale, 1978).

15. M. A. Tinker and D. G. Paterson, "Influence of Type Form on Speed of Reading," *Journal of Applied Psychology* 7 (1928).

16. J. Hartley, "Space and Structure in Instructional Text," paper given at the NATO Conference of the Visual Presentation of Information, Het Vennenbos, Netherlands, 1978.

17. E. C. Poulton and C. H. Brown, "Rate of Comprehension of Existing Teleprinter Output and Possible Alternatives," *Journal of Applied Psychology* 52 (1968).

18. E. C. Poulton, "Searching for Newspaper Headlines Printed in Capitals or Lower-case Letters," *Journal of Applied Psychology* 51 (1967).

19. A. G. Vartabedian, "The Effects of Letter Size, Case, and Generation Method in CRT Display Search Time," *Human Factors* 13 (1971).

20. H. Spencer, L. Reynolds, and B. Coe, *A Comparison of the Effectiveness of Selected Typographic Variations* (Readability of Print Research Unit, Royal College of Art, 1973).

21. M. A. Tinker, *Legibility of Print* (Ames, Iowa: Iowa State University Press, 1963), pp. 88–107.

22. D. Felker, *Document Design: A Review of the Relevant Research* (Washington, DC: American Institutes for Research, 1980), pp. 104–106.

23. M. Gray, "Questionnaire Typography and Production," *Applied Ergonomics* 6 (1975).

24. M. Gregory and E. C. Poulton, "Even versus Uneven Right-Hand Margins and the Rate of Comprehension in Reading," *Ergonomics* 13 (1970).

25. J. Hartley and P. Burnhill, "Experiments with Unjustified Text," *Visible Language* 3 (1971).

26. T. E. Pinelli, et al., "Preferences on Technical Report Format: Results of Survey," *Proceedings,* 31st International Technical Communication Conference (Society for Technical Communication, 1984).

27. J. Hartley, P. Morris, and M. Trueman, "Headings in Text," *Remedial Education* 16 (1981).

28. E. Kozminsky, "Altering Comprehension: The Effect of Biasing Titles on Text Comprehension," *Memory and Cognition* 5 (1977).

29. J. Hartley, J. Kenely, G. Owen, and M. Trueman, "The Effect of Headings on Children's Recall from Prose Text," *British Journal of Educational Psychology* 50 (1980).

30. H. Swartz, L. Flower, and J. Hayes, "How Headings in Documents Can Mislead Readers" (Pittsburgh, PA: Document Design Project, Carnegie-Mellon University, 1980).

31. P. Wright, "Presenting Technical Information: A Survey of Research Findings," *Instructional Science* 6 (1977), pp. 96–100.

32. L. T. Frase and F. Silbiger, "Some Adaptive Consequences of Searching for Information in a Text," *American Educational Research Journal* 7 (1970).

33. W. S. Cleveland and R. McGill, "Graphical Perception: Theory, Experimentation, and Application to the Development of Graphical Methods," *Journal of the American Statistician* 79 (1984).

34. W. S. Cleveland, "Graphical Methods for Data Presentation: Full Scale Breaks, Dot Charts, and Multibased Logging," *Journal of the American Statistician* 38 (1984).

35. A. S. C. Ehrenberg, "What We Can and Can't Get from Graphs, and Why," paper presented at American Statistical Association Meeting, Detroit, 1981.

36. M. MacDonald-Ross, "Graphics in Texts," in *Review of Research in Education,* Volume 5, ed. Shulman (Itasca, IL: F.E. Peacock Publications, 1978).

37. P. Wright and K. Fox, "Presenting Information in Tables," *Applied Ergonomics,* September 1970.

38. P. Wright and K. Fox, "Explicit and Implicit Tabulation Formats," *Ergonomics* 15 (1972).

39. P. Wright, "Tables in Text: The Subskills Needed for Reading Formatted Information" (Cambridge, UK: MRC Applied Psychology Unit).

40. E. R. Tufte, *The Visual Display of Quantitative Information* (Chesire, CT: Graphics Press, 1983).

41. P. Wright and F. Reid, "Written Information: Some Alternatives to Prose for Expressing the Outcomes of Complex Contingencies," *Journal of Applied Psychology* 57 (1973).

42. P. Wright, "Writing To Be Understood: Why Use Sentences?" *Applied Ergonomics* 2 (1971).

43. R. Kammann, "The Comprehensibility of Printed Instructions and the Flowchart Alternative," *Human Factors* 17 (1975).

44. D. Felker, *Guidelines for Document Designers* (Washington, DC: American Institutes for Research, 1981).

45. D. D. Feliciano, R. D. Powers, and B. E. Keare, "The Presentation of Statistical Information," *Audio-Visual Communication Review* 11 (1963).

The Art of the Interview

Eivind Boe

A job interview is a sales presentation of your best features. This article explains how to prepare for a job interview by anticipating questions, practicing answers, and finding information about the company. Try preparing the answers to some of these standard questions before your next job interview.

The ad was found; the résumé was sent; the eagerly awaited phone call was received: You're to go for an interview. Unless you're unquestionably the best or absolutely the worst insofar as qualifications go, your performance at the interview is what makes you or breaks you as far as the job is concerned. There is no getting around this.

As with everything else in life, there is no way to ensure success at an interview. You can buy the fanciest clothes, but they will not buy you the job. The firm handshake is not an automatic in; nor is any connection or pull you might have. But aside from your qualifications and maturity, some fundamental concerns will greatly increase the percentages in your favor.

For one thing, study up on your résumé, your reasons for wanting a job at that particular company, and the points in your past that you want to talk about. The best way to be ready for an interview is to have something to say. Having nothing to say at your interview is about as self-defeating as can be.

Perhaps the greatest temptation for young people at an interview is to act, to try to adjust their personality for each interviewer. Aside from creating impossible problems, you're best off being you. Any company worth working for isn't looking for only exuberant people; nor do they want meek submission, nor frenzied aggressiveness, nor Laputan eggheadism. They want mature, capable human beings. *That* is the only category you have to fit into. The trick is to be the best *you* you can be.

Manners are those things mother taught you that you dispensed with in college. They are really codified courtesy, and courtesy is one of those deeper qualities that make people want to have you around. Things like standing when the interviewer stands and forgoing smoking if the interviewer doesn't offer it—and doing these things with an easy grace—are what interviewers notice. Remember it is the interviewer's prerogative to be irascible, abrupt, or prying. Maintain your courteous demeanor—even if you must demand courteous treatment, which sometimes happens.

SELLING YOURSELF

Remember your manners when you make that all important "sales call." For even if you never, EVER, wanted to go into sales, when you interview, you have something to sell: yourself. To sell effectively you need three things: a good presentation, a unique product, and an unshakable belief in that product.

A good presentation consists of simply this: as many reasons to hire you, and as few reasons not to hire you, as possible. The interviewer is mainly concerned

465

with if you *can* do the job, if you *will* do the job, and if you're going to *get along* with the rest of the company. Inspire the interviewer with confidence in you; handle every question with aplomb. If the interviewer points out that you haven't done such and such, which is an integral part of the job, you can say, "This is true, but I've done this and this, which are quite similar. In the past I've always been able to adapt this way to new situations." Consider every question the interviewer puts to you an opportunity to show how good you really are.

A product has to be distinct from other products, and for it to sell, it must be distinctly better. If you feel like everyone applying for a position has exactly what you have, say, a B.S.E.E. and 4 years of experience, don't worry: No one else has the unique background you have. Your work experience inevitably has had special projects, unusual situations, trying circumstances. Your education includes special courses and activities (even those unrelated to engineering). Everything else you've ever done defines your unique character, and can show some positive attribute in you: Your participation in team sports shows a willingness to work with others; your active involvement in town politics shows your willingness to get involved. An interest in trout fishing evinces patience, even strategy; an interest in music manifests a desire to organize, a penchant for system. Every positive aspect about you can be turned to account.

Believing in the product is paramount. Why apply for a job if you don't think you can do it well? You have already passed many tests in life: What is it about this job that, through perhaps some effort, you couldn't master? You do, of course, already know a lot; you can, of course, learn almost anything you care to. Nothing really stops you from succeeding—at anything.

Try bringing some of these attitudes with you to an interview. They are at least as true as any negative attitudes you may have, and are far more likely to get you the job. Yet the problem may not be one of lack of confidence, but nervousness due to pressure.

If you're nervous before an interview, that's *good*. The stampeding herd of butterflies in your stomach, the apple in your throat, and the 2-lb weight tied to your tongue indicate that your mind feels doubt and is telling your endocrine system to pump out loads of adrenaline. Naturally it won't do to let this unfocused energy mess up your interview. The trick is to channel the energy and make it work for you. Learn how to turn it to positive action, rather than negative reaction.

Awareness of interviewers' standard stock of questions is another way to beat nervousness and build confidence. Being prepared for these questions allows you to free your mind to concentrate on more challenging issues. Here are the questions and some suggestions on how to handle them.

1. *Tell me about yourself.* Actually not a question, of course. In answering this, stick to your life at work: This tack reinforces your interest in the job.

2. *What is it about the job that interests you most?* If you launch into extolling the benefits you'll accrue if you get the job, you will have lost. Make the interviewer believe that you are interested in performing the work, using your knowledge and energy to help the company.

3. *Where do you see yourself five years from now?* A classic question. Probably best handled by something like: "Doing more of the same, only better." Perhaps you can think of something more imaginative. Just leave the impression that you know what you want.

4. *What do you consider your major strengths/weaknesses?* You know your strengths, so tell them without sounding boastful. As for your weaknesses, make them sound like strengths: Sometimes you're just too much of a perfectionist, or you get impatient when coworkers don't work as hard as you do.

5. *Why do you want to leave your present job?* Avoid saying that you hate your boss, or that you don't get along with your coworkers. Such remarks leave a bad taste in the interviewer's mouth. Wanting more money or a higher position, and being able to do more at a higher level than your present company can reasonably give you, are good answers here.

Rest assured that these aren't the only questions you'll hear. Nor are the suggested answers the only ones you can give. But be prepared for these specific questions, and you'll have started off the interview right.

WARMING UP

How does one practice interviewing? Try this simple idea: Get yourself a tape recorder, tape yourself in an interview situation, and listen to yourself. Either ask some of the standard interview questions yourself (in a different voice if you choose) or have a friend ask the questions, and then answer them.

There are certain things to listen for in the recording. Are you answering the interviewer's questions directly, or do you sound too much like you're dodging? Are there some bad habits there that you can correct, such as an overuse of hems, ums, or y'knows? Do you have a ready answer for every question? Are you perhaps talking too fast?

Granted, this is not a realistic situation. After all, you already know the questions, whereas in an interview you don't. But in most interviews there are stock questions, which are really opportunities for you to glow. Using a tape recorder can allow you to practice the answers to those questions.

KNOW THY PROSPECTIVE COMPANY

Of inestimable value when you go into an interview is knowledge about that particular company. The more you know, the more you appear to be the perfect, ready-made employee. You'll inspire your interviewer with respect for you, and by having something to say, will simultaneously remove a great deal of the burden of the interview from his or her shoulders, a fact that will dispose the interviewer to liking you.

The next question is where to find this knowledge. First of all, a company library or even the local library is a good start. Simply ask the reference librarian to help you. Also, check out the Dun & Bradstreet reports, and the *Reader's Guide to Periodical Literature* for any articles that may have been written on the company. For the latter source, don't give up if you don't find anything under the first heading you look at; try several headings, as many as you can think of. At least look under the company name, electronics, electrical engineering, microwaves, and radio frequency. The second source to tap is the company's annual report. Get one of these by contacting the company. A third source of information is through friends and contacts: Grill them!

CALL THE COMPANY

Do not despair if next to no information can be located. If this is the case, try calling the company itself, explain that you have an interview with them, and that you'd like to find out more about the company. Many executives and personnel officers will often be pleased to send you brochures, pamphlets, and other information. They will, in addition, remember your name come interview time.

It's a good idea to keep in mind that this information search takes a little time. When preparing for the interview, allow for the time it takes for mail to travel, and remember that libraries are open only during certain hours.

Having gotten this information from your various sources, carefully examine it to determine company trends, policies, and concerns. Look for the company's strengths and weaknesses. Set the knowledge against the background of your general knowledge of the field. Express an interest in these concerns during the interview, and to a certain extent, identify with these concerns. Think of possible solutions to the company's problems—or better yet, how *you* could help the company improve, meet goals, achieve important successes in the market.

These are the weapons you gird yourself with for confronting the question, "Why are you interested in *our* company?" This is the way to show the interviewer, "This guy's no slouch—he's done his homework."

Technical Documentation and Legal Liability

John M. Caher

This article describes a New York state legal case in which the court analyzed information included with a drug prescription to determine company liability after a patient committed suicide. In making a decision, the court examined the writer's prose for completeness and clarity.

If a technical writer's prose on a prescription drug data sheet is unclear, and a patient blows his brains out in a medicinally-caused fit of depression, is the pharmaceutical company liable?

That is exactly the question recently addressed by New York's highest court, the Court of Appeals, in a case underscoring the responsibilities and liabilities of the technical writing staff. The court's unanimous decision in *Martin v. Hacker* made two things perfectly clear: one, companies are definitely on the hook for financial damages when their product documentation is imprecise or inaccurate; and two, in this case the data sheet was sufficiently clear.

What makes this decision particularly interesting is the court's painstaking analysis of the verbiage contained in the data sheet and its effort to evaluate not only the content, but the context of the documentation. Although the decision is binding only in New York, opinions by the Court of Appeals traditionally carry great influence around the country and its legal precedents, procedures, and methodologies are often followed by other tribunals. Therefore, the ruling, dated Nov. 23, 1993, has indirect implications for technical writers and their employers across the country.

THE FACTS OF THE CASE

Eugene Martin was a retired New York State trooper under a doctor's care for high blood pressure. In 1981, Martin's physician prescribed a prescription drug, hydrochlorothiazide (HCT). A year later, a second drug, reserpine, was prescribed by the same doctor. The physician advised Martin of various side effects of reserpine, including the fact that the drug can produce depression, although usually would not do so in the dosage prescribed. It is unclear from the record whether the doctor informed Martin that HCT can exacerbate the side effects of reserpine.

On Feb. 13, 1983, Martin—who had no history of mental illness or depression—shot and killed himself in a drug-induced despondency. His widow sued various parties, including the doctor, Chelsea Laboratories (the manufacturer), and Rugby Laboratories (the distributor), alleging in part that the written warnings supplied with reserpine and HCT were insufficient as a matter of law.

THE LAW OF LIABILITY

Under the law, there are essentially three theories—contract, due care, and strict liability—under which a technical writer or manufacturer may be held responsible for an injurious result. Under the contract theory there is a binding agreement to perform

469

or provide a service. The due-care theory holds that a manufacturer knows more about a product than the consumer and therefore has a weightier responsibility. Strict-liability imposes the greatest burden of all. Under that theory, a manufacturer or employer can be held responsible for damages regardless of fault. The lawsuits against Chelsea and Rugby were brought as strict liability claims, predicated on the assumption that a prescription drug is by nature inherently unsafe. The legal issue in *Martin v. Hacker*, as framed by Judge Stewart F. Hancock, Jr., centered on a drug manufacturer's obligation to fully reveal the potential hazards of its products.

Since prescription drugs must be prescribed by a medical doctor, the information and warnings contained on package inserts are directed toward physicians. They must be written in accordance with labeling specifications of the Food and Drug Administration, which requires the following information in this order:

- Description
- Actions
- Indications
- Contraindications
- Warnings
- Use in pregnancy
- Precautions
- Adverse reactions
- Dosage and administration
- Overdosage
- How supplied

Eugene Martin's widow contended the package inserts were inadequate in at least three respects. She alleged: that the Warnings section was ambiguous as it relates to the type or category of patient at risk for suicide; that the Adverse Reactions section diminished the suicide caveat found in the Warning section; and that there was insufficient warning of the increased suicide risk when reserpine is prescribed in conjunction with HCT.

THE COURT'S APPROACH

The court's analysis is instructive and, perhaps, revealing.

Unsatisfied to merely scrutinize the package inserts from arm's length, the panel dissected the work of the technical writer and considered at the micro and macro levels not only what was said but what may have been implied or suggested in whole and in part.

"Whether a given warning is legally adequate or presents a factual question for resolution by a jury requires careful analysis of the warning's language," Judge Hancock wrote for the court as he began the analysis. "The court must examine not only the meaning and informational content of the language but also its form and manner of expression." Judge Hancock's prescription called for a surgical, tripartite examination of the package insert, with a focus on the warning's accuracy, clarity, and consistency. The court went to considerable lengths to spell out precisely the standard of review, carefully defining its own terms, as follows:

Accuracy—"For a warning to be accurate, it must be correct, fully descriptive and complete and it must convey updated information as to all of the drug's known side effects."

Clarity—In the context of a drug warning, the language of the admonition must be "direct, unequivocal and sufficiently forceful to convey the risk." The court went on to state:

"A warning that is otherwise clear may be obscured by inconsistencies or contradictory statements made in different sections of the package insert regarding the same side effect or from language in a later section that dilutes the intensity of a caveat made in an earlier section. Such contradictions will not create a question of fact as to the warning's adequacy, if the language of a particular admonition against a side effect is precise, direct, unequivocal and has sufficient force. The clarity of the overall warning may in such instances offset inconsistencies elsewhere in an insert."

Consistency—Essentially, the court said the whole is greater than the sum of its parts: "While a meticulous examination and parsing of individual sentences in the insert may arguably reveal differing nuances in meaning or variations in emphasis as to the seriousness of the side effect, any resulting vagueness may be overcome if, when read as a whole, the warning conveys a meaning as to the consequences that is unmistakable."

THE DOCUMENTATION AND THE ANALYSIS

The court analyzed and scrutinized the package inserts, pursuant to the allegations of insufficiency raised by the plaintiff. Judge Hancock specifically addressed the various sections of the inserts that gave rise to this lawsuit.

The Warnings Section

The Warnings section contains three declaratory sentences:

1. Extreme caution should be exercised in treating patients with a history of mental depression.
2. Discontinue the drug at the first sign of despondency, early morning insomnia, loss of appetite, impotence, or self-deprecation.
3. Drug-induced depression may persist for several months after drug withdrawal and may be severe enough to result in suicide.

Cynthia J. Martin, the widow, asserted that the first sentence set the parameters for the following sentences in the Warnings section. Namely, she argued that the caveats of the second and third sentences apply, or appear to apply, only to the patients described in the first sentence, those "with a history of mental depression." Mrs. Martin's contention was that the sequence of information— the pattern in which it was presented—made it unclear.

The court rejected her argument, described the third sentence as "direct, unqualified, and unequivocal," and added that it would "defy common sense and subvert the clear intendment of the third sentence to read it as limited by the first sentence of this section."

The Adverse Reactions Section

Under the FDA labeling specifications, the Adverse Reactions section should follow the Warnings section of drug package inserts. Mrs. Martin contended that a portion of the Adverse Reactions section served to dilute the third caveat in the Warnings section. The relevant portions read as follows:

> "Central nervous system reactions include drowsiness, depression, nervousness, paradoxical anxiety, nightmares. . . . These reactions are usually reversible and usually disappear after the drug is discontinued."

Mrs. Martin contrasted the final sentence in the above quote with the third admonition in the Warnings section, which advised that medication-induced depression may well persist after drug use is discontinued.

A contradiction?

The court said no.

It noted that the last section of the Adverse Reactions section pertains to the usual duration of the side effect, not to its seriousness. "Thus, the last sentence does not contradict the unequivocal and straightforward statement in the Warnings section that drug-induced depression may be severe enough to result in suicide."

Furthermore, the court looked to another section, the Actions portion, that precedes both the Warnings and Adverse Reactions sections. The Actions section states: "Both cardiovascular and central nervous system effects may persist for a period of time following withdrawal of this drug."

So, what we have here is the Actions section advising that the side effects may continue even though use of the product has ceased, the Warnings section admonishing that effects may persist after withdrawal and may be serious enough to result in suicide and the Adverse Reactions section offering that the reactions typically subside when drug use is curtailed.

Taken as a whole, the court said, those sections "are sufficient to convey to any reasonably prudent physician an unambiguous and consistent message" which "comports exactly with the risk of taking reserpine."

The Dosage and Administration Section

Mrs. Martin's final claim, that the reserpine insert does not sufficiently warn of the dangers inherent in ingesting both reserpine and HCT, was rejected by the court as meritless.

The Dosage and Administration section states that "concomitant use of reserpine with (other drugs) necessitates careful titration of dosage with each agent." Also, the HCT package insert includes a forewarning that the drug "may add to or potentiate the action of other antihypertensive drugs."

THE DECISION

The court dismissed the lawsuit against Chelsea and Rugby, holding that the package inserts "contained language which, on its face, adequately warned against the precise risk in question, i.e., depression-caused suicide." It upheld a lower court and found "no triable issues of fact regarding the warning provided to physicians by the package inserts accompanying these prescription drugs."

In other words, the tech writing staff did its part in adequately conveying information to the prescribing physician. The remaining question for a trial court jury is whether the physician did his part and adequately warned Eugene Martin of the danger of drug-induced despondency.

CONCLUSION

Gerald M. Parsons of the University of Nebraska, Lincoln, has written in this journal about the growing number of lawsuits focusing on the work of technical writers, and the increasing willingness of courts to carefully analyze, and perhaps second-guess, the writer's phraseology. *Martin v. Hacker* is progeny to this trend.

The potential exposure to the pharmaceutical companies involved in this case was enormous. But they escaped liability, precisely because the court was willing to take extraordinary care in analyzing the prose of the technical writer. It seems self-evident, for legal and moral reasons, that if the courts are willing to put that much effort into reading and evaluating a tech writer's work, then the author and employer must be at least as diligent in their construction of technical documentation. The stakes are substantial, and not just in a legal sense. When a technical writer's work is unclear, and an operator inadvertently reformats a hard drive, that's unfortunate. But if a technical writer's inaccuracy or imprecision claims a life, that's another matter altogether.

BIBLIOGRAPHY

Enterprise Responsibility for Personal Injury, Vol. II, *The American Law Institute,* Philadelphia, April 15, 1991.

Holzer, H. M., Product Liability Law: The Impact on New York Businesses, *Brooklyn Law School,* 1990.

Markel, M. H., *Technical Writing: Situations and Strategies,* St. Martin's Press, New York, 1992.

Martin, Cynthia J., Individually and as Executrix of Eugene J. Martin, Deceased, v. Arthur Hacker, et al., and Chelsea Laboratories, Inc., et al., *83 NY2nd 1,* Nov. 23, 1993.

Parson, G. M., A Cautionary Legal Tale: The Bose v. Consumers Union Case, *The Journal of Technical Writing and Communication,* 22:4, pp. 377–386, 1992.

There Ought to Be a Law: Product Liability in New York State, *The Public Policy Institute, Special Report,* June 1991.

Designing and Delivering Presentations and Workshops

Ric Calabrese

Many professional people have to make oral presentations or conduct workshops on the job. This article presents guidelines for planning and organizing a presentation, arranging the room, delivering the presentation, talking to listeners later, and conducting workshops. Use the preparation checklist to avoid last-minute problems before a presentation and the evaluation sheet to assess your own style after a presentation.

INTRODUCTION: KNOWLEDGE PLUS RISK EQUALS GROWTH

Today a significant responsibility included in the day-to-day life of many professionals includes making oral presentations and/or conducting workshops for groups of clients, customers, patients, other professionals, and the general public. Unfortunately, the skills needed to plan and deliver a message orally and articulately cannot be learned by reading alone; one must be prepared to digest the information and then have the courage to take risks.

While entire books are written on the broad and general subject of giving oral presentations, the purpose of this article is to develop and to discuss concisely the most salient principles occurring in the process of preparing and delivering oral presentations and workshops.

Following are suggestions for advance planning and organizing of a presentation, advance physical arrangements of the room, delivering the presentation, post-presentation actions, and conducting workshops.

ADVANCE PLANNING AND ORGANIZATION FOR THE PRESENTATION

Less is more when giving oral presentations. The key to holding an audience, particularly one with limited time to absorb the speaker's ideas, is to be coherent and to communicate simply; otherwise, their minds will wander. The secret of conciseness and simplicity is for the speaker to know his or her objectives prior to planning the talk. What does he or she want to accomplish? What changes in the attitude or behavior of the audience are desired? Does the speaker want them to perform a task or recall some information? A common mistake made among untrained presenters is to attempt to cover too much in the time allotted. Inexperienced speakers often feel the need to parade their expertise and thus they overload the audience with information.

Unlike reading, where one can go back and reconsider an idea, listening requires ongoing concentration. When the brain begins to feel overloaded and saturation sets in, it protects itself by shutting down. Has not everyone had the experience of pretending to be listening to an overly meticulous speaker while the imagination went elsewhere on holiday? Oral presentations need to be limited to a few major points that can be clearly explained and reinforced through details, examples, and a variety of media. Too much information and too many different points defeat the purpose. When listeners know where the presentation is going and are able to follow the presenter's reasoning, grasping examples with ease, they are much more likely to give their full attention.

Although presentations are often as brief as 10 minutes or as long as 90, presenters would do well to remember when adapting their goals to their group, what the Reverend William Sloane Coffin said about the length of an effective sermon: "No souls are saved after twenty minutes." Once the presenter has tailored the general and specific goals to a particular group, the next task is to organize them.

Introduction Critical to Speaker Credibility

Each of the three generally accepted divisions of a presentation (Introduction, Body, and Conclusion) requires its own internal organization and serves a specific function. The Introduction serves as the speaker's opportunity to establish credibility, to link himself or herself in some way with the audience, to let them know in what ways they will be better off as a result of having attended to the speaker, and to describe for them in some serial fashion what will be covered in the presentation.

Often when speakers are introduced, their credentials are presented in advance; however, there will be times when no one is present to introduce the speaker or, when "introducers" are available, they may neglect to mention important items related to the speaker's credibility. While self-serving comments delivered in a braggadocio manner may have a negative effect on audiences, audiences do, nevertheless, want to know that the person talking to them is worthy and knowledgeable. Presenters, therefore, should subtly let them know during the introduction that they are qualified. For example, one might say, "In an article I wrote last year for the journal XYZ . . . ," or "While I was completing my graduate work at . . . ," or "Of the several hundred accounts I have worked with in the past. . . ."

Audiences tend to be more attentive when they believe that the person speaking to them is able to relate to their circumstances. During the introduction, whenever it is possible, speakers would do well to underscore any connection they may have with a particular group. For example, the speaker might say, "I have lived in this community for fifteen years . . ." or "I see we are all baby boomers and share many of the same sentiments." If one gives it some thought, almost all audiences have some traits with which the speaker can identify.

During the introduction the speaker needs to let the audience know how the topic relates to their needs; in other words, *answer* the unasked question in everyone's mind, "What is in this for me?" Abraham Maslow has synthesized the basic human needs into five areas: physiological, safety and security, belonging and social activity, esteem and status, self-realization and fulfillment. When the presenter announces that after listening to the speech, the listeners will in some way be better able to control their health, be more secure, be in a position where others think better of them or respect them more, think more of themselves, or feel they have the knowledge to develop latent potential in themselves, the audience "perks up" and prepares itself to attend to the forthcoming message. Not every human need can be related to every topic, but as many as are possible and appropriate should be suggested during the introduction. During the "body" and "conclusions" of the speech as well, the speaker should remind the audience how what is being discussed can be related to fulfilling their own needs.

Finally, the last critical component to be included in the introduction is a list of topics that will be discussed. It might be presented something like this: "Today I intend to discuss three specific points. Number one, I will discuss the relationship of diet to heart disease; number two, I will illustrate the fat and cholesterol content of foods; and thirdly, I will model how to order at a restaurant." As mentioned above, not only does this help the audience to listen to the talk with an expectation of what is to come, but the organization itself adds to the "halo effect" and increases the audience's perception of the speaker's credibility.

Three Key Objectives of the "Body" of the Presentation

The Body of the presentation is the second major division and is where the points mentioned in the introduction are actually developed. Presenters need to have a rationale for the way they decide to organize this major section. The overall objectives generally are threefold: that the audience fully understand the message, that the audience believe, and that they be comfortable enough with the speaker to share their objections in the event that they are confused or wish to challenge the presenter.

To safeguard the first objective, understanding, speakers need not only to construct their messages clearly and concisely but also need to design visual aids, handouts, and/or participative experiences to enhance the audience's understanding. The second objective, audience belief, needs continuously to be reinforced throughout the presentation. Credibility or lack of credibility continues to be inferred from the presenter's style and the quality of all aids associated with the presentation. The third objective, to develop a rapport with the audience to the extent that they dare challenge or question, is critical. When objections are unexpressed, presenters may infer falsely that the audience agrees and understands, causing them to move too quickly from one point to another, leaving confused members behind.

A Presentation Can Be Concluded in More Ways than One

Like the first two, the third division of the presentation, the Conclusion, may be handled successfully in many different ways. The key is that all the ingredients be included somewhere. Ingredient one is for the audience to "feel" that the presentation is "winding down" and is about to end. This needs to be done gradually and smoothly. It sounds nonprofessional and haphazard to end with remarks like "any questions," "that's all folks," "thank you for your attention." Remember the presenter's credibility is influenced by the audience's perceptions of how well he or she is organized. Clues such as "In conclusion . . . ," "To summarize," "Before concluding, I want to leave you with one more thought," are helpful in letting the audience know that the presentation is about to terminate. If a summary is warranted, it should be given; if a final plea or pitch is warranted, that should be given; if a final quote, anecdote, or joke makes the point one more time, then that is appropriate.

One last word about conclusions is be proactive in asking if there are any questions. Of course there are, but people are often hesitant to ask. The speaker should prepare a few for the audience, and then call on a participant who has been paying close attention for a reaction. One might say, for example, "I noticed you looked confused when I was discussing the formula to determine appropriate profit levels. What is it you would like further discussion of?" After responding to that first ques-

tion generated by the presenter, it is often much simpler to get others to respond when the question is asked: "Are there any *other* questions or comments?"

Correlation Exists between "Form" and Speaker "Credibility"

Although the discussion of the presentation's design is generally divided into three areas of introduction, body, and conclusion, there is no one perfect way to organize. Speakers with different styles can be equally successful. There are, however, several points to consider when deciding upon a presentation's format. A fact that most people are not aware of is that the presentation's organization is critical primarily because it relates to the presenter's credibility.

For example, if a speaker were to deliver a talk to two different audiences, giving one audience ten slices of information in an organized way and giving the second audience the same ten slices of information in a disorganized way, both audiences would retain about the same amount of information after hearing the talk. But only one audience would consider it seriously or possibly change their attitude toward the subject matter.

When an audience hears an organized speaker, one who gives the audience a sense that the presenter knows exactly where he or she is going, with a defined beginning, middle, and end, they are more likely to infer that the speaker is competent in the area being addressed. On the other hand, many brilliant and qualified professionals are not taken seriously when giving presentations because they sound too "loose," too unprepared, too disorganized.

Media credibility is related to inferences regarding presenter's credibility. All media, the way they are designed, presented, and utilized, are an extension of the speaker and, consequently, reflect directly the speaker's credibility. Media include such things as handouts, blackboard, flip chart, pad or easel, overhead projector, 35 mm slides, motion pictures, sound recording, videocassettes, samples of products, models or mock-ups, and so forth. "Excellence" tends to be inferred from those that are obviously carefully put together. For example, a presenter whose overhead transparencies are executed with large print that can easily be read (as opposed to ordinary typewriter print, which cannot easily be read from a transparency) allows for the inference of an experienced and considerate presenter. Other signs include using stenciled letters in bold colors on posters, rather than sloppy printing or cursive writing. The condition of the poster itself leads either to positive or negative impressions of the speaker. Those that are discolored, bent, and old looking suggest that the presenter doesn't care enough to add fresh aids for his or her group.

Even the quality and color of the paper used in handouts can add or detract from the overall impression. If it is possible, the presenter is wise to try and coordinate all aids in colors that may be symbolic or meaningful. For example, a presenter giving a talk to a group on Saint Patrick's Day could make use of green; a talk to an Italian-American Club could be done in red, white, and green. This may sound superfluous, but audiences do respond on an unconscious level to the extra care and preparation the speaker has made in tailoring a presentation on their behalf.

An unfortunate judgment is often made regarding presenters who do not carefully proofread all their materials, including handouts, overhead transparencies, flip charts, posters, and the like, prior to the audience's exposure to them. While it is not rational, audience members do tend to make negative inferences about how

credible a presenter is in his or her area of expertise if he or she can't spell, count, or interpret statistics. PROOFREAD CAREFULLY.

Whenever presenters are going to be using audiovisual equipment with which they are unfamiliar, it is critical that they arrive early enough to study it beforehand. The most competent presenters may lose their credibility entirely by not knowing how to turn on a machine or advance a slide.

Language and Style of Oral Presentations Differ from Those of Written Presentations

The written text and the oral presentation are entirely different. There is no objection to a presenter writing out the entire talk, carefully organizing it according to topics, causes and effects, chronology, or whatever else seems appropriate. Once the talk is written, however, the speaker needs to recognize that the written manuscript represents the "science" of a presentation; the actual delivery represents the "art." Each time it is delivered, it should be somewhat different, using different words, different examples, different anecdotes, and so forth to suit each particular audience and situation.

The word "choice" in the spoken language tends to be different from the word "choice" used in the written language. Sentences in oral speech tend to be simpler, shorter, and sound more conversational, including common words and contractions, while the written manuscript may be more erudite and academic. The only way for speakers to develop the "art" of delivery is to rehearse from a simple outline and not from a manuscript, and to rehearse in front of real people who will react and comment, not mirrors, walls, or car windshields.

Oral presentations ought never to be read or memorized. There are good reasons for not rehearsing from a manuscript. The speech tends eventually to become memorized, and that can be deadly. Once a speech is memorized, speakers tend to become more "speaker-centered" than "audience-centered," which means that they tend to become more concerned about whether or not they can remember each line exactly as it is written on the manuscript and less concerned about whether or not the audience is enjoying, learning, listening, and understanding. Another problem that arises from manuscript speaking is that it is DULL! Because the facial expressions and vocal intonations are not spontaneous, the monologue tends to sound memorized and can easily become boring to listeners.

ADVANCE ARRANGEMENTS

Take control of seating the listeners before everyone settles down. It may be their boardroom, gymnasium, or meeting hall, but it is the presenter's "show." Conscious decisions should be made about whether to pull the group into a circle, half circle, rows, around tables, and so forth. When it is possible to know beforehand which persons are the most influential, their seats should be reserved and placed in the best position to see, hear, and appreciate any visual aids, as well as the speaker. A final checklist for presentations is found in Figure 1.

Creating positive impressions begins the moment the presenter enters the room. The presenter is being "sized-up" and adding to the presentation's ambience from the moment he or she enters the room. Therefore, the presenter should, whenever possible, arrive early and make an effort to meet people. The speaker's self-confidence, whether real or feigned, will relax the audience and increase their perceptions of his

Attend to details and prepare a final checklist. Listed below are a few questions that the presenter might consider in order to avoid last-minute problems.

Do I have my presentation notes?
Do I have all my supporting materials?
Have I enough copies for each of the attendees?
Will the facility be unlocked and open?
Are the tables and chairs arranged to suit my design?
Do I understand how to operate the lighting system?
Do I understand how to operate the ventilation system?
Do I know the location and operational condition of the electrical circuits?
Do I know how to work the projector?
Do I have an extra bulb, cassette, video, extension cord, etc.?
Will the projection screen be in place and adequate for this size group?
Do I have the type of sound system I require? Is it working?
Have arrangements been made to handle messages during the presentation?
Are there arrangements for hats and coats?
Will there be a sign to announce the place of the presentation?
Will someone be introducing me, and have I given him or her all the information I want shared with the group?

FIGURE 1   Final Checklist

or her desire to share information. Presenters should never volunteer any negative information regarding their own stress or fear of speaking. The audience wants to learn and enjoy, and when they are aware of the speaker's fragility or stage fright, they tend to become nervous themselves in sympathy.

The presenter, waiting to be introduced, seated among the audience or on stage, should be aware that those people who know he or she is the guest speaker will be watching his or her every move. That means that even before beginning the presentation, speakers must be careful to smile, look confident, and extend themselves to others. Once introduced, the way the speaker walks up to the podium is critical. During those first moments an initial impression is being created. The speaker should consciously walk confidently, looking and smiling toward the audience. Prior to uttering the first words to the audience, it is a good technique to spend a long three seconds just looking out at the audience, smiling and establishing eye contact with several individuals. This allows them to infer poise, confidence, and the speaker's desire to "connect" with them.

DELIVERING THE PRESENTATION

Never share internal feelings of fright or anxiety. Speakers experience themselves in the situation from the inside out; the audience experiences them from the outside in. Simply, that means that if asked if he or she is nervous, the speaker should always answer "NO!" The audience is picking up the "tip of the iceberg" from their observations of the "outside" of the speaker; they do not actually feel the intensity of the speaker's anxiety and will probably be totally unaware of it, unless it is brought to their attention through one's own confession. One must act confident, even when one may not feel it internally.

One of the worst things presenters can do is to admit to an audience that they are scared, ill prepared, missing material, or have done the presentation better in the past for other groups. The audience does not know what it might be missing, and are generally much less critical of speakers than they are of themselves.

"Stage fright" is a vestige from our ancient past. The feelings commonly referred to as "stage fright" may date back to the dawn of the human race, a time when our prehistoric ancestors had to survive by living in caves and sharing the food supply with other beasts. Faced by a predator, our ancestors had a genuine use for a sudden jolt of energy, which gave them the power to do battle or run, fight or take flight. The vestiges of this power, stemming from the secretions of the adrenal gland, still manifest themselves today when people sense danger. Who has not felt that ice block in the stomach while being reprimanded by the boss, or experienced the sweaty palms and racing heart while walking into a room full of strangers?

Occasionally one still reads in the newspaper accounts of individuals under conditions of fear or danger exhibiting superhuman strength; the father, for example, who lifts the car off his child, who has been pinned under the wheels. This is an example of the power that comes with the adrenaline jolt; however, when one is unable to fight, run, or in some other way utilize this surge, he or she may become overwhelmed by the internal feelings themselves. It is this feeling prior to and during a presentation that is commonly labeled "stage fright."

The best safeguard against stage fright is adequate preparation and rehearsal. The more one practices in front of *live others,* the less nervousness one will have. Other ways of dealing with this feeling include being active during the presentation and "acting" calm and confident. If one knows one is going to be full of extra energy because of one's adrenaline flow, one could plan to engage in demonstrations during the presentation, distribute handouts, use a pointer, or any other activity that involves motion. Motion is a release for the tension and anxiety and allows the audience to infer enthusiasm from the speaker's movement rather than fright, nervousness, or tension. It may not work for everyone, but many people can learn to control their public behavior if they visualize themselves as acting. When one is "on" giving a presentation, one is acting. Regardless of how one may feel, one can *act* confident, calm, and poised.

Movement should be intentional and meaningful. All movement should be meaningful. Do not pace. Presenters ought to look for opportunities to break the invisible barrier between themselves and their audience. Walking toward the audience, walking around the audience, walking in and out of the audience, are all acceptable ways of delivering a presentation. What is not acceptable is pacing back and forth, particularly with eyes down, pulling thoughts together before uttering them.

Movement into an audience is a communication vehicle in itself. When the speaker penetrates that invisible barrier between speaker and audience, he or she tells the audience of a desire to connect, to be close, to better "sense" what they are feeling about him or her and the content. In fact, as one walks among the audience, one can begin to be seen from a different perspective and may gain new insights into how to better clarify the presentation's points from this experience.

Unnecessary barriers between the presenter and audience should be omitted. Presenters do best when they omit all barriers between themselves and their audience. Avoid using a podium or lectern, even when one is provided by the sponsoring organization. Of course, there may be times when, because of the quantity of material, a place to store things may be required. Even under this condition, using a table to set handouts and other materials on is preferred to a podium.

A lectern should only be used when the speaker does not intend to move about; intends to lecture and needs a stand to rest against and place notes upon. Adults generally do not learn optimally through the lecture method and unless the speaker is extraordinarily good, straight lecture behind a lectern should be avoided. When one delivers the message standing in front of the group, without a barrier, one is more disposed to stop the talk to respond to their verbal or nonverbal feedback. Gestures and movement too can be more expansive and visible without the lectern barrier.

Voice cadence, pitch, variation, and rate are communication vehicles. Vocal inflection and variation add interest and add to the impression of speaker enthusiasm. For some people controlling this variation is simple and natural, but for others it is a challenge. Nevertheless, the presenter needs to attend to voice modulation. The goal when speaking in front of a group is to sound natural and conversational; however, what sounds natural and conversational when one is standing in front of a large group is not the same as what sounds conversational in a small face-to-face group.

"Natural and conversational" from the presenter's point of view is exaggerated. The highs need to be a bit higher and the lows need to be a bit lower. What may sound to the presenter's ear as "phony" and "theatrical" generally sounds far less so to the listener. In any case, a delivery that is of narrow range or monotone is difficult to attend to for more than a few minutes. The good news is that this trait can be fairly easily and quickly developed, even in those who recognize a problem in this area. It requires risking sounding foolish and exaggerated in front of trusted others, until adequate reinforcement has convinced the presenter that the increase is really an advantage that allows him or her to be attended to more easily.

When talking in front of a group, generally the speaker should attempt to speak more slowly than in ordinary conversation. What is an appropriate rate in a small face-to-face discussion is probably too fast for a group presentation. For some reason, there seems to be a correlation between the speech rate of the speaker and the size of the audience. What might be easily grasped at a more rapid rate in face-to-face conversation, isn't understood as quickly in large groups. Also, the speaker's slower rate allows him or her to scan the audience to see if the presentation is being understood, to see if some people need an opportunity to disagree, to see if he or she needs to talk louder or increase variation because some look bored.

Nonverbal behavior, the silent language, can be meaningful and controlled. It is good practice to keep hands away from the body and from one another. Allow them to be free to gesture, and avoid holding anything in them while talking, unless it is a useful prop like a pointer or a visual aid. After twenty-five years of teaching presentational speaking to college undergraduates and corporate professionals, this writer knows empirically that once speakers allow their hands to mesh together or to grasp one another behind their backs, there is only a slight chance of their being released to gesture. Often people feel awkward with their hands hanging loosely at their sides. Perhaps if they could see themselves on videotape in this posture, they would realize that it is natural looking, but even more importantly, they would probably see that one tends not to stay in that position. If speakers talk with their hands hanging loosely at their sides, eventually their hands begin to rise and gesture spontaneously to emphasize important points.

It is very dangerous to begin a presentation holding a pen, paper clip, rubber band, or other instrument not directly related to the presentation. Unconsciously, the fingers begin to play with the instrument, and the audience becomes fascinated in watching to see what the speaker will do. A former student actually straightened out a paper clip and began to stab himself while talking. Needless to say, for the remainder of his presentation the class couldn't take their eyes off the mutilation scene, and missed the speaker's concluding points.

As one speaks so will one be judged. Professional speakers attend to their diction, particularly when pronouncing words like "for," "can," "with," "picture," "going to," and "want to." In ordinary conversation one isn't likely to judge negatively a speaker who mispronounces common words and engages in sloppy diction saying, for example, words like "fer," "ken," "wit," "pitcher," "gunna," and "wanna," for the words listed above. When that speaker is in front of an audience, however, these mispronounced words often stand out and lead to negative inferences regarding the speaker. If one thinks of well-known television anchor men and women, one will be unable to recall any who have faulty diction. Professionals who present themselves in front of groups must attend to their diction because they risk losing credibility if it is poor. Logical? No! True? Yes!

Once one has decided to become conscious of one's diction and decides to improve it, several steps are required. Step number one is for the speaker to inform trusted others who are often around him or her to listen critically, and to stop him or her each time a diction error occurs. Only after one is made aware of common errors, can one begin to train one's self to hear them. That is step two. Because the human mind operates generally at five times the rate of human speech, it is possible to listen critically to ourselves as we speak. So those who are attempting to rid themselves of poor diction or some other vocalized interference ("um," "an," "and a," etc.) can train themselves to listen for the errors and to correct them. Like learning to ride a bicycle or to use a computer, this learning and training task is uncomfortable at first, but improvement comes quickly. Working on one's diction is an ongoing task. Professional speakers never stop listening to the way their words are coming out and planning ahead to pronounce them correctly.

The visage itself is a communication vehicle. Presenters need to train themselves to keep their faces animated, using a variety of facial expressions. For many of the same reasons expressed above, it is important that speakers use all the communication vehicles available to maintain the audience's attention. One's facial expression is itself a communication vehicle. When it is lively, animated, expressive, and changing regularly while the speaker reacts to the feedback coming from the audience, it enhances the verbal message and allows the audience to go on unconsciously inferring the speaker's audience-centeredness. Because of a natural dispositional personality, ethnic background, life experience, and so forth, this is easier for some people to do than for others; however, everyone can improve! Because it isn't easy for one to "act" expressive does not mean that one can't grow considerably in the ability to look expressive. Indeed one can.

Eye contact is a vehicle of communication. It should be used to see the audience and respond to their nonverbal feedback. It is surprising how many people seem to remember having learned some rule about being able to fool the audience into thinking that the speaker is seeing them while he or she is actually looking over the heads of the people in the last row. The point is that when speakers have the opportunity to present themselves and their ideas to an audience, they want them to understand, to believe, and to follow their recommendations. Speakers have the best chance of being successful in achieving those goals when they are able to interpret the audience's ongoing reaction to what they are saying. Even though presentation speaking is generally considered a one-way communication situation, with the speaker talking at the audience as they listen, it is, in fact, a two-way situation with audience and speaker communicating with one another constantly and simultaneously.

Trained speakers see almost everything from their position in front of the room. If they are alert and looking, they see people who are beginning to fidget and interpret their feedback. They might decide from this observation to give the audience a short break; they might liven up their own movements to regain attention; they might engage in a new activity, one perhaps that involves audience participation, and so forth. The speaker might see some people coming in late, looking awkwardly for a seat. This provides the opportunity to publicly welcome them and ask others to move over to provide seating. The speaker might see people who look angry. This provides the opportunity to say, "You look angry. What have I said to offend you?" In other words, speakers who use their eyes to "connect" with the audience make them a part of the presentation. The audience knows it too, and will begin to send signals when they realize the speaker is sensitive to them.

Facial expressions are important. Smile, and look like you are having a good time. Smiling can be rehearsed and may feel phoney, but it needs to be built into the design of the presentation. One does not need to be constantly grinning, but one does need to maintain an expression of gentleness, approachableness, and nondefensiveness. The easiest way to convey these impressions is to smile often. Unfortunately, it isn't easy to smile when one is unsure of the material. All the principles above can only be worked at after the speaker has sufficiently mastered the content and consciously, through rehearsal, developed skills.

Although individual situations may make this difficult, a general rule to remember is that when speaking for an hour or less, always plan on at least ten minutes for some audience interaction. In talks of more than forty-five minutes, actual audience participation activities should be planned where possible and appropriate.

POSTPRESENTATION

Speakers should remember to bring business cards and to remain afterwards for people who may want to talk. If they have done a good job with eye contact, smiling, and prompting the inference of warmth, people will want to talk with them. This is frequently a source of repeat talks to other groups, and it is an opportunity for the best kind of public relations, face-to-face. When there is a long line of persons waiting to talk and time is limited, this writer passes out his business card and tells everyone they are entitled to one call for free consultation. It is amazing how many people follow up on the offer.

WORKSHOPS

Workshops differ from presentations. There are significant differences between a presentation and a workshop or training session. The differences are in the amount of time needed, the amount of audience participation recommended, and the goals of the leader. Presentations generally run no more than ninety minutes, while workshops may run from ninety minutes to several days. Audience participation and training are an integral part of workshop design, and the goals of workshops are generally to teach and train, while the goal of a presentation often is to persuade the audience to accept a specific proposal. The suggestions below are particularly appropriate when designing workshops.

Workshop leaders should plan to use techniques that involve all participants and encourage open communication between themselves and the participants and among the participants. Ways to encourage participation include: dividing the larger group into smaller groups, giving them time in their small group to get to know one another, and then giving them activities related to the workshop topic. These small group activities may include: case studies, either real or hypothetical; role playing; and questionnaire completion and discussion. Occasionally a group may be given a preworkshop assignment to complete a questionnaire, read material related to the workshop, or some other task. Reactions to these tasks can be processed among the participants in small groups.

Frequently, the most important point in determining the climate and direction of the workshop occurs during the first twenty minutes. Some suggestions for using the opening minutes to establish an open climate include using a group introductory activity to promote a relaxed and open atmosphere. When the group is small enough (generally twenty or less), spending time to allow each participant to identify major concerns and questions tends to encourage this involvement. Workshop leaders can relieve participant anxiety by introducing themselves, sharing both personal and professional information, giving a brief overview of the objectives for the workshop, the main topics to be covered, their sequence, and approximate time span. They should also reinforce often that they do have expectations in terms of participants' cooperation and participation. Even when such introductory activities take as long as an hour, they are justifiable, because of their importance in establishing a common frame of reference with shared goals in a relaxed and receptive setting.

Leaders should be aware of signals of fatigue or boredom from participants. Some techniques used to avoid these problems include: identifying two or three participants whose behavior provides some type of clue to group climate, providing a variety of activities to break-up the routine, and providing a change of pace. Most successful workshops are a blend of information-presenting activities with "hands-on," experiential types of activities.

Another way to safeguard understanding and attention is to summarize regularly what has occurred, especially before moving on to a new topic. Continuity of training is enhanced, if there are purposeful and periodic reviews and summaries during the workshop. Leaders should note that it is not essential that they do the summarizing; in fact, having the participants themselves do it provides feedback as to whether or not the group has grasped the important points.

Anticipate from among the alternatives the appropriate conclusion for the workshop. Just as the introductory period to the workshop should not be rushed, so too should closure be carefully attended to. This depends upon how much time is available for the entire workshop, of course. But in a day's workshop of from six to eight hours, allowing a full hour at the end for closure is appropriate. During this time loose ends are tied; the group's original expectations are reviewed and assessed as to how well these expectations have been met. Requiring the group to complete an evaluation of the workshop during the time provided for the workshop is the method most likely to get the largest return. These evaluations are most helpful to leaders who want to continue to grow. They will process the evaluations and make changes in subsequent workshops based on the responses. A sample evaluation sheet is available in the "Appendix." The emphasis in a workshop is always on quality not quantity. It isn't how much the audience has heard; it is how much they will learn, will remember, and will use in the future that is the final measure of the workshop's success.

APPENDIX

Evaluation Sheet

Presenter: _____

Date: _____

Presentation (Check your response)

	Excellent	Good	Satisfactory	Poor	Unsatisfactory
1. How would you describe the presenter's knowledge of the subject matter?	____	____	____	____	____
2. How did you find the presenter's style of delivery?	____	____	____	____	____
3. Did the presenter encourage individual participation?	____	____	____	____	____
4. Did the presenter hold your interest?	____	____	____	____	____
5. How did you find the organization of the content material?	____	____	____	____	____
6. How useful did you find the visual aids?	____	____	____	____	____
7. To what degree did you feel that the content and exercises were relevant to your job?	____	____	____	____	____

8. Comments:

What Skills Will You Need to Succeed?

John R. Graham

Your technical knowledge and training may get you that first big job, but other elements are also important for on-the-job success. This article points out the five essential skills you will need to build a successful career and advance in your field.

What will it take to be a successful business owner or manager in the years ahead? As surprising as it may seem, it won't be such popular prerequisites as having the right connections, good financial relationships, or even a proven track record. The ability to choose the right people and the capability to manage both people and projects won't be at the top of the list, either. I would be naive to suggest that these qualities will be insignificant, but they will be less important than they were in the recent past.

What's Changed?   One factor has influenced the business environment for a long time—progress. Beginning with the start of the Industrial Revolution late in the 18th century, Western society has been dominated by the ideal of progress. The notion of progress has also fired the engine of business enterprise. In essence, the idea has gone something like this: By applying our knowledge, capabilities, and resources properly, we will enjoy the benefits of an ever-improving standard of living. What skills are now required to be effective in this new business environment? There are several to consider, but the following five are essential.

- **The ability to put it on paper.** Thirty years ago, a middle-aged, Harley Davidson-riding professor at the University of Wyoming said it very well: "Those who say, 'I know what I mean; I just can't express it; don't know what they mean.' " He's correct.

  In an expanding business environment, many people have been able to survive by virtue of their personality traits or their technical expertise. What many employees are discovering today is that they lack the critical communication skills necessary to get ahead. As a result, there's no place for them in tomorrow's business enterprise.

  Most people in business are in trouble because they are unable to express their thoughts in writing. This indicates that they have been able to get by on "fuzzy thinking" for a long time. Today, the standards are changing. Solid thinking is required to survive in the business world. If you can't put it down on paper, you're out of business.

- **The ability to present effectively to a group.** The other side of this coin is, of course, the skill required to communicate successfully with groups of people. For a long time we had erroneously concluded that working with people on a "one-on-one basis" is more important than working with people in groups.

  Many people would rather die, as one survey shows, than be required to express themselves in front of groups. In a sense, making an oral presentation to a group is the one "no excuses" act in life. If we fail a test, we can say

487

we didn't have time to study. If we don't get a promotion, we blame it on politics. But when we stand before a group, there can be no excuses. The ability to get the people on the team together and "put your arms around them" verbally is the one skill that really makes things happen.

- **The ability to develop original ideas.** For the most part, we rarely find ideas lying around in a business. Businesspeople see themselves as "doers," not "thinkers." Business and ideas seem to have an oil-and-water relationship.

    Why will original ideas be so essential in business in the years ahead? No longer can we afford to make mistakes. The ability to think through issues and to conceptualize our thoughts will make the difference between failure and success.

- **The ability to persuade others.** Persuasion is often equated with getting people to act in ways that may not be in their best interests. Actually, persuasion involves the ability to think totally from the other person's or other group's viewpoint. From a marketing perspective, persuasion involves understanding what the customer wants to buy, not what the business owner wants to sell.

    The old ideas—"just find their weak spot" or "play hardball if you have to"—are history because they resulted in too much waste. Today—and tomorrow—everyone is important because the supply of customers and prospects is anything but endless.

- **The ability to stay on track.** The 1980s will be a memorial to short-term goals which were more personal than corporate. What we are suggesting here is that they got off track because they had no vision of the future.

    The 1990s are quite different. The times now demand such personal qualities as inner trust, determination, and self-confidence. The ability to stay on track represents a sense of comfort with one's own vision of the future and then the stamina necessary to remain with it. These are the people who build businesses.

When you add these qualities together, it's easy to see how the whole is far greater than the sum of parts. These five leadership skills describe what it will take to be successful in the years ahead.

Send the Right Messages about E-Mail

Diane B. Hartman and Karen S. Nantz

Electronic mail is now a standard method of communication in most offices. This excerpt about e-mail style and etiquette is from an article reporting the results of a survey of 300 e-mail users in U.S. companies. The survey results indicated that most companies offered little employee training for using e-mail. The following tips will help you use e-mail effectively.

REMEMBER THE RECEIVER

When people use computers as communication tools, they sometimes forget that they are communicating with other people, not with machines. To keep your receiver's needs in mind, ask yourself the following questions before sending an e-mail message:

- What does my receiver know?
- What does my receiver need to know?
- What does my receiver want to know?
- What will my receiver think, say, and do in response to this message?
- Does my receiver have special needs to consider?

Consider carefully who needs to receive your messages. E-mail usually enables you to send messages to everyone in your organization, and sometimes to many people outside, as well. But should you?

When e-mail boxes become clogged with unnecessary messages, the system impedes communication instead of enhancing it. Most respondents to our survey report that they receive an average of 50 e-mail messages each day, and some receive as many as 200 a day. To avoid information overload, establish distribution guidelines. Usually, you need to share information only with people who will help solve a problem or make a decision. If you respond to a message that has been distributed to a group, think carefully about whether you need to reply only to the sender of the message or to the entire group. Automatically and unnecessarily replying to all members of a group bogs down the system, clutters people's e-mail boxes, and wastes time.

TO E(-MAIL) OR NOT TO E(-MAIL)

In some instances, employees should not use e-mail at all to communicate. Using e-mail might have negative consequences—for example, if a private message becomes public.

Suppose you must tell employees that your firm plans to downsize, and you plan to brief them about the effects of layoffs on their health insurance, sick leave, vacation, and retirement benefits. You could send a companywide e-mail message, distribute a memo, leave a message on a telephone voice-mail system, or talk with employees in person. If you send an e-mail message, you'll reach everyone quickly with this vital information. But because employees are likely to react emotionally and negatively to an announcement about layoffs, you probably would want to deliver the information face-to-face in small groups. Employees' needs for personal attention in the wake of distressing news outweigh the value of e-mail's speed and efficiency.

EXPRESS YOURSELF

One of the drawbacks when e-mail replaces a face-to-face conversation is that words on a computer screen often fail to convey intent or emotion. Nonverbal communication accounts for about 93 percent of an effective message. To compensate, e-mail users sometimes use abbreviations and "emoticons."

If you use such forms of e-mail shorthand, be sure everyone in the company understands them. If you use e-mail shorthand, define each abbreviation or emoticon the first time you use it: "LOL (laughing out loud) I could hardly contain myself." Some firms consider abbreviations and emoticons unprofessional and discourage their use, at least for external e-mail messages. In particular, if your company uses e-mail internationally, you should avoid shorthand as well as idioms and slang.

STRIVE FOR SUCCINCTNESS

Some e-mail experts compare the first screen display of an e-mail message with the first few seconds of a face-to-face conversation. In both instances, a first glance offers a brief opportunity to make a positive impression. Consider the following suggestions for capturing your reader's interest quickly:

> **Compose subject lines carefully.** In an e-mail message, the subject line is similar to the "regarding" line in a traditional memo. Except for the recipient's name, the subject line is the most important item in an e-mail message. Many e-mail users use the subject line as a tool for setting priorities. In the subject line, concisely indicate the content of the message. Instead of giving a general description ("E-Mail Training"), be specific ("E-Mail Communication Training, November 21, Training Room 3A").

> **Don't dilute your own message.** Stick to one topic when you send an e-mail message. If you try to cover too much ground, your reader might overlook some of your concerns. Practice writing complete but succinct messages by using the following "get-SET" technique:

> - State your purpose.
> - Expand it with pertinent details.
> - Tie the message up by summarizing or asking for action.

> When you reply to a message, remind the sender what he or she asked for. If necessary, include relevant text from the original message.

> **Use graphics judiciously.** Typographic elements such as bullets and lists can attract attention, but you should use them sparingly. And remember that some systems will not transmit italicized or boldface text. Do not type messages entirely in capital letters. Many users of electronic networks think of writing

in all caps as "flaming," or shouting. Messages typed entirely in capital letters also are harder to read than text written in capital and lowercase letters.

Write carefully. Write e-mail messages with the same care that you take with printed documents. Your grammar, spelling, and punctuation will affect others' perceptions of you.

Proofread. Reread all messages before you send them. If your message will reach many people, or if it is more than an informal note, print a hard (paper) copy and proofread it carefully. It's easier to read a hard copy than text on a screen.

E-MAIL ETIQUETTE

As electronic networks have become widely accessible, an on-line "netiquette" has developed. Keep these politeness pointers in mind when you communicate electronically.

When sending an e-mail message:

- Assume the message is permanent.
- Choose your recipients carefully; don't inundate people with information they don't need.
- Use a conversational but courteous tone. Offer any criticism kindly—don't insult people.
- Clearly indicate when you are expressing your opinion and when you are sharing facts.
- Do not rant or use offensive language.
- Get to the point. Limiting your message to one screen of text is a good rule of thumb.
- Use e-mail to foster connections, not to avoid face-to-face encounters.
- Use e-mail creatively; for instance, to offer feedback, to brainstorm electronically, and to give brief, on-line training sessions.

When receiving e-mail messages:

- Promptly forward messages intended for other receivers.
- Promptly respond to messages. (But if a message makes you angry or upset, give yourself time to relax and reflect before you answer.)
- Periodically purge your e-mailbox.
- Don't interrupt your work whenever messages arrive.

Barriers to Effective Listening

Jack E. Hulbert

Many communication problems are caused by poor listening habits. This article discusses the major barriers to effective listening and gives advice on overcoming them.

INTRODUCTION

Although listening is our most frequently used communication skill, it is perhaps our least effective communication skill. Research indicates that people spend approximately 70 percent of their waking hours communicating (i.e., listening, speaking, reading, and writing) and that about 45 percent of that time is spent in listening while only about 30 percent is spent in speaking, 16 percent in reading, and 9 percent in writing. Studies also reveal that immediately after listening to a ten-minute presentation, the average person has heard, understood, properly evaluated, and retained only about half of what was said and that within 48 hours retention decreases to only about 25 percent.

In business, the list of problems caused by poor listening is endless. Because of ineffective listening, letters have to be retyped, appointments have to be rescheduled, orders have to be reprocessed, products have to be remanufactured, and shipments have to be rerouted. Because of poor listening, employees cannot understand and satisfy customers' and clients' desires; and managers cannot understand and satisfy employees' needs. As a result, customers and clients are alienated; and unnecessary employee–employer conflicts disrupt operations and decrease productivity. Although it is impossible to calculate the exact cost, it has been estimated that poor listening costs American business billions of dollars annually.

To improve listening comprehension, one must overcome many barriers which interfere with listening efficiency. Understanding these listening barriers can help listeners surmount these obstacles and establish a climate conducive to effective communication. Listening barriers may be classified under the following headings: content, speaker, medium, distractions, mind set, language, listening speed, and feedback.

CONTENT

An obvious barrier to effective listening is the content of the message. Some listeners may feel that their knowledge of the subject is so extensive that they have little to learn from the speaker. They, therefore, pay little attention to what the speaker says.

Other listeners may feel that their background is too limited to provide an adequate basis for interpreting the speaker's remarks. They "tune out" at the first sign that the discussion will involve difficult intellectual or emotional content. Still other listeners are inclined to accept only information which agrees with their own beliefs and automatically reject any information which disagrees with their personal views and opinions. In these situations, poor listeners usually just sit back and wait for the speaker to finish; but little real communication occurs.

Effective listeners know that they must do more than passively allow sounds to enter their ears. They participate actively in the communication process by attempting to develop a positive attitude toward the speaker's message and consciously anticipate the importance of the message content. They discipline themselves to seek areas of interest in any message and constantly remind themselves that something of value can be learned from every message.

SPEAKER

The speaker has a significant effect on the listener's ability and willingness to listen. Even the speaker's delivery—enunciation, organization, clarity, speed, volume, tone, inflections, emotions, and appearance—affects the listener's willingness and ability to interpret the message. Research indicates that listeners are influenced more strongly by their attitudes toward the speaker than by the information presented. If listeners like the speaker, they are much more likely to empathize with his or her viewpoint, and, therefore, agree with—or at least more fully comprehend—the speaker's message.

Good listeners are aware of these pitfalls to effective listening and attempt to elicit maximum message meaning by concentrating on the "what" of the message rather than on the "who" of the speaker or the "how" of his or her delivery.

MEDIUM

Another variable affecting listening is the medium through which the message is transmitted—because the distance between the listener and speaker has a strong impact on the amount of listening effort required. Contrary to what might be expected, least listening effort is required when the speaker is not visible—as with radio or recorded messages. Increasing amounts of effort are required as the speaker becomes visible—as with televised or filmed messages. And, maximum listening effort is necessary when the speaker is physically present and speaking directly to the listener. This phenomenon occurs in face-to-face communication because the amount and variety of input or stimuli is a potential source of confusion and disruption of message meaning. In face-to-face conversation, the listener receives rich—and sometimes conflicting—verbal and nonverbal stimuli about the subject matter, the speaker's emotional state, and the speaker's feelings about the listener. Although face-to-face communication provides the richest variety of stimuli and, therefore, offers potential for multiple levels of meaning and deeper understanding, good listeners realize that face-to-face communication increases the listening effort necessary for message comprehension.

DISTRACTIONS

It is well known that listeners are easily distracted by almost any extraneous stimuli—sounds, lights, odors, mannerisms, voice inflections, or moving objects. Psychological studies indicate that a listener's attention span is sometimes no more than two or three seconds. If listeners' already short attention spans are disrupted by distractions, they may miss part or all of the message meaning by the time they refocus on what the speaker is saying.

In the broad sense, any factor that interferes with the accurate transmission and reception of a message may be classified as a distraction. Distractions may be caused by environmental factors, such as noisy equipment, loud traffic, or other talking; or they may be linked to physical problems, such as impaired hearing or vision. However, distractions are most frequently related to psychological factors arising from differences between the speaker's and listener's frames of reference, emotions, values, understandings, experiences, or cultural backgrounds.

Good listeners constantly monitor the listening environment in an effort to identify and eradicate distractions. If environmental distractions cannot be eliminated, they attempt to overcome these obstacles with increased concentration. In addition, they consciously endeavor to eliminate psychological distractions by freeing themselves from preconceptions, prejudices, and negative emotions in order to develop open minds receptive to new ideas.

MIND SET

Because listening is an extremely subjective process, obstacles to effective listening can arise from the listeners' attitudes about themselves, others, and the environment. People perceive the world through their own personal "mind filters" structured by their unique physical, mental, and emotional characteristics. Therefore, each listener approaches a message with a unique mind set which influences message comprehension.

The listener's mind set about the speaker or the subject matter can either magnify or diminish certain stimuli and thereby distort message meaning. If a listener expects to hear certain things based upon preconceptions about the subject or the speaker's personality and background, information conflicting with the listener's mind set is frequently ignored. On the other hand, the listener may attach unintended importance to some of the speaker's statements since the portion of a message to which the listener assigns greatest importance is largely determined by his or her mind set.

Effective listeners realize that differences in the speaker's and listener's mind sets can pose a major barrier to understanding. They know that listeners can be immobilized by emotional static when listening to a speaker whose mind set differs from their own. Therefore, they continuously strive not to allow their personal biases to interfere with message comprehension.

Good listeners have the courage to be objective and flexible and are, therefore, willing to permit others the freedom to hold their personal values and beliefs. They realize that attempting to understand another's viewpoint does not necessitate agreeing with it. They respect the rights of speakers with whom they disagree and are intellectually capable of acknowledging the feasibility of more than one acceptable point of view.

LANGUAGE

Although the primary function of language is to facilitate understanding, at times language can be a barrier to effective comprehension because ambiguity is an innate characteristic of any language.

Listeners rarely hear every word spoken and frequently attach different meanings from those intended by the speaker to the words they do hear. Obviously, listeners are apt to misinterpret words which are not part of their vocabulary. They are also likely to misinterpret words which are imprecise, emotional, technical, or overly intellectual. However, the greatest cause of misunderstanding is probably the fact that listeners interpret words according to their own personal definitions determined by their background, education, and experience—which are likely to be quite different from those of the speaker.

Listening efficiency can be improved if listeners realize that the same words frequently have different meanings for different people. Good listeners understand that words are simply symbols with little or no intrinsic meaning. They realize that the meaning of a word is in the speaker's and listener's minds, not in the word. They know that the meaning of a word is strongly affected by the context in which it is used and that that context is at least two dimensional when viewed from the speaker's and listener's unique perspectives.

LISTENING SPEED

Another major barrier to effective listening arises from the difference between listening and speaking speeds. The average person speaks at a rate of between 125 and 150 words a minute while the average listener can comprehend information at about 500 words a minute. This difference in speaking and listening speeds affords the listener a great deal of excess thinking time.

Instead of using this excess time to concentrate on the speaker's message, poor listeners indulge in daydreaming. When they finally return from their mental tangents, they frequently find they have missed part of what the speaker said and the speaker's meaning is confused, if not totally lost.

In contrast, effective listeners use this excess thinking time to:

- Outline mentally the speaker's message.
- Identify the speaker's purpose and determine how the speaker's points support that purpose.
- Evaluate the soundness of the speaker's logic.
- Verify and integrate information presented with past knowledge and experience.
- Maintain eye contact in order to observe and interpret the speaker's nonverbal signals.
- Formulate questions to ask at appropriate moments in order to verify the accuracy of their understanding.
- Provide encouraging verbal and nonverbal feedback.

In other words, effective listeners use their excess thinking capacity to elicit as much meaning as possible from the speaker's message.

FEEDBACK

When listeners provide inappropriate feedback, they hinder the speaker's ability to provide complete and honest information. In general, people are far more driven to speak than to listen and, therefore, listeners often respond with premature comments or evaluations before fully understanding the speaker's viewpoint. This premature feedback can cause speakers to say things they do not mean or divert them to irrelevant tangents. In addition, if listeners respond with indifference or color their feedback with emotions of resentment, defensiveness, or suspicion, they greatly decrease the possibility for effective communication.

Good listeners provide appropriate supportive feedback by:

- Demonstrating interest in what the speaker says.
- Maintaining appropriate eye contact.
- Smiling and showing animation.
- Nodding occasionally in agreement.
- Leaning toward the speaker to demonstrate an attitude of interest and confidentiality.
- Using verbal reinforcers like "I see" and "yes."
- Phrasing interpretations of the speaker's comments to verify understanding.
- Consciously timing their verbal and nonverbal feedback to assist rather than hinder the speaker.

Good listeners know that by providing appropriate empathetic feedback they can create a supportive listening atmosphere in which speakers are encouraged to provide complete, honest disclosure.

Summary

Listening is a highly selective, subjective process with many barriers to accurate comprehension. Because the average person has developed and reinforced careless listening habits through countless hours of social and recreational listening, it is difficult for many people to listen effectively in business or problem-solving situations. In fact, the message ultimately deciphered by the average listener frequently differs markedly from the speaker's original thought.

Awareness of the barriers to effective listening and how to combat these obstacles to accurate comprehension is vital to the development of efficient listening skills. Although research indicates that the average person listens at only about 25 percent efficiency, it is encouraging to note that in organizations that have instituted listening instruction employee comprehension has as much as doubled in just a few months.

Business Manners

Ann Chadwell Humphries

Successful professionals must understand appropriate etiquette for typical business situations. Knowing proper business etiquette will instill confidence and help you respond effectively to others in the workplace. This article reviews common etiquette mistakes and gives advice on how to avoid making them.

COMMON ETIQUETTE BLUNDERS

1. **Being rude on the telephone.** This, the most common business etiquette blunder, includes not returning phone calls promptly, not identifying oneself, and screening calls arrogantly. Always return calls within 24 hours—and preferably the same day. Identify yourself and the nature of your business up front; anticipate resistance and be helpful. And help people get the information they need. Avoid overly protecting the boss with questions too directly asked, such as, "What is the nature of your call?"

2. **Interrupting.** Let people finish their sentences, and ask permission if you need to interrupt their work. Don't barge into conversations or offices without giving a signal.

3. **Introducing people incorrectly.** Say the most important person's name first, then the secondary person's. In the workplace today, the most important persons—regardless of sex or age—are outside guests, officially titled people, and superiors. "Outside visitor, this is our company President." "Mayor, this is our Vice-President of Marketing." "Boss, this is an employee of 35 years."

4. **Wimpy or vise grip handshakes.** Wimpy handshakes or overpowering grips are no-noes. Grab your handshake high, around the thumbs, and shake in kind. Don't swoop on delicate folks, or withdraw from an acrobatic handshaker. And women—get your hand out there! Men hesitate to initiate this action. They've been taught to wait for a lady to extend her hand first. Handshakes are expected in business life. So learn to shake hands well, and offer yours easily.

5. **Incorrect eye contact.** In the United States, looking people in the eye means you have nothing to hide, that you are listening, that you are interested. In certain other cultures, however, direct eye contact is considered confrontational and disrespectful. Vary eye contact from short glances to longer holds of 3–5 seconds, but don't stare to make yourself look good. You will be overbearing.

6. **Poorly managed business meetings.** Start and end them on time. Distribute agendas ahead of time so people can prepare. If you are the leader, control the action. Don't suppress confrontation, or it will emerge elsewhere. But you can defer it to a more appropriate time. Last, limit telephone calls to the leader, so the group will not be held up.

7. **Poor or inappropriate appearance.** To the business executive, appearance is important. It's not the only measure of a person, but it does give visual interest to doing business and indicates your knowledge of, and respect for, the rules of the game. You must dress with understated distinction to be considered seriously in business. Invest in quality clothing, and be impeccably groomed.

8. **Forgetting names.** Ask anybody about his or her most uncomfortable business etiquette dilemma and forgetting names will emerge in the top five. To help you remember names, one positive strategy is to repeat the person's name as soon as you hear it, and to use the name at least once if you have a long conversation. Don't over-use a person's name, however.

But when you don't remember someone's name, there are several simple strategies to follow. Use your judgment about which is most appropriate for, and least embarrassing to, you and the other people involved.

a. **Introduce yourself first.** This is for the occasion—either in a one-on-one conversation or if you're part of a group—when you only vaguely remember the person. Introducing yourself helps take people off the spot.

b. **Stall for time.** When you know the person, but it takes a few minutes for your mind to compute the name, act friendly and don't withdraw. Don't sport the "Charlie Brown" nervous smile. Focus on them, not yourself.

c. **Introduce the people you do know.** Pause to let those whose names you don't remember introduce themselves. Or, say lightly, "I'm so sorry. I know who you are. I've just gone blank." Or, "I've just forgotten your name," with an implied, "Silly me." Keep the conversation going with what you do remember.

d. **Help out someone who looks as if he or she is struggling to remember *your* name.** This is not pompous or arrogant; it's considerate. Many people slur their names so they're unintelligible, or present themselves in an ordinary manner, so they aren't memorable. Take care when you introduce yourself.

Combating Speech Anxiety

Myles Martel

Most speakers suffer from anxiety before making an oral presentation. This article provides guidelines for controlling and de-emphasizing fear of public speaking. Read the guidelines before making an oral presentation.

Call it stage fright, speech fright, speech or communicator anxiety or apprehension, its symptoms are unmistakable and its significance as a barrier to effective presentations cannot be overstressed.

A quaking voice, trembling knees, erratic pacing or rocking, stomach butterflies, pronounced monotone, a deadpan facial expression, and lack of eye contact are common cues that the speaker is experiencing the malady I prefer to call speech anxiety—a tension-laden self-consciousness which dominates the speaker's concern for communicating ideas.

Few speakers are immune from this phenomenon. Leaders in all professions in all ages have experienced speech anxiety, regardless of status, sex, intelligence, age or income. Sir Winston Churchill remarked that when he began to speak he felt as if there were a nine-inch block of ice in the pit of his stomach. And Cicero said, "I turn pale at the outset of a speech and quake in every limb and in all my soul."

Communication experts and psychologists are not certain about the precise causes of speech anxiety. The most popular explanation, however, calls it a form of approach-avoidance conflict. On the one hand, the speaker may feel impelled to represent the organization, while on the other, feel pulled in the opposite direction by another dominant force, often by some fear of failure.

Speech anxiety has no sure-fire cures, but it can be alleviated by a proper attitude toward (1) the anxiety, (2) the self, (3) the audience, (4) preparation and practice, and (5) delivery.

ATTITUDE TOWARD SPEECH ANXIETY

1. Recognize that most if not all speakers experience some form of normal nervous anxiety. If you feel a little anxious, don't panic. Say to yourself that you have normal nervous anxiety, which you can control—not eliminate.

2. Consider the normal nervous anxiety to be potentially helpful. Your anxiety may motivate you to speak with greater forcefulness, and result in a more animated presentation.

3. Realize that your anxiety state is often much more obvious to you than to your audience.

4. Don't be afraid to admit to your speech anxiety in discussions with friends or colleagues.

Attitude Toward Self

1. Think "expert." With few exceptions you would not be making an appearance if the host did not feel you had something of value to share with your audience.

2. Assume a 100 percent attitude regarding your engagement. Many speakers have a tendency to take on a "less than" attitude toward the engagement, often not realizing that this attitude may reflect their own fear of coping with the challenge to communicate. The ability to "wing it" is a talent presumed by many but possessed by all too few.

Attitude Toward the Audience

1. Regard the audience as being composed mainly of friendly listeners with whom you will be engaging in an enlarged conversation.

2. Don't overreact to hostility, disagreement, lack of interest or apparent confusion.

Attitude Toward Preparation

1. Understand what a speech is, the specific means by which it can be prepared and practiced.

2. Avoid memorization. Fear of forgetting normally generates tension, self-consciousness and other unnatural delivery characteristics.

3. Learn how to speak extemporaneously from a carefully prepared outline consisting of key words and phrases. Conscientiously practice expressing each idea without "overscripting" yourself into memorized passages. Practicing with audio or videotapes while standing in front of one or more constructive critics can be especially helpful. Practicing in front of a mirror, despite the popularity of this advice, can be counterproductive; it can make you more concerned with your body than with your message.

4. Analyze the audience, occasion and setting well in advance. Learning about the demographic and attitudinal composition of your audience, the layout of the room and the specifics of the program can diminish your normal fear of the unknown.

5. Prepare a neat, well-spaced and well-selected set of notes with delivery advice and notations.

6. Devote extra efforts to creating within the speech itself an impactful introduction that captures the audience's attention, enhances your credibility and orients the audience toward your subject.

7. Do your best to be well-introduced. Send a suggested introduction to the host and always have a copy with you in case the host has lost the original.

8. Avoid major last-minute changes in your outline. The natural anxiety produced by the engagement may prevent you from handling such changes well.

9. Arrive early and mingle with the audience. This will help you to regard them as individuals with whom you can hold an enlarged conversation rather than as an unknown, fear-provoking mass of people.

10. Try relaxation exercises shortly before your appearance. Isometrics and deep-breathing exercises can be especially helpful.

11. To relieve your television or radio talk-show jitters it may help to have a friend ask you immediately before your appearance a few warm-up questions.

ATTITUDE TOWARD DELIVERY

1. Gesture and move around purposefully (when a lectern is not present) to reinforce the message physically, while you simultaneously create a natural outlet for your nervous anxiety.

2. Establish and maintain direct and distributed eye contact with the audience. The more you establish eye contact, the less you will be struck with fear of the unknown. Also, you will be better able to respond to their feedback with an enlarged-conversation frame of mind. The popular advice "pick a friendly face" may be helpful when you need visual reassurance, but don't concentrate on this person for too long.

3. Consider using visual aids. Flip charts in particular are effective means of inducing natural bodily movement.

Probably no one has ever conquered speech anxiety by just reading about it. Reading merely provides the insights to be applied in real speaking situations. The more you seek these situations and systematically prepare for them, the more confident—and compelling—you should become.

It's All in the Links: Readying Publications for the Web

Mindy McAdams

This article provides guidelines for creating useful hypertext links in electronic documents. The author includes cautions about common mistakes writers make.

If there were a single door leading to the World Wide Web, someone might hang a giant sign on it reading **EDITORS WANTED.** Adapting existing documents for use on the Web (or on an Intranet, an in-house-only version of the Web) is a distinctly editorial process that today is often handled by graphic designers or, in some cases, by automation.

Editors who want to work with Web documents should start by learning HTML (hypertext markup language), the code on which the World Wide Web is built. HTML isn't a programming language; it's a system of codes for tagging structural elements in a document. Motivated people can master basic HTML from a book in three or four days—it's no more complex than the editing codes that most newspaper copyeditors are required to learn.

HTML codes tag elements, such as headings and paragraphs, according to their purpose in the document. They can also define links between related documents like a set of pamphlets on employee benefits or the five parts of a serial newspaper article.

READABILITY CAN BE BUILT IN

The biggest difference between reading on-line and reading printed text is that on-line the text moves. You're scrolling up and down. As you scroll, you tend to scan the document. The environment urges you to speed-read, so if you don't see anything but plain text, you're likely to lose interest.

Two simple practices greatly increase the readability of on-line texts:

- Use headings and boldface more than you would in print.
- Keep paragraphs short.

Boldface headings enhance the reader's ability to scan text rapidly. In print, too many headings make a page look clunky and disjointed, but on-line headings disappear off the top of the screen as the reader scrolls down. As a rule of thumb, one heading per screen of text within a document works very well.

Headings aren't just window dressing. Each should provide a clear predictor of the content of the paragraphs below it. Try to spare speed-hungry on-line users from reading anything they aren't absolutely interested in.

Boldface or italics used to highlight key phrases in the text function much as pull-out quotes do in print, but without the redundancy. Boldface can eliminate the need for headings where they would be intrusive or inappropriate, as in brief documents (400 words or less).

Using short paragraphs with a line space between them also facilitates scanning. Just as you would break up a long printed article in which the writer had neglected to use any paragraphs, so in an on-line article you must break long paragraphs into two or three shorter ones.

HYPERTEXT LINKS ARE KEY

Hypertext, the most powerful feature of HTML, is fundamental and also unique to electronic publishing. A word or phrase in the text is underlined or highlighted. When you mouse-click on that word, a new document comes onto your screen. The highlighted text is similar to a footnote numeral—it refers you elsewhere—but it usually links to another large block of text, not a small note.

The text of a hypertext link can be a title (the link goes to a document with that title), a person's name (the link may go to a biographical sketch or résumé), a word (the link may go to a dictionary definition)—or any phrase or clause. Choosing or writing a good phrase or clause to use as a link requires editorial talent.

The cardinal sin of link-making is to use the words "click here." (You'll see those words all over the Web. Many people sin.) A link exists to be clicked, and to say so in the link text is a sorry waste of words.

WRITING STRONG LINK TEXT

The text used for the link should, first and foremost, produce a reasonable expectation in the user. If the link is a button that reads **HOME,** the user will expect to go to the site's home page (or first page).

If a link said, "Find out more about our product," would you be disappointed if that link went to an e-mail form that provided nothing new but invited you to write for additional information? A better link would say, "Contact us to find out more."

Consider this text:

Find out <u>who we are</u> and let <u>us</u> know what you'd like to see.

Can you guess, without following the two links, how "who we are" and "us" might be different? They actually lead to two different documents: "About This Site" and a page of Web staff bios. This would be a better way to write the links:

Find out <u>about our Web site</u> and let <u>us</u> know . . .

Link text can't always include active verbs, but a keen editor can often figure out a way to enliven a passive clause or dull phrase: "Our annual report is now on-line" can become "Read our annual report on-line," and "Membership form" can become "Apply for membership today."

AVOIDING CARELESS LINKS

It's a shame to waste the power of links by creating them randomly. Consider their cumulative effect on your on-line readers and avoid the following kinds of pitfalls:

Excessive Use of Links.   When links appear in almost every line of a document, users are less likely to follow *any* link at all (who has the time?). By eliminating links that are irrelevant, extraneous, or redundant, you do a great favor for busy, impatient users. Reference lists and search engines exist for anyone who wants to find every site related to a given topic.

Irrelevant or Extraneous Links.   My favorite example is the word *Washington,* which appeared as a link in a news article about an action in Congress. Clicking it took me to a page about tourist attractions in the U.S. capital. Yes, it was a page about Washington, but it wasn't directly related to the article where the link appeared. Such links waste users' time and erode their faith in your ability to lead them to something good.

Gratuitous Use of External Links.   You can fill a document with links that go to Web sites all around the world, but keep in mind that a person who leaves your site may never return. The more you send them away, the greater the impression that your own site has little to offer. Provide links to exemplary external sites as appropriate, especially when they add useful information that your site can't provide. But don't send people away without a good reason.

A Dearth of Link Options.   If a Web page has only one link, it may as well be printed on paper. Never try to force a single path on the user. Making choices is what interactivity is all about.

Breaking up Large Articles

In print a reader can flip a few pages and read the last paragraph (or read all the headings, or look at all the photos). A long article formatted as a Web page takes more time to load—to come on screen—than a shorter one. Because of the linear scrolling path from top to bottom, the user's ability to scan a very long article is reduced.

Careful use of hypertext removes this limitation and makes a longer article more pleasant to read on-line—and more work for an editor to prepare. The relationship is a direct one: The more effort an editor puts into breaking up a long article and linking the pieces intelligently, the more engaging that article will be.

Basic Tasks of Hypertext Editing

The four basic tasks a hypertext editor undertakes contribute much to the effectiveness and appeal of an on-line document.

1. **Finding appropriate places to break.** The writer may have already divided the article into sections, but the editor usually will have to split up the article even further. Base your decisions on content, on presenting a whole idea. Try to make each piece as independent as possible. Sometimes this means you'll delete or rewrite transition sentences.

2. **Deciding how long each piece should be.** The broken-out pieces don't have to be of equal length, but the goal is to keep them all relatively short (500 words is a good average, although it's too short for some kinds of material). In some cases, one piece will be much longer or shorter than all the others.

3. **Creating the link structure.** If there are very few pieces (three or four), they might be best handled as sidebars, with the titles of all related pieces listed (as links) at the end of each one. (That structure provides access to any part of the article from any other part, which is good.) A larger number of pieces

can be more intricately interwoven. Provide contextual links so that users can skip around, choosing their own paths, but also give them the option to follow a traditional path through the article (using "next" and "previous" as links, if appropriate).

4. **Providing an overview.** When an article is broken into a dozen or more parts, users appreciate the option of glimpsing the whole cloth before following a thread. The overview may be structured as a table of contents (list), a map (graphics), or an abstract or introduction (text) that has links to all the pieces on one page. Each piece of the article should include a link to the overview.

THE ON-LINE READER IS A MOVING TARGET

Construct your set of documents in such a way that users can easily skip the things they don't care about but won't miss the things they like.

Remember that users are always moving—scrolling up and down and jumping from link to link. They don't like to be still. They don't like to sit with their hands folded in their laps. This doesn't mean they are impossible to grab. They'll stop and read when something catches their eye. The trick is to hang onto them long enough.

Prepare, Listen, Follow Up

Max Messmer

For an effective job search, you need to gather information about opportunities in your field. This article provides guidelines for arranging and conducting an information-seeking interview with someone in your field.

Begin your informational interview campaign by writing down the names of people, organizations, and industries that interest you. Define the topics you want to explore. Clarify how these subjects relate to your work experience and career objectives. As you build your contact list and start making phone calls, remember to be persistent and maintain a positive attitude.

DEFINING YOUR OBJECTIVES

Many job seekers make the strategic error of phoning someone and immediately asking if there are any available positions. It's not likely a job will be open precisely when you call. It's more likely that your abrupt inquiry will place the person you're speaking with in the uncomfortable position of having to say, "No, I'm sorry, I can't help you."

Instead, let the contact know you're on a fact-finding mission to learn more about the industry. Productive informational interviews require listening. In most cases, people are flattered and receptive when asked to talk freely about their profession and experience.

A KNOWLEDGE-DRIVEN INQUIRY

In preparing for your informational interview, you should go through the same rigorous process you would undertake prior to a job interview. Be as thorough as you can in defining the topics you intend to discuss. Study and take notes on business publications, books, and corporate literature. Utilize resources on the Internet, CD-ROMs at libraries, and other databases for relevant information about the industries and companies you're contacting. This knowledge-driven approach will enable you to demonstrate both intellect and enthusiasm—two assets that must come across in any interview setting.

Another effective technique is to bring with you information of direct value to the person with whom you're meeting. It could be a book, an article, or even a report that you developed in the past. This is a no-lose opportunity. Be prepared to discuss your current situation—your skills, accomplishments, and current job-seeking objectives. You also should have available several copies of your resume and business cards.

GATEKEEPERS ARE YOUR ALLIES

As you make phone calls requesting informational interviews, you are likely to run into "gatekeepers" who will screen calls. Treat these professionals with the utmost

506

courtesy. Introduce yourself and politely try to establish a relationship. In the course of these short conversations, the gatekeeper might even tell you about others in the company who might be willing to meet with you. If you try to bypass gatekeepers, you run the risk of creating an adversarial relationship, thus damaging your cause.

CLARIFY TIME AND PURPOSE

Once the meeting begins, verify exactly how much time the person has available. It's also valuable to have an established agenda. Remind the person you're talking to that your objective is informational: You want to ask questions and learn more so that your job search is as productive as possible.

LISTEN CAREFULLY

Provided it is acceptable to the other person, you should take notes during your meeting so that you can retain as much information as possible. However, your note taking should not interfere with the flow of the conversation. Listen attentively, write down major ideas, and underline key points. You'll have time after the interview to transcribe your notes.

Typical questions to ask are:

- What are some of the challenges of working in this field?
- What skills or experience do you feel are most important for success in this industry/profession?
- What type of background is most suitable?
- How long have you been in this industry/profession? What did you do before?
- Why did you choose this field?
- What are some new developments in your industry? (You should have some knowledge of trends prior to the meeting.)

FOLLOW THROUGH IS CRITICAL

Monitor the length of your meeting. As it nears the agreed-upon finish, it is your responsibility to respect the other person's time by politely inquiring if he or she can talk further.

At the close of the interview, ask for names of others you could contact for information. Then within a day or two of your meeting, send a short thank-you note. In the weeks that follow, keep in touch with your new contacts by sending them relevant news articles that relate to their industry or profession, or phoning them to give them progress updates on your job search.

The time you invest conducting informational interviews will prove invaluable in expanding your career network. You will gain insight into various corporations, industries, and hiring trends, and you'll have a chance to practice talking about your own talents and experience in a less formal setting than an official job interview.

Meeting Technology: From Low-Tech to High-Tech

Mary Munter

This article describes a series of low-tech and high-tech options for use in meeting management and summarizes the advantages and disadvantages of each. These options include (1) face-to-face meetings, with choices of flipcharts, nonelectronic boards, electronic boards, handouts, still projectors, and mutimedia projectors; and (2) groupware meetings, with choices of audio- and videoconferencing, e-mail meetings, and electronic meetings.

From the long ago past, when people first met in their caves, to the future, when holograms may meet in collaboratories, the latest technological changes are only as effective as the people using them. Therefore, consider the ideas discussed in this article to make your use of meeting technology wise and productive. Thinking about the advantages and disadvantages of each technological option will help you make informed decisions, capitalize on advantages, and overcome disadvantages.

When you are choosing technologies to use in a meeting, however, always consider four general questions first:

1. *Group expectations:* What are the expectations of your particular group, organization, and culture? Some groups expect and always use a certain kind of equipment. For some groups, certain kinds of equipment would be perceived as too slick, flashy, or technical. For other groups, not using the latest technology would be perceived as too old-fashioned.

2. *Timing and location issues:* Do you need people to participate at the same or different times? Are they in the same or multiple locations?

3. *Group size:* Consider also the number of people in your audience. For example, a group of three might be easier to convene face-to-face; a group of fifteen might be easier to convene electronically.

4. *Resource availability:* Finally, be realistic about the equipment and resources you have available.

Then, consider the following meeting options: face-to-face meetings in the same site or groupware meetings in multiple sites (including teleconferences, e-mail meetings, or electronic meetings).

FACE-TO-FACE MEETINGS (IN THE SAME SITE)

Use the lowest-tech option—the face-to-face meeting—when nonverbal, human contact is especially important.

- *Advantages of face-to-face meetings:* Face-to-face meetings are appropriate (1) when you need the richest nonverbal cues, including body, voice, proximity, and touch; (2) when the issues are especially sensitive; (3) when the people don't know one another; (4) when establishing group rapport and relationships are crucial; and (5) when the participants can be in the same place at the same time. Because they are less technologically complex, systems are easier to use, less likely to crash, and less likely to have compatibility problems.

- *Disadvantages of face-to-face meetings:* Such meetings (1) do not allow the possibility of simultaneous participation by people in multiple locations; (2) can delay meeting follow-up activities because decisions and action items must be written up after the meeting; and (3) may be dominated by overly vocal, quick-to-speak, and higher-status participants.

When you are meeting face-to-face, choose from among various technologies—flipcharts, traditional boards, copy boards, electronic boards, handouts, or projectors.

Option 1: Using FlipCharts and Nonelectronic Boards

Flipcharts include large standing charts and small desktop charts; nonelectronic boards include blackboards and whiteboards. Charts and boards often elicit a great deal of group discussion because they are so low-tech that they are nonthreatening and unintimidating to certain kinds of participants and because they work in a brightly lit room. Additional advantages of flipcharts are that they can be taped up around the room for reference during the session and taken with you for a permanent record at the end of the session. On the downside, they may appear unprofessional and too low-tech for certain groups; they cannot show complex images; and they are too small to be used for large groups. Additional drawbacks of nonelectronic boards are that you must erase to regain free space and they do not provide hard copy.

Option 2: Using Electronic Boards

Electronic boards come in two varieties. Electronic "copy" boards look like traditional white boards, but they can provide a hard copy of what was written on them—unlike nonelectronic boards, which need to be erased when they are full. Electronic "live" boards provide digitized hard copy of documents, computer files, and other two-dimensional objects and can be annotated real-time.

Option 3: Using Handouts

Handouts also come in two varieties: paper or electronic. The advantage of all handouts is that they provide group members with hard copy, can show complex data, and can be used for participant notetaking. The advantage of electronic over paper is that participants can access the information when they want it from the network or disk, instead of having to carry paper with them. The disadvantage of handouts is that participants can read ahead of what you are currently discussing and become distracted. To overcome that disadvantage, give only those handouts you don't mind people reading ahead at the beginning of your meeting, give handouts on detailed information exactly when you are discussing it, and save detailed summary handouts you don't want your audience to read ahead until the end of the meeting.

Option 4: Using Still Projectors

You can also annotate on two kinds of still projectors, although some people associate such projectors with noninteractive presentations, so they may be less likely to talk. One option, overhead projectors, uses acetate sheets and special marking pens (which are not the same as flipchart markers). A second option, document cameras, also known as electronic overheads or visualizers, is more convenient because it uses regular paper (or any two-dimensional or three-dimensional object) instead of acetate slides, but the resolution is not as high as that of an overhead projector.

Option 5: Using Multimedia Large-Screen Projectors

Multimedia projectors (for computer or video images) come in three varieties: (1) three-beam projectors have the best quality and resolution, but are not portable; (2) self-illuminating LCD projectors have moderate quality and resolution (although they are improving); some are medium weight and compact enough to move; (3) LCD projectors that use an overhead projector as a light source have lower quality resolution than the others, but they are the easiest to move.

GROUPWARE MEETINGS (USUALLY IN MULTIPLE SITES)

Unlike the face-to-face meetings discussed so far, the following higher-tech kinds of meetings use different kinds of "groupware"—a broad term for a group of related technologies that mediate group collaboration through technology—that may include any combination of collaborative software or intraware, electronic- and voice-mail systems, electronic meeting systems, phone systems, video systems, electronic boards, and group document handling and annotation systems—variously known as teleconferencing, computer conferencing, document conferencing, screen conferencing, GDSS (group decision support systems), or CSCW (computer-supported cooperative work). Groupware participants may communicate with one another through telephones or through personal computers with either individual screens or a shared screen.

- *Advantages of groupware:* Groupware meetings are especially useful (1) for working with geographically dispersed groups—because they give you the choice of meeting at different places/same time, or different places/different times, or the same place/same time, or same place/different times; and (2) for speeding up meeting follow-up activities because decisions and action items may be recorded electronically

- *Disadvantages of groupware:* Such meetings (1) lack richest nonverbal cues of body, voice, proximity, and touch simultaneously; (2) are not as effective when establishing new group rapport and relationships are crucial; (3) may be harder to use and more likely to crash than low-tech equipment like flipcharts and overheads.

Groupware Option 1: Teleconferencing

Teleconferencing may take place on a large screen in a dedicated conference room with a dedicated circuit; on television screens in multiple rooms; on desktop computers with small cameras installed, using a shared resource like the Internet; or on telephones. Audioconference participants hear one another's voices. Videoconference participants see and hear one another on video. In addition, they may also be able to (1) view documents and objects via document cameras and (2) see notes taken on electronic live boards (some of which can be annotated in only one location, but viewed in multiple locations; others of which can be annotated and viewed in multiple locations and may have application-sharing capabilities as well).

- *Advantages of teleconferencing:* Teleconferences are useful (1) when the participants are in different places, but you want to communicate with them all at the same time; (2) when you want to save on travel time and expenses; (3) when you want to inform, explain, or train (as opposed to persuade or sell); (4) when you do not need the richest nonverbal cues, such as proximity and touch; and (5) in the case of audioconferencing when vocal cues are sufficient to meet your needs, you do not need the richer nonverbal cues of body language, or you need a quick response without much setup time.

- *Drawbacks of teleconferencing:* (1) They are usually not as effective as face-to-face meetings when you need to persuade or to establish a personal relationship; (2) fewer people tend to speak and they speak in longer bursts than in other kinds of meetings; and (3) in the case of audioconferencing, they do not include visual communication or body language.

Groupware Option 2: E-mail Meetings

E-mail meetings differ from other kinds of meetings in several ways. They differ (1) from electronic meetings because participants respond at different times and their responses are not coordinated through a facilitator; (2) from teleconferencing because responses usually consist of words and numbers only, with no nonverbal cues—except those provided by emoticons such as :-) and :-(or unless participants have the ability to scan in documents or animation; (3) from face-to-face meetings because participants may be in different places at different times and because they lack the richest nonverbal cues of body, voice, proximity, and touch. Although it may be possible to mediate e-mail meetings on some systems, I am using the term "e-mail meetings" to refer to unmediated meetings and the term "electronic meetings," as described below, to refer to mediated meetings.

- *Advantages of e-mail meetings:* At its best, e-mail can (1) increase participation because it overcomes dominance by overly vocal and quick-to-speak participants; (2) increase communication across hierarchical boundaries; (3) decrease writing inhibitions—using simpler sentences, briefer paragraphs, and a conversational style with active verbs and less pompous language than in traditional writing; (4) increase transmission time when you are circulating documents; and (5) speed up meeting follow-up activities because all decisions and action items are recorded electronically and can be distributed electronically

- *Disadvantages of e-mail:* At its worst, e-mail can (1) decrease attention to the person receiving the message and to social context and regulation; (2) be inappropriately informal; (3) consist of "quick and dirty" messages, with typos and grammatical errors, and, more importantly, lack logical frameworks for readers—such as headings and transitions; (4) increase use of excessive language and other irresponsible and destructive behavior—including blistering messages sent without thinking, known as "flaming"; and (5) overload receivers with trivia and unnecessary information. Two final problems with e-mail are that the sender cannot control if and when a receiver chooses to read a message and that, because the message is electronic, it is less private than hard copy.

Groupware Option 3: Electronic Meetings

Unlike e-mail meetings, electronic meetings utilize a trained technical facilitator who must be proficient at using EMS and at managing group control. Electronic meetings automate all of the traditional meeting techniques—such as brainstorming (sometimes called "brainwriting" when performed on-line), recording ideas on flipcharts and tacking them to the wall, organizing ideas, ranking ideas, examining alternatives, making suggestions, casting votes, planning for implementation, and writing meeting minutes—all electronically

Participants meet using a keyboard and screen, usually from their individual workstations, with information appearing and becoming updated real-time on all participants' screens simultaneously. However, in addition to the possibility of being at their workstations (different place/same time), participants can be in a dedicated room with a large screen (same place/same time) or at either place participating at their convenience (same place/different time or different place/different time).

Participants communicate by viewing and manipulating words, numbers, documents, spreadsheets, shared electronic files, and, sometimes, computer-generated graphics, presentations, or images.

- *Advantages of EMS:* Electronic meetings (1) like all the options except face-to-face meetings, are useful when the participants are geographically dispersed or when you want to save on travel time and expenses; (2) unlike email, are mediated and usually data are entered and viewed by all participants simultaneously, but can be used by participants at different times at their convenience; (3) can maximize audience participation and in-depth discussion because everyone can "speak" simultaneously, so shy members are more likely to participate and the "vocal few" are less likely to dominate the discussion; (4) unlike any other option, allow the possibility of anonymous input, which may lead to more candid and truthful replies, equalize participants' status, and increase participation among hierarchical levels (with some programs offering the choice to self-identify or not, and others making it impossible for even the facilitator to tell each participant's identity); (5) can lead to better agenda management and keeping on task; (6) can generate more ideas and alternatives quicker than with a traditional note taker; and (7) can provide immediate documentation when the meeting is finished.

- *Disadvantages of EMS:* EMS (1) cannot replace face-to-face contact, especially when group efforts are just beginning and when you are trying to build group values, trust, and emotional ties; (2) may exacerbate dysfunctional group dynamics and increased honesty may lead to increased conflict; (3) may make it harder to reach consensus, because more ideas are generated and because it may be harder to interpret the strength of other members' commitment to their proposals; (4) depend on all participants having excellent keyboarding skills to engage in rapid-fire, in-depth discussion (at least until voice-recognition technology, which converts dictation into typewritten form, is more advanced); and (5) demand a good deal of preparation time and training on the part of the facilitator.

Before your next meeting, weigh the advantages and disadvantages of each form of meeting technology.

Be Succinct! (Writing for the Web)

Jakob Nielsen

Research indicates that reading from a screen takes longer than reading from paper, and Web readers tend to print out documents that are longer than one screen. This article provides three guidelines for writing effective prose for Web readers.

The three main guidelines for writing for the Web are:

- Be **succinct:** write no more than 50% of the text you would have used in a hardcopy publication.
- Write for **scannability;** don't require users to read long continuous blocks of text.
- Use **hypertext to split up** long information into multiple pages.

SHORT TEXTS

Reading from computer screens is about **25% slower** than reading from paper. Even users who don't know this usually say that they feel unpleasant when reading on-line text. As a result, people don't want to read a lot of text from computer screens; you should **write 50% less text** and not just 25% less since it's not only a matter of reading speed but also a matter of feeling good. We also know that users don't like to scroll; one more reason to keep pages short.

The screen readability problem will be solved in the future, since screens with 300-dpi resolution have been invented and have been found to have as good readability as paper. High-resolution screens are currently too expensive (high-end monitors in commercial use have about 110 dpi), but will be available in a few years and common ten years from now.

SCANNABILITY

Because it is so painful to read text on computer screens and because the on-line experience seems to foster some amount of impatience, users tend not to read streams of text fully. Instead, users scan text and pick out keywords, sentences, and paragraphs of interest while skipping over those parts of the text they care less about.

Skimming instead of reading is a fact of the Web and has been confirmed by countless usability studies. Webwriters have to acknowledge this fact and write for scannability:

- Structure articles with two or even three levels of **headlines** (a general page heading plus subheads—and sub-subheads when appropriate). Nested headings also facilitate access for blind users with screen readers.
- Use meaningful rather than "cute" headings (i.e., reading a heading should *tell* the user what the page or section is about)

513

- Use **highlighting and emphasis** to make important words catch the user's eye. Colored text can also be used for emphasis, and hypertext anchors stand out by virtue of being blue and underlined.

HYPERTEXT STRUCTURE

Make text short without sacrificing depth of content by splitting the information up into multiple nodes connected by hypertext links. Each page can be brief and yet the full hyperspace can contain much more information than would be feasible in a printed article. Long and detailed background information can be relegated to secondary pages; similarly, information of interest to a minority of readers can be made available through a link without penalizing those readers who don't want it.

Hypertext should *not* be used to segment a long linear story into multiple pages: having to download several segments slows down reading and makes printing more difficult. Proper hypertext structure is not a single flow "*continued on page 2*"; instead, split the information into coherent chunks that each **focus on a certain topic.** The guiding principle should be to allow readers to select those topics they care about and only download those pages. In other words, the hypertext structure should be based on an **audience analysis.**

Each hypertext page should be written according to "inverse pyramid" principle and start with a short conclusion so that users can get the gist of the page even if they don't read all of it.

The Editor's Nightmare:
Formatting Lists within the Text

Gene A. Plunka

Lists in technical writing emphasize specific information for readers. This article provides guidelines for preparing stacked lists and lists within sentences. The article includes samples of how to format lists effectively and tips on how to punctuate lists and when to use bullets. Take the quiz in the article to test your knowledge of how to format lists effectively.

Every experienced editor has been confronted with the task of editing lists within the text. Almost daily, editors encounter writers who do shoddy work and turn in sloppy copy. However, even quite capable writers often do not know how to handle large blocks of information that must be compiled in the form of a list. Because there are no standard rules for the preparation of lists, writers must invariably create their own system (or systems) of notation.

Such "creativity" causes major problems for the editor, especially when the writer is not even consistent in preparing the same type of list. In addition, the editor, who usually has only a vague notion of how to edit lists properly, must make arbitrary decisions based on personal preferences. Such capricious marking raises doubts about the validity of the editorial changes, especially when there are many lists to edit, as is often true of scientific or technical material.

In this article, I provide guidelines for editors and writers when preparing or editing either vertical lists or lists within a sentence.

MISCELLANEOUS ERRORS

As a former editor, I can recall some of the most common errors that made the editing of lists a tedious and frustrating task. First, many writers create their own notation system, using dashes, asterisks, daggers, or other artistic "designs" to introduce listed items. When preparing lists, writers could help the editor considerably if they used only the standard punctuation marks that will be discussed later in this article.

The second major headache-producer for the editor is the shoddy writer's insistence on using "For example" to introduce a list, thereby writing in phrases rather than sentences. I am not suggesting that "For example" must be eliminated from a writer's vocabulary; instead, just be sure that when "For example" begins a statement, the two words will be followed by a sentence and not by a colon.

The third major fault is the long list that is not grammatically parallel—e.g., participial phrases mixed with noun phrases, infinitive phrases with adverbial phrases, etc. The following example indicates why many editors cringe at the thought of editing technical manuscripts full of lists.

Our expenses included the following costs:

1. Mail—$500
2. Telephone—$230

515

3. Using the Printer—$200

4. Copier Fees—$75

Obviously, lines 3 and 4 need to be changed to "Printer" and "Copier" to maintain parallel structure. In short, when the editor has to worry about both formatting the lists for consistency and correcting for parallel structure, the editing of lists becomes that much more demanding, time consuming, and frustrating.

WHEN TO CREATE LISTS

First, try this quiz to test your knowledge of how to format lists. Choose the column number that represents the proper method for formatting the list in the following sentence:

The elements in the test included

I	II	III
1. zinc	(1) zinc	1) zinc
2. lead	(2) lead	2) lead
3. tin	(3) tin	3) tin

IV	V	VI
a) zinc	a. zinc	zinc
b) lead	b. lead	lead
c) tin	c. tin	tin

This example illustrates the types of decisions editors must make when correcting lists. The solution to the puzzle is that none of the six columns is the best choice. The writer should not have created a list at all. Instead, the sentence should read, "The elements in the test included zinc, lead, and tin." Most lists are superfluous. Scientists, engineers, and technicians frequently create lists when they could have otherwise saved space and avoided excessive formatting decisions. Thus, writers should first ask themselves whether there is a significant need for the vertical list that is being considered.

Lists within a sentence are often preceded by a colon. Most style manuals or grammar texts recite a rule that should be memorized by "list-happy" authors: **Do not use a colon between a verb or preposition and its direct object.** Often, however, writers assume that colons must automatically precede long lists, even when a verb introduces the list. To avoid violating the rule above, writers may merely add the words "as follows" or a similar variation after the verb. For example, instead of writing *The criteria were: (1) cost, (2) quality, (3) reputation, and (4) service*, the author should be consistent in applying the rule: *The criteria were the following factors: (1) cost, (2) quality, (3) reputation, and (4) service.*

Similarly, writers who use a colon after a preposition (e.g., *He supplied the scientists with: pipettes, bunsen burners, and ether*) should instead write *He supplied the scientists with the following materials: pipettes, bunsen burners, and ether*, or more simply, without the colon, *He supplied the scientists with pipettes, bunsen burners, and ether.*

Some writers insist on following the old rule that the first word after a colon is capitalized if a complete sentence follows the colon. Today, however, writers have the option of capitalizing or lowercasing the first word of a complete sentence following a colon; they must, of course, be consistent in following the chosen option throughout the text.

Elements in a list can be specifically enumerated to prevent misreading, to clarify a complex or lengthy series, or to highlight the listed items. Enumerations within a sentence should be introduced and identified only by numbers or lowercase letters, not by capital letters or roman numerals. In *A Manual for Writers of Term Papers, Theses, and Dissertations,* Kate L. Turabian notes that numbers or letters in a list stand out better when they are surrounded by parentheses rather than when they are followed by periods [1]. *The Chicago Manual of Style* concurs with Turabian's assessment and suggests double parentheses surrounding numbers or lowercase letters [2].

Following the colon that introduces the list, a comma or semicolon may be used to separate enumerated entries; again, the most important factor is consistency of style throughout the manuscript. Of course, when there are commas within the items of the list, semicolons must be used for clarification.

Thus, models to follow for enumerations within a sentence would be these four examples:

The report consisted of four sections: (1) introduction, (2) discussion, (3) results, and (4) conclusion.

The report consisted of four sections: (1) introduction; (2) discussion; (3) results; and (4) conclusion.

The report consisted of four sections: (a) introduction, (b) discussion, (c) results, and (d) conclusion.

The report consisted of four sections: (a) introduction; (b) discussion; (c) results; and (d) conclusion.

When writers use letters or numbers in a sentence list, they should keep in mind that a line that ends in (1) or (a) is considered a poor line break. Many editors will, by habit, mark such errors, even in draft copy, as carry-over lines to run over the letter or number to the rest of the list on the following line. By paying closer attention to inappropriate line breaks in the middle of lists, writers could simplify the editor's tedious and time-consuming job of correcting and marking errors concerning typography.

Vertical Lists

Lists that contain four or more items in a series may be prepared vertically, set off from the sentence that introduces the list. Again, the rule to follow is that a short list should be incorporated into the sentence of which it is a part, not into a vertical list. Vertical lists are usually introduced by a colon; however, if the list is preceded by a complete sentence, a period may follow the sentence and thereby introduce the list. Dashes or other punctuation marks should not introduce vertical lists.

Introducing and Enumerating Vertical Lists

Writers who seek clarification with regard to the rules for enumerating vertical lists will discover a potpourri of contradictory information. *The Chicago Manual of Style* uses numbers and periods in its examples of such lists, yet no guidelines are provided. The *Publication Manual of the American Psychological Association* suggests the use of arabic numerals followed by a period but not enclosed or followed by parentheses [3]. The editors of *Words Into Type* also support the use of numerals with periods [4]. *The Council of Biology Editors Style Manual* states that lowercase roman numerals, arabic numerals, or lowercase letters in single or double parentheses may be used, or the writer may prepare the list "in accordance with the style of the journal" [5].

The other style manuals, including the *U.S. Government Printing Office Style Manual,* the *MLA Handbook, The Associated Press Stylebook and Libel Manual,* and *The New York Times Manual of Style,* offer no advice on the preparation of vertical lists. The consensus is that the format adopted for vertical lists should be arabic numerals or lowercase letters (be consistent as to which you use) followed by periods. The style therefore differs from the formatting of lists *within* sentences where double parentheses are suggested to make the items easier to differentiate for the reader.

Sometimes vertical lists may be introduced by phrases instead of sentences, or the items in the list may be needed to complete the sentence. In such instances, no colon is used to introduce the list items, thereby precipitating different rules to follow with regard to punctuation and numbering. The following sentence is an example of such a list:

The hydroponic flooding system included

a sealed reservoir,
an aquarium vibrator air pump,
an automatic household timer, and
a plant container

Such lists cause numerous problems with regard to punctuation, numbering sequence, and capitalization. In addition, the editor must worry about whether or not the list's format is consistent with similar vertical lists displayed elsewhere in the text.

A good rule is to use the colon to introduce all lists (i.e., use complete sentences) preceding vertical lists) so as to develop a degree of consistency in formatting vertical lists throughout the manuscript. When the colon is used to precede a list, rules can be followed. However, the lack of a colon usually leads to arbitrary rules with regard to style and formatting.

In vertical lists, numerals or lowercase letters are aligned by periods and can be set flush left or indented. Any run-over lines in the list should be aligned with the first word following the numeral, rather than aligned with the number, lowercase letter, or period. The writer has the option of either capitalizing or lowercasing the first word of each list item, provided that the style is adhered to consistently throughout the manuscript. An editor's work will be substantially increased when a writer capitalizes first-word list items in one sentence and then lowercases the next time around, and if the manuscript is of book length, obviously, errors of this sort will be more difficult for the editor to catch.

Punctuating Vertical Lists

Punctuating vertical lists is often a major source of contention among editors and writers. If the listed items are complete sentences, periods may follow each separate entry in the list. Otherwise, no punctuation marks should be included in the vertical list. The advantage of this simplified method of punctuation is that it eliminates semi-colons or commas between entry items. The disadvantage is that no period ends the sentence, which is annoying to many writers and editors [*including this one, who ends lists with a firm period.-FRS*]. An example of the suggested format is found below.

Chapter Four includes the following information on flight dynamics:

1. Regional defenses against multiple ICBM attacks

2. Minimum energy and nonoptimum ICBM elliptic trajectories

3. Dynamic equations of interceptor rockets

4. Free-flight phases of ballistic missile trajectories

In this example, lowercase letters could be used to replace arabic numerals. In addition, each entry in the list could conceivably begin with a lowercase letter instead of a capital letter.

Using Bullets in Vertical Lists

During the past 25 or 30 years, bullets have been used increasingly to enumerate vertical lists. A bullet is a typographical mark, a solid dot, used to distinguish elements in a list. I have been unsuccessful in tracing the exact origin of the term, although I am fairly certain that it is not of British derivation. *The Oxford English Dictionary* does not refer to "bullet" in relationship to printing or proofreaders' marks. In addition, Judith Butcher, chief subeditor of Cambridge University Press and author of *Copy-Editing*, an important reference work for editors, does not mention "bullets" in her list of editorial marks.

In the United States, "bullet" did not appear as a typographical mark in *Webster's Second International Dictionary*, first printed in 1934 and reprinted in 1949. However, the first printing of *Webster's Third New International Dictionary* in 1961 defines the term as "a large solid dot so placed in printed matter as to call attention to a particular passage [6]." Thus, the term probably evolved in the United States sometime between 1949 and 1961.

The exact origin of the bullet is a mystery. In his humorous approach to the subject, Frederick P. Szydlik amused us with possible origins that he speculated upon in his 1986 article in *Technical Communication* [7]. In July 1983, the editors of *The Editorial Eye* suggested that bullets evolved from printers' center dots, but no specific date of origin was mentioned [8]. Robert Compton, writing in the October 1983 issue of *The Editorial Eye,* stated that representatives of the Burger writing course refer to bullets as "Burger dots" in honor of author/teacher Robert S. Burger, who claims to have invented them [9]. Burger has been teaching businessmen how to write since 1958, so he could be a likely candidate for authorship.

Style manuals and editing texts do not help much since most of them, including the *U.S. Government Printing Office Style Manual, The Chicago Manual of Style,* and Karen Judd's *Copyediting: A Practical Guide,* do not even list the bullet as a typographical symbol. Even *The Associated Press Stylebook and Libel Manual* refers the reader to "Weapons" when one looks up "Bullets" in the body of the sourcebook.

Bullets are generally used as flagging devices, for they call attention to, and readily distinguish, items in a list. Writers choose bullets instead of numbers or letters when the items in the list have no special rank, sequence, or significance—in other words, when all of the elements in the list are equally important. In addition, bullets should be included when the listed information in each entry is composed of more than one line, e.g., one long sentence, two or more sentences, or a paragraph. In short, bullets are not used in lieu of numbers or letters; instead, they serve a distinct and different purpose in the enumeration process and should be used sparingly. As Szydlik wryly points out in his précis, poor writers are apt to substitute bullets for complete sentences, thereby turning some reports into long bulleted lists that put facts together in piecemeal fashion. In effect, what we are witnessing in private industry is that writers who have trouble constructing sentences are using bullets to convey ideas in the form of phrases.

Writers should take the time to format bulleted lists properly. There are essentially four ways to use bullets. First, bullets can be flush left with the margin, with the text also running over flush left. Second, bullets may be flush left, with the text running over only to the beginning of the first word in the copy (hanging style). Third, bullets may be indented from the left margin, yet when the copy runs over, it is flush left. In the last form, bullets start flush left, the copy extends flush left, but the bullets are run-on in such a way that they follow each sentence in the middle of the paragraph. The following examples differentiate the four methods of using bullets.

• XXXXXXXXXXXX	• XXXXXXXXXXXX
XXXXXXXXXXXXXX	XXXXXXXXXXXX
XXXXXXXXXXXXXX	• XXXXXXXXXXXX
• XXXXXXXXXXXX	XXXXXXXXXXXX
XXXXXXXXXXXXXX	• XXXXXXXXXXXX
Flush	Hanging

• XXXXXXXX	• XXXXXXXXXXXX
XXXXXXXXXXXX	XXXXXXXXXXXX
XXXXXXXXXXXX	XXXXX • XXXXX
• XXXXXXXX	XXXXXXXXXXXX
XXXXXXXXXXXX	XX • XXXXXXXXX
Indented	Run-On

Writers should decide which style is most appropriate to save space and make for easier reading; then they should avoid combining the various styles, thereby pleasing editors as well as attentive readers.

CONCLUDING REMARKS

As an increasing amount of our literature is becoming more scientific and technical, writers are including more lists in their manuscripts. Until there are standardized rules for the compilation of such lists, inconsistencies will increase in the formatting of scientific and technical articles and books. Writers could assist editors in reducing the number of formatting errors in lists by asking themselves these questions:

1. Is there a need for a vertical list, or will a list within a sentence be sufficient?

2. How should the list be punctuated?

3. Should numbers, letters, or bullets be used to format the list?

4. Have I been consistent in preparing all similar lists in the text the same way?

5. Are all of the items in the list parallel in structure?

Astute writers who pay attention to all five questions will improve the quality of their writing, develop an eye for detail, and spare their editors the extra antacid needed to get them through yet another manuscript.

REFERENCES

1. Kate L. Turabian, *A Manual for Writers of Term Papers, Theses, and Dissertations,* 4th ed. (Chicago: The University of Chicago Press, 1973), 28.

2. *The Chicago Manual of Style,* 13th ed. (Chicago: The University of Chicago Press, 1982), 245.

3. *Publication Manual of the American Psychological Association,* 3d ed. (Washington, D.C.: American Psychological Association, 1983), 68.

4. Marjorie E. Skillin and Robert M. Gay, *Words Into Type,* 3d ed. (Englewood Cliffs, NJ: Prentice-Hall, Inc., 1974), 175.

5. *Council of Biology Editors Style Manual,* 4th ed. (Arlington, VA: Council of Biology Editors, Inc., 1978), 111.

6. *Webster's Third New International Dictionary* (Springfield, MA: G. & C. Merriam Co., 1961), 294.

7. Frederick P. Szydlik, "The Bulleted List in Technical Communication: A High-Caliber Paradigm," *Technical Communication* 33, no. 2 (Second Quarter 1986): 93.

8. "Ask the Eye," *The Editorial Eye,* July 1983, 7.

9. Robert A. Compton, "About Those Bullets," *The Editorial Eye,* Late October 1983, 4.

Ideology and Collaboration in the Classroom and in the Corporation

James E. Porter

Collaboration among company departments is necessary to produce accurate product information. This article describes a problem in labeling that developed when a company's individual departments did not collaborate to ensure consistency.

In composing important, large-scale publications such as product information, packaging, and advertising, corporations usually rely on some kind of collaborative model—and it is the nature and effectiveness of these models that I have begun investigating in recent research.

We know that collaborative writing involves ideology because ideology is a component of all language practice, including classroom practice. Collaboration itself is ideological, John Trimbur (1989) argues, because it involves a group organizing itself to produce common work. Any such organization presupposes the existence of a political / ethical philosophy (or philosophies): that is, a set of beliefs about why the group exists, how it will function, and what it will do. Any collaboration adopts or determines an end, a goal, a purpose—whether that purpose is assigned by the teacher (or department supervisor) and whether the group agrees (tacitly or not) about that purpose.

Ideological issues are not matters of classroom interest only. Through policy or practice, corporations develop their own "mega-composing" processes—strategies for producing public documents (like product information) collaboratively—and ideology certainly influences this collaboration.

A recent lawsuit illustrates the influences of disciplinary ideology on corporate composing. Several fertilizer companies were sued by a competitor for mislabeling their bags of composted manure. One of these companies countersued, on the basis that the plaintiff's product was similarly mislabeled. Although the plaintiff's bags contained identical contents (7% sheep manure, 33% pig manure, and 60% cow manure), some bags were titled "sheep manure" and others "cattle manure." Is this a case of misleading labeling or simply harmless descriptive license?

The interesting thing about this case is that the law suit did not come from outraged customers. The dispute arose among competing fertilizer companies, which accused each other of unfair competitive practices. The case was settled out of court, but not before considerable legal expense and inconvenience to all parties involved. Several of the companies revised the information on their fertilizer bags.

What caused this problem in the first place? By what process were these "mislabeled" bags produced? It is easy to see how a labeling problem of this kind could arise in an organization with a compartmentalized notion of product responsibility. If the operations division (i.e., the technical people, such as agricultural chemists) sees itself as responsible only for the contents of the bag, and if marketing sees itself as responsible only for bag design (and not contents), then who takes responsibility for assuring referential accuracy?

The problem illustrates the tension that can exist between separate functions within the corporation. Collaboration in the corporation can, and often does, occur at the departmental or functional level. The operational function has responsibility for filling the bag with a salable product. The marketing function has responsibility for producing a bag labeled for consumers. The legal function has responsibility for assuring compliance with fair labeling standards. If these functions operate as separate political units and if they manufacture, promote, and distribute their product following a strictly linear, "division of labor" collaborative model (Killingsworth & Jones, 1989)—that is, operations makes fertilizer, marketing sells it, lawyers check the bag—problems are bound to result. Even if operations objects to the technical inaccuracies in labeling, in a strictly linear model of authority, marketing would have the final say on the label, and would not need to collaborate with operations. Legal collaboration is supposed to prevent these difficulties—and certainly packaging ought to be "edited" from a legal point of view, in light of state and federal regulatory restrictions on labeling. But an editing check of the label might not reveal the referential problem of a package not containing what it says it contains.

What might help the entire process is a more dynamic and interactive collaborative model, with opportunity for recursion built in, or a model that includes a coordinated holistic perspective. Such a perspective might be provided by a professional writer, with political allegiance neither to operations or marketing, who would track the product from design to manufacture to packaging and shipping, insuring that package labeling, package contents, and regulatory guidelines are all in mutual accord. A major computer software company, conscious of how a strictly departmentalized political outlook can threaten collaboration, has instituted strategies designed to counter such departmentalization. In the traditional, strictly linear model of composing, the computer specialist would design the software first; then the technical writer would take the completed software and write documentation for it. This company challenges that model by hiring writers who are capable of doing design and writing together (i.e., who have technical expertise as well as writing skills). The writer becomes an equal partner on the software development team and serves as an advocate for the user. This company is aware that a management ideology which supports a hierarchical and compartmentalized view of composing can block rather than promote effective collaborative writing.

References

Killingsworth, M. J., & Jones, B. G. (1989). Division of labor or integrated teams: A crux in the management of technical communication? *Technical Communication, 36*(3), 210–221.

Trimbur, J. (1989). Consensus and difference in collaborative learning. *College English, 51*(6), 602–616.

The Practical Writer

Written documents often fail to achieve their purpose because they confuse or irritate readers. This article discusses how to achieve effective, clear style through careful word choice, using active voice instead of passive, and using concrete words instead of abstract ones whenever possible.

From time to time most educated people are called upon to act as writers. They might not think of themselves as such as they dash off a personal note or dictate a memo, but that is what they are. They are practising a difficult and demanding craft, and facing its inborn challenge. This is to find the right words and to put them in the right order so that the thoughts they represent can be understood.

Some writers deliberately muddy the meaning of their words, if indeed they meant anything to begin with. When most people write, however, it is to get a message across. This is especially so in business and institutions, where written words carry much of the load of communications. The written traffic of any well-ordered organization is thick and varied—letters, memos, reports, policy statements, manuals, sales literature, and what-have-you. The purpose of it all is to use words in a way that serves the organization's aims.

Unfortunately, written communications often fail to accomplish this purpose. Some organizational writing gives rise to confusion, inefficiency, and ill-will. This is almost always because the intended message did not get through to the receiving end. Why? Because the message was inadequately prepared.

An irresistible comparison arises between writing and another craft which most people have to practise sometimes, namely cooking. In both fields there is a wide range of competence, from the great chefs and authors to the occasional practitioners who must do the job whether they like it or not. In both, care in preparation is of the essence. Shakespeare wrote that it is an ill cook who does not lick his own fingers; it is an ill writer who does not work at it hard enough to be reasonably satisfied with the results.

Unlike bachelor cooks, however, casual writers are rarely the sole consumers of their own offerings. Reclusive philosophers and schoolgirls keeping diaries are about the only writers whose work is not intended for other eyes. If a piece of writing turns out to be an indigestible half-baked mess, those on the receiving end are usually the ones to suffer. This might be all right in literature, because the reader of a bad book can always toss it aside. But in organizations, where written communications command attention, it is up to the recipient of a sloppy writing job to figure out what it means.

The reader is thus put in the position of doing the thinking the writer failed to do. To make others do your work for you is, of course, an uncivil act. In a recent magazine advertisement on the printed word, one of a commendable series published by International Paper Company, novelist Kurt Vonnegut touched on the social aspect of writing: "Why should you examine your writing style with the idea of improving it? Do so as a mark of respect for your readers. If you scribble your thoughts any which way, your readers will surely feel that you care nothing for them."

In the working world, bad writing is not only bad manners, it is bad business. The victim of an incomprehensible letter will at best be annoyed and at worst decide that people who can't say what they mean aren't worth doing business with. Write a sloppy letter, and it might rebound on you when the recipient calls for clarification. Where one carefully worded letter would have sufficed, you might have to write two or more.

Muddled messages can cause havoc within an organization. Instructions that are misunderstood can set people off in the wrong directions or put them to work in vain. Written policies that are open to misinterpretation can throw sand in the gears of an entire operation. Ill-considered language in communications with employees can torpedo morale.

A Careful Writer Must Be a Careful Thinker

In the early 1950s the British Treasury grew so concerned with the inefficiency resulting from poor writing that it called in a noted man of letters, Sir Ernest Gowers, to work on the problem. Out of this Gowers wrote an invaluable book, *The Complete Plain Words,* for the benefit of British civil servants and anyone else who must put English to practical use. (Her Majesty's Stationery Office, London, 1954.)

Gowers took as his touchstone a quotation from Robert Louis Stevenson: "The difficulty is not to write, but to write what you mean, not to affect your reader, but to affect him precisely as you wish." To affect your reader precisely as you wish obviously calls for precision in the handling of language. And to achieve precision in anything takes time.

Gowers suggested that the time spent pursuing precision more than cancels out the time wasted by imprecision. People in administrative jobs might well protest that they were not hired as writers, and that their schedules are crammed enough without having to fuss over the niceties of grammar and the like. The answer to this is that it is an important part of their work to put words on paper. It should be done just as thoroughly and conscientiously as anything else for which they get paid.

No one should be led to believe writing is easy. As great a genius as Dr. Samuel Johnson described composition as "an effort of slow diligence and steady perseverance to which the mind is dragged by necessity or resolution." Writing is hard work because *thinking* is hard work; the two are inseparable. But there is some compensation for the effort invested in trying to write well.

The intellectual discipline required to make thoughts come through intelligibly on paper pays off in clarifying your thoughts in general. When you start writing about a subject, you will often find that your knowledge of it and your thinking about it leave something to be desired. The question that should be foremost in the writer's mind, "What am I really trying to say?" will raise the related questions, "What do I really know about this? What do I really think about it?" A careful writer has to be a careful thinker—and in the long run careful thinking saves time and trouble for the writer, the reader, and everybody else concerned.

The problem is that many people believe that they *have* thought out ideas and expressed them competently on paper when they actually haven't. This is because they use nebulous multi-purpose words that may mean one thing to them and something quite different to someone else. Gowers gave the example of the verb "involve," which is used variously to mean "entail," "include," "contain," "imply," "implicate," "influence," etc., etc. "It has . . . developed a vagueness that makes it the delight of those who dislike the effort of searching for the right word," he wrote. "It is consequently much used, generally where some more specific word would be better and sometimes where it is merely superfluous."

THE RIGHT WORD WILL ALMOST TELL YOU WHERE IT SHOULD GO

There are plenty of other lazy man's words lurking about, threatening to set the writer up beside Humpty Dumpty, who boasted: "When I use a word, it means just what I want it to mean." It is therefore wise to avoid words that can be taken in more than one way in a given context. This ties in with the first commandment of practical writing, which is: "Be Specific." "Specify, be accurate, give exact details—and forget about fine writing and original style," Rudolph Flesch says in his book, *How to Be Brief*.

Style tends to take care of itself if you select the right words and put them in the most logical order; so, to a large extent, do grammar and syntax. Find the right word, and it will almost tell you where in a sentence it should go.

This is not to say that grammar and syntax are not important. Words scattered on a page at the discretion of the writer simply would not be comprehensible. The rules of language usage also exert a degree of discipline over your thinking about a subject by forcing you to put your thoughts in logical order. Many grammatical conventions are intended to eliminate ambiguity, so that you don't start out saying one thing and end up saying something else.

Most literate people, however, have an instinctive grasp of grammar and syntax that is adequate for all ordinary purposes. The rules of usage (in English more so than in French) are in any case flexible, changeable, and debatable: new words are invented as the language lives and grows, and a solecism in one generation becomes respectable in the next. So while grammar and syntax have their roles to play in written communications, they must not be adhered to so slavishly that they interfere with intelligible expression. Gowers quoted Lord MacAulay with approval on this score: "After all, the first law of writing, that law to which all other laws are subordinate, is this: that the words employed should be such as to convey to the reader the meaning of the writer."

VOCABULARY IS USUALLY THE LEAST OF A WRITER'S PROBLEMS

Since words come first, an ample vocabulary is an asset in conveying meaning. Oddly enough, though, people who have difficulty getting their written messages across rarely lack the vocabulary required. They know the apt words, but they don't use them. They go in for sonorous but more or less meaningless language instead.

People who are perfectly able to express themselves in plain spoken language somehow get the idea that the short, simple words they use in everyday conversation are unworthy to be committed to paper. Thus where they would say, "We have closed the deal," they will write, "We have finalized the transaction." In writing, they "utilize available non-rail ground mode transportation resources" instead of loading trucks. They get caught in "prevailing precipitant climatic conditions" instead of in the rain. They "utilize a manual earth removal implement" instead of digging with a shovel. When so many words with so many meanings are being slung about, nobody can be quite sure of just what is being said.

The guiding principle for the practical writer should be that common words should always be used unless more exact words are needed for definition. The reason for this is so plain that it is all but invisible. It is that if you use words that everybody knows, everybody can understand what you want to say.

A common touch with language has always distinguished great leaders. Winston Churchill comes immediately to mind; he "mobilized the English language and sent it into battle," as John F. Kennedy said. Churchill mobilized the language in more ways than in his inspiring speeches. As Prime Minister of Great Britain, he was that nation's chief administrator at a time when governmental efficiency was a matter of life and death for the democratic world. In August, 1940, while the Battle of Britain was at its peak, Churchill took the time to write a memo about excess verbiage in inter-departmental correspondence. It read:

> Let us have an end to such phrases as these: 'It is also of importance to bear in mind the following considerations . . .' or 'Consideration should be given to carrying into effect . . .' Most of these woolly phrases are mere padding, which can be left out altogether or replaced by a single word. Let us not shrink from the short expressive word even if it is conversational.

Churchill's own wartime letters and memos, reproduced in his memoirs, are models of effective English. It is interesting to speculate on how much his clarity of expression, and his insistence upon it in others, helped to win the war. He was, of course, a professional writer who had earned a living from his pen since he was in his early twenties. He was something of a literary genius. In the light of this, it may seem ridiculous to exhort modern white-collar workers to write like Winston Churchill. Nevertheless, the principles of writing which Churchill followed are not at all hard to grasp.

Churchill was an admirer of H. W. Fowler's *A Dictionary of English Usage,* to which he would direct his generals when he caught them mangling the language. Fowler set five criteria for good writing—that it be direct, simple, brief, vigorous and lucid. Any writer who tries to live up to these is on the right track.

By keeping in mind two basic techniques you can go some way towards meeting Fowler's requirements. These are:

Prefer the active voice to the passive. It will make your writing more direct and vigorous. It's a matter of putting the verb in your sentence up front so that it pulls along the rest of the words. In the active voice you would say, "The carpenter built the house;" in the passive, "The house was built by the carpenter." Though it is not always possible to do so in the context of a sentence, use the active whenever you can.

Prefer the concrete to the abstract. A concrete word stands for something tangible or particular; an abstract word is "separated from matter, practice, or particular example." Churchill used concrete terms: "We have not journeyed all this way, across the centuries, across the oceans, across the mountains, across the prairies, because we are made of sugar candy." If he had couched that in the abstract, he might have said: "We have not proved ourselves capable of traversing time spans and geographical phenomena due to a deficiency in fortitude." Again, there are times when abstractions are called for by the context because there are no better concrete words, but try not to use them unless you must.

Sticking to the concrete will tend to keep you clear of one of the great pitfalls of modern practical writing, the use of "buzz words." These are words and expressions that come into currency not because they mean anything in particular, but merely because they sound impressive. It is difficult to give examples of them because they have such short lives; the "buzz words" of today are the laughing stocks of tomorrow. They are mostly abstract terms (ending, in English, in *-ion, -ance, -osity, -ive, -ize, -al,* and *-ate*), but they sometimes take the form of concrete words that have been sapped of their original meaning. The reason for giving them a wide berth is that their meaning is seldom clear.

Jargon presents a similar pitfall. It has its place as the in-house language of occupational groups, and that is where it should be kept. It too consists mostly of abstract words, and by keeping to the concrete you can shut out much of it. But jargon is contagious, so it should be consciously avoided. Never use a word of it unless you are certain that it means the same to your reader as it does to you.

The combination of the active and the concrete will help to make your prose direct, simple, vigorous, and lucid. There is no special technique for making it brief; that is up to you.

The first step to conciseness is to scorn the notion that length is a measure of thoroughness. It isn't. Emulate Blaise Pascal, who wrote to a friend: "I have made this letter a little longer than usual because I lack the time to make it shorter."

Use your pen or pencil as a cutting tool. No piece of writing, no matter what its purpose or length, should leave your desk until you have examined it intensely with a view to taking the fat out of it. Strike out anything that does not add directly to your reader's understanding of the subject. While doing this, try to put yourself in his or her shoes.

Be hard on yourself; writing is not called a discipline for nothing. It is tough, wearing, brain-racking work. But when you finally get it right, you have done a service to others. And, like Shakespeare's cook, you can lick your metaphorical fingers and feel that it was all worthwhile.

The Writer as Market Researcher

Lee Ridgway

Writers who prepare instruction and reference manuals for products must be fully aware of the readers and their needs. This article explains how to interview product users and determine how they use the product in their work and what they need in manuals. Use the sample interview questions to generate your own set of appropriate questions for interviewing potential readers.

As technical writers, we have often defined our audience of readers. An article written for *Scientific American,* for example, is read by a well-defined audience with known characteristics and known variation. Any successful technical publication must know its readers, either through conventional market research techniques (such as reader surveys), association and contact (particularly for specialized trade or hobby magazines), or inspired guesswork by the editor (pretty risky). When we write for such a publication, therefore, we have a good audience description when we start.

But those of us who write instruction and reference manuals for manufacturers have been in a somewhat dangerous position. The people who bought the products (from can openers to software systems) received the information without any effort on their part. Furthermore, if they needed the information, they had to use the material, whether or not it was fun to read, whether or not it was useful, whether or not they understood it. In fact, the primary (buying) audience was the technical people who had built the product. If they didn't like the material, it didn't reach the customers. Everyone assumed that the users were just like the developers, and that developers' reviews were appropriate. So we wrote for an audience of developers.

For complex products, this approach often worked very well. Because only experts were expected to use the products, the developers were in fact very like the users of the products.

For simple products, people simply ignored the information. They used reference material as a last resort, when experimenting was not successful. Sometimes they drew inferences from pictures of the product. Frequently, such logic was enough.

But increasingly, ordinary people are being expected to master complex equipment and learn complex concepts. For many products, logic and past experience do not provide a basis for intuitive understanding. So we need to provide palatable information that ordinary people can cope with.

THE NORMAL WRITING PROCESS

Normally, at the beginning of a project someone tells us who the buyers of the product will be. This identification is made by marketing and sales people and is based on some form of crystal-ball gazing. Somehow, given the predicted buyers, we deduce who the actual users will be. During the original writing, reviewing, and testing stages of the manuals, we assume that the identified audience is the real one. We base our information design on that audience, and we use various techniques to see whether the design is acceptable.

Writers use their skills to write truthfully and in a way that is useful to the specified reader. We review for accuracy and completeness, we test for readability, we test for usability, and the test results help us present appropriate information in a helpful way for the assumed audience. When the information is complete, it has already been exposed to all sorts of checking. The information is fine for the audience as we or the product planners defined it.

But did we define it correctly?

INTERVIEWING THE AUDIENCE

When the products have actually become available and there are people actually using them, you have the opportunity and the duty to see whether the users are as you defined them and whether the tasks they perform are the ones that you supported. To do this, you must take on another role. You must become an interviewer, visiting customers and finding out how they do their work using the product.

Interview Techniques

Being a successful visitor requires a good deal of tact. Frequently visits are very structured, with you and your readers sitting in a conference room together. They are aware that they are criticizing your work and may be quite apologetic about their comments. You have to project genuine interest and acceptance and avoid defensiveness. If you argue, the users will stop volunteering opinions, or they will become angry and uncooperative. You may ask for clarification but must take care that the request doesn't sound challenging. ("I dare you to show me a place where that is true.")

When you ask questions, you should phrase them in such a way that the users do not know what answer you want (which may affect the reply). If it is quite obvious what the "right" answer would be, you may phrase a question in a way that invites another answer. ("I wasn't sure about the presentation of topic. How could it have been made clearer?" Or "I thought about putting in a diagram of the phlisbug. Do you think that would be a good idea?")

Especially during early use of the product, interviews give you the only feedback available, so you want to cover the right ground and talk to the right people. It often helps to have an outline or questionnaire to refer to. If you are asking about a specific manual, questions to ask are like these:

- How frequently do you use this manual?
- Under what circumstances do you use it?
- When did you last use it?
- What tasks are you doing when you use it?
- How do you use it? Do you sit down and read it, or do you refer to it while you are doing something else?
- How would you rate it (excellent, good, fair, poor, awful)?
- What do you like best about it?
- What would you change about it?
- Do you have marginal notations in it?

- Who else uses the manual?
- Do you know what they use it for?

When there is a set of manuals for a product, you may be interested in the library structure and the placement of information within manuals. You may ask questions like these:

- How easy was it to find the information you wanted? Did you
    1. always find the right manual right away
    2. sometimes try another manual before the right one
    3. almost always try the wrong manual first
    4. hunt through several manuals to find the information
    5. mostly not find it
- When you had the right manual, how easy was it to find information in it?
    1. very easy
    2. pretty easy
    3. took more than three tries
    4. had to leaf through looking
    5. never found it
- Were the titles of the manuals
    1. very descriptive
    2. descriptive
    3. all right
    4. not very descriptive
    5. not at all descriptive

If people admit to making marginal comments, and if you can persuade them to share them, you will find them invaluable. Information that people have added for themselves is obviously important to them. The way they organize the information and the level of detail that they add tell you how expert they are and how they want information to be presented. But people are often shy about their notes, because they are hastily or sloppily written. The notes often contain simple information that they feel they should not need, and they are embarrassed to show it to you.

Uses and Advantages of Interviews

During interviews, you are finding out something about the people who are using your material and about the tasks and responsibilities they have. But during these interviews, you see only a few of your readers and you must not generalize too much from the ones you meet and talk to. You can, however, learn about the mental set that at least a few readers have, and try to find out whether the writer and reader share the same assumptions.

Readers are usually not able to pinpoint what they dislike or would change. They know that they are dissatisfied with something, but they often do not know why they are dissatisfied. They are uncomfortable because their expectations (which may not have been conscious) have in some way not been met.

You have to listen carefully to deduce their unfulfilled expectations. Perhaps they thought that the product would be "like a typewriter," meaning that they could sit down and use it immediately. The 300-page user's guide makes them suspect that this is not true. They may then react by saying "The guide is too big," when what they mean is that the product requires too much information and it really isn't like a typewriter at all.

Often people have some analogy in their minds when they deal with something new ("It's a blender, really" or "It's an overgrown adding machine"). When the analogy fails in some crucial way, they feel that they have been misled. You need to understand what analogy they were making, whether you encouraged and supported it, and whether it failed or succeeded. If it failed, you need to discourage other readers from thinking along the same lines.

You are also trying to find out whether your understanding of the users' environment and duties is correct. If possible, you should observe users in their work setting, actually using information. You have to be very careful not to interfere with normal activities or to make people feel self-conscious by watching them too closely. But you might ask to see where the manuals are kept, or where the product is located, and see some of the environment that way. During a discussion, you might try to get a description of how things are done, establishing a scenario, as it were, of a day in the life of a terminal operator, or what the procedures are for running the payroll, to help you understand the real tasks.

To sum up, visits enable you to meet real readers, and to get a detailed picture of some readers and some work environments. You find out where your information fits and does not fit a few users. You may get new ideas from your reader sample. However, you have only seen a small sample of your readers. You must decide whether the sample is representative and whether it is complete enough to be useful.

SURVEYING THE AUDIENCE

Many products depend on mass markets, so that a few users may or may not be representative. What would suit one customer perfectly would suit only that one customer. To find out about the whole customer group, you have to prepare questionnaires and survey representative customers. You don't personally need all the skills of statisticians and market researchers, which include how to select samples and how to analyze the statistical significance of data. You do need to be advised by someone who has these skills, if you don't have them.

The selection of the sample is very important because it determines whether the results of the survey apply to the whole customer set. A sample can be the whole set, it can be customers chosen at random, or it can be representative customers. You need advice on sample selection to balance cost, time, and reliability. An appropriately chosen representative sample can yield more reliable results than a random sample of the same size, for example.

Surveys can be done by mail, by telephone, or in person. Mail is the most convenient but the least reliable and the least likely to get responses. You get few responses (sometimes only a few percent), and the people who reply are mostly people with very strong opinions (not necessarily representative). The sample is self-selecting, because every user chooses whether to respond and become a part of the sample. However, mail questionnaires can be longer and more detailed than telephone surveys, and may bring good results if used appropriately.

Telephone surveys have a much higher response rate, and the sample is chosen instead of choosing itself. The results are more reliable, but telephone survey questionnaires have to be written carefully, because the interview may be conducted by someone who does not know the topic at all. Questions have to be simple enough for answerers to understand them without explanation. Any list of choices must be short enough for the answerer to remember on one hearing.

However, you can be comforted by two facts about telephone surveys. First, people (surprisingly) are very cooperative about being interviewed over the telephone. Even so, they probably have an upper limit of about 20 minutes for question answering, except by special arrangement. (Many people do not like to talk on the telephone for long periods, so that their patience wears thin. They might also be very busy.) Second, there are professional market research companies that specialize in telephone surveys. They can help you with the questionnaire, do the actual telephone interviews, and gather and tabulate replies.

Personal-interview surveys are the most expensive and most difficult, but they can also be the most fruitful. The advantage is that a skillful interviewer can find out a great deal in a personal interview. The disadvantages are the cost and the need for a very skillful interviewer. The same considerations of personal interaction that affect visits also affect face-to-face surveys to a smaller degree. Interviewers are less likely than you to signal what they would like to hear. But sending trained interviewers to users can be very expensive, if a large sample is needed or users are spread thinly.

A variation of the face-to-face interview is the round-table discussion, where a number of customers discuss questions in the presence of an interviewer. The group interaction makes it easier for people to express opinions that they feel may not be flattering, but group pressure may give a false impression of unanimity. The interviewer tries to make sure that no one is dominating or dominated to a misleading degree.

USES AND ADVANTAGES OF SURVEYS

From surveys, you can get a broad picture of who the real users of the product are, what environment the product is used in, and how satisfied the users are with the product. Although you do not get an in-depth knowledge of any single user (unless the survey was done by personal interviews), you have a lot of sketches of users, and a high degree of confidence that the users sketched are a realistic picture of the various user types.

In addition, surveys can verify task definitions. Although you learn more about actual tasks in detail from visits and long interviews, you can check that those tasks are realistic by survey questions. As a result, task-oriented instructions can be refined if necessary to reflect the way tasks are really done.

Don't expect surveys to give you facts about how long it takes a user to do a task, or find a piece of information, or correct a mistake. People's perception of time depends on how anxious they are, how interested they are, how impatient, or worried, or tired. Their time sense is affected by how long they expected something to take. Five minutes can be a very long time or a very short time, and depending on circumstances will be seen by the user as much too long or very quick. Time estimates will be unreliable. People can tell you whether they were happy or unhappy with the time they spent doing a task. You can then deduce what tasks need to be redesigned so that they can be done more quickly.

At this point, you may go back to the testing lab to find the facts that users could not give you. You can compare how long a task takes in testing with the users' evaluation (too long, very short, etc.) to uncover problem areas and to provide a basis for measuring improved performance. This testing may not test the same tasks that were tested during development. Task descriptions may have been redefined as a result of customer visits and surveys.

You may change users' expectations by changing the description of the task. One description may make the task sound trivial, while a different description can make it seem reasonable that the task should take longer. You may break the task into two parts, describe checkpoints, or give the user a distraction. Tell the user that there will be 10 messages before the task is done, and the user may count the messages instead of being impatient.

In short, you use survey results to verify definitions of tasks and users and to gather user opinions about the information. These opinions, although highly subjective, can be shown to be valid if the sample is large and representative. By structuring the survey questions carefully, you or your statistics expert can find out what factors affected users' judgments and deduce what improvements will have most effect.

Summary

Collection and analysis of feedback are new skills for the technical writer when they are undertaken in a systematic and formal manner. Technical writers working for manufacturers need to be very much aware of their audience and its needs. Since the usual indicators of acceptance do not apply very well to manufacturer supplied material, technical writers must depend on customer interviews and surveys to gauge their success. They therefore must develop interviewing skills and an understanding of statistical methods—another accomplishment of the Renaissance technical writer.

Six Graphics Guidelines

Typographic elements can help readers understand and use information efficiently. This article explains how to use specific typographic elements, such as type size, white space, and capital letters. Notice the samples of type style and size.

In the first part of this article, we present six graphics guidelines that the Document Design Center has developed to help writers and graphic artists produce documents that are both visually appealing and easy to read. Good graphics can help readers to overcome resistance to a text or even help them to understand the material more easily.

1. Use Highlighting Techniques, but Don't Overuse Them.

Highlighting techniques are a way of emphasizing important aspects of your document by calling attention to them visually. Some highlighting techniques are: *boldface, italics, and white space.* The six guidelines are printed in boldface. The list of highlighting techniques in this paragraph is printed in italics. We have used all of those techniques in *Simply Stated.*

In addition to emphasizing a part of your document, highlighting techniques generally contribute to the attractiveness of your document by providing visual relief in what might otherwise be a uniform page of text.

You can use highlighting techniques to emphasize important points, set off examples from the rest of the text, or set off sections of text by calling attention to headings.

Be careful, however, not to overuse any highlighting technique. If too much of your text is highlighted, the purpose of highlighting will be defeated. For example, if a whole section is in italics, it will not stand out; in fact, it will be more difficult to read than text set in regular type. If too much is in boldface, your text will also become more difficult to read, because the page will look too black and heavy. Also be careful not to use too many different highlighting techniques in one document. This can make your text look cluttered and can lead to confusion. Finally, make sure you are consistent in the way you use a particular technique. For example, if you are going to use boldface for a certain level of heading, be sure always to use it for that level.

2. Use 8 to 10 Point Type for Text.

For most documents, 8 to 10 point type is the most readable size. If your type is too small, your document can look crowded and uninviting. Your readers may skip over text, or they may get eyestrain.

If your type is too large, your text will use more space than it needs to. If you have constraints on space, you may have to cut down on important information. If you choose to add pages to accommodate the large type, it can get expensive. Inappropriately large type can even make a text more difficult to read.

In addition to considering point size (see "Measuring Type"), you must consider the look of the type you choose. Some typefaces look larger than others of the same type size. For example:

This is an example of 10 point Souvenir type.

This is an example of 10 point Avant Garde type.

Simply Stated is set in 10 point Century Schoolbook. See how much more difficult it would be to read if it were set in 6 point type of the same style.

Simply Stated is set in 10 point Century Schoolbook. See how much more difficult it would be to read if it were set in 6 point type of the same style.

3. Avoid Making Your Lines of Type Too Long or Too Short.

The best line length for most text is 50–70 characters. Experience has shown that this length is less tiring to the eye than either short lines, which make the eye jump back and forth, or long lines, which strain the eye as it tries to stay on course. With either extreme, the eye is likely to jump to another line.

The lines in *Simply Stated* average about 48 characters. If we were to keep the same type size but lay out *Simply Stated* in four columns, the line length would be too short. The short lines would make awkward breaks in the text and cause the eye to jerk back and forth. The change would make for uncomfortable reading.

If we were to keep the same type size and lay out *Simply Stated* all the way across the page, with no column breaks, the long lines would be difficult to follow, and the text would look too densely packed to make pleasant reading. It would even appear to have less leading between the lines. (See "Leading.")

4. Use White Space in Margins and Between Sections.

If you use white space well, you can make your document look better and easier to read. The term "white space" refers to any of the blank space on a document, such as the margins and the space between sections, or the space that sets off an example. A text with too little white space can look cramped.

Use white space as an integral element in designing your document, and use it functionally. For example, the white space between sections helps the reader to see how the document is organized. The white space surrounding a title or an example isolates it and emphasizes its importance.

In *Simply Stated* we use white space to isolate the masthead and the titles of the articles. We leave adequate margins and separate each paragraph from the next with white space. If the margins were narrower and there was no space between paragraphs, the text would look cramped and less inviting.

5. USE RAGGED RIGHT MARGINS.

When all the lines of text begin at a left margin but end at different points on the right, the right margin is "ragged." *Simply Stated* is set with a ragged right margin.

When the lines all end in the same place, the right margin is even. The text is "justified." This paragraph is justified, or set "flush left" and "flush right." To get the lines to come out even on the right, the typesetter had to put extra spaces between words and letters all along the line.

Many document designers today prefer ragged right margins, because they are less formal than justified text and create a more relaxed, contemporary look that many readers find inviting. Tastes do change, however, and ragged right margins may go out of fashion.

There are practical advantages to ragged right margins, however. Some printers have found that they reduce production costs, because it is easier to make corrections on unjustified type. It is not necessary to change every line in a paragraph in order to add or take out a word in one line. Some readers find that ragged right margins make a text easier to read. When lines end at different places, it is easier for readers to keep their place in the text. They are less likely to go back and reread the same line twice, because the right profile distinguishes one line from another. Also, the eye does not have to adjust to different spacing between letters, as it does with justified type.

6. AVOID USING ALL CAPITAL LETTERS.

Some documents use ALL CAPS, or uppercase letters, for emphasis. But ALL CAPS interferes with the legibility of text. We recommend other highlighting techniques instead, such as boldface, italics, or color.

All caps make text harder to read because the shapes of the letters do not vary very much. One of the ways that readers differentiate among letters is by their shape. Lowercase letters have more distinctive shapes than uppercase. Compare the shape of these two sets of words:

FLASHLIGHT BATTERY

Flashlight battery

When a whole block of text is printed in ALL CAPS, it takes up more space and takes longer to read. Also, the highlighting effect of the uppercase letters is lost because it is overused. See how this paragraph would look in ALL CAPS.

WHEN A WHOLE BLOCK OF TEXT IS PRINTED IN ALL CAPS, IT TAKES UP MORE SPACE AND TAKES LONGER TO READ. ALSO, THE HIGHLIGHTING EFFECT OF THE UPPERCASE LETTERS IS LOST BECAUSE IT IS OVERUSED. SEE HOW THIS PARAGRAPH WOULD LOOK IN ALL CAPS.

A Typography Primer

In this section, we describe the basic features used in typesetting.

Serif and Sans Serif Type

Type comes in many styles, but there are two basic ones: serif and sans serif. Serif type has short, horizontal strokes that project from the tops and bottoms of the letters. *Simply Stated* is printed in a serif typeface. Serifs enhance the horizontal flow of a line of type, making it easier to read across a line. Serifs also make the individual letters easier to distinguish. Ancient Roman stone cutters used serifs to make their hand cut lettering look more even and horizontal. Serif typefaces are generally considered to be formal and traditional.

Sans serif type is type without serifs. It has a clean, contemporary look, and is generally considered to give an informal feeling. The clean design of sans serif type makes it easy to read, but because it does not have serifs to enhance the horizontal flow, a sans serif typeface requires more space between lines of type than a serif typeface of the same size.

serif Typography

sans serif Typography

Families of Type

Most styles of type are available in six different versions. The *style* is the same, but the letters vary in thickness, width, or slant. For example, here are six versions of Helvetica, a sans serif typeface.

Light	typography
Regular	typography
Bold	**typography**
Condensed	typography
Extended	typography
Italic	*typography*

These six versions form a "family" of type. If you want to emphasize individual words or short passages, you can use bold or italic type of the same family as the rest of your text. Titles can be in a larger size of the same face. (See "Measuring Type.") You can mix light, regular, bold, and italic type, as long as they are in the same family. But do not mix condensed or extended type with regular type; the shapes of the letters differ too much to look good together. In addition, condensed and extended faces have their own families of light, bold, and italic.

Measuring Type

Graphic artists work with two basic measurements: picas and points. They use picas to measure the length of a line or the width of a column. There are six picas to an inch, twelve points to a pica, and 72 points to an inch.

Points are used to measure the size of the type itself—the individual letters. Typefaces are identified by *point size* and *style*; for example, *Simply Stated* is printed in 10 point Century Schoolbook. The point size measures the whole letter, including *ascenders* (the tops of the "T" and the "h") and *descenders* (the tails of the "y" and the "p").

Graphic artists also speak of the "x-height" of a letter. This is the height of the body of the letter *without* ascenders or descenders, or the height of a small letter like an "x." When you are choosing a type size, it is important to consider the "x" height of your typeface. Although two different styles of type may both be 9 point, one may have a smaller "x-height" than the other. If you choose that face, you might need to go up to a 10 point size to get as readable a text as you would with a 9 point size and a larger "x-height." "X-height" will also influence how much space or "leading" you need between lines of type. (See "Leading.")

Leading

The space between lines of type is called *leading*. This term derives from the practice of setting hot metal type. When the type is set, strips of lead are laid between the lines of type. Although phototypesetting is more common than hot metal today, graphic artists still use the term "leading" to describe the space between lines. The leading, like the type itself, is measured in points. A text set in 10 point type with 11 point leading is said to be set "10 on 11," or "10/11." *Simply Stated* is set 10/11.

The amount of leading you use can affect the legibility of your text. If your text is *set solid,* with no extra space between lines, it will look too heavy and difficult to read. If you put in too much leading, your lines of type will appear to drift apart, making it difficult for the reader to follow the text.

Features of the type will affect your leading. Very small type and bold type require extra leading to relieve the density of the text. Sans serif type requires more leading than serif type of the same size, because it does not have serifs to carry the horizontal flow of the line and establish a clean break between the lines. Long lines require more leading than short lines in the same typesize; the extra leading helps the reader to follow across the long lines.

Look how much easier it is to read this passage in 7 point type when it is set with 8 point leading, as opposed to 7 (set solid). But see how it floats apart when it is set 7/11. (This is set 7/8.)

Look how much easier it is to read this passage in 7 point type when it is set with 8 point leading, as opposed to 7 (set solid). But see how it floats apart when it is set 7/11. (This is set solid.)

Look how much easier it is to read this passage in 7 point type when it is set with 8 point leading, as opposed to 7 (set solid). But see how it floats apart when it is set 7/11. (This is set 7/11.)

Listen Up—Tips from the Top on Talks

Terry C. Smith

Most effective speakers "listen" to the audience by checking for comprehension and watching for restlessness. This article gives advice on responding to audience questions during an oral presentation and creating a decision-making atmosphere. Review the ten tips before giving an oral presentation.

Recently I interviewed several general managers from a large aerospace electronics corporation concerning advice they would give presenters. What better way to improve our speaking skills than to identify the likes and dislikes of one of our most important audiences? I wasn't disappointed.

One piece of advice that kept coming up in the interviews seemingly had little to do with speaking—but a lot to do with communication. It was LISTEN. In fact one GM's response was "*LISTEN, LISTEN, LISTEN!*" Another's went even further, pointing out that speakers should listen with their eyes (observing audience body language, etc.) as well as their ears. This particular GM suggested that speakers "measure their audience constantly to tell—

- Whether they are interested or bored
- Whether you're talking over or beneath the key players.

Then be willing to adapt on the fly, hitting key points, skipping details, asking if your points are making sense."

LISTEN AS YOU SPEAK

Most of us have our hands full merely giving a presentation. Being a good listener while giving a talk will be a lot easier if you follow a few of the GMs' simple tips. First, keep your head up, maintaining eye contact rather than staying buried in a script. Better still, throw away the script by learning to extemporize. Put your key points and statistics on a single sheet, in large type, as a life preserver for use only if needed. (Practices, dry runs, and dress rehearsals will make this seem easy.) Secondly, work in a few pauses so the audience will have an opportunity to get a word in edgewise.

Before you start, let the audience know you welcome questions during your presentations. (Top management is unlikely to wait until the end anyway.)

Remember, your objective is to convey thoughts, issues, solutions—whatever, and a monologue may not do the trick. Delivery intermingled with questions and answers is far more likely to achieve your objective. For example, a key member of the audience engaging you in dialog and then reaching concurrence may have more *real* impact on others in the audience than your entire presentation delivered without interaction. (Of course, if that key person does not reach concurrence, or is perceived by the others not to have reached concurrence, you may have a problem. But it's better to know now than to find out later.) Whatever you do, never leave an issue hanging. Restate the situation and strive for concurrence that will be clearly evident to others, but be careful to do so without putting the person in an uncomfortable position.

Having *thoroughly* done your homework is a must for having things go smoothly. If you do run into difficulty and think you might be about to stumble, be willing to lateral to a team member. But do so advisedly. Establish eye contact to make sure your teammate looks like he or she knows the answer. Don't toss anyone the ball if the person's eyes are closed. A prearranged hand signal from a team member will tell you that your teammate is ready and allow you to control the lateral rather than be interrupted. (Particularly bad if the wrong person jumps in trying to be helpful because you waited too long or appeared too desperate.)

Once your team member has answered the question satisfactorily, regain control by expressing thanks and/or asking the questioner if his or her needs were satisfied. Then move on to your next point.

If both you and your team members are stumped, don't guess or speculate. Be willing to say you don't have the information, but you will get it. Then *always* follow up. And follow up with the entire audience, even if the information may only be relevant to one or two individuals. Credibility is your number one asset. Perhaps some easier questions asked earlier will have built up a credibility balance in your account that will carry you over the tough one you couldn't handle.

Even if a question is an easy one, don't cut the questioner off in a rush to show how smart you are. In addition to being rude, you may wind up giving an answer that's correct, but not the answer to the question that would have been asked had you allowed the person to finish. In many presentations you can't accomplish your objective until the audience starts talking. How foolish to cut off that flow with a snap answer.

One GM went so far as to say *never* give a one-way presentation. Find a way to make it two-way. Then there is much less risk of being accused of arrogance, talking down, or patronizing. "Polished speakers," he added, "know when to let it free wheel and when to control the interchange. Finally, they know when to stop talking: when they've convinced the audience and further talking may result in a step backwards."

This last point would seem a function of time as much as anything else. If you can present your ideas in 10 minutes, do so. If the audience wants more, they'll let you know by the questions. By all means avoid going beyond 20 minutes unless it's a training session or the subject matter is complicated. Even then, keep in mind that the purpose of most business presentations is to put forth ideas for consideration and not to provide step-by-step proof. The detailed proof can be provided in a handout or kept in reserve in the form of extra visuals to be used if needed. Having a few extra visuals set aside in case someone says "How do you explain . . ." or "Wait a minute" can have a great effect on an audience.

Don't get upset or lose your cool if you find yourself being challenged, particularly if your proposal involves big bucks. The people holding the purse strings have a right and a duty to probe deeply. As a minimum, you'd better be prepared to answer, "What is your confidence level in . . . ?"

So far this column has concentrated on the dialogue engaged in during a presentation. That's where the GMs I talked to placed the most emphasis and where there was the most agreement. Suggestions on other areas will be found in the accompanying checklist. Certainly these men and women practice what they preach.

Over the years I have watched each of them enter the ranks of management and progress upward. Anyone aspiring to move up the ladder of success would do well to follow their advice.

TEN MORE TIPS FOR SUCCESSFUL TALKS

1. Never be wishy washy about accepting an assignment to speak. Your acceptance should be an indication of the enthusiasm you will bring to the actual presentation. Consider it an opportunity to sell yourself and your ideas.

2. If there are other speakers, find out as much as you can about them and their talks in advance—particularly if they will precede you on the program. If you are in the same organization, sit in on their practice session. If they are outsiders, ask for a draft or at least a hard copy of their visuals. Offer yours in return.

3. KISS! Keep it short and simple. (No more than three main points.) Make it fun. Try to sell weddings instead of funerals.

4. Recipe for a talk . . .
   Add portions of Who, What, Why, Where, When, and How. Blend in the Problem, Approach, Results, Conclusions, and Recommendations. Concentrate on "What Happened?" and "So What?" Tell "What It Is," "What It Does," and "How It Does It." Drain complexities and discard. Sprinkle generously with Benefits. Finish with a Call to Action.

5. Still battling butterflies? If you've really done your homework, that fact should give you confidence. So should the fact that you have something worthwhile (benefits) to say. The practice/dry run/dress rehearsal approach means you've already given the talk at least three times. Get there early to check out *all* the mechanics and greet the audience as it arrives. Take a few deep breaths, pick out somebody who looks friendly, and start talking.

6. Watch out for slang, poor grammar, tasteless jokes (racist, ethnic, sexist, off color), and any appearance or dress factors that will make you appear less polished.

7. Give viewgraph projectors some room. After placing material, step away at least three feet to avoid blocking the image. Using a pointer will give you an opportunity to step away from the projector toward the side of the screen. But be sure to avoid the temptation to gaze lovingly at the screen with your back to the audience.

8. Avoid using the phrase, "As you can plainly see. . . ." while showing visuals that would send even a .300 hitter to the closest Pearle Vision Center. Remember that an illustration prepared for a report or a proposal will probably have too much detail and too small type to make a good visual for a presentation.

9. Use the end of your talk to cover all the bases. 1. Tell them what you told them (summarize). 2. Ask for the order (call to action or close). 3. Thank them for their time and attention (and perhaps wish them good luck). 4. Ask

for questions and then WAIT long enough to give them time to respond. If there are none, consider adding some of your own as a way to cover a few key points one last time.

10. After the presentation, follow up by sending extra information, or at least a thank-you note for their time. If you didn't get an answer to your call for action at the end of your presentation (quite likely), this may help jog them.

Editing for an International Audience

Judith H. Tarutz

> *Writers must be aware of pitfalls in writing for international audiences. This excerpt from a book about technical editing provides guidelines for preparing documents that will be used by international readers.*

If you work for a multinational company or one that sells internationally, chances are the documentation you edit will either be used by foreign nationals or translated into other languages.

If internationalization is important where you work, you may even do a separate editing pass to ensure that the material is suitable for translation or use by a non-American audience.

Editing for an international audience requires a sensitivity to language, cultural, and technical differences.

LANGUAGE CONSIDERATIONS

Here are some ways you can make manuals easier to read and use for nonnative speakers of English:[1]

- Use simple, clear sentences.

- Use more illustrations.

- Provide an expanded glossary.

- Provide constant confirmation. For example, instructions for a call-forwarding service for a telephone could say, "When you press the # button, you hear a short beep. The beep confirms that the call-forwarding feature is activated."

- Use consistent terminology. Don't use more than one name for the same thing without a valid technical reason.

Here are some ways we inadvertently make manuals more difficult to read for our international audience:

- Changing voice within a paragraph.

- Using slang, idioms, colloquialisms: *stripped down version, jumping to conclusions, stop short, on the other hand.*

- Using industry jargon. (Be aware that readers outside the U.S. may be using the English of ten years ago; their technical dictionaries and glossaries—if they have them—may be out of date. For example, the term *unbundling* was being used in the U.S. to refer to a pricing and distribution practice for hardware and software long before the practice and the term became known in Europe and Asia.)

---

[1] These are good guidelines for material destined for domestic audiences, too.

545

- Using words that have more than one meaning, particularly verb forms with prepositions; for example, *make up* can mean *to compose* or *to reconcile; exhaust* can mean *to tire* or *to use up*.
- Using noun strings. Even if English is your native language, "logical operator precedence" and "DNA fingerprinting study results" are difficult to parse.
- Using nouns as verbs or using words that can be either nouns or verbs, such as *result* and *order.*
- Splitting infinitives, splitting verbs and adverbs. For example: "put down the telephone" is easier to read than "put the telephone down."
- Using abbreviations (even **Y** for *yes*) and acronyms, which are sometimes impossible to translate.

CULTURAL CONSIDERATIONS

Here are some ways we can be more sensitive to cultural differences:

- Avoid showing human figures, if possible, because of race, gender, and other stereotyping.
- Give metric measurements, followed by U.S. equivalents.
- Give the metric equivalent of the size of U.S.-based tools.
- Use culture-neutral examples, with respect to names, dates, numbers, and monetary systems. Tell what format (for dates and numbers) or system (monetary) you're using.
- Recognize that not all speakers of the same language are culturally the same. For example, there are cultural differences among French speakers in Canada, Switzerland, and France, just as there are cultural differences among English speakers in the United States, England, Australia, and the Philippines.
- Remember that humor doesn't travel easily.
- Use generic terms instead of trademarks, such as *photocopy* instead of *Xerox*. (Besides, you should not be using a trademark as a common noun or verb. A trademark is an adjective, as in Xerox copier.)
- As a matter of courtesy more than correctness, you might include non-Anglo-Saxon names in examples.
- Remember that not everybody knows U.S. geography. For example, the reference, "On the east coast" makes sense to a North American but probably doesn't to anyone else. If you need to refer to such a region, use a more definite reference, like, "On the east coast of North America."

TECHNICAL DIFFERENCES

Here are some production technicalities to consider:

- International paper sizes differ from "standard" American sizes, so you may need to adapt the page design to accommodate the different text image area.
- Many manuals in the U.S. are drilled with three holes. Binders in other countries vary in the number of holes.

- English is a concise language; when translated into other languages, text requires on average 30% more space. Ensure that illustrations have space for translated callouts and labels.

Here are some technical details to consider:

- Ordering is often culture-bound. For example, if the text says, "list the days of the week in order," an American would put Sunday first, but some Europeans would put Monday first. If it matters, make sure you spell out which day should be first.

- Americans would read the date 10/9/88 as October 9, 1988; Europeans would read it as September 10, 1988. The Japanese often format dates in year/month/day order. If you're editing a sample program that uses dates, make sure the text specifies the order expected for input or output.

- Time is culture-bound. Many countries use the 24-hour clock to express written times (although when speaking, people often still use the 12-hour clock). If you're using an American-style time, make sure you include AM or PM to avoid confusion.

- Be careful with time zones. Sometimes documentation refers to the time when daylight savings time begins but doesn't mention the specific date. The date can vary from country to country, and some countries don't go on daylight savings time at all. If the specific date is important, make sure you spell it out, rather than just imply it.

- If you give engineers feedback on the user interface, make sure there is enough room to display translated text in help screens, prompts, error messages, and menus. Editing instructions for a small screen—such as a copier—will be quite a challenge!

- When you organize information—such as reference pages—alphabetically, you may be giving the translator more work.

- Be aware that the American *billion* is 10^9; in the British system it is 10^{12}. The names of other high numbers (such as trillion, quadrillion) are likewise different in the two systems. Instead of using these terms, express the value as a power of 10.

Here are some technical details just for computer manuals:

- Make sure references to the ASCII character set are correct. In some cases, references to ASCII are justified; in others, they're holdovers from the days before companies supported larger character sets.

- Think about when you mean *byte* and when you mean *character*. The two terms are often used synonymously, but in an internationalized system, a character can consist of more than one byte. For example, you may be used to saying that a filename can have up to 256 characters, but that isn't correct if you're using a 16-bit character set.

- Watch for case conventions. Ideographic languages such as Japanese and Chinese have only one case—there are no separate uppercase and lowercase versions of characters. In addition, not all characters in alphabetical languages have uppercase and lowercase versions. Keep these differences in mind if your text includes references to case conversion. The conversion may be impossible to do.

- If your products support European languages, common references such as "Identifiers can include any alphabetical character (A–Z)" may not be correct. Several European languages, Danish for one, have characters that occur *after* Z. Of course, A–Z as an all-inclusive range doesn't even begin to encompass all the possibilities in ideographic languages.

- Check references to sorting order. The text might read, "The utility sorts the names in alphabetical order." But "alphabetical order" differs from language to language—or doesn't exist at all for many Asian languages. For example, the Spanish alphabet begins *a, b, c, ch, d*. The correct wording differs according to what the software you're describing *actually* does. It might sort characters in code-set order, or in language order, or (for ideographic languages) in stroke order, or any number of different ways.

Tips, Tricks and Pitfalls to Avoid When Doing Business in the Tough but Lucrative Korean Market

Although Koreans have adopted many Western business practices, there remain many significant differences. This article from Business America, *a publication of the Department of Commerce, discusses some important distinctions between North American and Korean business practices.*

- Koreans have a great respect for the family and hierarchy, and also a great respect for anyone senior in age. They will intuitively establish their hierarchical position relative to others based on age and social position.

- The majority of working women, many with top university degrees, are relegated in Korean companies to secretarial jobs, assembly work positions, or educational work. Many women, hence, welcome the opportunity to work as a professional with a foreign company where attitudes toward gender equality and professional respect prevail.

- American business representatives should be prepared to answer what the Koreans may regard as common curiosity but foreigners may regard as personal intrusion, such as questions regarding age, marital status, income and salary. Be ready to mix business with pleasure as the Koreans base their business relationships on personal ones.

- When doing business, Americans should be sensitive to the Korean historical relationship with Japan, which made a virtual colony of the Korean peninsula. Because of the Japanese colonial period, Koreans have an emotionally intense reaction at times to things Japanese, though there is an admiration for Japanese business acumen.

- Korea still observes Confucian ethics based on a strong association to a group. Whereas Americans may think in individual terms—"what is in my best interest?" Koreans often think in group terms—"what is in the best interest of the group?" For this reason, the majority of Koreans are intensely patriotic, calling Korea by the term *"oo-ri-na-ra"* (our country).

- For Koreans, relationships are critical: "cold calls" don't work and introductions are crucial! Koreans want to do business with people with whom they have formed a personal connection.

- The exchange of business cards is very important and a means by which Koreans learn about the name, position and status of the other person. Koreans observe a very strict hierarchical code, whereby Koreans will generally meet to discuss business with persons of the same, parallel rank. Always have your—preferably bilingual—business card at the ready and treat the exchange and your counterpart's card with some respect. (It is customary to receive and present items with both hands.)

- An important point to keep in mind concerns the nature of reaching an agreement with a Korean firm. Westerners attach great importance to a written

549

contract which specifies each detail of the business relationship. Koreans, on the other hand, value a contract as a loosely-structured consensus statement that broadly defines what has been negotiated, but leaves sufficient room to permit flexibility and adjustment.

- Most Koreans have three names. These names usually follow the Chinese pattern of a surname followed by two given names. In addressing Koreans, foreigners should stick to the use of surnames (Mr. Kim; Ms. Lee), using formal titles if possible (Dr. Yoo; Director Song). The most common last names are Kim, Lee, and Park.

Color: The Newest Tool
for Technical Communicators

Jan V. White

Appropriate colors in a technical document can direct readers to specific kinds of information, focus attention on particular elements, and establish consistency. This article excerpt discusses color as an editing device to help readers find useful information.

One of the myths of publishing is that readers are readers. Seldom is that true. Of course, there is a group of publications that are bought for the pleasure of reading (novels, whodunits, literary magazines), but they are a tiny segment of the total number of printed pages produced in a given time. Technical documentation uses much more paper, even if it does get less publicity.

Except for the true literati, readers are nothing of the sort: they are *searchers*. To do their searching, they start out as *viewers* or *lookers*. They flip pages, scan, hunt and peck, searching for the nuggets of information that they need and that might prove valuable to them.

CATCH YOUR READERS' ATTENTION

Overworked, in a hurry, saturated with "information," and perhaps a bit lazy, too, technical readers need to be lured into reading. Perhaps *persuaded* might be a better word than *lured*, because luring implies a little bit of bamboozling, and duplicity has no place in technical documentation. The least trace of cheating or trickery is self-defeating, because it destroys the potential reader's trust in the probity and seriousness of the document.

The only kind of persuasion that is credible must be based on the presentation of the values that are inherent in the message. Exposing those values and making them easily accessible does not destroy their dependability or credibility, for honest values are demonstrable. Making them easily accessible helps to make the document useful and liked. Combining accessibility (that is, making things easy to find) with speed makes the document a useful, dependable tool.

Where do people begin reading? Where do **you** begin? Observe your own reactions when you pick up a piece of printed matter, because you are typical. You probably don't always start at the beginning. In fact, you very seldom start at the beginning.

Like you, most people enter a document at a place where something catches their interest. If there is a picture, the first thing they look at is the image. But a caption, a word, a phrase, a concept, even a title can also catch their eye and fascinate them into paying attention. The trick is to find the valuable highlights that you know will be helpful to your audience, and deliberately display them. That is the way to make documents helpful and therefore irresistible.

COLOR CAN HELP OR HINDER

Unfortunately, color is a material so beset with silly misunderstandings and imagined magic that it is the editor's worst temptation. It is perhaps even more difficult to exploit color simply and forthrightly than to use type simply and forthrightly. True, you can have a lot of fun with type . . . but you probably know simply from experience how far to go before making a fool of yourself. Everyone is more familiar with type because it has been around for so long as the fundamental black-and-white raw material.

But color is a material that has only lately become widely available. It is such an alluring material, it is so beautiful, so cheerful, so different, such a treat to work with. Look at all those magazines and posters and movies and videos bubbling with visual excitement. What an opportunity to be creative!

Please avoid that trap. Technical documentation is a serious product, and there is no place in it for amusement and evanescent trendiness.

Furthermore, today's audiences (those "readers") are so sated with visual excesses that whatever may be exciting to you and an innovation in the day-to-day techniques at your disposal is not nearly as exciting to them. Color may be new to you, since you have not had an opportunity to use it before, but it is old hat to them. It saturates whatever they look at all around. Therefore, color as plain, simple colorfulness carries little attraction any more.

A third depressing negative: However hard it may try, technical documentation is doomed to look like a poor cousin next to publications in which colorfulness is a functional and integral part of the product. Color is vital in *Vogue, Sports Illustrated,* and *National Geographic.* It is part and parcel of the message there. In some instances, color itself is the substance of the message. What fun it must be to work with material like that.

Alas, it is seldom fun to work with technical documents—unless you make it happen by clever and insightful analysis. You'll need a lot of thought and a lot of self-restraint, because color is such an amusing material to work with. If ever that cliché about "less being more" applied, here is that instance.

How cleverly you handle what you have to work with is the difference between mediocrity and greatness. There are no rules. There are only criteria by which to judge. Every communicator has to stand alone in his or her judgment as to the rightness or wrongness of a technique. Is red better than blue? It depends on what you are trying to do.

Should the background be in color and the foreground in black, or should the background be in black and the foreground picked out in color? It depends on what you are trying to do.

Everything always depends on what you are trying to do. That is what makes communication so exciting and challenging. That is also what makes it perfectly possible for a nondesigner to be confident of making the right decisions about the daunting esoteric process of Design.

Color judgment should not be based on subjective, personal "liking." It must be used deliberately, fulfilling specific needs and purposes. It is not an artistic material but a communication material.

Here are some of the fundamental intellectual underpinnings for using color functionally—and appropriately—in the area of technical communication. You could think of them as criteria for judgment. Perhaps you could even use them as a mental checklist. If the way you intend using color fulfills one of these purposes, you are reasonably safe. At least you can rationalize its use. If it fulfills two of them, you can be confident that you are on the right road. If it fulfills three or more, you have nothing to worry about. Go!

Does the Color Focus Attention on an Element That Is Worthy of It?

Color is different from black. (Not a brilliant insight, but you would be amazed how often the most obvious is overlooked.) Since most of the surroundings are usually black and white and are expected by the viewer to be so, anything that departs from the norm is bound to attract attention to itself.

Three question you have to ponder is whether that element is worthy of the attraction color gives it. Headings are often done in color. Why? They are already different from the body copy by virtue of their size and blackness. What quality does color add by making them even more different?

Perhaps it might add value, if you can honestly say yes to the next question.

Does the Color Establish Understanding Through Color-keyed Associations?

If some headings are in color because they belong to a subset of some sort (whether in ranking, quality, subject, or any other grouping), then their color is a mark of differentiation. They remain headings, but they become special. Color is a means of making them so.

But this recognition only works if you can say yes to the next question.

Does the Color Establish Identity Through Logical Consistency?

People are keenly aware of differences in color: red apples and yellow apples in a bowl are immediately sorted into Red Delicious and Golden Delicious, and a green Granny Smith obviously stands out as another variety. True, they are all apples, but they are sorted into kinds by color at first glance.

If you make some headlines red, some blue, and others green for no better reason than exuberance and because the colors are technically available, the viewer will not be able to sort them out. The result will be confusing. (Incidentally, black plus three other colors is the maximum that most people can easily remember as distinguishing characteristics for purposes of sorting, unless you provide a color key as a frequently repeated reminder.)

Does Color Rank Value by the Sequence in Which Elements Are Noticed?

Bold type screams and tiny type whispers. Those are qualities everyone understands, so they are used for fast communication by editors, writers, and designers; they rank information and attract attention.

Again, there is nothing startling about this concept. It has an exact parallel in color, where some hues jump off the page and others hide. Alas, however, the concept is a little more complicated than mere brightness ("chroma"). The **effect** of color depends on proportions and relationships to the surroundings. A huge area of very bright color is so loud that it repels, whereas a small spot of the identical hue may be just right. A tiny area of a pale, wan color may not be noticed at all, whereas a large area may be perfect as an identifying background for a box on the page.

It is impossible to generalize or make rules. But the principle is valid. Be aware of the comparative degrees of urgency your colors create, and apply them in such a way that the viewer is guided by them to understand the information in the appropriate sequence.

Does Color Facilitate Comprehension of the Document's Structure?

One of the most depressing characteristics of technical documentation is the apparent length of each volume. User manuals are especially daunting by their weight and the very number of their pages. If their enormousness is broken into segments, they become less terrifying, for even the longest journey starts with but a single step.

Color can be used to subdivide. Let's assume you print the glossary on blue, the index on green, and the introduction on yellow. Three units have been separated from the rest, making the residue appear shorter and more user friendly.

Now take your chapter openers, make them all a full spread and run red ink or toner full bleed all around. Such a strong organizational signal cannot be missed, especially when the document is held in the hand and examined—and the slivers of red are visible on the outer edge. (It is vital to have chapter starts use a full spread, so the color can appear on the edges of both left-hand and right-hand pages. That way it is noticeable in both directions).

Does the Color Imply the Right Connotations?

Colors carry cultural associations. Again, there are no general rules nor are the implications universal or standardized. They are based on common sense and knowing the culture of the demographic segment you are communicating with.

Take the case of bananas: They are yellow, but when flecked with brown they are ripening, yet an all-brown banana is over-ripe and a black one is rotten (especially if it has a few patches of green). A pale-green banana is unripe, and a blue one is frozen. A purple banana is a child's version of bananahood, and a striped banana is surprising (like a purple-and-green-striped zebra). A silver banana is inedible because it is a piece of sculpture, while a polkadotted one is a joke. And a red banana is not a banana at all but a plantain.

So which color do you use? The one that gets the right story across. Don't pick out dollar numbers in red: the company might be interpreted as being in the red. Beware of picking a color just because you like it. The color may skew the meaning in a given context. Green also means Go; amber, Caution; red, Stop.

Does the Color You Want to Use Fit Into the Corporate Idiom?

Your choice of hue may well be limited by the palette determined by the designers who produced the corporate style for the organization. As in most companies, it is very likely that these determinations were made for everything other than technical documentation. They were probably originally intended to create an identity in the marketing and advertising sphere, were then extended to include signage, the marking of vehicles, and then someone remembered, Oh yes! How about all that technical stuff? Oh well, let them figure that out for themselves, because it doesn't really matter.

Ah, but it does matter very much indeed. The way the techdocs look is a vital link in the total impression a company makes on the competitive world. Learn the rules, understand the need for discipline, and realize that the more restricted the variety of materials used, the stronger and more obvious the corporate image becomes. It is senseless to rail against the restrictions. It is far better to accept them and work with them.

Does Color Help to Give Order to Information Chaos?

- Does it explain relationships by the way segments relate to one another?
- Does it analyze data visually so they are obvious to the casual looker?
- Does it draw the looker into becoming interested, involved, and perhaps even into reading?
- Does it help that reader to understand the information?
- Does it enliven the atmosphere of the product, while making the information clearer?
- Does color add intellectual value?

If you can find a way to fulfill those purposes, you will have achieved something of inestimable value. The frustrating thing is that none of this is quantifiable. The first and most obvious reaction of everybody on looking at a page is whether it is pretty or not, irrespective of whether it works. Color is too often mistaken for cosmetics. Avoid that trap.

Use color to make the ideas on the pages clear, no matter whether the color adds deliberate prettiness or not. If you apply color functionally, you will discover to your amazement and delight that it also adds a degree of excellence that is in fact visually satisfying and perhaps even beautiful. However, that happens only if you do not pursue beauty as a goal. If you pursue clarity, you will find that beauty is an inevitable byproduct.

Having found the answer, standardize it. Repeat and repeat and repeat, because patterning creates clues for the viewer, who is taught how to react to the elements you are presenting on the pages. Besides, repetitive patterning also helps create personality for your product, a vital characteristic in the marketplace. So avoid the temptation to add, embroider, or make changes for the fun of it (or because you are afraid the viewers will get bored. They won't, even if you do, because they don't have to live with your product as long as you do.) Don't show off, don't be original for the sake of being original. On the contrary, guard your system carefully against erosion or dilution.

None of this is designing for Art's sake. That is why you need not be afraid of color. All it does is to exploit the capacity of design to help the user. As such, it is an integral part of editing for the reader. That is our profession.

Ethical Reasoning in Technical Communication: A Practical Framework

Mark R. Wicclair and David K. Farkas

Technical writers often confront ethical problems just as lawyers and other professionals do. This article discusses three types of ethical principles—goal based, duty based, and rights based—and then describes and analyzes two cases in which a writer had to face an ethical dilemma. Notice that the third ethical case has no suggested solutions. Consider what you might do in these circumstances.

Professionals in technical communication confront ethical problems at times, just as in law, medicine, engineering, and other fields. In recent years STC has increased its effort to generate a greater awareness and understanding of the ethical dimension of the profession.[1] This article is intended to contribute to that effort.

To clarify the nature of ethical problems, we first distinguish between the ethical perspective and several other perspectives. We then discuss three types of ethical principles. Together these principles make up a conceptual framework that will help illuminate almost any ethical problem. Finally, we demonstrate the application of these principles using hypothetical case studies.

THE NATURE OF ETHICAL PROBLEMS

Typically, when faced with an ethical problem, we ask, "What should I do?" But it is important to recognize that this question can be asked from a number of perspectives. One perspective is an attempt to discover the course of action that will best promote a person's own interests. This is not, however, a question of ethics. Indeed, as most of us have discovered, there is often a conflict between ethical requirements and considerations of self-interest. Who hasn't had the experience of being tempted to do something enjoyable or profitable even while knowing it would be wrong?

A second non-ethical perspective is associated with the law. When someone asks, "What should I do?" he may want to know whether a course of action is required or prohibited by law or is subject to legal sanction. There is often a connection between the perspective of law and the perspective of self-interest, for the desire to discover what the law requires is often motivated by the desire to avoid punishment and other legal sanctions. But between the perspectives of law and ethics there are several significant differences.

First, although many laws correspond to moral rules (laws against murder, rape, and kidnapping, for instance), other laws do not (such as technicalities of corporate law and various provisions of the tax code). Furthermore, almost every legal system has at one time or another included some unjust laws—such as laws in this country that institutionalized racism or laws passed in Nazi Germany. Finally, unethical actions are not necessarily illegal. For example, though it is morally wrong to lie or break a promise, only certain instances of lying (e.g., lying under oath) or promise breaking (e.g., breach of contract) are punishable under law. For all these reasons, then, it is important to recognize that law and ethics represent significantly different perspectives.

One additional perspective should be mentioned: religion. Religious doctrines, like laws, often correspond to moral rules, and for many people religion is an important motive for ethical behavior. But religion is ultimately distinct from ethics. When a Catholic, Protestant, or Jew asks, "What should I do?" he or she may want to know how to act as a good Catholic, Protestant, or Jew. A question of this type is significantly different from the corresponding ethical question: "How do I behave as a good human being?" In answering this latter question, one cannot refer to principles that would be accepted by a member of one faith and rejected by a member of another or a non-believer. Consequently, unlike religiously based rules of conduct, ethical principles cannot be derived from or justified by the doctrines or teachings of a particular religious faith.

THREE TYPES OF ETHICAL PRINCIPLES

To resolve ethical problems, then, we must employ ethical principles. We discuss here three types of ethical principles: goal-based, duty-based, and rights-based. Although these do not provide a simple formula for instantly resolving ethical problems, they do offer a means to reason about ethical problems in a systematic and sophisticated manner.[2]

Goal-Based Principles

Public policies, corporate decisions, and the actions of individuals all produce certain changes in the world. Directly or indirectly they affect the lives of human beings. These effects can be good or bad or a combination of both. According to goal-based principles, the rightness or wrongness of an action is a function of the goodness or badness of its consequences.

Goal-based principles vary according to the particular standard of value that is used to evaluate consequences. But the most widely known goal-based principle is probably the principle of utility. Utilitarians claim that we should assess the rightness of an action according to the degree to which it promotes the general welfare. We should, in other words, select the course of action that produces the greatest amount of aggregate good (the greatest good for the greatest number of people) or the least amount of aggregate harm. Public-policy decisions are often evaluated on the basis of this principle.

Duty-Based Principles

In the case of duty-based principles, the focus shifts from the consequences of our actions to the actions themselves. Some actions are wrong, it is claimed, just for what they are and not because of their bad consequences. Many moral judgments about sexual behavior are in part duty-based. From this perspective, if patronizing a prostitute is wrong, it is not because of harm that might come to the patron, the prostitute, or society, but simply because a moral duty is violated. Likewise, an individual might make a duty-based assertion that it is inherently wrong to lie or break a promise even if no harm would result or even if these actions would produce good consequences.

Rights-Based Principles

A right is an entitlement that creates corresponding obligations. For example, the right to free speech—a right that is valued and protected in our society—entitles people to say what they want when they want to and imposes an obligation on others to let them speak. If what a person says would be likely to offend and upset people, there would be a goal-based reason for not permitting the speech. But from a rights-based perspective, the person is entitled to speak regardless of these negative consequences. In this respect, rights-based principles are like duty-based principles.

While many people believe strongly in the right to free speech, few would argue that this or other rights can never be overridden by considerations of likely consequences. To cite a classic example, the consequence of needless injury and death overrides anyone's right to stand up and cry "Fire!" in a crowded theater. Nevertheless, if there is a right to free speech, it is not permissible to impose restrictions on speech every time there is a goal-based reason for doing so.

APPLYING THESE ETHICAL PRINCIPLES

Together these three types of ethical principles provide technical communicators with a means of identifying and then resolving ethical problems associated with their work. We should begin by asking if a situation has an ethical dimension. To do this, we ask whether the situation involves any relevant goals, duties, or rights. Next, we should make sure that ethical considerations are not being confused with considerations of self-interest, law, or religion. If we choose to allow non-ethical considerations to affect our decisions, we should at least recognize that we are doing so. Finally, we should see what course, or courses, of action the relevant ethical principles point to. Sometimes, all point unequivocally to one course of action. However, in some cases these principles will conflict, some pointing in one direction, others in another. This is termed an "ethical dilemma." When faced with an ethical dilemma, we must assign priorities to the various conflicting ethical considerations—often a difficult and demanding process.

We now present and discuss two hypothetical case studies. In our discussion we refer to several goal-, duty-, and rights-based principles. We believe that the principles we cite are uncontroversial and generally accepted. In saying this, we do not mean to suggest that there are no significant disagreements in ethics. But it is important to recognize that disputes about specific moral issues often do not emanate from disagreements about ethical principles. For example, although there is much controversy about the morality of abortion, the disagreement is not over the acceptability of the ethical principle that all persons have a right to life; the disagreement is over the non-ethical question of whether fetuses are "persons."

We believe, then, that there is a broad consensus about many important ethical principles; and it is such uncontroversial principles that we cite in our discussion of the following two cases.

Case 1

Martin Yost is employed as a staff writer by Montgomery Kitchens, a highly reputable processed foods corporation. He works under Dr. Justin Zarkoff, a brilliant organic chemist who has had a series of major successes as Director of Section A of the New Products Division. Dr. Zarkoff is currently working on a formula for an improved salad dressing. The company is quite interested in this project and has requested that the lab work be completed by the end of the year.

It is time to write Section A's third-quarter progress report. However, for the first time in his career with Montgomery Kitchens, Zarkoff is having difficulty finishing a major project. Unexpectedly, the new dressing has turned out to have an inadequate shelf life.

When Yost receives Zarkoff's notes for the report, he sees that Zarkoff is claiming that the shelf-life problem was not discovered earlier because a group of cultures prepared by Section C was formulated improperly. Section C, Yost realizes, is a good target for Zarkoff, because it has a history of problems and because its most recent director, Dr. Rebecca Ross, is very new with the company and has not yet established any sort of "track record." It is no longer possible to establish whether the cultures were good or bad, but since Zarkoff's opinion will carry a great deal of weight, Dr. Ross and her subordinates will surely be held responsible.

Yost mentions Zarkoff's claim about the cultures to his very close and trustworthy friend Bob Smithson, Senior Chemist in Section A. Smithson tells Yost that he personally examined the cultures when they were brought in from Section C and that he is absolutely certain they were OK. Since he knows that Zarkoff also realizes that the cultures were OK, he strongly suspects that Zarkoff must have made some sort of miscalculation that he is now trying to cover up.

Yost tries to defuse the issue by talking to Zarkoff, suggesting to him that it is unprofessional and unwise to accuse Ross and Section C on the basis of mere speculation. Showing irritation, Zarkoff reminds Yost that his job is simply to write up the notes clearly and effectively. Yost leaves Zarkoff's office wondering whether he should write the report.

Analysis. If Yost prepares the report, he will not suffer in any way. If he refuses, he will damage his relationship with Zarkoff, perhaps irreparably, and he may lose his job. But these are matters of self-interest rather than ethics. The relevant ethical question is this: "Would it be *morally wrong* to write the report?"

From the perspective of goal-based principles, one would want to know whether the report would give rise to any bad consequences. It is obvious that it would, for Dr. Ross and her subordinates would be wrongly blamed for the foul-up. Thus, since there do not appear to be any overriding good consequences, one would conclude that writing the report would contribute to the violation of a goal-based ethical principle that prohibits actions that produce more bad than good.

Turning next to the duty-based perspective, we recognize that there is a duty not to harm people. A goal-based principle might permit writing the report if some good would follow that would outweigh the harm to Dr. Ross and her subordinates. But duty-based principles operate differently: Producing more good than bad wouldn't justify violating the duty not to harm individuals.

This duty would make it wrong to write the report unless some overriding duty could be identified. There may be a duty to obey one's boss, but neither this nor any other duty would be strong enough to override the duty not to harm others. In fact, there is another duty that favors not writing the report: the duty not to knowingly communicate false information.

Finally, there is the rights-based perspective. There appear to be two relevant rights: the right of Dr. Ross and her subordinates not to have their reputations wrongly tarnished and the company's right to know what is actually going on in its labs. Unless there is some overriding right, it would be morally wrong, from a rights-based perspective, to prepare the report.

In this case, then, goal-, duty-, and rights-based principles all support the same conclusion: Yost should not write the report. Since none of the principles furnishes a strong argument for writing the report, Yost is not faced with an ethical dilemma. But he is faced with another type of dilemma: Since refusing to write the report will anger Zarkoff and possibly bring about his own dismissal, Yost has to decide whether to act ethically or to protect his self-interest. If he writes the report, he will have to recognize that he is violating important goal-, duty-, and rights-based ethical principles.

Case 2

Susan Donovan works for Acme Power Equipment preparing manuals that instruct consumers on the safe operation and maintenance of power tools. For the first time in her career, one of her draft manuals has been returned with extensive changes: Numerous complex cautions and safety considerations have been added. The manual now stipulates an extensive list of conditions under which the piece of equipment should not be used and includes elaborate procedures for its use and maintenance. Because the manual is now much longer and more complex, the really important safety information is lost amid the expanded list of cautions. Moreover, after looking at all the overly elaborate procedures in the manual, the average consumer is apt to ignore the manual altogether. If it is prepared in this way, Donovan is convinced, the manual will actually lead to increased numbers of accidents and injuries.

Donovan expresses her concern in a meeting with her boss, Joe Hollingwood, Manager for Technical Information Services. Hollingwood responds that the revisions reflect a new policy initiated by the Legal Department in order to reduce the number of successful accident-related claims against the company. Almost any accident that could occur now would be in direct violation of stipulations and procedures described in the manual. Hollingwood acknowledges that the new style of manual will probably cause some people not to use the manuals at all, but he points out that most people can use the equipment safely without even looking at a manual. He adds that he too is concerned about the safety of consumers, but that the company needs to protect itself against costly lawsuits. Donovan responds that easily readable manuals lead to fewer accidents and, hence, fewer lawsuits. Hollingwood replies that in the expert opinion of the Legal Department the total cost to the company would be less if the manuals provided the extra legal protection they recommend. He then instructs Donovan to use the Legal Department's revisions as a model for all subsequent manuals. Troubled by Hollingwood's response, Donovan wants to know whether it is ethically permissible to follow his instructions.

Analysis. From the perspective of goal-based principles, writing manuals that will lead to increased injuries is ethically wrong. A possible good consequence is that a reduction in the number of successful lawsuits could result in lower prices. But neither this nor any other evident good consequence can justify injuries that might have been easily prevented.

A similar conclusion is arrived at from a duty-based perspective. Preparing these manuals would violate the important duty to prevent unnecessary and easily avoidable harm. Moreover, there appear to be no overriding duties that would justify violating this duty.

Finally, from a rights-based perspective, it is apparent that important rights such as the right to life and the right to health are at stake. It might also be claimed that people have a right to manuals that are designed to maximize their safety. Thus, ethical principles of each of the three types indicate it would be morally wrong to prepare the manuals according to Hollingwood's instructions.

Because Case 2 involves moral wrongs that are quite a bit more serious than those in Case 1, we now go on to consider an additional question, one not raised in the first case: What course of action should the technical communicator follow?

An obvious first step is to go over Hollingwood's head and speak to higher-level people in the company. This entails some risk, but might enable Donovan to reverse the new policy.

But what if this step fails? Donovan could look for a position with a more ethically responsible company. On the other hand, there is a goal-based reason for not quitting: By staying, Donovan could attempt to prepare manuals that would be safer than those that might be prepared by a less ethically sensitive successor. But very often this argument is merely a rationalization that masks the real motive of self-interest. The company, after all, is still engaging in an unethical practice, and the writer is participating in that activity.

Would leaving the company be a fully adequate step? While this would end the writer's involvement, the company's manuals would still be prepared in an unethical manner. There may indeed be an obligation to take further steps to have the practice stopped. To this end, Donovan might approach the media, or a government agency, or a consumer group. The obvious problem is that successively stronger steps usually entail greater degrees of risk and sacrifice. Taking a complaint outside the organization for which one works can jeopardize a technical communicator's entire career, since many organizations are reluctant to hire "whistle blowers."

Just how much can be reasonably asked of an individual in response to an immoral situation? To this question there is no clear answer, except to say that the greater the moral wrong, the greater the obligation to take strong—and perhaps risky—action against it.

CONCLUSION

The analyses offered here may strike the reader as very demanding. Naturally, we are all very reluctant to refuse assigned work, quit our jobs, or make complaints outside the organizations that employ us. No one wishes to be confronted by circumstances that would call for these kinds of responses, and many people simply would not respond ethically if significant risk and sacrifice were called for. This article provides a means of identifying and analyzing ethical problems, but deciding to make the appropriate ethical response to a situation is still a matter of individual conscience and will. It appears to be a condition of human existence that to live a highly ethical life usually exacts from us a certain price.[3]

Case 3

This case is presented without analysis so that readers can resolve it for themselves using the conceptual framework described in this essay.

A technical writer works for a government agency preparing instructional materials on fighting fires in industrial settings. Technical inaccuracies in these materials could lead to serious injury or death. The technical writer is primarily updating and expanding older, unreliable material that was published 30 years ago. He is trying to incorporate recently published material into the older material, but much of the recent information is highly technical and some of it is contradictory.

The technical writer has developed some familiarity with firefighting through his work, but has no special training in this field or in such related fields as chemistry. He was hired with the understanding that firefighting specialists in the agency as well as paid outside consultants would review drafts of all the materials in order to catch and correct any technical inaccuracies. He has come to realize, however, that neither the agency specialists nor the outside consultants do more than skim the drafts. Moreover, when he calls attention to special problems in the drafts, he receives replies that are hasty and sometimes evasive. In effect, whatever he writes will be printed and distributed to municipal fire departments, safety departments of industrial corporations, and other groups throughout the United States.

Is there an ethical problem here? If so, what is it, what ethical principles are involved, and what kinds of responses are called for?

NOTES

1. Significant activities include the re-establishment of the STC Committee on Ethics, the preparation of the STC "Code for Communicators," the group of articles on ethics published in the third-quarter 1980 issue of *Technical Communication* (as well as several articles published in other places), and the continuing series of cases and reader responses that have appeared in *Intercom*.

2. The arguments justifying ethical principles as well as ethics itself are beyond the scope of this essay but can be examined in Richard B. Brandt, *Ethical Theory: The Problems of Normative and Critical Ethics* (Englewood Cliffs, NJ: Prentice-Hall, 1959) and William K. Frankena, *Ethics,* 2nd ed. (Englewood Cliffs, NJ: Prentice-Hall, 1973). Other informative books are Fred Feldman, *Introductory Ethics* (Englewood Cliffs, NJ: Prentice-Hall, 1978) and Paul W. Taylor, *Principles of Ethics: An Introduction* (Encino, CA: Dickenson Publishing Company, 1975). All of these books are addressed to the general reader.

3. STC might develop mechanisms designed to reduce the price that individual technical communicators have to pay for acting ethically. For their part, individuals may have an obligation to work for the development and implementation of such mechanisms.

Index

CREDITS *(continued from copyright page)*

Pages 38–39. Revised and adapted from Charles Groves, "Safety Guidelines for Workers Renovating Buildings Containing Lead-Based Paint." Reprinted with permission of the author.

Pages 57–60. "Arthritis (brochure)." Reprinted with permission of the American Academy of Orthopaedic Surgeons, Rosemont, IL.

Page 62. From "Installation Instructions," *Maintenance and Troubleshooting Manual ACS:180.* Reprinted with permission of Ciba Corning Diagnostics Corp.

Page 64. Ko, H. C., and Brown, R. R., from "Enthalpy of Formation of $2CdO.CdSO_4$." Report of Investigations 8751. (Washington, DC: U.S. Bureau of Mines, U.S. Department of the Interior, 1983).

Page 87. Adapted from "Protecting Workers in Hot Environments," OSHA Fact Sheet 95-16, U.S. Department of Labor, January 1, 1995.

Page 109. "General Layout of Coal Cleaning Operations." From *Steam: Its Generation and Use,* 40th ed. Barberton, OH: Babcock & Wilcox Co., 1992. Reprinted with permission of the Babcock & Wilcox Company.

Page 110. "Mass Burning Schematic." From *Steam: Its Generation and Use,* 40th ed. Barberton, OH: Babcock & Wilcox Co., 1992. Reprinted with permission of the Babcock & Wilson Company.

Page 110. "One-Leg-Stand Test," from U.S. Department of Transportation, National Highway Traffic Safety Administration, *Improved Sobriety Testing,* 1984 (Washington, DC: U.S. Government Printing Office, 1984).

Page 111. U.S. Congress, Office of Technology Assessment, *Marine Minerals: Exploring Our New Ocean Frontier,* OTA-0-342 (Washington, DC: U.S. Government Printing Office, July 1987).

Page 111. From *Spacelab J, Microgravity and Life Sciences,* NASA, Marshall Space Flight Center, n.d.

Page 113. Callis, R. R. *Housing Vacancies and Homeownership Annual Statistics: 1992,* U.S. Bureau of the Census, Current Housing Reports, Series H111/92-A U.S. Government Printing Office, Washington, DC 1993.

Page 113. Photograph of HealthRider. Reprinted with permission of HealthRider, Inc., Salt Lake City, UT.

Pages 123–124. "Pure Touch, The Filtering Faucet System." Reprinted with permission of Moen Incorporated, North Olmstead, OH.

Page 126. "Hunter Original." Reprinted with permission of Hunter Fan Company, Memphis, TN.

Page 128. "Aurora Australis." NASA HgL-303, n.d.

Page 168. Epoxy definitions from *West System User Manual.* Reprinted with permission of Gougeon Brothers, Inc., Bay City, MI.

Page 170–172. "Appendix 6: Waste Disposal: Solid Hazardous Wastes," from *Lead-Based Paint: Interim Guidelines for Hazard Identification and Abatement in Public and Indian Housing,* Office of Public and Indian Housing, Department of Housing and Urban Development, September 1990.

Page 189. From "Comets," NASA. Available: http://starchild/nasa.gov/docs/comets.html [4 August 1998].

Page 192. "400 Wood Stove." Reprinted with permission of Heatilator, Inc., Mt. Pleasant, IA.

Pages 469–473. Caher, John M. "Technical Documentation and Legal Liability," *Journal of Technical Writing and Communication,* 25(1) (1995). Reprinted with permission of Baywood Publishing Company, Inc., and the author.

Pages 474–486. Calabrese, R., "Designing and Delivering Presentations and Workshops," *The Bulletin of the Association for Business Communication* 52 (June 1989). Reprinted with permission of the author.

Pages 487–488. Graham, J. R. "What Skills Will You Need to Succeed?" *Manager's Magazine* 67 (1), 1992. Reprinted with permission of LIMRA International.

Pages 489–491. From Hartman, Diane B., and Nantz, Karen S. "Send the Right Messages about E-Mail," *Training & Development* 49(5), May 1995. Reprinted with permission of the American Society for Training and Development.

Pages 492–496. Hulbert, J. E. "Barriers to Effective Listening," *The Bulletin of the Association for Business Communication,* 52 (2) (June 1989). Reprinted with permission of the author.

Pages 497–498. From Humphries, A. C. "Business Manners," *Business & Economic Review* 36(3) (April–June 1990). Reprinted with permission of *Business & Economic Review,* published by the University of South Carolina College of Business Administration, Division of Research.

Pages 499–501. Martel, M., "Combating Speech Anxiety." Reprinted with permission from the July 1981 issue of *Public Relations Journal.* Copyright 1981 by the Public Relations Society of America.

Pages 502–505. McAdams, Mindy. "It's All in the Links," *The Editorial Eye* 19(6), June 1996. Reprinted with permission of the author.

Pages 506–507. Messmer, Max. "Prepare, Listen, Follow up," *Management Accounting* 78(8), February 1997. Reprinted with permission of the Institute of Management Accountants.

Pages 508–512. Munter, Mary. "Meeting Technology: From Low-Tech to High-Tech," *Business Communication Quarterly* 61(2), June 1998. Reprinted with permission of the Association for Business Communication.

Pages 513–514. Nielsen, Jakob (1997 March). "Be Succinct! (Writing for the Web)." *Alertbox* [On-Line}, Available: www.useit.com/alertbox [7 July 1998]. Reprinted with permission of the author.

Pages 515–521. Plunka, G. A., "The Editor's Nightmare: Formatting Lists within the Text," *Technical Communication* 35 (February 1988). Reprinted with permission of the Society for Technical Communication.

Pages 522–523. From Porter, J., "Ideology and Collaboration in the Classroom and in the Corporation," *The Bulletin of the Association for Business Communication* LIII(2) (June 1990). Reprinted with permission of the author.

Pages 524–528. "The Practical Writer," *The Royal Bank Letter* 62 (January/February 1981). Reprinted with permission of The Royal Bank of Canada.

Pages 529–534. Ridgway, L., "The Writer as Market Researcher," *Technical Communication* 32(1) (1985). Reprinted with permission of the Society for Technical Communication.

Pages 535–540. "Six Graphics Guidelines," *Simply Stated* 30 (October 1982). Reprinted with permission of the Document Design Center, American Institutes for Research.

Pages 541–544. Smith, T. C., "Listen Up—Tips from the Top on Talks," *Technical Communication* 38(4) (November 1991). Reprinted with permission from *Technical Communication,* published by the Society for Technical Communication, Arlington, VA.